The Elusiveness of the Ordinary

The Elusiveness of the Ordinary

Studies in the Possibility of Philosophy

Stanley Rosen

Yale University Press
New Haven & London

Copyright © 2002 by Yale University. All rights reserved. This book may not be reproduced, in whole or in part, including illustrations, in any form (beyond that copying permitted by Sections 107 and 108 of the U.S. Copyright Law and except by reviewers for the public press), without written permission from the publishers.

Set in Adobe Garamond type by The Composing Room of Michigan, Inc., Grand Rapids, Michigan.

Printed in the United States of America.

Library of Congress Cataloging-in-Publication Data

Rosen, Stanley, 1929–
  The elusiveness of the ordinary : studies in the possibility of philosophy / Stanley Rosen.
      p. cm.
Includes bibliographical references and index.
ISBN 0-300-09197-4 (hardcover : alk. paper)
1. Ordinary-language philosophy.   I. Title.
B945.R526 R67   2002
149′.94—dc21
                                        2001008406

A catalogue record for this book is available from the British Library.

The paper in this book meets the guidelines for permanence and durability of the Committee on Production Guidelines for Book Longevity of the Council on Library Resources.

10 9 8 7 6 5 4 3 2 1

Contents

Acknowledgments, vii
Introduction, 1

1 Politics and Nature in Montesquieu, 14
2 Husserl's Conception of the Life-World, 54
3 Kant and Heidegger: Transcendental Alternatives to Aristotle, 94
4 Wittgenstein, Strauss, and the Possibility of Philosophy, 135
5 Moore on Common Sense, 159
6 Austin and Ordinary Language, 182
7 What Do We Talk About? 204
8 The Attributes of Ordinary Experience, 259
9 Concluding Remarks, 290

Notes, 305
Index, 317

Acknowledgments

In writing this book, I was assisted by a sabbatical fellowship from the Earhart Foundation of Ann Arbor, Michigan, and a sabbatical from Boston University in the spring semester of 2001.

Portions of this book have appeared elsewhere. The material on Kant in chapter 3 was published in slightly different form in German as "Kant über Glückseligkeit" in the Festschrift for Gerold Prauss, *Systematische Ethik Mit Kant,* ed. Hans-Ulrich Baumgarten and Carsten Held (Munich: Alber Verlag, 2001), pp. 355–80. The material on Heidegger in chapter 3 also appeared in slightly different form as "Phronesis or Ontology: Aristotle and Heidegger," in *The Impact of Aristotelianism on Modern Philosophy,* ed. Riccardo Pozzo, Studies in Philosophy and the History of Philosophy (Washington, D.C.: CUA Press, 2001).

An earlier version of chapter 4 was published in the *Review of Metaphysics* 53 (March 2000): 541–64. Even earlier versions were delivered at three conferences devoted to the thought of Leo Strauss, held at the University of Paris (1998), Middlebury College (1999), and the New

School (the 1999 Hannah Arendt/Reiner Schürmann Colloquium). I am grateful to all those who commented on those papers, and more generally, to the occasions themselves, each of which led to modifications in my text. The present version of the chapter differs in important respects from its predecessors.

Introduction

In *Sense and Sensibilia,* John Austin warns us that we must always bear in mind the non-arbitrary character of ordinary words. He adds that we must never tamper with them before careful investigation: "Tampering with words in what we take to be one little corner of the field is always *liable* to have unforeseen repercussions in the adjoining territory."[1] Austin is in effect recommending that ordinary language play a regulative role in the evaluation of philosophical discourse. This is a particular version of the more general tendency in twentieth-century philosophy to take one's bearings by, or to place central emphasis on, the correct conceptual treatment of ordinary, everyday, pretheoretical experience. In the following pages, I propose to investigate the implications of this tendency.

In particular, I shall be concerned with the question of the elusiveness of the ordinary. Some philosophers have devised elaborate technical machinery for the capture and analysis of the ordinary; but even those who claim to find it ready to hand are forced to engage in theoretical justification of the function they assign it. We are accordingly led to ask whether the ordinary is not necessarily replaced within philosophical analysis by a theoretical artifact. Austin, for example, implies (with certain prudential qualifications) that to be "ordinary" means to be directly accessible to the plain man or average speaker of everyday language, say English. At the same time he recognizes, and again demonstrates, that the senses of ordinary words are complex and subtle; they do not reveal their treasures to the naked gaze of the plain man but require careful analysis by someone with unusually acute linguistic perception. In other words, the very "ordinariness" of ordinary words is in large part an illusion.[2] The ordinary is accessible, but it has the disconcerting feature of turning into the extraordinary even as we grasp it. The thesis that ordinary language ought to and indeed must serve as the standard against which to measure the legitimacy of philosophical diction (with the exception of technical terms and stipulated meanings) is itself problematic. The ordinary is something that we pursue.

My investigation is primarily concerned with two opposing, yet related, responses to the problem of the ordinary in modern and contemporary philosophy. These responses are the attempt to acquire conceptual mastery of the ordinary by employing the paradigm of modern scientific method, on the one hand, and, on the other, to rescue the ordinary from what is perceived to be the distortions of that same method. There are two versions of the first or scientific response, namely, the Enlightenment's pre-Kantian version, and the version that reflects the pervasive influence of Kant. It is a testimonial to the importance of Kant for late-modern and contemporary philosophy that his influence is also fundamental among those who approach ordinary language and experience more directly, as a topic that is not amenable to scientific methods.

I shall proceed through studies of thinkers who represent the aforementioned orientations to the problem of the ordinary, in order to determine whether their theoretical methods are successful, or indeed even plausible. These studies will serve as the basis for some reflections of my own on the pursuit of the ordinary. The studies, to repeat, are representative, not exhaustive, and they are analytical, not primarily historical. I am almost entirely concerned with modern and in particular contemporary thinkers. But it is appropriate in an introduction to begin with a somewhat panoramic view of the problem.

According to the tradition, the first wise men were concerned either with the practical activity of *techné* and politics or with the formulation of general maxims about the conduct of life. Parmenides and Heracleitus, who devoted themselves to theoretical and speculative investigations of nature, paramount among which was the inquiry into being and becoming, seem not to have been interested in, and even to have belittled, everyday life and the ordinary opinions of common sense. Socrates was apparently the first to bring together what was eventually to be called "theory" and "practice" as the two dimensions of philosophical reflection. He is represented most famously in the Platonic dialogues, engaging in careful analyses of the speeches and deeds of everyday life, usually with young men and sophists, but sometimes with practitioners of the arts and professions. The city, or more precisely the life of the citizen, serves in these dialogues as the framework that unites philosophical investigation, even when philosophy pursues theoretical questions that go beyond the demands of political and practical life. The dramatic form of the Platonic dialogue exhibits the tacit thesis that theory and practice are not so much two distinct lives as two aspects of human life, at least in its best manifestations. They are not ways of understanding life so much as ways of living.

Nevertheless, theory and practice are not the same. As Socrates tells the story, philosophy emerges not from a careful analysis of everyday life and language, and not even from reflection on politics, but in wonder at the heavens and their regular movements. This wonder is deepened but at the same time made more difficult by the famous doctrine of the erotic nature of philosophy. The god (or daimon) Eros stands for the power that raises the human soul up from everyday life to the transuranian domain of the pure forms or Platonic Ideas. It is only after this erotic revelation of the extraordinary that the philosopher returns to the surface of the earth and the cities of human beings, where he or she attempts to illuminate the ordinary, and thus to direct nonphilosophers to the central question of the nature of the good life.

The *Dialogues* exhibit the Platonic conviction that philosophy is an extraordinary activity at which only a few can excel, but at the same time that human beings are philosophical animals. All human beings can therefore strive for what Socrates calls the Ideas, whether they know they are doing that or not. In other words, Plato's *Dialogues* show us that philosophy both transcends and is deeply rooted in ordinary life. Wonder directs us to cosmology, physics, mathematics, and (as we now call it) metaphysics, but these theoretical investigations are conducted by human beings, not gods, and their progress depends on the flourishing of the city, or, as we can also say, on the cooperation if not the unity of theory and practice.

Nor is this simply a matter of convenience or prudential caution. Although wonder is directed toward the heavens, the study of nature, or the attempt to transform wonder into knowledge, begins in the mastery of what is close at hand, and the structure of knowledge is already visible within the procedures of the most ordinary arts and crafts. Even the order of the heavenly bodies is incorporated into human life through such everyday activities as measuring the land, the seasons, the periods of the day, and the course of a sea-voyage. Stated succinctly, common sense must indeed be illuminated by erotic madness, but madness requires the sobriety of common sense. The question is how these two are related within the harmony of human life. Otherwise put, what has the theoretician to learn about the structure of intelligibility from the poet, the craftsman, or the statesman? Is there something about everyday life that serves not merely as the basis for its own transformation into the arts and sciences but as a standard of excellence for philosophical knowledge?

The history of philosophy after Plato's Socrates may be understood as a debate between two different responses to these questions. Some hold that philosophy is radically detached from ordinary experience, whereas others contend that the first originates in and develops from the second. One might be tempted to call these the characteristic replies of metaphysics on the one hand and of empiricism on the other. The point I wish to emphasize is that Socrates' response differs from both these replies. As he presents the situation, philosophy originates from above, that is to say, through an erotic "revelation" that is needed in order to clarify the implicitly philosophical content of ordinary life and language. This clarification has theoretical as well as practical significance. Ordinary experience without revelation is blind, but revelation without ordinary experience is empty. I believe that this point has been obscured in the modern epoch because of the radical split between the natural sciences and philosophy, a split that led in the Enlightenment to the attempt to grasp the ordinary, or what was still called the political, within the methods and concepts of the mathematical and experimental sciences.[3] But even in this violent form we can still discern something of the Socratic (or Platonic) conviction that theory is not radically sundered from practice. What is perhaps not quite so visible is the Socratic view that theory and practice are united by human life, and so by practice, not by theory.

The history of philosophy during the past three centuries is to a large extent, although certainly not entirely, the story of the effort to bring ordinary life under the rational control of theory, whether "theory" be understood as systematic and speculative metaphysics, or as the political and social sciences conceived in the image (or shadow) of physics. This effort has led to significant contrary attempts to make ordinary experience, if not completely regulative, at least decisive for the preliminary orientation of philosophy. A striking feature of twentieth-century philosophy is the importance of such terms as "the lifeworld," "average everydayness," "ordinary language," "commonsense reason," and most recently "folk psychology," to mention some of the most famous examples. These expressions are not synonymous, nor do their partisans interpret them uniformly. Let us say that they exhibit a family resemblance rather than a formal or conceptual unity. Furthermore, the members of this family are not at all on good terms with one another. Some philosophers insist on the need to seek the meaning and value of science, or paradigms for the analysis of philosophical discourse, or the existential context within which philosophy emerges in ordinary, pretheoretical, commonsense experience and language. For others, the interpretation of everyday life is relegated to the level of prescientific folklore, or subjected to purification by formal analysis of the logical or mathematical kind; the regulative function of ordinary experience is thus rejected on behalf of the construction of scientific models. What is decisive here is, as it were, the "deconstruction" of the ordinary.

The situation is further complicated in two ways. We must first distinguish between those who seem to regard the pretheoretical domain as directly accessible through attention to ordinary language, and those for whom access to the structure or essence of everyday life depends upon the application of sophisticated technical tools. Second, however, advocates of the replacement of ordinary by scientific or logico-mathematical languages themselves conduct their technical discourse within the context of, and in explicit dependence on, the "intuitions" and "background theories" of common sense. This is perhaps especially clear in Quine, who says that "science is a continuation of common sense, and it continues the common-sense expedient of swelling ontology to simplify theory."[4] To deny this continuity is to arrive at the inversion of scientific technicism exhibited by the more extreme postmodernists, for whom every discourse is a new creation.

Speaking very generally, I believe that the views of contemporary partisans and enemies alike of ordinary experience suggest that that experience can no longer be regarded as "ordinary"—another paradox—or that the ordinary has become problematic for twentieth-century philosophers, whether their intention is to resuscitate it or to reject it. In both cases, albeit in different ways, we have either lost touch with or become detached from ordinary experience, even as we continue to take it for granted. There would, for example, have been no need for "ordinary language philosophy" or for Wittgensteinian linguistic therapy if it were evident that "ordinary language is all right," that it is in order as it is.[5] The pursuit of the ordinary is a sign of decadence, not of simplicity. Unfortunately, what was naturally accessible to us at the beginning of the Western philosophical tradition has today become "sedimented" (Husserl's phrase) and hard to discern, so much so that one is tempted to regard its pursuit as a kind of romanticism. However this may be, nothing could be *less* simple and straightforward than the language within which so many of our contemporaries celebrate the virtues of ordinary experience and language.

To continue with this general reflection, the scientific rationalism of the Enlightenment directs us toward the future, the privileged tense in Heidegger's existential analysis in *Being and Time,* despite his attempt to adapt Husserlian desedimentation in his own idiosyncratic return to the origin. Because this return assumes its extreme form in the period subsequent to *Being and Time,* one can say that the latter work is still influenced by the Enlightenment, with fundamental ontology the technical surrogate for mathematical rationalism. The connection with the Enlightenment is of course much more evident in Husserlian phenomenology. Perhaps the main point is that both thinkers accept the need to recover the origins of human experience, that is, to remove the sediment deposited by traditional rationalism. All differences to one side, both thinkers seek to neutralize the distortions of traditional philosophy by a return to everyday life that is oddly reminiscent of Wittgenstein's approach. But whereas Husserl and Heidegger share the scientific bias toward the future and a taste for technical or extraordinary language, Wittgenstein's advocacy of customary or ordinary language seems to be opposed to technical innovation, and hence to favor a conservative retention of contemporary idiom, which is to say that he seems to be inclined toward the past, which is the mother of the present.[6] Nevertheless, Wittgenstein's own language is anything but ordinary; it is not only radically innovative but paradoxically baroque in its obscurity. This tendency is less dramatically visible in an important parallel movement, ordinary language philosophy, of which the outstanding representative is probably John Austin. However, Austin differs from (the later) Wittgenstein most notably in his belief in positive philosophical results based on the careful analysis of linguistic distinctions.[7]

In short, Husserl and Heidegger return to the past in order to find the right way into the future, whereas Wittgenstein and the various partisans of ordinary language philosophy must necessarily favor a previously established discursive orthodoxy; in that sense, the present, or "how we speak now," is a mask for the past. This is not to say that they are unaware that ordinary or customary language itself changes.[8] But this change produces, as it were, a series of new pasts, none of which has a theoretical or explanatory significance for the present, except as the authority of tradition. How we speak is just that: how we speak now. Ordinary language may be all right, but it carries no philosophical weight, and certainly no normative significance outside the penumbra of one's linguistic community. The inclination toward the past is obvious from the fact that the present cannot be in continuous change; if it were, no postmodern thesis of continuous spontaneity would be sufficiently radical to capture the truth about human discourse, since there would be no coherent discourse. Emphasis on the usual or customary is necessarily a turn to and preference for the past.

Let me summarize these introductory remarks in two points. The first is that those who reject the scientific or philosophical relevance of everyday discursive experience themselves presuppose a good bit of this experience in the construction of their theories. Without the reliable accessibility of ordinary experience, no one would know how to deviate from it in a scientific manner, nor would it be clear what precisely is the function of a scientific theory. Theory construction would become indistinguishable from poetry. The second point is that both extremes, the critics and the champions of ordinary experience, are characteristically associated with a censoriousness toward, and often a rejection of, traditional philosophy, which is said to be riddled with logical and grammatical improprieties arising on the one hand from carelessness with respect to the common rules of linguistic use that govern our natural languages, and on the other from scientific ignorance, religious superstition, and even political interest.

Suppose that we accept this critique, if only for the sake of argument. It would seem to entail one or the other of two consequences. Either there is a common experience that has been obscured by false philosophical or primitive scientific theories, and to which we must return through the purification, and perhaps even the elimination, of our philosophical language. Or else common experience is itself a kind of scientific error that requires to be rectified together with the elimination of prescientific philosophy. But even those who ridicule ordinary experience as the domain of folk psychology will not go so far as to deny that science is about something external to itself. They do not assert that it is mere talk, of however sophisticated a variety, but hold rather that it is a correct analysis of the nature of the external world, albeit a world that is accommodated to the human neurophysiological system, which takes the role assigned by Kant to the transcendental ego. And "external" means here something like "not subjective" or "not phenomenal." On this alternative, a new, scientifically purified common experience is substituted for the old, primitive domain of folk science. This purified common experience is the historically evolving milieu of scientifically enlightened humanity. And it is itself not a series of equations but the rhetorical atmosphere within which we persuade ourselves that we are "up to date" in the never-ending journey toward universal scientific enlightenment. Those whom Plato's Eleatic Stranger calls the hardheaded materialists must grant a world of everyday life precisely as they reject our ordinary interpretation of it. It is the ordinary world in which they announce their triumph in the stentorian tones of scientific rhetoric.

I understand that science is not theoretically homogeneous, and that there are alternative theories that cover the same phenomena. I also understand that scientific theories are as much the product of imagination and conjecture as of discovery and the generalization of observations. And finally, I know that many theoretical entities are unobservable at the level of ordinary human perception. But none of this alters the fact that science arises from the attempt to grasp the nature of everyday experience. It is true only up to a point that such a grasp entails the replacement of ordinary modes of reasoning by the extraordinary technical procedures of science. We may supplement our understanding of Newtonian and Einsteinian physics with quantum mechanics and field theories, just as we replace or supplement Darwinian biology or behaviorist psychology with contemporary genetics and neurophysiology. But we do not replace ourselves with quarks, and try as we may, I believe that we shall not succeed in replacing ourselves with computers (although our computers may some day do this for us). The underlying problem of the pursuit of the ordinary, whether to be guided by it or to transcend it, is nothing less than the question of human nature.

My main concern, accordingly, is not with science as an ongoing enterprise but with the question whether we can identify a common experience, sometimes called "ordinary" or "pretheoretical" (again, these terms are not synonymous), that produces, or plays a decisive role in the production of, science and philosophy. Let me say at once that the results of the following investigation will be mixed. The attempt to provide an analysis of ordinary experience is subject to two great difficulties. Either one converts the ordinary by its very analysis into a technical artifact of a formalist philosophy, or one runs the risk of seeming to remain at the level of impressionistic and arbitrary anecdotes. It remains to be seen whether I can navigate between Scylla and Charybdis. I am tempted to add that ordinary experience is by its nature anecdotal. On either alternative the attempt to elicit the formal structure, logical or ontological, of everyday life, takes us very soon outside the perimeter of ordinary experience and into the domain of systematic philosophical theories. But how do we choose between rival models if we do not have direct, pretheoretical access to the phenomena of everyday life?

Rather than appearing controversial, the assumption that there is a common pretheoretical experience that serves as the womb of our diverse cognitive activities, philosophy among them, may seem to many philosophers entirely trivial. How else could theories arise if not from the gradual refinement of the observation, measurement, and analysis of everyday phenomena? Unfortunately, this triviality (if it is a triviality) does not provide us with a theoretically neutral description of the preconditions of theory. Otherwise stated, if we assume the "triviality" thesis, we have to admit that the refinement of ordinary experience leads to a wide variety of theories, if not finally to all philosophical expositions of human life. Furthermore, if ordinary experience is where we begin, it does not follow that the beginning remains regulative for all subsequent theoretical refinements. This is the position of those who see science as a steady progress away from the primitivism of "folk psychology."

In attempting to gain clarity on this ostensible triviality, which turns out instead to be one of the most intractable of philosophical problems, I have changed my mind about the proper formulation of the problem, not to mention its possible solution, on more than one occasion. On balance it has seemed best to me to spend some time in the careful study of representatives of the most important approaches to a solution. Only then will I venture to provide some samples of the approach I favor. Let me however warn the reader in advance that a final solution is no more possible here than it is with respect to any fundamental philosophical problem. The phrase "final solution" has unpleasant overtones that are not philosophically irrelevant. The most we can hope for is "correct opinion," not *epistémé,* and this is because life is not a science.

By far the most influential method for capturing, as opposed to merely pursuing, the ordinary is the effort to grasp it in the conceptual web of science. Two examples of this method that will concern us at some length are the origin of sociology in Montesquieu's work, and Husserl's and Heidegger's creation of the phenomenological description of the life-world. Essentially the same situation obtains, however, in radically less formal approaches to ordinary experience, approaches in which everyday discourse is constantly referred to as if it were a familiar friend waiting at our side to spring into action as the standard of permissible language, a friend whose exact identity is never given but only suggested in one particular quotation after another.

Perhaps the account of ordinary experience is itself both extraordinary and theoretical not because we arbitrarily presuppose what is to be discovered but because it is perfectly ordinary for human beings to engage in philosophy. In this case the impossibility of separating the ordinary from the extraordinary would not prevent us from distinguishing between them, thereby understanding how life is a continuous transformation from one into the other. On the contrary, separating them would enable us to describe the transformation and to try to determine the degree to which it regulates our philosophical views. In other words, the study of ordinary experience cannot be extra- or metaphilosophical, because the prefixes derive their sense from philosophy. The attempt to choose between two philosophical positions is itself necessarily philosophical. What we must therefore subject to preliminary scrutiny is not an ordinary language that is independent and regulative of philosophical discourse but the genesis of philosophical discourse itself. The view I am proposing is that language is both ordinary and extraordinary in its response to the varieties of human experience. The ordinary is not determined in advance by linguistic rules; instead, the rules are determined by our experience. I do not mean by this that there are no "deep linguistic structures" that determine the most general forms of language, but rather that these deep structures are the foundation for the diversity and creativity of language. Syntax is more like permission to speak than an invocation to silence.

If this is right, and I believe that it is right, then there can be no rigorous, technical, systematic, logically and conceptually complete construction of a theory of ordinary experience. Stated very generally, ordinary experience is saturated with the extraordinary. The two are not independent entities; one cannot hold the ordinary against the extraordinary like a ruler to a line or a tailor's pattern to a bolt of cloth. Less poetically, it is possible to employ ordinary language as a tool in the analysis of extraordinary philosophical discourse, but nothing philosophically interesting is accomplished unless one shows the basis for the authority of the ordinary over the extraordinary. After all, the reverse may be the case, just as it so frequently, perhaps always, is in science. What we need here is not the plain man, the legendary passenger on the Clapham bus, but the "bilingual" philosopher who actually speaks the language of everyday life, as distinguished from its technicist reconstructions, in its two quite different and yet related dialects.

I would be more reluctant than I am to set out on the quixotic task of pursuing the ordinary if I had not been encouraged by the most powerful thinkers of our century to believe that something decisive is involved, something that is both as plain as the nose on one's face and as invisible, and perhaps, as has often been suggested, invisible because it is as plain as the nose on one's face. The ambiguous phenomenological location of the nose also casts its shadow over what lies just beneath our noses.

The chapters that follow may be read as independent investigations, but they are intended to fit together as a sketch of the problematic nature of our certitude about the ordinary. It is this certitude that leads to reliance on or repudiation of the ordinary. But it also conceals a slightly deeper problem about the extraordinary, which itself seems to be either rejected or else transformed into the ordinary, thanks to the ordinal role we assign it. This is the contemporary destiny of both scientific rhetoric on the one hand and the rhetoric of the surrealist partisans of new modes of discourse on the other. It would surely be as extraordinary to replace our everyday discourse with the language of neurophysiology and cybernetics as it would to employ post-Heideggerian or deconstructionist litanies of uniqueness.

In the first six chapters of this book I study leading representatives of the main responses to the problem of knowledge of ordinary experience. The first two figures, Montesquieu and Husserl, exhibit the beginning and the end of the Enlightenment project to acquire a scientific understanding of human nature. In keeping with the older tradition, Montesquieu takes his bearings from the emergence of political life. He provides us with a detailed picture of the tension, intrinsic to modern scientific rationalism, between two different conceptions of nature, one human, the other cosmological. In Husserl, already a late modern, politics is submerged within the general and abstract structures of the "life-world." The standpoint is that of everyman, and it invokes the anonymity of scientific description. Human nature is replaced by, or rather assimilated into, the quasi-mathematical structures of pure form.

The third study is devoted to a contrast between Kant and Heidegger on the one hand, and Aristotle on the other. The two former thinkers are quite conscious of the incompatibility of scientific reason and the understanding of human life as it is actually lived. In Kant, the later modern depreciation of politics is already visible in his separation of ethics from the domain of "prudence" or, as Kant calls it, "cleverness" (*Klugheit*). Kant follows Aristotle in connecting ethics to common human experience, but he differs from his pagan predecessor in retaining decisive elements of the biblical interpretation of that experience. In addition, as is already indicated by his critique of prudence, Kant remains under the influence of modern mathematical science in his conception of practical reason. In Heidegger, ethics and politics are both replaced by an ontological abstraction rooted in elements of pagan and biblical thought as interpreted through the filter of a post- (or even anti-) Husserlian phenomenology.

Chapter 4 is dedicated to two thinkers who are not normally treated together, Ludwig Wittgenstein and Leo Strauss. They are united by a certain antitheoretical bias and a conviction that the depths are contained in the surface. In other words, they advocate a return from the theoretical to the pretheoretical understanding of ordinary language in the first case and to commonsense ethical and political understanding in the second. Wittgenstein's attempt to employ ordinary language as a safeguard against the existential and discursive corruptions of scientific rationalism is presented as a kind of syntactical exercise that is hard to distinguish from the historicism of phenomenological hermeneutics. Strauss makes the most extensive attempt to return to the perspective of Aristotle, or let us say to rehabilitate the wisdom of the ancients as a vital weapon in our attempt to purge modernity of its defects. But his attempt is marred by its deep ambiguity concerning both the nature of philosophy and the validity of the claim that the ancient Greeks provide us with a paradigm of ordinary or commonsensical reason unsullied by ideological and philosophical doctrines.

Chapter 5 attacks the problem of common sense with the assistance of a consideration of some of the leading ideas of G. E. Moore; in chapter 6, I approach more directly the problem of ordinary language through an analysis of passages from the philosophical papers of John Austin. Let me emphasize that these chapters do not pretend to be exhaustive interpretations of the philosophies of Moore and Austin; I have chosen for study those views that bear most directly upon my central theme: the elusiveness of the ordinary. I emphasize that the first six chapters are meant to be representative, not exhaustive. It would have increased the size of an already long book to deal with Scottish Common-Sense philosophy or pragmatism, which I neglect here. I hope to have covered the major themes at play, if not in all their various manifestations, by my choice of figures for discussion. These figures are, as it were, "ideal types" intended to regulate what is not so much a history as a philosophical investigation.

The last three chapters are intended to serve as samples of how we can think about the ordinary without transforming it into a theoretical artifact. My aim has been to convey something of the unity within difference of human life, and not at all to construct a system. At the same time I argue against those who would eliminate extraordinary discourse through unsatisfactory refutations of metaphysics that are rooted in the same everyday characteristics of experience as metaphysics itself.

As the reader will see, the theme of common sense plays both an explicit and implicit role in these final chapters, a role that has both similarities to and differences from the function of common sense in thinkers like Moore and Austin. Perhaps the most important difference between my view and theirs stems from my conviction that common sense is a bridge from the ordinary to the extraordinary, but a reliance on common sense is not a license for the repudiation of what we have become accustomed to call "metaphysics." It is, however, an indispensable element in the process of adjudicating rival metaphyscal claims.

In chapter 7, the longest of the three, I take my bearings from a text by Bertrand Russell written during his adherence to logical atomism. But the purpose of the chapter is not historical; Russell figures as the provocation for an extensive reflection on what it is within ordinary experience that we "actually" talk about. Chapter 8 is devoted to a discussion of the fundamental properties of ordinary experience, and to how these properties provide the matrix for the articulation of experience into intelligible entities. Chapter 9 restates in summary form the main theme of this book.

My goal in these last three chapters is to exhibit how common sense assists us in deciding among competing metaphysical claims. I do not attempt the impossible and self-contradictory task of providing a theoretical reconstruction of the nature and limits of common sense. In the last analysis, it is the apparent success of our pursuit of the ordinary that demonstrates its elusiveness.

Chapter 1 Politics and Nature in Montesquieu

A dispute concerning the philosophical authority of science marks the decisive character of the pursuit of the ordinary in the twentieth century. Those for whom ordinary experience is still understood as fundamentally political in the broad sense of that term differ from those who assign no special prominence to politics but arrive at a theoretical abstraction of "the plain man" or the life of "average everydayness," to mention two prominent examples. In the first case, "ordinary experience" is inseparable from the older view, going back to Aristotle, that human beings are by nature the sole political animals. Ordinary life is in this tradition the manifestation of what is common to human beings, not in a purely biological sense, or even merely as private individuals engaged in everyday discourse concerning the pretechnical context of practical life, but as citizens rather than as isolated or self-centered psychological atoms. Political life is primarily the domain of *doksa,* belief or opinion, and the most important of these beliefs are, in the Aristotelian tradition, the *endoksa* or views of the most serious and experienced citizens. In this honorific sense, *doksa* is very close to common sense.

In the second case, the role of politics is minimized. One detects instead the influence of the Christian preoccupation with the destiny of the individual person, or alternatively, the increasing anonymity of late-modern life that is dominated by technology, industry, and the other features of mass society. In this context, the "ordinary" comes to mean the inner life of everyone and anyone, soon submerged by the anonymity of modern society, and reappearing as a locus of theoretical structures, whether these be sociological, phenomenological, or ontological. There is obviously a social and political background to the theoretical devices known as the ordinary speaker or the plain man, even if these mythical personages are not conceived explicitly as "the average citizen."

Contemporary representatives of these competing orientations have a forefather in Montesquieu, a paradigmatic example of the eighteenth-century Enlightenment, who himself revised the older, explicitly social and political conception of ordinary experience. Montesquieu is, of course, a political philosopher, and perhaps the grandfather of sociology, not a theoretician of the life-world. But we can see very clearly in his great work, the *Spirit of the Laws,* the founding of the attempt to explain everyday human practice by means of the inspiration and even some of the techniques of the new experimental and mathematical sciences. This inspiration underlies many of the most influential contemporary philosophical approaches to the pursuit of the ordinary, independently of whether they are explicitly concerned with the political as such. Montesquieu provides us with a classic statement of this approach and enables us to see its intrinsic deficiency with great clarity.

The statement is most fully visible in book 2 of the *Spirit of the Laws* (hereafter, *SL*). Montesquieu stands at the intersection between the Aristotelian tradition of practical judgment (*phronésis*) and the generation in which the model of the natural sciences stimulates the development of the social and political sciences. The ordinary, commonsense, or "doxic" life of the citizen is thus pulled in two differing explanatory directions. The result of this inner tension is not a "science" of states and societies in the sense determined by the model of mathematical physics but almost the reverse: the philosophy of history. The result of the attempt to master everyday life by the rigors of scientific reasoning leads paradoxically to the dissolution of nature into history. The presumed function of history is to supply us with examples from which the natural laws of human practice may be inferred. In the absence of an appropriate model of human nature, however, namely, one that underlies history rather than being inferred from it, we soon become enthralled by the multiplicity of difference. The scientific model is inadequate to the task of eliciting the intelligible structure of social and political life. This is the forerunner of the failure of scientific or ontological theories to explain ordinary experience in the twentieth century. Or so I will argue.

I am in no way claiming that Montesquieu addresses the question of ordinary experience in the style of twentieth-century philosophers. My claim is rather that contemporary partisans of formal analysis, whether scientific in the strict sense or not, are repeating in principle the error that Montesquieu and his generation are the first, or among the first, to make. And the more rigorously our contemporaries exclude social and political content from their analyses in favor of complex abstract structures and transcendental foundations, the less human is the ordinary speaker or plain man who dwells in their doctrines; and the more moribund the life-world of that person, the emptier his or her zone of average everydayness.

Montesquieu is an exemplary representative of the attempt to reconcile the traditional, prudential study of politics and legislation with the spirit of the new natural science. This attempt is characteristic of the early, or moderate, eighteenth-century Enlightenment. By "moderate Enlightenment" I refer to the absence of revolutionary fervor and also to a belief in infinite progress, as well as in the possibility of avoiding war through commerce and in so doing, combining virtue and material comfort. The key to this attempted reconciliation lies in the success or failure of the associated interpretation of the laws of human nature in the light of the conception of natural laws that characterizes Cartesian and Newtonian science. The central question is thus whether there can be a "science" of politics (or for that matter, of society) that articulates the deductive structure of natural and positive law without sacrificing the prudential commonsense experience on which political and moral judgments have always been based, and in accord with which we have tried to construct our social institutions.

Montesquieu himself calls our attention to the difficulty of his text in a passage that deserves to be quoted in full: "I ask a favor that I fear will not be accorded me; that is not to judge by a moment's reading the work of twenty years, [and also] that one approve or condemn the book as a whole and not some few phrases. If one wants to seek the design of the author, one can find it only in the design of the work" (229).[1] Unfortunately, it has not been easy to find this design. I cannot say that I have discovered a concealed deductive structure beneath the somewhat disheveled surface of the *SL*. Most scholars are struck by the peculiar arrangement of Montesquieu's subject matter, the sometimes arbitrary-looking nature of his transitions, and the apparently random character of his collections of examples. Certainly Montesquieu's practice leaves us in no doubt that the "design" of a work in political philosophy is quite different from that of a treatise on physics or the laws of mechanics.

It has seemed best to me to follow the written order of the text rather than to gather together passages on similar topics for discontinuous analysis. This decision allows me to follow Montesquieu's thought as he himself presented it, and so to allow for the discovery of an inner plan, should one be indicated, rather than to obscure the author's order with an external hypothesis.

What does Montesquieu mean by "esprit" in his title? The laws are themselves "alive" and are sustained by the constitution, by the articulation of the motivating principle of each form of government, but also by "the mores, climate, religion, commerce, and so forth" of each particular political organism. Laws are dead if separated from this living organism, and the organism is in turn derived from its principle. Furthermore, the laws do not determine but rather are determined by the factors mentioned in the full title. It follows that the spirit of the laws is similarly determined. One cannot legislate the climate, which has an effect on the kind of laws that are appropriate for a given geographical region. As to the other factors, Montesquieu means that a people's customs, religion, and even commercial relations have already been determined by the time these people are ready to engage in self-conscious legislation.

For example, a land with a sea coast and natural harbors will develop maritime commercial practices: wharves, fishing, shipping, import and export, maritime law, and so forth. Religions arise rather early in the history of a people; they are not normally legislated into existence but crystallize out of myths, rituals, legends, and from long-standing practices. The prophetic religions, and in particular Christianity, seem to interrupt tradition, but they are not the product of legislative reflection. Religions may be subsequently regulated by laws, but they cannot be created by them. People are accustomed to behave in certain ways, which move them to pass laws of such and such a kind; or alternatively, the ways in which they behave are best served by laws of such and such a kind. It is the task of the political philosopher to determine which laws are best suited to the organisms that emerge in the manner I have just sketched.

It follows from this that Montesquieu is not a "revolutionary" legislator.[2] Laws are produced in accord with *nature,* a term that has a broad but not an indefinite range of meanings. Nature in this broad sense is revealed by history. In other words, human nature is always the same, but it is diversely individuated by circumstance. Hence we need a knowledge of history in order to see both that different circumstances require different adaptations of natural principles, but also that there are natural principles. Furthermore, these principles are not uniformly applicable in all cases. Instead, they serve as a guide for the improvement of those laws that express the spirit of the local situation. One could say that the regularity of ordinary experience expresses itself in the diversity of custom. Regularity is the basis of science, as is diversity of history. The problem is that these two bases form an unstable conjunction.

So much for the title. It is entirely characteristic of Montesquieu's style that he opens his treatise with a point of terminological clarification, yet in such a way as to produce ambiguity. The word *Avertissement* does not here mean simply "preface" or "foreword." It is literally a warning to the reader. The "preface" follows this warning. A proper understanding of the first four books of his work, Montesquieu says, depends upon the observation of how he uses the term "virtue" (*vertu*). No such warning is necessary in the case of "spirit" or even of "laws." Each of these terms has a conventional and noncontroversial sense that will no doubt be refined as we proceed but that is satisfactory to orient us in our study of Montesquieu. "Virtue," however, is the potential source of controversy because it designates distinct and even conflicting senses of "excellence." Montesquieu wishes to distinguish between political and moral or religious uses of the term. We can detect here a resonance of the tradition that begins with Machiavelli and is institutionalized by Hobbes. The scientific study of politics requires that it be separated from the moral and religious dogmas of a particular nation. I hardly need emphasize that Montesquieu must be particularly sensitive to the authority of the Catholic church and the French monarchy. But his concern goes beyond this. If the analysis of political virtue is confused with an account of moral and religious virtue, Montesquieu could be made to speak absurdities "which would be revolting in every country in the world, because in all countries in the world, people want morality" (227).

Reference to "excellence" has immediate moral implications, even and perhaps most of all when it is being used in a morally neutral sense. Montesquieu wishes to emphasize that his terminological distinction is not intended to contradict traditional morality. But the fact that he feels required to issue this warning is itself a sign that the distinction is dangerous. It remains to be seen whether moral virtue supervenes over political virtue. Even further, it remains to be seen whether the expression "political excellence" can be understood independently of moral and religious considerations. If the term is totally neutral, then a dangerous split opens between politics and morality: science or political philosophy in the spirit of modern science is shown to be politically dangerous. But if the term is not totally neutral, then it has moral and religious implications that are potential rivals to the traditional beliefs of the nation. Montesquieu was in fact subjected to extensive criticism by those who spoke for the tradition and by officials of the Catholic church; his masterpiece was placed on the Index in 1751.

Let us now look more closely at the terminological distinction itself. All questions of morality to one side, the distinction as presented by Montesquieu is ambiguous. By separating political virtue from both moral and Christian virtue, he thereby implies, or at least leaves open the possibility, that these two are not identical. But there is a more important ambiguity. In Machiavelli, the distinction between political and moral *virtù* can be justified on pragmatic grounds that are themselves not scientifically precise, and for that reason allow a certain movement between the two terms. For Montesquieu, however, the distinction is technical, and it is intended to be rigorous. Ambiguity in the definitions of these crucial terms must necessarily be transmitted throughout the work. This seems to be the case with respect to what is arguably the single most important conception in the SL, namely, political virtue.

The second point of importance is that Montesquieu identifies political virtue as "the mainspring" (*ressort*) that drives the republican government, just as *honor* is the mainspring that moves the monarchy. It is not until the beginning of book 2 that he introduces his main division of regimes into republican, monarchic, and despotic (239). He also says there that aristocracies and democracies are both republics. Assuming that this classification is already in play, the mainspring of these two regimes is accordingly political virtue. That there is some ambiguity here is already evident from the definition of political virtue in the *Avertissement* as "love of country and of equality." It is, to say the least, initially implausible to associate love of equality with the motive force of aristocracies. That it is also undesirable, and perhaps impossible, to separate love of country and of equality from virtue is shown by the fact that the principle of an aristocracy is moderation founded upon virtue (254). I note in passing that the high praise bestowed elsewhere by Montesquieu upon moderation at least suggests the possibility that he preferred aristocracies to monarchies (and England, which he admired, although not unqualifiedly, was as much an aristocracy as a monarchy).[3]

The identification of honor as the mainspring of monarchies is certainly plausible, although the separation of aristocracies from monarchies raises some questions. One could argue that honor is also the mainspring of aristocracies. Montesquieu goes on to say that simply because a certain principle is not the mainspring of a regime, it does not follow that the principle is absent from that regime. Granting, however, that honor is also present in aristocracies, we shall have to be told how its role differs in the two regimes, and in particular how one could attribute the love of equality to an aristocracy. Montesquieu later identifies the mainspring of despotisms as fear.

Despite his adoption of the descriptive, analytical, or scientific approach, Montesquieu is by no means free of a normative dimension. The distinction between honor and fear, and so between a monarchy and a despotism, for example, is implicitly evaluative, especially in contrast with Hobbes, according to whom "they that are discontented under *Monarchy,* call it *Tyranny.*"[4] But even more striking is the implicitly evaluative nature of the pivotal expression "political virtue." It is plainly Montesquieu's intention to identify the possession of political virtue in a regime as superior to its absence. One might suggest that Montesquieu means here by "virtue" simply the ability to survive in accordance with the original principle of the form of government. There cannot be any doubt that something of this sort is intended by Montesquieu, but the problem of his terminology remains, to say nothing of the value-judgments that are to be found throughout his work. Montesquieu does not simply praise survival above destruction; he praises certain types of survival over others. The least one can say is that his new use of the word "virtue," if it is new, inevitably invokes the old senses as well. "Political virtue" is not a term like "quantity of energy" or "force of gravitation" that carries no moral connotations or expressions of political superiority. How could it, and still be *political?* This is another facet of Montesquieu's problem of how to associate traditional normative expressions like "patriotism," "love of equality," and "honor" with a purely mechanistic conception of human nature in general and political laws in particular.

In the *Prince,* Machiavelli wishes to separate political virtue, or the capacity to found and preserve a state, from traditional and especially from Christian morality. But Machiavelli's distinction is in the interest of justice and political stability, not of a mechanistic analysis of the action and reaction of morally neutral political forces. As the *Discourses* make clear, Machiavelli was a republican in the classical Roman sense. We are not yet in a position to say anything similar of Montesquieu, but surely his juxtaposition of political virtue and honor is suggestive of the Machiavellian resonances of the ostensibly novel term "political virtue." For example, Montesquieu does not distinguish between moral virtue and the *virtù* of the gifted political "captain" or combination of founding father, general, and statesman, nor does he use "virtue" in the sense of the archaic Greek *areté*, that is, the "excellence" or manliness of the noble warrior. The separation of political virtue from honor implies a preference for peace, although this should not be exaggerated at the present stage of our investigation. We can, however, safely infer an ambiguity in the sense of "political virtue" as it applies to aristocracies and democracies. The former cannot be characterized as lovers of equality.

Montesquieu's claim to novelty is also Machiavellian, and one finds it reiterated in all of the major thinkers of modern European philosophy. In the case of Machiavelli, the claim refers primarily to the repudiation of the political wisdom of the ancient philosophers; it is a claim to have understood human nature and political life as it is, was, and will be. In this sense, Machiavelli is appealing to a uniform and ahistorical nature that is accessible to experience, observation, and rational reflection. In this very important sense, he is in agreement with the pagan philosophers, however much his analysis of politics deviates from their doctrines. This is why he appeals regularly to the great captains and statesmen of pagan antiquity, whose deeds and speeches are entirely pertinent to modern times but whom the ancient philosophers have misrepresented for their own purposes.

Montesquieu shares the traditional philosophical view that human nature, although various in its particular manifestations, is essentially everywhere the same in its fundamental appetites and motives. He is, however, unambiguously a partisan of the new science, which is based upon the Galilean distinction between primary and secondary attributes, or in more accessible terms, upon the difference between scientific truth and human experience. As we have also seen, there is a conflict in Montesquieu's thought between the reductive claims of modern physical and mathematical science on the one hand, and the commonsensical irrelevance of mathematical physics to the conducting and understanding of political life on the other. But Montesquieu now detaches common sense from scientific truth, and accordingly, from a rational conception of nature. In the modern epoch, it becomes progressively more difficult to appeal to a conception of unchanging human nature. In the classic formulation of Aristotle, the polis is a community of animals that perceive good and evil, just and unjust.[5] If one denies that this perception is by nature and insists that it is the perception of an illusion, then differences of behavior and judgment become random motions, governed if at all only by laws analogous to those of matter in the void. Human reality is a perturbation on the surface of chaos. The so-called laws of politics then become a branch of mechanics and possess no political meaning whatsoever, in any rational sense of "meaning." We are then free to interpret chaos as we like. Odd though it may sound initially, the age of universal hermeneutics begins with Galileo.

In the final statement on political virtue in the *Avertissement*, Montesquieu defines its possessor as "the man who loves the laws of his country, and who acts through love of the laws of his country" (228). This is presumably an addition to, rather than a substitute for, the original definition. We must also assume that whereas this love of one's own laws, like political and moral virtue, can also be found to a lesser degree in monarchies, the intensity is insufficient to count as a principle of the regime. This may be because citizens in republics are closer to the production and administration of the laws than in the monarchy.

The distinction between political and moral virtue is plainly designed to distinguish the analysis of political from that of religious and moral phenomena. Montesquieu can claim that he is concerned with the former, not with the latter, and that there is no reason why a state cannot possess both. That this claim was not persuasive is evident from the various defenses that Montesquieu was forced to mount against charges that he had failed to define the virtuous regime as Christian, and even that he was an advocate of Spinozism (a term used to connote atheism).[6] Montesquieu's Christian critics could reasonably assert that the separation in question allows not only for the presence of Christianity in a politically virtuous state but also for its absence. As I have emphasized, the distinction between politics and morals not only imports a quasi-scientific objectivity into the study of politics but at the same time blurs that objectivity by associating political virtue with attributes that are normally also given a moral value. Is it not a moral judgment to say that political and moral virtue are distinct, or that it is a contingent matter whether a politically virtuous country is Christian or not? In sum, Montesquieu both separates and blends together moral and political virtue. This may be partly attributed to a desire to conceal what could and did look to his contemporaries as amoralism, but I believe that the ambiguity is intrinsic to Montesquieu's doctrine and was not fully appreciated by him. Whether or not this is right, it is certainly correct that the terms used by Montesquieu to distinguish political from moral virtue show that the two are inseparable. But this is not the same as to say that they are identical.

We turn next to the preface to the *SL*. Once again Montesquieu begins in a somewhat unexpected manner. Instead of stating his general theme, he initiates a defensive maneuver. If anything in his book offends the reader, that was not his intention. "I do not at all have by nature a disapproving spirit" (229). In a characteristically ambiguous statement, Montesquieu thanks heaven (*le ciel*) that it has arranged for him to be born in the government in which he lives "and that it has made me obey those whom it has made me love." This is a rather elegant way of not explicitly saying that it is the members of the government of France that he obeys and loves. The discussion of politics is much more dangerous than that of mechanics (although the connection between mechanics and theology may indeed be a dangerous topic). I am reminded here of Spinoza's *Tractatus Theologico-Politicus,* the preface to which begins with a criticism of superstition and ends with a willingness to submit everything in what follows to the judgment of the rulers of Holland, a willingness that is repeated at the end of the treatise. Despite this transparent maneuver, I think it is fair to say that Spinoza is bolder than Montesquieu. This cannot be due solely to the difference between the regimes under which the two philosophers lived. It is another sign of the greater daring evinced by what I shall call the "Cartesians" of the seventeenth century in comparison to the more moderate thinkers of the early Enlightenment.

In contrast to the Cartesians, Montesquieu is not advocating the mastery and possession of nature. He is not a prophet of revolution. One sign of this is that he does not employ biblical hermeneutics in the manner of Hobbes and Spinoza, or citations from the pagan historians in the manner of Machiavelli, to inculcate the institution of a new political order. The antibiblical views of Hobbes and Spinoza were relatively easy to discover by their contemporaries, who by and large discerned their general political programs. One cannot advocate a revolution by means of documents that are so esoteric as to be intelligible only to a small minority of readers.[7] Montesquieu is without doubt much more obscure a writer on politics than were these three predecessors. For the time being it must suffice to say that Montesquieu's rhetoric of concealment is not compatible with the intention to initiate a revolutionary shift of world-historical proportions. This shift had already taken place in the seventeenth century, thanks in particular to Locke, Hobbes, and Spinoza. Montesquieu does not simply continue in this tradition; he seeks to modify it and so to moderate it. But neither is he simply endorsing views that would be immediately acceptable to the political and religious authorities of his day. Montesquieu had his troubles with the censors, but these were relatively minor in comparison with those faced by Spinoza or Hobbes.

One can make a general observation about Montesquieu's rhetorical strategy by relating it to the main principles of his philosophy. I begin from the fact that nature obeys laws in all of its domains, human and nonhuman. There is however an obvious difference between the two domains. Let me put the point by a comparison with Plato. According to the Platonic dialogues, human beings are by nature sick or divided within their very souls in a way that prevents them from living just lives in well-ordered cities. Reason is nevertheless capable in principle of understanding not only human sickness but also health; this is represented somewhat hyperbolically in the metaphor of the philosopher-king. The well-ordered soul is a natural paradigm, however difficult it may be to achieve that orderliness in practice. In order to achieve it, we should have to possess knowledge of nature altogether, as represented by the doctrine of Platonic Ideas, and not just political knowledge.

In sum, Plato's doctrine is revolutionary in the precise sense that it predicates the solution to the political problem upon the overthrow of all existing regimes, or on the replacement of convention by the knowledge of nature. But it is not enough to say that we require knowledge of nature. It is after all nature that is responsible for our sick and divided condition, and so nature by itself will not make us well. The very acquiring of knowledge is already an activity, and the transformation of knowledge into political action is constructive. We are thus required to act contrary to nature in the attempt to heal ourselves, but the directions we follow in so acting are themselves furnished by nature.

This fundamental disjunction in nature is still present in Montesquieu. Whatever exists, follows the laws of its own nature, and this is true of human beings as well. But human beings differ by nature from all other beings in the possession of self-consciousness and intelligence. As one could express this, human beings are free by nature to deviate, both intentionally and unintentionally, from the very laws that, if followed, would guarantee a virtuous life in the moral and political senses of that term.[8] The task of the philosopher is accordingly to understand the laws of human or political nature. This includes the ability to explain why these laws are being disobeyed and how the legislator should act in particular circumstances in order to eliminate this disobedience.

It is entirely unclear in Plato precisely how a knowledge of the Idea of justice would compel its perceiver to act justly, and even more unclear how that perception would reveal what is just in the particular case. What is clear, however, is that just action must be compelled. Reason requires the mediation of spiritedness in order to rule the passions within the individual soul, even within the philosopher's soul. In Montesquieu, the Platonic Ideas are replaced by laws of nature, but the disjunction within nature remains. There is then at best only an analogy between physics and politics in Montesquieu. Just as physicists must know the laws of mechanics if they are to understand the motions of inanimate bodies, so political philosophers and legislators must know the laws of political behavior if they are to understand and rectify the actions of human beings. It should be emphasized that the physicist does not legislate; this is a function reserved for God. But the political philosopher is dealing with beings that are "sick" or disobedient. Political philosophers must therefore legislate, or they must make recommendations that will facilitate legislation by others.

By dispensing with metaphysical entities such as Platonic Ideas, and replacing them with natural laws of political action (the counterpart to inanimate motion), Montesquieu has a much easier task in formulating recommendations for political legislation. On the other hand, by attempting to assimilate human natural laws as much as possible with nonhuman natural laws, Montesquieu has a more difficult task in identifying a standard or foundation for the determination of what is politically natural. I have introduced the comparison with Plato at this point for a more restricted reason. There is in Montesquieu no natural basis on which to advocate a radical revolution analogous to that envisioned by Plato. This can be expressed in terms of the difference between Platonic Ideas and natural laws. At the same time, Montesquieu is too moderate, and one could even say too Aristotelian, a political thinker to advocate a purely historical conception of revolution as perpetual change.

However difficult it may be to explain their efficacy, the Ideas underwrite the power of human reason to transform the polis or to bring it into greater accord with beauty, goodness, and justice. Laws of nature, where nature is essentially that of modern physics, lack this efficacy. To the extent that they bind our action, they reduce us to the level of inanimate bodies. One cannot here speak of freedom and so not even of obedience in the political sense of the term; hence there can be no talk of justice or morality. But to the extent that the laws of nature do not bind our action, they leave us free to do as we please. In this sense and to this degree, it is no longer intelligible to speak of "laws of nature." Montesquieu may explain and recommend on the basis of experience, common sense, or historical, geographical, and anthropological knowledge, but this is not the same as an appeal to nature, whether in the Platonic or the Newtonian sense. It is largely an appeal to tradition and custom. The shift from construing nature as the ancient philosophers did to understanding it as do modern physicists deprives political philosophers of a standard by which to validate traditional or customary standards. It leaves open the possibility of the creation of new values and standards, or in other words of new interpretations of political life. If the conservative objects that human beings have always behaved in such-and-such ways, or that rational persons have always adhered to this or that standard of justice and morality, the radical replies that traditional behavior was regulated by superstition, ignorance, or timidity, and that we are now free to overthrow the past and to act as well as judge in new ways.

Montesquieu advocates a moderate implementation of the new science for the amelioration of the human condition, a goal that is to be carried out peacefully rather than by war or the forceful overthrow of existing laws. "I do not at all like persons who overturn the laws of their country."[9] Montesquieu must explain the spirit of the laws without excessively disturbing the spirits of those whom heaven has wished that he obey. Despite his objections to revolution, and his understanding that no revolution takes place as it was intended,[10] Montesquieu is engaging in a campaign of political revisionism that has greater revolutionary implications than he allows for. This, I think, is the main reason for his peculiar style. It is neither radically revolutionary in the Platonic manner nor is it a thoroughly traditional defense of the *ancien régime*. As a defender of natural laws, Montesquieu is a son of the Enlightenment. In his explanation of the political implications of the analogy between physics and politics, Montesquieu practices a certain prudent obfuscation.

It is as a son of the Enlightenment that Montesquieu speaks next. Despite the infinite diversity of laws and mores, human beings do not live by their fantasies; there is an underlying regularity in human lives. "I have posed principles, and I have seen the particular cases submit to them as though by themselves; the histories of all nations are nothing but the consequences [of these principles], and each particular law is linked to another law or depends upon one that is more general" (229). This being so, why cannot Montesquieu write his study of laws in the same manner as a study of mechanics? Again, the obvious problem is that of giving offense. The underlying order is deductive, but the mode of presentation is "political" or rhetorical. This implies that Montesquieu might have written his book quite differently, in a quasi-mathematical or deductive form. Instead, he proceeds in what sometimes looks like a haphazard manner, piling up particular examples and not at all following a deductive order. It is as if someone were to have written a book on universal mechanics by stating the principles he or she had uncovered, followed by the diverse manifestations of those principles in widely differing types of physical bodies, without noting that these bodies are related by custom rather than by inner forces or natural laws.

Nevertheless, Montesquieu insists on the necessary structure of the consequences of his principles. He also emphasizes the difference between his principles and his prejudices. The principles are not "fantasies" but are "posed" on the basis of his "examination" of human beings. He adds that these principles are derived from "the nature of things" (229). In sum: we are to be given a rhetorical presentation of a scientific discipline. The link between Montesquieu and Descartes (as well as Newton) is thus visible at the very beginning of the work, but so too is the difference between politics and physics. It would be going entirely too far to say that Montesquieu conceives of politics as if it were mechanics or, à la Spinoza, the study of "lines, planes, and solids."[11] The need to conceal the deductive teaching is itself a sign that the understanding of politics cannot be entirely deductive. Whereas the circumstances of daily political life can be reduced to laws and studied as deductive consequences of first principles, this knowledge cannot be implemented as a deductive science.

Montesquieu refers explicitly to the dangers inherent in an unrestrained enlightenment: "But in a time of enlightenment [*lumière*], one trembles even when one effects the greatest goods. One senses the ancient abuse; one sees the correction. But one sees also the abuse of the correction itself. One leaves the evil, if one fears what will be worse; one leaves the good, if one is in doubt of something better" (230). This is hard to distinguish from traditional conservatism. The early Enlightenment is thus for Montesquieu the wrong time to introduce radical political changes because European constitutions are sufficiently good that one runs the risk of replacing them with something worse. Change is desirable only when prevailing conditions are marked by ignorance and manifest deficiencies.

Montesquieu thus claims that he would like to give reasons to all citizens "to love their duties, their prince, their country, their laws," and an augmentation of knowledge to each ruler concerning what he ought to prescribe. In general, he would be the happiest of mortals if he could free humankind of its prejudices, namely, "that which makes one ignorant of oneself." Montesquieu tends to downplay the practical consequences of what is ostensibly a work of pure theory, not only to avoid conflict with the authorities but because he disapproves of radical change. His aims are nevertheless not only theoretical but philanthropic. Montesquieu says: "It is in attempting to instruct human beings that one may practice that general virtue which includes the love of all. Man, that flexible being, submitting in society to the thoughts and impressions of others, is equally capable of understanding his own nature whenever one points it out to him, and of losing even the sentiment of it when one conceals it from him" (230). It is the very "flexibility" of human beings that separates politics from physics and makes it impossible to write a purely theoretical study of politics. If human nature may be concealed, is this not the practical equivalent to the admission that it may be changed? As an infant without a mother (the Latin epithet *prolem sine matre creatam* follows the title) who also says of himself *io anche son pittore* ("I too am a painter"), Montesquieu is not only aware of but prides himself upon his originality. And that in itself is an omen of the replacement of nature by art.

The formal structure of the *SL* is complicated and almost scholastic. It divides into parts, books, and chapters. Part 1, with which we are primarily concerned, treats laws in general and the fundamental principles of government. Part 2 considers the relation of the laws to factors internal to the state. In part 3, Montesquieu introduces one of his most famous themes: the relation of the laws to the geographical characteristics of the country; the concluding book in this part turns to the spirit, mores, and manners of the nation. Part 4 is largely but not exclusively concerned with commerce; it closes with a heterogeneous treatment of the relation of the laws to the size of the population. Part 5 groups together religion and a more general discussion of the various kinds of laws. In part 6, Montesquieu discusses the origin and revolution of Roman and French civil law and then turns in book 29 to a general treatment of the manner of composing laws. This book fits awkwardly into the context and seems to be a general conclusion to the entire work rather than a separate topic. It is followed by a long, historically oriented study of the feudal laws of the Franks and the establishment of the French monarchy. The last book of part 6 studies the relation of these same laws to the revolutions of the monarchy. The last chapter of the last book has the odd title "Continuation of the Same Subject," and it closes with a quotation from Virgil's *Aeneid:* "*Italiam, Italiam* . . . I finish the treatise on fiefs where most authors have begun" (995). It looks as though Montesquieu is commenting on his work as a whole. We arrive at the shores of Italy by understanding that the art of politics is the application of Montesquieu's doctrine to one country and historical time after another.

It is entirely outside our present concern to endorse any conclusions about the organization of the work, but some points are obvious at the outset. Montesquieu follows a loose but discernible route from the general to the particular. The practical result of this plan is to conceal, or at least to render less visible, his conclusions. The final 111 pages of the work are devoted to a kind of historical or sociological exhibition of the practical application of Montesquieu's doctrine, rather than to a summary of the doctrine itself. Finally, instead of discussing foreign affairs in general, and war in particular, as a separate part following the discussion of the internal structure of the state, Montesquieu takes up the central theme of commerce. The "official" discussion of war is contained in a single short chapter of less than a page (377) in part 2, entitled "Of War." The entire book, which is devoted to the theme of the laws in their relation to the offensive force (i.e., the army) of the state, is only fifteen pages long. This is of course not to say that the topic of war does not occur regularly in the midst of discussions of other topics. But it is given very little attention as a fundamental element in the art of legislation. This is in accord with Montesquieu's belief that an expanded commercial activity will bring peace; the solution to the problem of human bellicosity is material comfort.

Part 1 will require very close study. Book 1 contains just three chapters, of which the first two are of special interest to us. Montesquieu moves from "laws in their relation to diverse beings" to "natural laws" and thus to "positive laws." The first chapter affirms that all beings are governed by laws; the second and third chapters discuss the two main species of law. Laws, in the broadest sense of the term, "are necessary relations which derive from the nature of things" (232). Everything has laws because everything has a nature; everything is something or another of such and such a kind, as Aristotle might put it. But to be of such and such a kind is to be involved in positive and negative relations with things of other kinds. This has nothing to do with teleology but is a straightforward ontological consequence of what it is to be anything at all. The same properties that define something as this sort of thing, also determine the consequences of the interaction (or in the mechanical idiom, collision) of things of the same and different kinds. We should note that not only are laws themselves relations, but that Montesquieu regularly studies laws in their relations to the main themes of government. The nature of existence in general, and human life in particular, is that of a series of relations of relations, and this makes it difficult to isolate the "natures" or independent identities of any of the elements of these relations.

It would seem that the definition of law in the extended sense of the term identifies all laws as natural laws, but Montesquieu is going to follow the traditional distinction between laws that human beings make and those that they do not. To look ahead for a moment, he will say in chapter 3, "Of Positive Laws," that "the law in general is human reason, insofar as it governs all the peoples of the earth; and the political and civil laws of each nation are nothing but the particular cases in which this human reason is applied" (237). Montesquieu is referring here to the laws we devise, positive laws; obviously we do not legislate the natural forces that combine to produce us as self-legislating beings. Nor is he speaking here of the laws of mechanics. The passage does imply, however, that positive law is not divine. Positive laws are an expression of human nature in the sense that we can trace them back to human characteristics as these are modified by circumstances of climate, custom, religion, and so on. In other words, the defining human characteristics exhibit the so-called natural laws, despite their relativity to time, place, and circumstance. The intelligibility of nature underlies the power of reason to produce laws that are appropriate to the local manifestation of the general.

In chapter 1, Montesquieu says that it is impossible that intelligent beings should have been produced by a blind fatality. He therefore takes it for granted that there is a deity or creator that he calls "une raison primitive," i.e., original or primeval, not "simple." His God is presented here in such a way as to be scarcely distinguishable from the laws of natural science; the laws according to which God has created things are those by which he preserves them. God is here not a religious but an ontological entity, not an object of worship but a rhetorical expression of scientific order. Let us notice the statement that God knows his rules because he has made them. This is a very common theme in modern philosophy; in fact it goes back to the Middle Ages. In the modern period, the axiom is transferred to human beings and strengthened or narrowed to say that we know *only* what we make, such as definitions of theoretical terms or principles in morality (Hobbes, Locke, Vico), or objects of perception in the Kantian transcendental philosophy. The assertion already anticipates the strong constructive element in the modern scientific standpoint.

To continue, these laws of creation and preservation are invariable, since they are the expression of the natures of beings as the things that they are. If the laws were contingent, so too would be the natures of things. In general there are two views about the relation between the will and the intellect in God. The first view is that of Descartes, who claims that God could have made all things other than they are; the second is that of Leibniz. Montesquieu sides with Leibniz and holds that the very subsistence of the world is an expression of the invariability of the laws of creation. But this is a non sequitur, since God could will to preserve what is inherently contingent. We are not going to get very far in choosing one view or the other on theological grounds, nor are these of any real importance for Montesquieu. What counts for him is that if this world were replaced by another, then laws would be different, but there would still be laws. Without laws, there is no world. This is our world, and so these are the laws that we must understand. We might ask why Montesquieu is not concerned about the possibility that God will suddenly change his mind and with it, the world and its laws. The answer, I suspect, is not only that Montesquieu is no metaphysician but that God is for him a figure of speech for the laws of physics. But this cannot be established by straightforward textual quotation.

Montesquieu speaks first of the relations of mass and speed that obtain between physical bodies; here the Newtonian horizon is unmistakable. He then goes on to deal with particular intelligent beings. Before their existence, he says, these beings were possible, and so the laws or relations that govern their natures were also possible. In other words, necessity holds at the level of possibility as well as of actuality. A possible human being is governed by possible laws; all actual laws were initially possible. Therefore it is wrong to say, for example, that there is no justice or injustice until human beings actually legislate or produce positive laws. We misunderstand the significance of the fact that human beings can pass positive laws in accord with diverse senses of justice. All these senses are rooted in the possibility of the human being, i.e., in what it is to be a human being. The senses of justice cannot therefore be so diverse as to include injustice. In slightly different terms, human beings cannot live together except on the basis of a common conception of justice, which is itself an expression of human nature for which "possibility" is here a virtual synonym. Hence the comparison to a circle. To say that there is no justice before actual or positive laws are promulgated is like saying that before a circle is drawn, all of its radii are not equal.

In sum, when Montesquieu refers to possible laws of possible beings, he does not mean that human beings and the laws that express their natures could have been otherwise. "Possible" means here "not actually existing." There is a kind of anticipation here of Kant's "transcendental" possibility, which actualizes as necessary rules. Montesquieu concludes: "One must admit therefore that there are relations of equity anterior to the positive law that establishes these relations" (233). He gives some examples. The line of argument, already stated, is that to be is to be something of such and such a kind. As a being of such and such a kind, each thing has relations with things of other kinds as well as with things of its own kind. These relations constitute the behavior of the beings, and these are in principle accessible to our intelligence.

Let me now emphasize a non-Aristotelian aspect of a concept that looks initially Aristotelian. Montesquieu's natures are not substances or essences but relations. The traditional essence is replaced by its external acts, positive or negative. In the last analysis, to be is to be a relation. This shows us also that Montesquieu has not really thought through the metaphysical or ontological implications of his position. The replacement of essences or substances by external relations leads inevitably to the replacement of necessity by contingency. This is because a relation is a logical form that can unite many different terms; it is not an essence or a substance in the Aristotelian sense.. The same problem is of course visible in Aristotle, who attempts to solve it by his doctrine of intellectual intuition. I do not suggest for a moment that Montesquieu is concerned with questions of this sort. But we should understand how the shift from one metaphysical paradigm to another leads to a new way of conceiving beings in the world. Montesquieu belongs to the champions of the modern paradigm, but he seems to be unaffected by the skepticism that one finds already in Hume. This is the self-confidence of the modern scientific world-view in its classical form.

Next, Montesquieu distinguishes between physical bodies and intelligent beings. The intelligible world has laws which are by their nature invariable, exactly like the physical world. However, the intelligible world, i.e., the world of political life, does not follow its laws constantly, as the physical world follows its laws. "The reason is that particular intelligent beings are limited by their nature, and are consequently subject to error; and from another side, it is their nature that they act by themselves" (233). Montesquieu's remark seems at once obvious and ambiguous. He is obviously referring to the fact that intelligent beings possess a will, that is, we can deviate from laws that we have passed. Human beings cannot deviate from the laws of their nature; they cannot do without food and drink, they must reproduce themselves in a determinate manner, they cannot live together except in accord with a principle of justice, and so on. But they can choose to abstain from nourishment and so perish; they can refrain from reproduction; they can behave unjustly and destroy, or contribute to the destruction of, society. What is traditionally called "freedom of the will" is here called by Montesquieu a limitation of nature, and one that subjects mankind to error. This sounds as though we would be better off if we lacked free will and functioned entirely in accord with the laws of mass and speed that govern physical bodies.

However this may be, our freedom to deviate from the laws that govern our nature does not negate the status of these laws. If someone draws an ellipse instead of a circle, that does not change the geometrical nature of the circle. Montesquieu is therefore making the following claim. What we need to understand is human nature: we need to understand the laws that not simply govern but that constitute that nature. These laws are the same in possibility as they are in actuality. However, they cannot be discovered in abstraction from knowledge of the rich diversity of details that make up human existence. But neither can they be discovered simply by recording those details at random. At some point it is necessary to arrive at principles that make possible a rational deduction of the laws in an order of decreasing generality. We arrive at these principles through a combination of good sense and experience.

Montesquieu says nothing about the logical or psychological process by which we arrive at principles. He simply presents us with the principles that have enabled him to organize experience, that is, to explain the spirit of the laws. No doubt he would say that things are as they are; either we understand them or we do not. If we do, then we can arrange in a deductive manner the laws that govern the world of politics. The proof of the soundness of our principles and of our deductions is simply their explanatory power. Nothing is added by supplementing this analysis with a metaphysical doctrine, and so nothing is subtracted by refraining from metaphysics. In this vein, Montesquieu does not comment on the significance of his emphasis upon laws, relations, or deductive completeness because they are what make science possible, and in the particular case, political science. This is obvious for him.

I can be very brief in noting Montesquieu's remarks about the brutes. The main point is that they lack our advantages but possess others of their own. They cannot hope, but neither can they fear. In particular, they have no foreknowledge of death. In addition, most of them can attend to their self-preservation more efficiently than we can attend to ours, and they do not make as bad a use of their passion as we do. It needs no emphasis that for Montesquieu the brutes are closer to inanimate nature than we are. His reference to the fear of death suggests that in human beings fear outweighs hope. To say this in another way, hope is rooted in memory, whereas the brutes forget almost immediately whatever they have not learned by instinct.

A discussion of forgetfulness concludes the first chapter. Just as freedom to choose is inseparable from the possibility of making the wrong choice, so apparently the capacity to learn is associated with the defect of forgetfulness. Laws express our nature in two analogous ways. They define our relations with other beings, but they also restrict our errors by compelling our memory. This is of course quite different from the function of the laws that govern physical bodies. Human being is by nature free to misinterpret and to forget the laws. Montesquieu is clearly thinking of moral and political laws. His book is concerned not simply with the spirit of the laws but with *the laws of the spirit*. Today we know, as Montesquieu presumably did not, that we are also capable of ignoring or changing the laws that govern our bodies. But this is in a sense always evident; for example, human beings can starve themselves to death or take poisonous substances intentionally. It is not so easy to say which technical modifications of the body and its environment are an expression of, or at least compatible with, the nature of humanity, and which are not. What we can say is that freedom, the distinctive human condition, is a natural attribute of the spirit: not just of intelligence but of desire and the will. But it is not an unmitigated blessing. Religious, moral, and political laws are necessary not so much as an expression of, but as a restriction on, human freedom. They prevent us, as Montesquieu puts it, from forgetting God, ourselves, and our fellow human beings. This is another indication of the fact that Montesquieu is not a revolutionary. The frequently expressed view that Montesquieu replaces virtue with liberty requires considerable qualification. It would be more accurate to say that he prepares the way for this replacement.

In chapter 2 of book 1, Montesquieu takes up the laws that govern human beings in the state of nature, that is, "prior to the establishment of societies" (235). This is the first of many passages that make clear the priority of society to politics. Human beings do not move directly from the state of nature into a political state. Before we can make formal constitutional and legal arrangements, we must pass through a process of socialization, and it is in this process that our religious beliefs, traditions, customs, and manners are all developed. Montesquieu emphasizes throughout that the founding of the state and all subsequent legislation must adjust itself to this pre-political complex of factors. But this leaves unanswered the question of what properties the human beings must have possessed by virtue of our nature alone, such that the entrance into social units was itself possible.

In general, Montesquieu follows Locke in his description of the state of nature. The fundamental thesis is the primacy of self-preservation. Montesquieu grants that there is a law which imprints in us the idea of a creator and directs us toward him. Whereas this law is the most important, it is not the first in the order of human experience. "Man in the state of nature would possess the faculty of knowing, rather than knowledge itself. It is clear that his first ideas would not be at all speculative ideas; he would think [*songerait*] about the conservation of his being before seeking its origin" (235). Montesquieu cited this passage in his favor when he was subsequently accused of atheism, but it is not difficult to see why the charge was leveled. The religious instinct is in effect excluded from the set of natural laws that are intended to explain the essential character of political legislation.[12]

For Montesquieu, as for Locke, self-preservation is the fundamental law of nature.[13] Locke's conception of natural law is notoriously ambiguous, but it will suffice for our purposes to say that he regularly emphasizes self-preservation, peace, sexual reproduction, and the security of private property. In an important passage from his reply to Filmer, Locke derives the right to property from the right (granted in the Bible) to use inferior creatures for the subsistence and comfort of life.[14] Montesquieu differs from Locke on a crucial point. According to Locke, the laws of nature are laws of reason, and they can be administered in the state of nature by all human beings.[15] Montesquieu on the other hand defines natural laws as desires or sentiments. The desire for self-preservation is fundamental to all of these laws, of which Montesquieu gives the first four: a sentiment of feebleness with an accompanying desire for peace, the sentiment of the need for nourishment, the charm of sexual pleasure, and, following the recognition of sentiment, the desire to live in society, which originates in the acquisition of knowledge (236). It is interesting to note that Montesquieu does not explicitly include the right to private property as one of the laws of nature. Nevertheless, on balance, Montesquieu can be described as a follower of Hobbes and Locke in the pursuit of comfortable self-preservation.[16]

It is reasonable to assume that the need for food, shelter, sex, and protection against other animals must have driven human beings to congregate in groups of various sizes. But this assumption is also trivial. The more interesting question concerns the psychological or cognitive properties that transform human congregations into societies rather than into packs or herds. This question is not invalidated by the errors of those who read back into the natural condition of the human animal attributes that could have arisen only in society, and sometimes only in advanced societies or political associations. For example, Montesquieu criticizes Hobbes for attributing to humankind in the state of nature the desire to subjugate one another. He says that "the idea of empire and domination" is too complex and depends upon too many other ideas to be on the original level of human motivation (235).[17] It would nevertheless be useful to know whether *homo sapiens* is by nature peaceable or warlike, and not only for theoretical purposes. There is not much point in designing the constitution of a state for primarily peaceful ends if our nature drives us to war and eventually to "empire and domination." One might wish that human beings were pacific or even claim that they *ought* to be so. But even if a beneficent political founder were legitimately to try to pacify his or her subjects, knowledge of their original nature would be essential in that founder's formulation of laws and institutions, including the taking of measures to protect citizens within the domain from external enemies.

This example shows the serious weaknesses in the doctrine of a state of nature. The doctrine entails that human nature is not accessible to the naked eye or even to the scientific methods of observation and experiment by which we confirm the natural laws that govern inanimate bodies. The ostensible laws of human nature are covered over by historical accretions, namely, by the very social and political customs and institutions that we are attempting to explain. We cannot control the behavior of human beings in order to isolate uniform causal relations, as is done regularly in the experimental sciences. And even if we could control human behavior, the result would be a despotism, which is not in accord with the goal of political virtue and liberty. In other words, there is no way short of the destruction of political life to establish controlled experiments designed to understand the laws that govern political life. Either the laws of nature are visible to us within a given society and state, or they are not. If they are visible, scientists should agree concerning their nature, just as they agree about the laws of mechanics. But if such laws are not visible, then all inferences from society back to the state of nature are pure speculation. That is, we are forced to speculate, not merely on the particular natural laws themselves, but on whether human beings have a presocial nature at all, in any sense beyond the biological. We therefore turn to history as a substitute for experiment.

Montesquieu's unstated implication is that he is the Newton (or more accurately, the Descartes) of politics, and that he has discovered the natural laws of politics as Newton and his fellow savants have discovered those of the heavenly bodies. But the laws of motion can be confirmed experimentally to very high degrees of precision. In this way, no competent disagreement is allowed. This is not true of the laws of political nature, which are disputed more violently by the experts in this domain than by the average person. Closely connected to this is the fact that political laws do not allow for prediction, or that they leave it to a matter of opinion whether predictions have been confirmed. But if the laws do not allow for accurate predictions, then they are not laws, or at least not laws in the sense of the laws of mechanics. The universal methods of science make it possible to resolve disagreements between physicists about the laws of motion. There are no such methods for resolving the disputes of Hobbes and Montesquieu about the state of nature.

I do not mean to imply that I regard all talk of political nature as circular or empty. My point is rather that the false analogy between physics and politics that underlies Montesquieu's treatment of natural political laws vitiates his orienting theoretical claim. From the fact that human beings have innate psychological and cognitive properties, e.g., a peaceful or a warlike inclination, no natural laws whatsoever may be derived. This is because peaceful people may be rendered martial and martial societies pacified, thanks to the fact that human beings are, in Montesquieu's words, "this flexible being" (230). And if, by "law," Montesquieu means not what must happen but what ought to happen, this in turn cannot be inferred from how human animals behaved in the state of nature. The existence of human history is thus a demonstration of the radical difference between physical motions and political actions, rather than of a universal domain of natural laws. From the standpoint of natural law theorists, history is the story of human disobedience. But if history is the record of human behavior, and if this behavior deviates from "natural law," then in what sense are these laws binding? And how did we discover their existence, if human conduct does not exemplify them?

The principal error in Montesquieu's reasoning, or more accurately, in his implied line of reasoning, is the claim that our innate traits explain our political actions in the same way that the laws of mechanics explain the motions of natural bodies, but that we are also free to deviate from these laws. It does not follow from this error that there are no laws of any kind that govern political behavior. No one could deny that there is a certain regularity in human behavior, and that this regularity makes political life possible. But these laws are more like positive than natural laws in the very important sense that we can disobey them. If Montesquieu says that we pay a penalty for disobedience, this is a value judgment, not a statement of scientific fact. And even if in fact we pay such a penalty, that does not interfere with our freedom to disobey. One could therefore say that Montesquieu's error arises from a failure to have thought through the problem of the relation between freedom and necessity. But how could one remove the problematic nature of this relation? The two terms seem to be mutually exclusive. We might be free in some respects and determined by necessity in others, but we cannot be both with respect to the central question of the natural laws of politics.

So much for the flaw in Montesquieu's implicit reasoning. Despite the excessive reliance on the example of mechanics, there is a more reasonable way in which to formulate Montesquieu's central thesis. Human beings are the only animals who can exit the state of nature by their own efforts. Furthermore, the main cause of our entrance into society is not sentiment, as we have just seen. The fourth law of nature, namely, the desire to live in society, is rooted in the link that arises among human beings through the acquisition of knowledge. This is decisive for the origin of society in a way that sexual attraction is not. We could reproduce in the state of nature, but we could not expand our knowledge. Sex becomes centrally important when it is politicized, but this obviously depends upon the establishment of society. Montesquieu does not elaborate at all on what he means by "knowledge" in this context, but it is safe to say that it cannot be pure natural science. Political society is marked in its essence by the phenomenon of interpretation or ideology, that is, the interpretation of how to live, given that we are free to express our sentiments in such a seemingly infinite variety of ways, as Montesquieu himself testifies.

Only human beings are free in this precise sense of the term. We possess a unique nature; one could say that we are partially detached from nature. This is our openness, and by this I mean something more than flexibility. Our flexibility allows us to cope with our openness, but it must be implemented by laws in order to prevent us from falling through that openness or entirely out of nature. On this point there is no difference between Montesquieu and Rousseau. The social contract is the safety net against the very openness that allows us to emerge from the state of nature. But for Rousseau, this net is itself an artifact, whereas for Montesquieu it is natural. In other words, the two thinkers disagree about the state of nature. Rousseau's explanation of the exit from the state of nature into society is problematic, and the results are negative to a considerable degree.[18] The state is thus a kind of artificial device that is designed to rectify as much as possible these negative consequences, whereas for Montesquieu, the state is a natural consequence or perfection of the human condition in the state of nature. One obvious sign of this difference that is especially pertinent to our inquiry is the different assessment by the two philosophers of the relation between material comfort and virtue in both its senses.

Montesquieu anticipates Rousseau by criticizing Hobbes's account of humankind in the state of nature. The first law of nature that we acquire is not speculative but practical: we are concerned with self-preservation before we begin to think about our origin. Nevertheless, as we have seen, one of the laws of nature "imprints in our minds the idea of a creator" and "draws us toward him" (235). Montesquieu does not say that we conceive the law of nature "God exists" but that the law imprints the idea of God on our intellects. In other words, we are by nature inclined to arrive at such a conclusion. We have intelligence before we acquire knowledge. Furthermore, we begin to acquire knowledge in the state of nature, and this is the decisive factor for the shift into society. The knowledge may be quite simple, as for example with respect to the use of tools. But this is enough to engender the long process that culminates in Enlightenment.

It thus turns out that Montesquieu is only partially in disagreement with

Hobbes. He does follow Locke in holding that human beings are feeble, and so timid rather than warlike, in the state of nature. "Everything makes them tremble; everything makes them flee" (235). This is a rather dubious conclusion, since it seems to be based upon the encounter between civilized persons and savages in the forests of Europe (again, an anticipation of Rousseau's "anthropologism"). In any case, Montesquieu claims that, in the state of nature, "each person regards himself as inferior; he scarcely regards himself as equal" (i.e., to the other savages). "They do not seek to attack; peace is the first natural law."

Let us pause here for a moment. If human beings initially regard themselves as inferior and unequal in the state of nature, then the desire for peace is a consequence of that natural inequality. In other words, it looks as if Montesquieu must here reject the Hobbes-Locke thesis that human beings are by nature equal. And in fact, he makes equality the principle, or part of the principle, of just one type of regime, the republic. On the other hand, a universal feeling of inferiority amounts to a sentiment of negative equality. We feel unequal to our perceived enemies, namely, everyone, and so we "equalize" ourselves by seeking peace.

A brief contrast between Montesquieu and Hobbes is instructive at this point. Hobbes, like his critics, emphasizes the primacy of fear in human life. But he infers from this the priority of war to peace, whereas for his critics, peace is prior to war. If life is primarily war, fear leads us to desire domination or the imposition of peace through universal power: Hobbes' monarchism leads through the pressure of modern science and technology to Alexandre Kojève's universal homogeneous state. This is equivalent to the political restriction of the passions and desires. If life is primarily peace, fear is mitigated by timidity. The task of the legislator is therefore to mitigate timidity rather than to induce it. Otherwise put, human beings must be encouraged to cooperate in order to preserve themselves. This cooperation is achieved by the mutual satisfaction of the passions and desires, i.e., of private interests (to use a famous eighteenth-century term). Since human beings are not by nature "interested" in domination, they can attend to the amelioration of their natural condition.

Hobbes is thus the founder of a centralized, state-controlled economy, whereas his critics are the champions of commerce and manufacture on the part of private citizens. For the Hobbesian, the function of the state is to regulate commerce and manufacture; for the Lockean, the function of the state is to encourage commerce and manufacture. In one last formulation: Hobbesian politics is designed to make fearful human beings secure and comfortable, whereas Lockean politics (and Montesquieu belongs in this camp) is designed to achieve security through encouraging the acquisition of items of comfort. Hobbes thus retains fear within political life, whereas Locke, Montesquieu, and other Enlightenment thinkers seek to banish fear from political life.

Hobbes attributes ideas and concerns to human beings in the state of nature that could not arise before the establishment of societies. The ideas of empire and domination are all too common within society, and Montesquieu knows that we cannot return humankind to the state of nature in order to prepare the proper political laws that will guarantee the continuation of natural pacifism. The decision about the priority of peace to war, and in fact the entire discussion of the state of nature, taking it in its most reasonable sense, is a schematized way of presenting Montesquieu's analysis of the laws of human nature as they are visible within actual political life. Peace is more natural than war, but when we step outside nature, or in other words exercise our freedom, we fall into war. The problem faced by the political philosopher is how to restrict war. Montesquieu's answer is not: destroy the existing state and rebuild correctly. It is rather that the natural development of the state is leading us to a restriction of the desire for domination, if not to a complete replacement of it, by the desire for comfort. I mention here once more Montesquieu's importance in the development of what we now call "the philosophy of history." The natural priority of peace to war makes violent revolution unnecessary as well as dangerous. This is the sense of "Enlightenment": we are evolving toward peace. Still, that evolution is not uniform, as I noted previously.

In accord with the principal laws of nature, our desires for peace, nourishment, sex, and knowledge compose the fundamental structure of our political nature. So war, hunger, loneliness, and ignorance are contrary to nature; they are the result of freedom and we have to protect ourselves against them by positive laws. Again we see that it is a mistake to exaggerate Montesquieu's preference for liberty over moral and even political virtue.

The third and last chapter of book 1 treats of positive law. The state of nature is peace. This peace is rooted in the timidity and even fear that is the result of a feeling of inferiority. But now Montesquieu seems to deny that the state of nature represents the structure of social existence. Previously he said that everyone in the state of nature feels inferior and, with difficulty if at all, equal. But now he interprets this feeling of inferiority as itself a form of equality. When everyone feels inferior, no one seeks to obtain power over the others. The shift from the state of nature to society is accompanied by a loss of the feeling of feebleness or inferiority. Accordingly, the previous equality is lost, "and the state of war begins" (236).

On this interpretation, human beings are equal in the state of nature; in society, however, equality is the principle, or more accurately, part of the principle, of republics, and it must be established by positive law. In this limited degree, the principle of the republic would then be in accord with the state of nature as the principles of the other regimes are not. It looks as if the state of nature is an expression of the human ability to deviate from the laws of that nature. The state of nature is a metaphor for the correct understanding of the laws of human nature. The ambiguities of political life are thus a reflection of the ambiguities in the very constitutive sentiments and desires of human nature. What must be the case is that the laws of human nature are visible within past and present political activity, together with the many deviations from them that are made possible by our freedom. In other words, for Montesquieu, human beings are not free simply to invalidate the laws of nature, or to replace them with entirely new laws, or, finally, to live without laws at all. Freedom is freedom to deviate from the laws of nature in ways that are themselves law-like.

I do not believe that this reply, assuming that it would be endorsed by Montesquieu, resolves the problem of the assimilation of the laws of politics to those of physics. But it is sufficient to provide us with a working hypothesis as to how freedom and law may be reconciled within the political domain. The political model of the state of nature functions at a lower level of theoretical generality than does the physical model of a comprehensive structure of laws. The model of the state of nature is designed to express the innate causes of the practical uniformity of human conduct that has been noticed by all students of politics, and that is empirically confirmed by the apparently universal presence, within societies of widely differing positive laws and customs, of a finite set of ends, motives, and appetites. The onus of proof is on those who claim that uniformity in the past was a matter of historical contingency, and that no inferences can be drawn from the rule of convention to an enduring human nature.

The conventionalist, in order to refute Montesquieu, must demonstrate that new modes of communal life that differ radically from those of the past are possible, and that the apparently universal desire for justice, glory, power, or wisdom, however differently these may be conceived in the details, is no longer operative. The argument is not one of mathematics or logic; it is not simply on the other hand an arbitrary opinion or subjective perspective but rather an interpretation of empirical facts. Montesquieu cannot demonstrate his interpretation of human nature to a higher degree of precision than the matter allows. But he has a case to be made. The most profound problem in Montesquieu's philosophy is not with his political observations and recommendations as such, but with the underlying theoretical conception of universal natural law. The inner inconsistencies of this theoretical conception lead to problems like that of the status of political recommendations in what is ostensibly a work of scientific objectivity, essentially like mechanics.

To repeat the main point, the natural political laws are distorted by society as it actually exists. That social existence is a consequence of our freedom or openness, of our falling out of nature. This fall is the aforementioned shift from peace to war. What is the precise reason for this shift? I do not believe that Montesquieu makes this entirely clear. He says: "Every particular society comes to feel its force, which produces a state of war between nations. Individual persons within each society begin to feel their force; they seek to turn to their favor the principal advantages of this society; this produces a state of war between them" (236). So the cause of the shift from peace to war is the sentiment of force. In nature, we feel feeble; in society, we feel strong. The cause of the shift from peace to war must be the same as the cause of our exiting from the state of nature into society. Let us remind ourselves of how we enter into society in the first place. This must be inferred from our analysis of the laws of nature themselves. Our desires for peace, nourishment, sex, and knowledge bring us together; we learn how to satisfy our desires and how to protect ourselves against our weakness. Hence we become braver as well as cleverer. And this in turn excites our desires so as to drive us to seek further gratification. Obviously the gratification of this drive is encouraged by the sense of strength that comes from the size of the association. But in itself, it is not an explanation, since a social group could feel weak and inferior with respect to other social groups. When all the aforementioned factors obtain, the result is, or soon becomes, the pursuit of war. Something like this must be what Montesquieu has in mind.

There is also an ambiguity in the natural freedom arising from the will, that is, from our openness and flexibility, from our capacity to modify our behavior in order to satisfy our desires. Freedom institutes war; it is therefore not an unmitigated good. It is also not an unmitigated evil, because the same freedom allows us to ameliorate our natural condition. The most important example is the progress of comfort and knowledge that follows the exit from the state of nature. The political problem is how to ameliorate our natural condition while suppressing war and promoting peace. Since war is caused by the sentiment of force, it follows that peace will require a restriction of this feeling. Montesquieu's doctrine is the reverse of Nietzsche's celebration of the will to power. Or rather one could say that whereas Montesquieu recognizes the will to power as a human characteristic, he equates it with society rather than with nature. Think here of Rousseau's famous opening sentence to the first chapter of the *Social Contract:* "Man is born free, yet everywhere he is in chains."[19] Montesquieu is in effect saying that human beings are born in peace, yet everywhere they are at war with one another.

The expression of our natures leads to the transition from nature to society. This transition is both good and bad; otherwise stated, the bad elements of the transition have good consequences: perpetual peace, at least in the state of nature, would mean perpetual stagnation. This transition is of course accompanied by the creation of positive law, the primary function of which is to regulate the feeling of force in such a way as to preserve society from dissolution. The task of the political philosopher is to recommend modifications of the positive law that will rectify the bad consequences of nature, that is, of the openness of human nature. I note in passing that the ambiguity of the relation between nature and freedom extends into each term. It is not clear whether openness, and so the distortion of natural law, is itself natural or whether it is precisely freedom from nature. Is nature opposed to freedom or divided within itself into necessity and freedom? Montesquieu does not ask questions like these. Perhaps he would regard them as too metaphysical. Unfortunately, they are imposed upon us as soon as we think carefully about his teaching.

We thus have to reconcile, or at least to combine, two aspects of Montesquieu's fundamental doctrine. The understanding of political life is a science that consists in the deducing of positive laws from the natural principles that are their source. This tells us why positive laws are as they are in particular kinds of states. It also tells us how to modify defective laws or how to bring them back into conformity with their principle. But just as the defective laws owe their deficiencies to human freedom, so with the modifications or corrections. Science may be the mastery of nature, but it is itself an art. Just as physical scientists require machines in order to study nature, machines that allow them to modify nature's intrinsic behavior, so too the analysis of the spirit of the laws allows us to modify the natural consequences of freedom, namely, war. But oddly enough, whereas the goal of physical science is to increase our power to satisfy our desires through control and transformation of the environment, the goal of political science is to restrict that power. Political science is thus an art by which we regulate nature, not so much to become masters and possessors of nature as to return to our own natures, that is, to our intrinsic peacefulness, but in a more comfortable manner. We produce the circumstances for *douceur de vivre,* and in that sense we modify nature. We return to nature by means of art. It would be going too far to call this art the will to powerlessness, but the difference between Montesquieu and Nietzsche is evident. And in saying this I mean to be understood as distinguishing Montesquieu from the radical or late French Enlightenment.

The closest Montesquieu comes to the Nietzschean doctrine of self-overcoming is in the advocacy of increasing comfort. And this is not very close, since Nietzsche would have abhorred the interpretation of self-overcoming as a steady increase in comfort. I bring up this contrast between Montesquieu and Nietzsche in order to illuminate the difference between prerevolutionary and postrevolutionary modernity. In *Natural Right and History,* Leo Strauss refers to Locke's understanding of human life as the "joyless quest for joy."[20] Oddly enough, Locke is in this sense closer to Nietzsche and in general to nineteenth-century thought than is Montesquieu. In Hegel's fine expression, "the peculiar restlessness and dispersion of our modern consciousness" has both a positive and a negative role to play.[21] There is a touch of this in Montesquieu, as we just saw in the discussion of freedom. On the whole, however, Montesquieu attempts to domesticate restlessness. He combines Aristotelian prudence with Newtonian scientific confidence. If I am not mistaken, this is the reason that Montesquieu is far less studied and appreciated today than are Hobbes, Locke, and Rousseau. Tocqueville is also very popular today because he exhibits the disillusionment of the alienated intellectual, albeit in the idiom of the prudential aristocrat, who is led by his disillusionment to an attempt to come to terms with democracy. Thus he is appreciated today by liberals and conservatives alike.

I have suggested that Montesquieu can be understood as one of the initiators of a series of efforts that evolves into twentieth-century doctrines like sociology on the one hand and Husserl's account of the scientifically determined structure of the life-world on the other. It is of course true that the science in question is for Husserl his own phenomenology, and that he is not concerned with prudence or the ordering and legislation of actual political life but with bringing to light the "transcendental" (i.e., theoretical) sources of the meaning and value of science in human life generally. But this is just to say that twentieth-century phenomenologies and ontologies, very much like the parallel philosophies of linguistic and conceptual analysis, exhibit clearly the difficulty intrinsic in the attempt to develop a science of *praxis.* The more scientific the analysis or description of human acts, the further we move from the commonsense and ordinary phenomena with which we began and that we intend to clarify.

A second and correlative intention of the present study has been to show how the modern attempt to acquire a scientific theory of politics leads to the replacement of the original paradigm of physics or cosmology by the new paradigm of history. What was known in the eighteenth century as natural history was transformed in the twentieth century into the history of nature. There is a curious parallel in the science of linguistics, which uses the expression "natural language" to refer to the dialect of the native speaker of a historical language. "Nature" here refers to growth and change in everyday use. The term is also used by Chomsky and his students in a quasi-Cartesian sense to designate the universal innate laws of syntax, but whether these exist or not is irrelevant to our own investigation. The Chomskyan project itself is an interesting example of the late-Enlightenment attempt to transform linguistics into an exact science, but it is not concerned with the philosophical explanation of ordinary experience. Chomsky's "natural laws" purport to tell us how languages are constructed but not what we say within them, other than that we must follow certain rules of transformation in order to express ourselves properly. In this chapter, I have been primarily concerned with Montesquieu's doctrine of the nature of law as it bears upon everyday human practice in the presocial "state of nature," and thus with the origin of society and the state. It seems advisable, however, to conclude with a summary statement that places the *SL* within the general philosophical context of its time.

In 1751 Rousseau published his *Discourse on the Arts and Sciences*. In this discourse, Rousseau raises the question that the most important figures of the early or (what I call) moderate Enlightenment attempt to answer in the affirmative: Is virtue compatible with unrestricted technological and scientific progress? The characteristic affirmative answers to Rousseau's question are all based on a relaxed interpretation of moral virtue and even, as is true of Montesquieu, on a distinction between political and moral virtue. This distinction is at least as old as Aristotle, but in its modern form it is closely associated with an enhanced appreciation of commerce, wealth, and the comfort or "softness" (*douceur*) of modern life, to employ Montesquieu's term.

Montesquieu is therefore of interest not simply as a founding father of sociology, and so as a test case for the compatibility of scientific *logos* with society in its everyday course. He is also to my mind the most penetrating advocate of what I call "comfortable virtue." To understand him is necessarily to arrive at a judgment as to whether comfort, the steady amelioration of the material conditions of human life, is compatible with virtue. And this of course requires a deliberation on the term "virtue," which, as Montesquieu insists, has more than one sense. Is the goal of "comfortable virtue" coherent? Can we enlighten ourselves in a moderate rather than an extreme manner, and so not sacrifice virtue to comfort? This is not a question of purely academic interest. It is true that we now live in an accelerated version of the mature Enlightenment. It has been more or less clear for some time, and to some from the very beginning of the Enlightenment, that this process of acceleration has deleterious consequences for the very ends to which it aspires. An excessive intensification of light is a hindrance to, rather than a prerequisite of, acute vision. One should not, however, leap from one extreme to the other. No sensible person advocates a return to "darkness," and I have no wish to repudiate the principles of the moderns or to advocate a return to "the wisdom of the ancients" that is not only historically impossible but, in an extreme form, undesirable as well.

By studying Montesquieu we inquire not merely into the application of the model of natural science to everyday life but also into a subtle and complex version of the principles of society that predominates among contemporary defenders of the Enlightenment. Our itinerary is thus both theoretical and practical. To the extent that we are able to give the practical consequences of Montesquieu's theoretical assumptions, this double route is an advantage. I have previously described these consequences as moderate. Let me now try to render more precise what I mean by the expression "the moderate Enlightenment."

I accept the widely held view that there were several Enlightenments and that it would be a serious error to ignore the various differences separating the Scottish-English, French, German, and Italian versions from one another, to give only the leading examples. But the names by which these versions are designated have an essential feature in common. All refer to the attempt to eliminate restrictions placed upon bringing to light the truth about human experience. This attempt is connected in all cases to the wish to increase the scope of personal freedom in the political as well as the intellectual senses of that expression. Stated in general but not misleading terms, the various versions of Enlightenment are designed to reduce the power of religious dogma and authoritarian government. Correlatively, they are all associated with the effort to extend the authority of human reason, and in particular, of the rationality typified by the new mathematical and experimental sciences. Hence the great importance of the words "freedom" and "autonomy" in the official vocabulary of the Enlightenment.

It would be tempting to add to this cautious formulation that the various versions of the Enlightenment represent different but related attempts to institutionalize or render popular the great scientific, philosophical, and religious rebellion of the seventeenth century against the allegiance between the Christian religion and pagan theory. The temptation should be resisted, however, if not altogether discarded. This is mainly because of the difference between the "moderate" and the "extreme" or "mature" Enlightenment, at least with respect to the French *siècle des lumières*. Its most characteristic representatives were d'Alembert, Diderot, Voltaire, and Condorcet, as well as lesser figures like La Mettrie, Helvétius, and d'Holbach. I cite the French Enlightenment because I take its mature form to be the direct precursor of the dominant version of the Enlightenment in our own time, namely, the "triumph" of scientific and technological rationalism, a triumph that we cannot resist even as we become ever more aware of its limitations and dangers.

What interests me here is the rhetoric of the mature French Enlightenment. Its contemporary version has assimilated and redefined important elements of other versions of the Enlightenment, as for example the flourishing of economics, commonsense empiricism, and appeals to sympathy and prudence. No one could say that Shaftesbury, Hume, Smith, Mandeville, or Montesquieu himself adopted without reservation the mathematical paradigm of reason that underlies the transformation of almost every aspect of social and political life during the past three centuries. This transformation testifies to the inability of other conceptions of rationality to resist the mathematical paradigm, without doubt because of the technological consequences of mathematics, consequences that can hardly be deduced from or attributed to common sense, prudence, or sympathy.

The moderate or early Enlightenment, on the other hand, and not only in France, is characterized fundamentally by the belief that the new science can be united with and regulated by more traditional versions of political and philosophical moderation. This view is also to be found in Rousseau, ostensibly the great enemy of the Enlightenment but in some ways more properly seen as a philosophical cousin of Montesquieu and Hume. One can say that the early Enlightenment is marked by a failure to understand the extraordinary forces of transformation that were set loose by the founding fathers of the modern age. In important ways, Montesquieu and Hume are far less radical than Descartes, presumably because they were not by nature and education deeply versed in the new natural sciences. Nor was Montesquieu, despite the fact that he was influenced by Descartes in his own scientific studies as well as in the general project to discover the laws of nature.[22]

The early Enlightenment was moderate. It exhibits the process by which steps were taken to initiate a moderate improvement of the human condition. The new science thus assumes a subordinate or instrumental role: it is to be employed for the sake of comfortable virtue. There is no question here of the mastery and transformation of nature advocated by Descartes, nor, in the case of Montesquieu (Hume is another story), of the associated implication that the previous master must be disinherited. No doubt that is the main reason why, despite the praise of commerce and manufacture, we do not find in the early Enlightenment a clear picture of the economic consequences of the scientific and technological revolution. This is certainly true of Montesquieu, for whom, as Raymond Aron notes, economy is essentially agriculture and commerce, to the neglect of industry.[23]

Montesquieu, together with Hume and Adam Smith, is one of the three greatest representatives of the early or moderate Enlightenment, understood as a political program in the broad sense of the term. He is neither an epistemologist nor an economist, and his interest in the experimental sciences is essentially that of the well-educated amateur. On the other hand, he has a comprehensive view of human life, reminding us at some crucial points of Aristotle's ethical and political writings. The *SL* is an attempt to preserve the moderation and prudence of Aristotelian political thought while at the same time rejecting Aristotle's conception of nature, and in particular of human nature. As Montesquieu says near the end of his work, "I say it, and it seems to me that I have written this work only to prove it: the spirit of moderation should be that of the legislator; the political good, like the moral good, is always found between two limits." He goes on to illustrate this important principle by noting that the formalities of justice, although they are necessary for liberty, may be so cumbersome as to interfere with it, in which case they must be curtailed (865). One of the most important features of Montesquieu's philosophy is the combination of Aristotelian *phronesis* with a Cartesian, even mechanistic, conception of nature. He attempts to insert a classical conception of unchanging human nature, of which the principles are directly accessible to the careful observation of all historical epochs, into a framework of natural law that is derived from modern physics, not medieval jurisprudence and political philosophy. This combination, as I hope to have shown in detail, is unstable, and it leads directly to the dissolution of the conception of an unchanging human nature, common to most of the leading thinkers of the Enlightenment. Montesquieu sets out to show us how humankind is everywhere the same; he ends by creating, or contributing fundamentally to the creation of, historicism and the philosophy of history. In this way he anticipates the fate of our understanding of ordinary experience and language in the twentieth century.[24]

From another perspective, Montesquieu could be understood as having attempted to effect a synthesis of the ancients and the moderns by preserving the best features of the two conflicting agendas.[25] In this sense, he is a successor of Leibniz and Spinoza and a precursor of Hegel, although he is, to repeat, primarily a political thinker rather than a metaphysician or system builder. This is for us an advantage rather than a limitation. It has been my express intention in this study to understand Montesquieu as a precursor of the tension between modern science and ordinary experience and the contemporary destiny of that tension. This exercise is easier to conduct on a text that eschews metaphysics and approaches human nature from the standpoint of politics.

I want now to say a final word about the Aristotelian component in Montesquieu's thought. This component is, so to speak, spiritual rather than corporeal. I of course do not suggest that Montesquieu was a disciple of Aristotle. It would be more accurate on many crucial points to see him as a student of Machiavelli. Nevertheless, there is something unmistakably Aristotelian in his devotion to moderation and in the correlative tendency to define political wisdom as a mean between two extremes. Montesquieu gives an Aristotelian twist to the doctrines of Machiavelli. Montesquieu's "virtue" is much closer to Machiavelli's *virtù* than it is to Aristotle's *arete,* but it is nevertheless a *virtù* that is moderated and rendered more gentle by *arete.* One can make this point somewhat more precise by noting that Montesquieu's conception of "political virtue" is closer to Aristotle's *Politics* than to the *Nicomachean Ethics.* It is the virtue that is relative to the republican regime rather than that of the perfect "gentleman" whose nobility and goodness could be harmonized only with the best regime. Furthermore, no virtue expresses for Montesquieu the fundamental spirit of the monarchy or despotism, as one certainly does for Machiavelli. The spirit of violent innovation that permeates Machiavelli's most famous work, *The Prince,* is entirely absent from Montesquieu.

Montesquieu resembles Aristotle in another way while at the same time deviating from him. Aristotle's definitions of virtue and prudence are rooted in his doctrine of human nature. This doctrine is often said to depend upon the order of the cosmos.[26] If this is true, then politics is for Aristotle a branch of physics, which is itself inseparable from metaphysics. But this is not how Aristotle describes the situation. He separates practical from theoretical intelligence in such a way as to make moral virtue a refinement of the "opinions" (*endoksa*) of sensible persons. This is exhibited most dramatically in his rejection of the Platonic paradigm of the philosopher-king. Practical intelligence and the regulation of a virtuous life at the political and personal levels in no way require knowledge of physics or metaphysics. But this does not prove that the sound philosophical understanding of ethics and politics is independent from a sound grasp of psychology, physics, and metaphysics.

We must not confuse two distinct points. The commonsense understanding of ethics and politics as articulated by "serious" or good and sensible persons is not the same as Aristotle's elaborate analysis of ethics and politics. Furthermore, it may not be necessary for the statesman, and still less for the citizen, to be a physicist or metaphysician, but only someone with a theoretical grasp of human nature would be able to confirm that the practical maxims of good and sensible persons are something more than conventional or historically conditioned "folk wisdom."

There is then a deep ambiguity at the heart of Aristotle's ethical and political writings that turns upon the exact relation between theory and practice. Practice seems to be both dependent upon and independent of theory. Human nature seems to be distinct from and governed by the principles of cosmological nature. Whereas it would be impossible from an Aristotelian standpoint to give a theoretical account of practice, there is clearly some intermediate account that makes use of distinctions like that between nature and convention. It is not clear that one can understand human nature without understanding nature in a sense broader than that of practice, yet narrower than that of physics or cosmology.

This much does seem clear. If we are to retain the conviction that human beings are in a practical sense always the same, then it cannot be adequate to say with Aristotle that the principles of practice are changeable. There must be some basis on which to decide when these changes are to be approved and when they are to be rejected. But this requires principles that go beyond those of practice, that is, beyond the *endoksa* or beliefs of the serious and good pretheoretical observers of everyday life. And this in turn opens the door to the danger of reductionism, of reducing practical to theoretical principles: of reducing politics to physics. Or else we must embrace a radical dualism of human and cosmological nature. Montesquieu vacillates between these two alternatives. He attempts to sustain a prudential and early modern conception of unchanging human nature in a framework of laws that express the spirit of modern mechanics. The substitution of Cartesian or Newtonian for Aristotelian physics radicalizes the problem, already visible in Aristotle, of the natural basis for politics.[27] It is this problem that leads to historicism.

More generally, modern political philosophy from Machiavelli to Montesquieu takes it largely for granted that human nature is the same in all periods of political history. The transformation in physics and metaphysics does, however, have an obvious effect on the particular interpretation of human nature. To mention only one crucial example, there is a marked shift, especially apparent in Descartes, Hobbes, and Spinoza, from virtues to passions as the foundation for the analysis and evaluation of human behavior. This shift is one consequence of the replacement of the classical dualism of body and soul with the modern dualism of body and mind. The soul is silently forgotten; modifications of character are accordingly interpreted physiologically (as in Descartes' *Passions of the Soul*) whereas practical intelligence comes to be understood as cleverness at achieving gratification of the bodily desires. If the mind is restricted to conceptual thought, or to determining the formal structure of reality, then "good" and "bad" lose their rational element and are taken to express the desire or antipathy of the passions.

A similar situation exists in Montesquieu. In very general terms, the inner tension in Montesquieu's thought is already visible in the title of his masterpiece. The "spirit" of the laws is not accessible within the framework of mathematical physics. Montesquieu goes beyond Aristotle by including in the *SL* an introductory discussion of the laws of nature in general. He then draws a formal analogy between mechanics and politics. So doing, he falls short of the excellence of Aristotle's political writings, because there is no analogy between mechanics and politics. If there were, the distinction between virtue and vice would become meaningless, and this is true of political as well as of moral virtue. It is hard to see how Montesquieu could have overlooked this difficulty, especially since it was obvious to him that human beings can and do violate the so-called laws of nature. The least one could say is that there is a disjunction between human and nonhuman nature. It is this disjunction that allows for, and indeed requires, political philosophy, or a doctrine that teaches us how to construct laws that will allow us to live in accord with nature, both human and nonhuman. In fact, human life is unintelligible except as the pursuit of freedom and the good life, in a sense of "good" that includes virtue of the moral as well as the political type. But the laws of mechanics are of no assistance to this pursuit, except perhaps as a metaphor for the underlying regularity of human nature. Even as a metaphor, however, the paradigm of the uniformity of the laws of nature is radically defective. Just as Aristotle's statesman does not require a knowledge of physics and metaphysics, neither does Montesquieu's doctrine of politics require from its practitioners a knowledge of mathematical physics. The political philosopher, however, requires what one could call a popular conception of the structure of natural laws. There are so to speak two spirits in the law, one political and the other scientific.

The lesson to be derived from our study of Montesquieu is that modern mathematical and experimental science, among the greatest accomplishments of the human spirit, cannot serve as a foundation to explain or to guide the life of the human spirit. Instead, that science tends inevitably to destroy that life when placed in that role. Montesquieu both did and did not know this. The sense in which he knew it is evident in the way he detaches his political thought from its scientific presuppositions, just as in the case of Aristotle. The sense in which he did not know it is also evident in his turn to anthropology and history, and in particular in his deductions of the political implications of differences in climate and terrain as well as in customs, religious views, and so on. In one more formulation, Montesquieu tries to overcome the disjunction between human and nonhuman nature by approximating as closely as possible to the detachment and objectivity of the natural scientist. Montesquieu is a theoretician of the practical. But it is unclear how his theory clarifies practice. In particular it is unclear whether Montesquieu is describing or recommending, as has often been noted. Montesquieu thus fluctuates between the unity of description and recommendation that characterizes the commonsense or practical approach of Aristotle, and the attempt to deduce the consequences of nature in a purely scientific manner. To say this is not to assert that Aristotle's approach is without defect or ambiguity. The main problem for both thinkers is how to ground the art of politics in a conception of human nature that is appropriate to the phenomena of politics. And this leads to the fundamental philosophical question of whether human beings possess a nature in any sense beyond those that physics and biology explore. For the time being, I have to leave it at this: Do the phenomena of politics themselves provide us with an affirmative answer to this question? Is the political articulation of ordinary experience our best and perhaps our only path toward human nature?

As a corollary to the previous discussion, I add the following observation. Montesquieu distinguishes between political and moral virtue and says that he is exclusively concerned with the former. This sounds as though he is rejecting the Aristotelian approach, but I do not take him in that sense. It is Montesquieu's view that moral virtue is not possible except where there is political virtue, and this is actually Aristotle's view as well. The differences between their two formulations of this point can be explained, first, by Montesquieu's adherence to modern natural science, and second, because Montesquieu emphasizes the difference between the private and the public, in keeping with the modern emphasis on the subject as *ego cogitans*. On the other hand, Montesquieu's conception of personal freedom is not only political but much closer to Aristotle's than to the conceptions of more extreme figures of the later Enlightenment.[28]

As a postscript to the present chapter, I want to make a brief comment on the connection between Montesquieu and sociology. Sociology is literally the science of society. This science rests upon a sharp distinction between politics and society. But it also assumes that politics is intelligible only on the basis of the science of society. This has to be emphasized: sociology does not simply assume that there is a science of *praxis* but it further assumes that *praxis* is not fundamentally political. Sociology also tends to reduce morality to an epiphenomenon of social institutions and customs, or in other words, it reduces morality to historical contingency. In his excellent commentary on the *SL,* Thomas Pangle explicitly and completely denies that Montesquieu is a sociologist, on the grounds that Montesquieu does not explain politics via society. He bases this contention on the fact that society plays at best a derivative role in Montesquieu, and that society is derived from the principles of government.[29] I think that this goes too far. As I have shown, there is for Montesquieu a stage intermediate between the emergence from the state of nature and entrance into the political state that can only be called "social," a stage from which the polity as a legal entity emerges. This is precisely why Montesquieu emphasizes the dependence of the lawgiver not only upon geography and climate but upon the customs and beliefs that govern human associations in families or herds prior to the formation of the state.

Let me immediately qualify this affirmation of the link between Montesquieu and sociology. The most important reason for studying Montesquieu is that he exemplifies Nietzsche's adage that philosophers are commanders and lawgivers of mankind. Montesquieu stands squarely in this tradition, which of course originates with the Socrates of the Platonic dialogues. Montesquieu is himself legislating for the legislators. In thinking about the *SL,* we are also thinking about the nature of philosophy. In other words, Montesquieu has not yet succumbed to the view that philosophy is replaceable by political science, comparative politics, or sociology, even though he takes steps that set into motion the development of these disciplines.

Chapter 2 Husserl's Conception of the Life-World

Husserl's analysis of the life-world is one of the most thorough attempts in the past hundred years to ground philosophy in everyday or pretheoretical life. At the same time, it is the most prominent example of the consequences of applying the Enlightenment model of scientific rationalism to the explanatory description of human affairs. A careful study of the essential elements of this analysis will supplement what we have learned about the ordinary from Montesquieu.

I want first to say a word of explanation concerning the order in which I study the thinkers in chapters 2 and 3. I wanted to study Heidegger in contrast with Kant, and it seemed desirable to treat Husserl before Heidegger, although there is some controversy about which of the latter two influenced the other in their treatments of the life-world. It also seemed useful to deal consecutively with the two main versions of the scientific Enlightenment. I shall say something about Kant's transcendental doctrine in the present chapter when my discussion of Husserl requires it, but my treatment of Kant's practical philosophy is reserved for chapter 3. The order of figures discussed is thus conceptual rather than purely historical. Kant combines transcendental arguments with a repudiation of the scientific analysis of human life, and so does Heidegger. In this sense, both fall between Montesquieu and Husserl on the one hand, and Wittgenstein and Strauss on the other.

For our purposes, Husserl's doctrine of the life-world is marked by three main assumptions. The first is that the sense or meaning (*Sinn*) and the validity (*Geltung*) of science is rooted in the everyday structures of pretheoretical experience. Second, philosophy in the traditional sense must itself be replaced by a science that is appropriate to the task of uncovering these roots. Third, although Husserl speaks of senses, he is not engaged in a semantics of the traditional sort, whether ontological or linguistic. Instead, he defines the grasping of senses as a form of intellectual intuition, which is clearly modeled after sense-perception, although the senses in question are purified, generalized, or idealized, and thus remind us of the Platonic Ideas. Unlike Plato's Ideas, however, Husserlian essences are internal to, and indeed constituted by the activity of, a "transcendental subjectivity" that is plainly related to the Kantian doctrine of the transcendental ego. For Kant, however, the transcendental ego is not a self-conscious entity or absolute ego but a set of logical conditions for the possibility of the cognition of a world like ours by beings like us. Husserl's transcendental subjectivity is not this, but rather a descendant of the absolute ego of post-Kantian German Idealism.

Husserl's term "scientific," when used in conjunction with "phenomenology," refers to a transcendental, apodictic, or strictly grounded description of the essences that make up the structure of human experience. Perhaps the best way to begin is by clarifying the Kantian origins of Husserl's conception of "transcendental," as it determines the meaning of the term "world" in the expression "life-world." The "world" is for Kant the product of transcendental subjectivity. In the First Critique, Kant defines "world" as "the mathematical sum [*Ganze*] of all appearances and the totality [*Totalität*] of their synthesis." (B446). This sounds like Wittgenstein's opening statement in the *Tractatus* that "the world is everything that is the case." Wittgenstein goes on immediately to qualify this assertion: "The world is the totality of facts [*Tatsachen*], not of things [*der Dinge*]." This world is in turn a logical space that contains all the possible relations of objects, thanks to their forms.[1] In sum, the world for Wittgenstein is the logical or formal condition for the possibility of substantive or empirical or objective existence. And this is what Kant means by "the world." Alternatively expressed, the world is "transcendental" because it contains the conditions for the possibility of experience for creatures like us, who cognize through a combination of sensation and conceptual thinking. I emphasize the important fact that "world" is for Kant, Husserl, and Wittgenstein a concept of totality, albeit not in the same sense for all three thinkers. For example, in Wittgenstein, the world seems to be the totality of logically possible propositions, whereas for Kant, it includes all objects of experience.

As Henry Allison observes, all of Kant's uses of the term "world" make this same point.[2] The thought of the sum of all items must be accompanied by the thought of these items as actually constituting a whole. This constituting is a synthesis, more precisely, a transcendental synthesis. There are in Kant no unities independent of our synthesizing them. Kant always speaks of synthesis and analysis, but he does not speak of intuition as a separate apprehension of what is given as unified or totalized in itself, independent of the activity of cognition. Intuition is of course used by him to refer to the apprehension of the pure forms of space and time.

In short, Kant defines "world" as the place in which human beings have experience, but it is also the concept we have of the totality of all possible experiences. In this transcendental sense, we make the world and our experience in it. It is true that Kant speaks of the world of the noumena, but whatever he may mean by this expression, it is not a world in which we have cognitive experience. I pass by the difficult question of the sense in which morality can be noumenal and nevertheless transpire within the phenomenal world. Classical philosophy, as we can refer for convenience to philosophy before Kant, tends to speak of the whole, the all, or the cosmos as including human beings but not as dependent on their cognitive activity. Strictly speaking, there is no concept of "world" in classical thought, if we understand this term in its modern or Kantian sense. In the modern idiom, we can of course speak of "worlds" quite informally, as in referring to life on other worlds, by which we presumably mean other planets or solar systems. For the most part, however, "world" carries with it an allusion to subjectivity. A world is defined by common perception, interests, or intentions: the world of entertainment, the world of sports, and so on.

A cosmos, then, is not a "world" because it is not *produced* by the activity of cognition. It is accordingly not a "synthesis" in the peculiar Kantian sense. Neither does it constitute the boundary between "phenomena" or how things appear to us, and how they are in themselves. The cosmos does not, as Heidegger puts it, "open the horizon" within which we enact our experience; it is instead always open by its nature to the appearance of beings like us. The subjective aspect of the world is already visible at the colloquial level, when we speak, for example, of the world of finance. This world is constituted by the interests and activities of those who engage in the professions of banking, investment, and so on. It does not exist prior to the exercise of such interests and activities.

The first thing to be said about Husserl's life-world, then, is that it is a product of transcendental subjectivity, and as such, it is a theoretical artifact rather than the domain of pretheoretical or everyday life. Husserl accordingly conceives of the task of phenomenology as that of isolating and describing the structures of this artifact. The contingent or unstructured character of ordinary experience is ignored or eliminated by reduction. A scientific study of the structure of the life-world is thus something entirely different from the inspection of ordinary experience. If the sense of philosophy is held to originate within the life-world, this sense can become accessible only through a phenomenological description of the transcendental source of the constituting or creating of sense. The structures of the life-world are themselves understood as the product of the sense-constituting activity of transcendental subjectivity. Among the other consequences of this way of seeing things, we study "senses" as objects of scientific inquiry, not as subjectively experienced or intended. There is an *Ausschaltung* or switching-off of the process of experiencing senses from within the lived values, hopes, or purposes of the conscious human being.

In sum, as human beings, we *have* experience, whether ordinary or extraordinary. As phenomenologists, we *describe* experience. Although we, as phenomenologists, purport to be describing the inner flow of subjectivity, we are in fact not within this flow but in some neutral dimension that seems to be neither within nor outside subjectivity. This strange place is the transcendental standpoint of the phenomenologist. We are like beings from another planet who are engaged in the scientific study of the subjective activity of human beings. As such, we no more live this experience than human psychologists live the experience of rats in their laboratories. Psychologists reconstitute the intentional life of rats from the outside. And so too with the phenomenologist. He or she does not live or evaluate or function in response to philosophical eros. It is a strange fact that the motivation that drives the phenomenologist to study the life-world derives from that life-world, but is not allowed to function during the actual study itself. One of the great puzzles of Husserlian phenomenology is how the perception of a sense by means of transcendental subjectivity can itself invoke in us the lived sense of everyday life, by which the sense of science is itself to be rescued from reification. The analogous question with respect to Plato, who somehow underlies the Husserlian doctrine of eidetic perception, is why the pure intellectual vision of, say, the Idea of justice should make us just in political life, or still more precisely, show us what is just in the particular case.

Husserl's main discussion of the life-world is to be found in his *Crisis of the European Sciences*.[3] We are primarily concerned with part 3, section A of this work, but in order to set the context for our analysis I shall begin with some orienting remarks about the introduction and two earlier parts. David Carr, the English translator of the *Crisis,* emphasizes on page xvi of his introduction "the fact that the work is incomplete and that the text available to us is not a finished version and in some places is almost fragmentary in character." The *Crisis* is more like a collection of related essays and preliminary exercises or sketches of proposed sections than a final manuscript. The German edition contains a collection of additions and supplementary texts, some of which have been translated by Carr.

Despite the somewhat disheveled condition of the manuscript, Husserl's general intentions in the *Crisis* are, I think, more accessible than some of his other works: the *Ideas,* the *Cartesian Meditations,* or the *Formal and Transcendental Logic.* Husserl is a very difficult, even careless, writer with a peculiar and not always well-defined technical terminology. We cannot read the *Crisis* as though it were a Platonic dialogue. But we must be as careful as possible to grasp accurately Husserl's main points, and where this accuracy is not available, to verify that the difficulty lies primarily in Husserl's faulty exposition.

The first part serves as an introduction to the entire project. Husserl begins somewhat hesitantly. There is today much talk of a crisis in the sciences, but is this not an exaggeration? How could one say that the very method of science has become questionable, as would have to be the case if there is a genuine crisis? "This may be true of philosophy, which in our time threatens to succumb to scepticism, irrationalism, and mysticism" (3). It may also be true of psychology, to the extent that it makes philosophical claims for itself and is not content to remain one of the positive sciences. But the humanistic sciences, despite any difference between their method and the exact procedures of the natural sciences, are also apparently flourishing: "The scientific rigor of all these disciplines, the convincingness of their theoretical accomplishments, and their enduringly compelling successes are unquestionable" (4).

The opening statement thus seems to locate the problem within philosophy rather than in European science as a whole. Whereas there may be no scientific crisis in general, there is an unmistakable difference between the unscientific character of philosophy, and the scientific character of the humanistic sciences, to say nothing of the mathematical and physical sciences (4–5). This assertion could be given a positivist interpretation by taking Husserl to be on the verge of saying that the crisis can be avoided by making philosophy scientific. I want to emphasize that this remains a serious problem in understanding Husserl, despite his rejection of positivism.

In section 2, Husserl is about to identify the crisis as one in which science has lost its meaning for life. Yet he will advocate throughout this and his other works the ideal of philosophy as a rigorous science (the title of one of his earlier essays). If Husserl is not a positivist, he is certainly not an existentialist or a humanist. The question is therefore how a rigorously scientific philosophy can restore to science its meaning for life. In other words, is not the rigor of science the cause of its loss of meaning for life?

A negative allusion to Heidegger is apparent in the opening remark about the current state of philosophy as threatened by irrationalism and mysticism. This tacit allusion becomes more pronounced in section 2, where Husserl makes explicit his wish to rectify the loss in contemporary thought of the relevance of science for life. We can anticipate his general point by saying that Husserl wishes to rehabilitate the great Enlightenment program of universal reason, whereas Heidegger wishes to destroy it. Both have in mind a revolution in philosophy as the necessary first step, but their conception of the new form of philosophy is as different as their attitude toward classical and modern forms of rationalism.

Husserl's critique of the sciences, which the current crisis makes necessary, will leave untouched "their primary sense of scientific discipline, so unimpeachable within the legitimacy of their methodic accomplishments" (5). Husserl is in fact about to recommend phenomenology, the revolution in philosophical method, which is designed to make philosophy truly scientific as well as to restore the human relevance of science. It is not entirely clear what is to be left untouched in science by Husserl's investigation. As his casual remark about psychology suggests, there seem to be problems within scientific method, and even within the mathematical sciences; he is no doubt alluding to the discussion with Frege on psychologism. But this opens the question of the need for a revolutionary new logic, and so for a new approach to the foundations of mathematics. However, Husserl does not develop the observation further.

Instead, he continues with his main theme of the humanly debilitating consequences of nineteenth-century positivism. The very success of the positive sciences has led them to turn away from the deepest human questions and instead to accumulate ever more facts. The disaster of the first World War has produced a climate within which we, and especially the younger generation, are consumed by the most burning questions "of the meaning or meaninglessness of the whole of this human existence" (*Sinn oder Sinnlosigkeit dieses ganzen menschlichen Daseins,* 6).[4] The following passage must be cited in full. "Do not these questions, universal and necessary for all men, demand universal reflections and answers based on rational insight? In the final analysis, they concern man as a free, self-determining being in his behavior toward the human and extra-human surrounding world and free in regard to his capacities for rationally shaping himself and his surrounding world. What does science have to say about reason and unreason or about us men as subjects of this freedom?" (6).

In short, the questions of freedom and the meaning of life have come to be regarded as antithetical to scientific rationalism. But Husserl rejects this view. He does not, however, simply reiterate the assumptions of the seventeenth- and eighteenth-century Enlightenment. Descartes took it for granted that scientific and technological advancement would lead to the rejection of political institutions and moral practices based upon ignorance, superstition, and the traditions affiliated with an absurd Scholastic science and metaphysics. Husserl, with the experiences of the first third of the twentieth century behind him, can no longer rest content with this assumption. According to his diagnosis, however, the root of the difficulty does not lie inside the scientific method, or with the general program of the Enlightenment, but in the fact that science has lost touch with its origins in everyday life. It is therefore disconnected from the original intentions and estimations of significance and value that motivate the universal conception of rationality.

I find Husserl's introductory statement of the problem to be ambiguous. On the one hand, he wishes to retain the methodology of the modern sciences and the conception of universal reason that underlies them. On the other, he recognizes that the sciences, including the humanistic sciences, are concerned with facts, not with values or "all questions of the reason or unreason of [the sciences'] human subject matter and [their] cultural configuration" (6). If science is a neutral tool that has been constructed for the exclusive purpose of gathering facts about the world, then it would seem that we need a new philosophical conception of the rationality of that purpose. Husserl seems to locate the source of that rationality in everyday or pretheoretical life, that is, in extrascientific and evaluative reason, in what is normally called "practical intelligence" or *phronesis*. All this being so, we need to restrict sharply the scientific conception of rationality, perhaps in the style of Kantian, if not of Aristotelian, practical judgment. But for Husserl, this would apparently be the same as invoking irrationality and mysticism. He refuses to surrender the Enlightenment conception of the inner link between human freedom and universal reason.

In one more preliminary statement, Husserl is about to begin a critical analysis of the modern epoch that shows how the origins of scientific reason have been covered over by the positive results of science. The foundation of these results is the mathematical model of the world that stems from Galileo, or let us say, from the generation for which Galileo is the outstanding representative. But the mathematical model, which underlies the entire Enlightenment project, is itself the cause of the detachment of science from questions of value and the meaning of life. Therefore one must either reject the model as inconsistent with human values, or else supplement it with some additional type of rationalism or science that will both preserve the integrity of positive science (to use that name for convenience) and re-attach it to its human roots. We would expect this additional type of rationalism to be practical or normative. But, rather oddly, Husserl says that we require another science, that of phenomenology, which will describe the natural world, i.e., the pretheoretical world of everyday life, in scientifically objective and exact terms. This scientific description will then presumably reveal to us the original values and meaning for life of scientific rationalism, and so, of the positive sciences. To anticipate, it looks as if Husserl is claiming that a scientific description of values and meanings will be tantamount to re-instituting the value and meaning of science. But this is to claim that the perception of a value is itself the enactment of a valuation. And this seems implausible, to say the least.

In the first paragraph of section 3, Husserl seems to address himself directly to my question. "It was not always the case that science understood its demand for rigorously grounded truth in the sense of that sort of objectivity which dominates our positive sciences in respect to method and which, having its effect far beyond the sciences themselves, is the basis for the support and widespread acceptance of a philosophical and ideological positivism. The specifically human questions were not always banned from the realm of science; their intrinsic relationship to all the sciences . . . was not left unconsidered" (7). So presumably science once subscribed to a different and broader conception of "rigorously grounded truth" than the late-modern paradigm of objectivity. There was, as it were, an additional dimension of rationality within which the specifically human questions could be asked, among them the question of the human value of science.

The sequel leaves it somewhat unclear which historical period Husserl has in mind. He begins by recalling the Renaissance project to revitalize the ancient conception of humanity. And this means to accept the model of "the 'philosophical' form of existence: freely giving oneself, one's whole life, its rule through pure reason or philosophy" (8). I note that this whole paragraph contains an exaggerated version of the rationalism of the ancient conception of humanity. In particular, it seems to reduce practice and production to theory. However, it is with the Renaissance appropriation of classicism that Husserl is concerned. He understands the appropriation to be a universal rationalism, that is, the investigation of every sphere of human experience by a reason altogether free from prejudice. In this renewed Platonism, theoretical freedom is extended to practice. Ethical, political, and social existence "must be fashioned anew through free reason, through the insights of a universal philosophy" (8). So, to Husserl, science in the Renaissance seems not to have been restricted by the kind of positivism that limits and disfigures late-modern rationalism.

I leave it an open question whether Husserl's romantic portrait of the Renaissance is historically accurate. Husserl shifts his attention once more to the early modern, or post-Renaissance period represented by Descartes. The Cartesian ideal is that of encompassing "in the unity of a theoretical system, all meaningful questions in a rigorously scientific manner, with an apodictically intelligible methodology, in an unending but rationally ordered progress of inquiry" that will solve all "problems of fact and reason, problems of temporality and eternity" (8–9). Husserl's exposition supports the inference that the Cartesian program is a continuation, perhaps an expansion to systematicity, of the Renaissance renewal of Platonism. It must therefore be within this period of the Renaissance and early modernity that Husserl finds the "demand for rigorously grounded truth" in some sense other and broader than the objectivity of late-modern positivism. The breadth seems to lie in the universal scope of its investigation. In other words, Cartesianism considers metaphysical and religious questions as well as those of ethics, politics, and society. It does not consider merely the facts of the natural universe. But Husserl does not tell us *how* this consideration differs from the methods of mathematics and physics. He needs to tell us how an investigation by free reason of the sense and value of science differs from the investigations of the various sciences themselves.

In his immediately following statement Husserl himself indicates that the shift from Cartesianism to positivism is one of a narrowing of focus. Positivism is a "*residual concept*. It has dropped all the questions which have been considered under the now narrower, now broader concepts of metaphysics, including all questions vaguely termed 'ultimate and highest'" (9). These questions, of which important examples are the (Kantian) trilogy of God, freedom, and immortality, have their inseparable unity in the problem of reason. Problems of reason are higher than problems of fact. "Positivism, in a manner of speaking, decapitates philosophy" (9). But it does not do so by changing the methodology of science. Husserl never suggests that the higher and even ultimate questions of reason are to be treated in some way that differs from the ways appropriate to the science of facts. And yet, given his own critique of positivism, this must be the case.

It is apparent from the outset that there is a central confusion in Husserl's mind as to the nature of the problem and the method of its resolution. The difference between "facts and values," to use Husserl's own terminology, is sufficiently great that we require two different kinds of reasoning in order to address both elements successfully. Husserl never says this. Instead, he concentrates upon the difference in kind between the two classes of questions. Cartesianism asks both kinds of questions, but applies one universal method of rational investigation in both cases. Positivism asks only one kind of question. But it does not employ some method other than that of systematic rationality.

Husserl gives no sign, in the opening pages of the *Crisis,* that he disagrees in any way with the Renaissance desire for a systematic philosophy based upon a true, universal method and culminating in a *philosophia perennis* that includes metaphysics (9–10). Neither has he given us any indication of the nature of that method, which, thus far at least, must be that of modern science in its Platonist, Cartesian, and positivist manifestations. Of course, he has said nothing as yet of phenomenology and the phenomenological method. But if this method is to conform to the scientific ideal of the Enlightenment, which Husserl evidently endorses, it remains to be seen how this method can circumvent the methodological limitations of positivism. It cannot be by applying positivist methods to metaphysical questions.

In section 4 Husserl states explicitly the central problem of the Enlightenment. The ostensibly universal method it employed "could bring unquestionable successes only in the positive sciences" (10). Husserl's wording is a bit vague; it is compatible with allowing for questionable successes, i.e., successes that cannot be universally verified or confidently incorporated within a universal system. But these would presumably not be rational. The need for a new method is in any case now obvious. There must be at least two methods, one for the positive sciences and one for the human, metaphysical, and religious sciences. But this seems to guarantee dualism, not the unity of science. It seems to direct us back to ancient philosophy rather than forward into the unending progress of universal reason.

Needless to say, this is not the direction in which Husserl is moving. He has a general conception of history as a cumulatively progressive concern with the "problem of the genuine ideal of universal philosophy and its genuine method," as he describes "the innermost driving force of all historical philosophical movements" (12). The initially "untouchable" status of the positivist sciences is eventually compromised by the crisis in metaphysics, because the meaning of the factual sciences lies within "the indivisible unity of philosophy" (11). To make a long and all too familiar story as short as possible, "the crisis of philosophy implies the crisis of all modern sciences as members of the philosophical universe: at first a latent, then a more and more prominent crisis of European humanity itself in respect to the total meaningfulness of its cultural life, its total *Existenz*" (12). In other words, he decries the rise of existentialism, which is for Husserl the wrong response to the right problem. We need to preserve universal reason, not to replace it with irrationalism and mysticism.

If we lose our belief in a universal philosophy of reason, which replaces belief (*doksa*) by knowledge (*episteme*), then we lose all meaning in life. Husserl describes this alternative in powerful language that makes clear his deep conviction of the impossibility of establishing the human value of science, and more broadly, the value and significance of human existence, by any method other than that of a universal, systematic, and unified rationalism. We are called upon "to initiate a new age, completely sure of its idea of philosophy and its true method, and also certain of having overcome all previous naïvetés, and thus all skepticism, through the radicalism of its new beginning" (14). The close similarity between Husserl's program and his own account of the Cartesian ideal is unmistakable. In section 6 this takes the form of an endorsement of metaphysics, which is in effect identified with universal philosophy: "To bring latent reason to the understanding of its own possibilities and thus to bring to insight the possibility of metaphysics as a true possibility—this is the only way to put metaphysics or universal philosophy on the strenuous road to realization" (15). Husserl sees this result as the culmination of Greek philosophy, and so as the telos of European history, a view that is surprisingly reminiscent of Hegel's teleological conception of the history of Western philosophy.

I must cite one more passage from this section: "To be human at all is essentially to be a human being in a socially and generatively united civilization; and if man is a rational being (*animal rationale*), it is only insofar as his whole civilization is a rational civilization." (15). This is the dream of the scientific Enlightenment, and it is the dream of Husserlian phenomenology. It is the dream of "a universal philosophy which grows through consistent apodictic insight and supplies its own norms through an apodictic method" (16).

Section 7 is a beautiful example of Husserl's great-souled nature and his utter naivety. In it, he silently identifies his own project with the universal task of all genuine philosophers, who are not or should not be the inventors of private philosophies but are rather "the functionaries of mankind" (17). We cannot sacrifice the possibility of universal knowledge. In other words, Husserl never considers the possibility that this goal is based upon his misunderstanding of the nature of philosophy. Husserl assumes from beginning to end that there is one universal method, one science, one philosophy, and one system, and the whole of it is rooted in the apodictic results of phenomenology. He has obviously sublimated his personal destiny into a conception of himself as the manifestation of the world-spirit, just as Hegel did before him, and no doubt as Heidegger was in the process of doing, albeit in a radically different style and in service of a radically different doctrine. "We cannot seriously continue our previous philosophizing; it lets us hope only for philosophies, never for philosophy" (17). This complaint is at least as old as Hobbes, and it is entirely typical of those for whom science, or *mathesis universalis,* is the paradigm of rationality.

Husserl says that the first step is to reflect back through history in order to inquire "what was originally and always sought in philosophy." The answer, of course, is his own phenomenological method. This requires that "the total sense of philosophy, accepted as 'obvious' throughout all its historical forms, be basically and essentially transformed" (18). Again: "all the philosophy of the past, though unbeknown to itself, was inwardly oriented toward this new sense of philosophy" (ibid.). This requires no further comment.

I close this section with a very brief summary of the process by which, according to Husserl, the life-world was covered over by modern mathematical science. I begin with Husserl's view that there are two stages or kinds of concealment. The first stage is the concealment of the pure consciousness by the empirical or natural ego. Phenomenological purification is required in order to ascend from empirical to essential or apodictically certain apprehension of universal essences and their encompassing structures. But access to the life-world is blocked at the empirical level because of the mathematicizing of our experience. We cannot view phenomenologically the structure of the life-world if we have no empirical perception of it.

The first task of the *Crisis* is therefore to explain the historical process by which modern human beings have lost touch with the roots of their own experience, that is, the process by which the everyday experience that produced modern science has been replaced by a mathematical or technical artifact. It is this replacement or concealment that has robbed our lives of human significance, and in so doing, destroyed the value of science and rationalism itself. This process begins (or can be regarded for all practical purposes as beginning) with Galileo and is initially addressed to nature, the physical world of bodies in motion. The same process is extended to cover the human soul, which is accordingly studied by studying the body, and is eventually reduced to or eliminated in favor of the body. An important step in this process is the algebraicizing of geometry, a step that takes us entirely away from sense experience and replaces the world of experience with an idealized abstract world of mathematical equations. The sensory content of these mathematical forms is interpreted as the result of the oscillation of bodies. The mathematical is the ideal representation of the sensed object; each sense quality has a "mathematical index" in the ideal world of forms (37).[5]

Let me emphasize the crucial point. The life-world, which is in fact the source of scientific investigation, is replaced by the mathematical artifact of the subsequent development of science (43, and *Beilage* 1).[6] Having lost touch with the very origin that validates it, science is transformed into positivism. This is the result of the arithmeticizing of geometry and the algebraicizing of arithmetic (43f.). Universal formulae replace determinate measurements. Practical or everyday life no longer is regarded as constitutive of sense. The empirical reality of the practical life-world is replaced by an infinite series of verifications of infinite hypotheses (41f.). Life, so to speak, is replaced by an infinite historical process of approximations to an ideal state of mathematical structure. The sensory content as well as the practical intentionality that constitutes the most fundamental or grounding stratum of human existence, has no mathematical status and is in effect discarded as lacking in rational significance. But this makes it impossible for us to determine the source of the human significance of science, which cannot be supplied by mathematics itself.

Thus far we have been concerned in the *Crisis* with what might be called Husserl's philosophical rhetoric and his program for phenomenology. I want now to consider certain difficulties intrinsic to the phenomenological method.[7] On the one hand, Husserl wishes to circumvent the separation of the subject and object that was introduced by modern philosophy, and to return to "the things themselves." This sounds initially like a rejection of Kant and a return to Greek "realism" (to use a non-Greek word). In one point, and it is a crucial point, we could say that this impression is correct. For Husserl, philosophy is fundamentally, if not exclusively, the intellectual intuition of pure essences.[8]

If anything, Husserl goes further than the Greeks on this point, since for him, intuition has access to the essences of every intentional entity whatsoever. An intentional entity is an object or content of any cognitive act of the human consciousness. As the Greeks might say, to think is to think of something. The "something" in question is, in Husserl's language, an intention. Intentions entered philosophy by way of Brentano, who adapted them from medieval philosophy. Husserl wishes to bypass modern epistemological constructions that stand between the mind and the entity by bringing the essential entity, the *noema* or *eidos,* to full presence. We can see here something of Aristotle's contention that the soul becomes "somehow" the beings.

On the other hand, whereas Greek essences are *of* "separate substances" or independently existing things, Husserl's essences are *of* anything whatsoever, including things that would for the Greeks be contingent or accidental, i.e., modes of substances, and of imaginary as well as real entities, and so of things that exist in the everyday or natural world as well as things that do not. This is connected to a central ambiguity in Husserl's doctrine: What is the connection between our perceptions and the essences that present themselves to the mind at the end of a series of phenomenological purifications that supposedly *remove* obstacles between the mind and the entity rather than construct them? It looks as though Husserl starts from ordinary perceptions of the external world and proceeds to explain how we can purify those perceptions of all contingent properties. This purified essence is said to be "constituted." As such, however, it is not a grasping of the direct "presence" of the external object but of its "representation" at the level of transcendental subjectivity.

Husserl does not mean that essences of existing perceived objects are created by the imagination, but he certainly never explains how we can verify that our perceptions give us direct access to the external world. This access cannot be by way of the essences, which are in the transcendental domain, not that of the natural world. So Husserl is open to the criticism that his essences are at best the structure of the world as British empiricism construes it: a world produced by impressions, sensations, imaginations, and so on. Otherwise put, how do we distinguish between imaginary essences and essences of actually existing external entities? Or in a slightly different formulation, why is Husserl not a Kantian, who synthesizes the objective world out of sensations on the one hand, and out of concepts, rules, categories, schemata, and ideals, or some selection of these, on the other?

This problem should always be kept in mind as we study Husserl. He apparently wishes to verify "apodictically" or with full "evidence" the structure of intelligibility, that is, of intelligible experience, and so of the real world; and this seems to put him on the side of the pre-Kantians or Greeks. But the road to the external world is at every point through consciousness, and even transcendental consciousness, i.e., consciousness purified of every vestige of psychology, epistemology, history, and of course, personal or historical consciousness. And this is the road from Descartes through Kant to German Idealism.

The simplest way in which to summarize Husserl's method is as follows. Think of something. Then vary it imaginatively by changing one property after another. At each step, ask yourself if the entity you thought of is the same as it was before you varied its properties. If the answer is "no," then you have an essential property. I do not say that this is all there is to phenomenology. But it is a basic component of phenomenology. And, in my view, it is defective. To state only the most obvious reason, everything depends upon our ability to imagine the object in a variety of guises. How do we know that we have proceeded far enough with our variations? Just because we are certain that we now see the pure essence of something, how can we or others verify this self-confidence?

Husserl himself frequently emphasizes the endlessness of the task of arriving at a phenomenologically pure description of an essence. This endlessness extends not merely to our grasping the essences of objects but also to our grasping the essences, the structures, of transcendental subjectivity themselves. In Kant, science can endlessly continue to gain knowledge of objects of experience, but the determination of the transcendental conditions for the possibility of knowledge is said to be complete. Rightly or wrongly, Kant claims completeness on the basis of logical or conceptual analysis of the aforementioned conditions. Because of Husserl's adherence to perception as central to his method, no such completeness is possible. This renders ambiguous his constant striving for ever-higher levels of descriptive rigor. Husserl demands that we see mentally the structures of subjectivity, but also that we see ourselves in the act of seeing.[9]

It is a corollary to Husserl's adoption of the paradigm of perception that his conception of the phenomenological method has much in common with the Cartesian conception of *mathesis universalis;* that is, phenomenology is based upon intuition rather than deduction. We have to see each step of our analysis of perception. And so we have to see the connection of these steps within a unified whole.[10] Husserl does not construct deductive arguments so much as he describes the content of intuition. This is why he regularly refers to phenomenological *description*. And the ultimate purpose of this description is to return to the origin or last ground of philosophy in the pure consciousness of the "I myself" (*Ich selbst*), the universal and absolute consciousness that is the ostensible source of all scientific meaning (97–100). This is obviously an idealist interpretation of the Cartesian *ego cogitans*.

It should also be emphasized that, for Husserl, the unification of deduction and intuition carries with it the unification of science and philosophy, and so it is the basis for the unification of human life. In other words, Husserl wishes to unify meaning and value. One of Husserl's deepest convictions, which he shares with the scientific Enlightenment, and for which he never in my view gives a satisfactory argument, is that the unification of science and philosophy in the sense-constituting faculty of absolute consciousness will also overcome the Humean dualism of facts and values; that is, it will provide a rational meaning and value to human existence.

We should not therefore be misled by Husserl's critique of the deterioration of the scientific spirit, or his thesis that the life-world has been covered over by a mathematical artifact or ideal formal structure. We must recognize his complete commitment to a scientific renaissance. The desedimentation of the life-world has as its goal, not the orientation of ontology by the structural features of human praxis (as is the case in Heidegger's *Being and Time*) but the vindication of science by returning it to the sources that bestow meaning and validity. It is true that these sources lie embedded within the life-world, which has a certain superficial resemblance to Heidegger's conception of average everydayness. Husserl, however, takes it for granted that the meanings and values of life are expressed in scientific terms, and yet scientific terms are precisely the terms that led initially to the concealment of the life-world. Heidegger is more consistently Husserlian than Husserl on this particular point, although his exposition of sense and validity has very little to do with the meanings and values of ordinary experience, which is for him "ontic" rather than ontological.

I turn next to the problem raised by the historical dimension of Husserl's philosophy. In order to return to the life-world as the source of human intentionality, and so too as the ground for the meaning and value of modern science, it is necessary to reverse the historical development of the contemporary scientific world, a process that Husserl calls "desedimentation." Husserlian "desedimentation" is reminiscent of Heidegger's "destruction" of Western philosophy and of the Derridean "deconstruction" of the world of finite, unified subjects and objects. Both Heidegger and Derrida wish to liberate us from the reification of human life by scientific rationalism (a rationalism that is extended backward to Plato). And both deny that their intention is to destroy or obliterate science and rationalism; instead, they wish to free it of its faults and liberate it for new and salutary forms of development. Husserl, although he is an enemy of positivism, intends rather to return to the rationalist conception of the Enlightenment, and to restore it to health by showing how it derives its universal sense and value from the intentional activity of the life-world.

Human beings are historical beings, and science itself has a historical origin. But the inner structure of that historical origin is not historical; it is absolute or transcendental. The ground of the intentional production of meaning and value in everyday life is not the historical but the transcendental ego. Husserl also holds, however, that transcendental consciousness produces history in a teleological sense. The universal spirit of the Enlightenment is an expression of the ideal of reason; this spirit must enact itself by stages, that is, as a historical process. But the completion of the teleology of universal science lies in phenomenology, the science that exhibits the meaning, value, and unity of human life as the locus of the universal formal structures of reality (70–73). The phenomenologist, that is to say, Husserl himself, is thus not an individual philosopher advocating a personal doctrine or ideology. The phenomenologist is the spokesperson and functionary of the human race whose task is to break through the crust of the history of philosophy in order to find "the inner sense, its hidden teleology" (16–18). Phenomenology is the telos of modern scientific rationalism.

The general problem that this raises is how to establish the value of transcendental history for human beings as residents of the natural world, and so of empirical history. Why is phenomenological formalism the discovery or validity of the value and significance of human life? Stated with brutal simplicity, what is *good* about universal reason? Why should we not remain within the life-world, once Husserlian desedimentation has excavated it from its rationalist grave, just as Wittgenstein seems to recommend that we remain, as philosophers or ex-philosophers, within the ordinary language to which his linguistic therapy, or destruction of theoretical philosophy, has returned us?

The controlling paradigm of intentional activity in general is for Husserl the constituting of an object of perception. The phenomenological method is intended to allow us to achieve a pure view of pure form, and this is also true of meanings and values as well as of the forms of empirical objects, mathematical relations, causal laws, and so on. One question that Husserl does not answer, so far as I can see, is how perception of a form conveys value. I can, as it were, "see" the value of justice without myself being just, and without placing any value upon justice. In fact, it seems to be impossible for a phenomenologist to move beyond the description of the form of justice to the enacting of the value of justice in a particular human context, namely, in the life-world. As we have seen, the method of phenomenology itself requires us to "detach" ourselves from any immersion within the pulse of historical existence. It therefore seems that the actual evaluation of science, the affirmation of its sense for human life, is extraphenomenological.

But this is exactly the situation with modern scientific rationalism and technicism, which Husserl criticizes so radically. The pure formalism of the mathematical physicist leaves no room for the affirmation of the value or sense for human existence of the structures he or she studies. This affirmation must come from outside science. And it must also come from outside phenomenology. What then is the source of the value of the telos of universal science? How can we infer value from a perception of a pure form? In my opinion, the utility of the Husserlian paradigm of perception breaks down precisely in the context of his most brilliant insight into the shipwreck of modern scientific rationalism. Husserl is like a prophet who discovers a promised land, but prevents us from occupying it by the very process through which he discovered it.

I emphasize that for Husserl, the life-world is the pretheoretical environment of intentional action, in which there are no ideal mathematical objects and in which the dominant mode of reasoning is induction rooted in the directly accessible objects of ordinary experience. Husserl defines this mode of reasoning as *Voraussicht*, "foresight": "We may therefore say that all of human life rests upon foresight, upon induction" (51).[11] In other words, the practical articulation of foresight and induction is always the same, despite the particular historical epoch in which we consider it. Elsewhere Husserl says that the life-world corresponds to the Greek *doksa*. We can understand this to mean that it corresponds to the human nature of everyday life, which is always the same, and which serves as the universal foundation for all historical activity, including the progress of science. But *doksa* is belief, not knowledge. That is to say, for Husserl, "nature" and *episteme* must be understood in their modern senses. The only knowledge of the life-world that Husserl recognizes is the pure phenomenological description of its constituting formal structures. The clarification of the life-world is the turn away from its mathematical surrogate, the logicized or formalized world of modern positivist science; but this turn is not to *doksa*. Instead, it is the description of the "unity and sameness of the world as the same, that alters only in its historical content" and so is the ground of the unity and sameness of the intentionality of philosophy.[12] The phenomenologist describes "the mode of being peculiar to the life-world and its essential formal structure, as that which is apodictically invariant in all the change of the life-world, in all of its relativity and relatedness to possible human knowers."[13]

In order to carry out this investigation, we as phenomenologists must detach ourselves (perform an *epoche*) from the activity of logicizing that characterizes modern scientific rationalism. But we must also detach ourselves from the life-world itself. The phenomenologist must "place himself above the life-world, instead of immersing himself in its normal everyday interests, or instead of entering into worldly life in the natural way."[14] In other words, instead of acting as a natural scientist or a resident of the prescientific life-world, one must stand outside both modes of engaged existence and take on the standpoint of the pure observer. Instead of the scientist who observes the forms of nature, we have the phenomenologist who observes the forms of the life-world. But this remains science. Our concern as phenomenologists remains the accurate description of formal structure. We are explicitly enjoined against the process of evaluation or affirmation of sense that is the defining characteristic of residents of the life-world. The upshot is as follows. At best, we arrive at a scientific description of the procedures of the life-world and the forms that underlie them. But we ourselves, who arrive at this description, do *not* do so as residents of the life-world. There remains a discontinuity between activity within the life-world, upon which the meaning and value of science depends, and scientific activity itself. As givers of value and meaning, we are not scientists. As scientists, we are not givers of value and meaning.

The *epoche* with respect to the life-world is thus only one of a series of detachments that are the necessary preconditions for ascent to the transcendental standpoint of the phenomenologist. In the *Phaedrus,* Socrates describes an ascent to the roof of the cosmos; the philosophical soul stands on the roof of this moving sphere and looks up to the hyperuranian beings or pure Platonic Ideas that are like the fixed stars in contrast to the moving solar system. In other words, the Ideas are detached from the world, and so too from the philosopher who attempts to contemplate the order of the world. In Husserlian phenomenology, we detach ourselves from the world, but also from the natural or historical ego, from "myself" as a resident within the world; we do not stand on the roof of the world but outside it, as it were, in hyperuranian space. But it is the pure or transcendental or absolute consciousness that occupies hyperuranian space, not separate Platonic forms. The forms are visible *within the flow of transcendental consciousness.* In the full phenomenological *epoche,* we do not view from outside, but are ourselves the theater within which the intentional original of every aspect of human experience shows itself fully and apodictically, i.e., with complete evidence.

This process is a radicalizing of the Cartesian method of doubt, a method that, according to Husserl, suffers from the fatal defect that it does not detach the observing consciousness from the natural world of the ego that is a resident of that world. Descartes does not rise from psychology to phenomenology (see especially sections 17–19, and *Beilagen* 7 and 8). The Cartesian ego contemplates the conscious correlates of things in the natural world, as these appear to and depend upon the inner-worldly observer. Husserl wishes to achieve the standpoint of God, so to speak; one could almost apply to him Hegel's metaphor in the *Science of Logic,* that we think the thoughts of God as he thinks them prior to creating the universe.

The main features of Husserl's doctrine of the life-world, as they have emerged in our analysis to this point, may be summarized as follows. Like Kant, Husserl wishes to describe the universal structures of possible experience. The elements of these structures are accessible to consciousness through a process of successive purifications of its own activity. This activity is fundamentally perceptual, or modeled after perception; in this respect, it reminds us of the pure intellectual intuition of Platonism. But the task of phenomenology is not merely to elicit the forms of intelligible experience. These forms have content, namely, the subjective coordinates to the endless events of experience itself. A phenomenological description of intelligibility cannot rest content with identifying the categories, rules, ideas, ideals, and schemata through which our discursive intelligence gives objectivity to what would otherwise be a mere rhapsody of impressions, imaginations, and the like. The impressions and images of the individual objects can themselves be purified; that is, we can extract the essence of contingent particulars, whether real or imaginary, by what is fundamentally the same process through which we arrive at the general structures of intelligible experience. And by "contingent particular," I mean every element in experience that we can conceive of, including values, social institutions, and historical and political entities, not just objects of spatiotemporal perception.

I turn now to this essential step of purifying the impressions and images of individual objects in order to extract their essences. The step in Husserl's argument is in principle a rectification or extension of Kant's transcendental philosophy. I begin with two remarks from the *Crisis*. The first is from section 25: "Kant speaks of the 'Humean problem.' What is the actual problem, the one that drives Hume *himself?*" Husserl replies to his own question as follows: "How is the *naive obviousness* of the certainty of the world, the certainty in which we live—and what is more, the certainty of the *everyday world* as well as that of the sophisticated theoretical constructions built upon this everyday world—to be made comprehensible?" (96). The second appears somewhat later, at the end of section 30: "All objective consideration of the world [*Weltbetrachtung*] is consideration of the 'exterior' [literally, "in the exterior": *im 'Aussen*] and grasps [*erfasst*] only 'externals', objective entities [*Objektivitäten*]. The radical consideration of the world is the systematic and purely internal consideration of the subjectivity which 'expresses' [or "externalizes"] itself in the exterior" (113).

I am not interested in whether Husserl is right to attribute this problem to Hume. The two passages just cited, when taken together, provide us with the basis for an introductory formulation of Husserl's own problem. The world of modern mathematical and experimental science is a theoretical construction that is rooted in the everyday world, the intelligibility of which we take for granted. In order to understand the full significance of the scientific world, we must understand the everyday world that is the source of that significance. The objective world of science is a construction of the inner subjectivity of the scientist; more precisely, the objective or external world is constituted by the transcendental subjectivity. But so too is the inner world of the everyday. In order to understand the world-constituting activity of transcendental subjectivity, we must bring that subjectivity to pure contemplation, we must see it as it is, namely, as subjectivity, and we must do so without distorting subjectivity into objectivity.

I would say that Husserl's own problem is how to find a nonobjectifying mode of the phenomenologist's objective contemplation of subjectivity. Husserl cannot rest content with purely subjective contemplation, because the subjective life-world is directly perceived or experienced as it is, whereas this is not the case with the objective world. At first glance, it would seem that the direct perception of the subjective life-world is incapable of being brought to pure contemplation, precisely because it is not objective, that is, because it is directly perceived in different ways by different individual subjects. But Husserl is tacitly adopting the Kantian distinction between sensation and perception here, whether intentionally or not. He is not interested in the "subjective" characteristics of subjectivity, i.e., in the content that is personal or peculiar to each of us as individuals. Husserl wants to bring to pure contemplation, and thus to intelligibility, just that which can be genuinely intelligible, namely, structure. The content of the direct perceptions or experiences to which Husserl refers is not at all subjective experience in the informal or psychological sense of the term, but the particular essence that holds together the subjective perception as an identifiable kind of entity. This use of "essence" comes close to the Platonic conception of an Idea, or even an Aristotelian species-form, but Husserl extends the concept to cover any coherent, identifiable, and so re-identifiable item.

It is fair to conclude that when Husserl speaks of subjectivity in this context, he is actually referring to intersubjectivity. The individual sentient being is constituted from subjectivity and objectivity, or interiority and exteriority. I experience objectivity through my body and thus by participating in the spatiotemporal world. But the experience of objectivity is itself subjectivity. To experience an object is to intend it, to constitute it with a sense that is within a stratified structure of senses known collectively as the world, a collectivity that is perceived differently by different egos or points of subjectivity, but by a process that is common to them all. It is this latter process that Husserl wishes to isolate and describe in the phenomenological description of the life-world. This description extends beyond the powers of the Kantian transcendental ego to the structures in and through which the personal subject exists *as* a person.

In the naive, natural, or pre-phenomenological attitude, we regard the objectivity of the world as immediately intelligible, and so as requiring no explanation (96). This naivety is lost when life itself is placed under inspection. Hume, in other words, anticipates Kant and follows in the footsteps of Descartes by regarding the world from the standpoint of the *ego cogitans* as "its own *Lebensgebilde* that has come into being within itself" (96). A *Lebensgebilde* is a life form, life creation, or life structure. Incidentally, we see here the Kantian origins of Wittgenstein's conception of a life-form. The difference, of course, is that Wittgenstein rejects the distinction between the interior and the exterior and attempts to explain the construction of the life-form entirely as communal discursive activity. For Kant, however, I produce the world by the process of my inner existence. But Hume cannot discover the origin of the world in "subjektive Leistung," i.e., in subjective work or performance (96). The reason for this, I believe, is that for Hume, subjective activity is primarily sensation. The ego is as much a product of sensation as the world. The shift from Descartes to British empiricism brings about the dissolution of the *ego cogitans* by its own activity, rather than its transcendental actualization. Subjectivity is subordinated to chance and custom.

One would think that the problem is solved, or at least that a solution is offered, by the transcendental philosophy of Kant. But from a Husserlian standpoint this is not so. The reason is that Kant takes as self-explanatory how the world of inner experience is constituted, that is, how the subjective world within which the transcendental machinery operates (to lay down the objective structure of scientific knowledge) is constituted (97). Husserl explains how he uses the term "transcendental." "I myself use the term 'transcendental' *in the broadest sense* for the original motif . . . which through Descartes confers meaning upon all modern philosophies . . . It is the motif of inquiring back (*Rückfragens*) into the ultimate source of all the formations of knowledge (*Erkenntnisbildungen*), the motif of the knower's reflecting upon himself and his knowing life, in which all the scientific structures that are valid for him occur purposefully, are stored up as acquisitions, and have become and continue to become freely available."

From this passage it is immediately clear that, whereas Kant uses "transcendental" to refer to the formal knowledge of rational constituting of the world, Husserl employs it to designate the inquiry into the root of subjectivity. Despite all talk in Kant of the transcendental ego, what is for him transcendental is not subjectivity but formal actualization; that is to say, *objectivity*. Furthermore, Kant is concerned with the forms as structures, not with the process by which they are actualized. One could say that Kant, in his role as transcendental philosopher, is not fundamentally concerned with subjectivity at all, and so not with subjective experience, certainly not with the subjective experience of the everyday. This type of experience does not present him with a proper object for scientific knowledge; it does not lie within the horizon of rationality in the sense of rule-governed cognition.

We should therefore not be confused by the Kantian-sounding terminology with which Husserl articulates his deepest concern. Husserl continues: "Working itself out radically [the aforementioned self-reflection] is the motif of a universal philosophy which is grounded purely in this source and thus ultimately grounded. This source bears the title *I-myself,* with all of my actual and possible knowing life and, ultimately, my concrete life in general. The whole transcendental set of problems circles around the relation of *this,* my 'I'—the 'ego'—to what it is at first taken for granted to be—my *soul* and, again, around the relation of this ego and my conscious life to the *world* of which I am conscious, and whose true being I know through my own cognitive structures (*Erkenntnisgebilde*)" (98).

For Husserl, it is not possible to understand the rational structure of the world as a pure transcendental form; one has to understand it as the form produced or constituted by the rational activity of a subjectivity that is fully conscious of itself as the root of the knowledge of the formal structure. And note especially: whereas the ego does not produce the world, it does produce the Being of the world. Being is not ontic but ontological. It is not a property of beings that we encounter or discover by observing them; it is rather a property that we produce within our consciousness as knowledge. Being is knowledge. But it is the knowledge of living subjectivity. Kant neglects this facet of the situation and concentrates upon the knowledge; for him, in other words, the transcendental ego is a set of logical conditions for the possibility of rationally cognizing a world. "Being" is a logical rather than a real predicate; it is nothing more than the position of the object within the conceptual structure of the world of scientific knowledge. Whereas one could say that, for Kant, we "produce" Being, the latter is not a property that is accessible to objective, or scientific, knowledge. For Husserl, the possibility of rationally cognizing a world belongs to self-consciousness or subjectivity. What one might call the "donation" of Being is thus for Husserl an epistemic or sense-constituting activity of transcendental subjectivity. He calls this subjectivity "transcendental" but his sense of this term is quite un-Kantian. For Kant, the term means something like "universally valid entirely apart from personal subjectivity." For Husserl it means "universally valid for me personally." Of course, to be a "me" is for Husserl to exhibit intersubjectivity; nevertheless, intersubjectivity is constituted by individual egos who participate in absolute knowing through the self-affirmation or self-validation by direct phenomenological vision and description of both the formal structure of the world and the subjective processes by which these formal structures are constituted.

And this is why Husserl turns to the life-world as Kant does not. The Kantian transcendental turn is a turn away from the life-world to the structures of modern mathematical science and so of the syntax of rational language. Husserl's transcendental turn is a turn "backwards" into the depths of subjective activity, and so into the subjective activity that is the medium in which the Kantian forms are actualized but that those forms cannot grasp. In one more formulation: Husserl reflects the post-Hegelian concern with process in two senses (i) the formation process (that is, the process that constitutes formal structure) and (ii) the process of subjectivity. Kant is not interested in process; he remains within the ambit of the same traditional emphasis on pure formal structure that characterizes the pre-Copernican philosophy.

Thus, when Husserl uses the Kantian-sounding phrase "Ich selbst" as the name of the source of all knowledge-formations, he is again doing so in a quite un-Kantian sense. For Kant, the "I think" is an empty logical condition by which thoughts are unified within a single horizon of pure synthesis. It plays a critical role in turning our attention away from ourselves as empirical, subjective, personal egos. To say "I think" is not to say that the world is my product but that it is unified as a world by my act of thinking it. I stand at the switch, as it were, and I am necessary to hold open the circuits of transcendental world-constitution; but I myself am of no other interest. For Husserl, on the contrary, "I myself" refers to subjective life, to the life of knowing, *Erkenntnisleben,* and the life of the formation of knowledge as *my* knowledge, namely, as emerging from within my own consciousness and so as present to me, as validated by me, through my very act of thinking. The "me" is again transcendental, but it is no longer a mere logical condition for the effectuation or guarantee of the synthetic unity of apperception. "I" am the God who creates the world of Being, and the phenomenologist must achieve full evidence with respect to the process of creation in order to validate the structures or forms that have been created.

It therefore becomes impossible to ignore the subjective circumstances under which the formation of knowledge transpires. Husserl says, "But Kant, for his part, has no idea [*Vorstellung*] that in his philosophizing he stands on unquestioned presuppositions, and that the undoubtedly great discoveries in his theories are there only in concealment; that is, they are not there as finished results, just as the theories themselves are not finished theories, i.e., do not have a definitive scientific form" (103). In particular, Husserl accuses Kant of being unable to ground the "intuitive *Umwelt*" or nonobjective, that is, prescientific or everyday aspects of the phenomenal world (110 f.). For this reason, Kant's doctrine, although ostensibly of subjectivity, is in fact a doctrine of the world as external and objective, whereas radical world-contemplation is systematic and pure inner contemplation of subjectivity that 'externalizes' itself in the exterior." (113). Husserl repeats his main point in the next section [sec. 30; 114 ff.]: all transcendental concepts, i.e., all the rules by which scientifically cognized objects are constituted and known, are formed within inner experience. But according to Husserl, Kant ignores this inner experience itself, which is the ground of scientific objectivity.

This seems to me to be a misunderstanding of Kant. For Kant, the thinking of transcendental forms, and so the constituting of objectivity, does not take place within inner temporalized subjectivity, as Husserl claims here, but is instead extratemporal. It does not take place in immanent personal subjectivity but, so to speak, in eternity, at the transcendental level. Kant would therefore deny that scientific objectivity is grounded within the intuitive *Umwelt* or in the personally experienced life-world. Husserl on the other hand relates the validity of objective constituting to the evidence (or full presence) of the constituting acts. He relates that validity to the contemplation of the phenomenologist as pure *ego cogitans*.

From a Kantian standpoint, Husserl has misunderstood the nature of transcendental cognition. This cognition is not subjective experience; it is not the direct presentation of an essence or sense to the intellectual eye of the individual ego. It is neither immanent nor transcendental "experience" or "perception" but the condition for the possibility of experience and perception. In other words, whereas Husserl claims that the transcendental activity of constituting the world must be validated by a transcendentally purified description of everyday subjectivity, Kant claims that everyday subjectivity is validated by transcendental constitution. There is for Kant no such thing as transcendental subjectivity but only immanent subjectivity. And as such, in itself, or taken apart from its objective structuring by the transcendental conditions of cognition, it is of no scientific or philosophical interest. It is the mere flow of impressions of British empiricism, bounded only by psychological laws of association or custom.

Husserl's misunderstanding of Kant to one side, Husserl goes Kant one step better by demanding a transcendental validation of what I call subjective subjectivity. He is not referring to the contingent events transpiring in this or that historical person, but rather to the general processes that are common to all personal inner experience. For Kant, there are transcendental structures that constitute objectivity: what it is to be an object of science or of rational knowledge. For Husserl there are also transcendental structures of personal subjective and everyday inner experience. Husserl further claims that the thinking by which transcendental structures of objectivity are engaged, is carried out within everyday personal or subjective experience and that the validity of objectification depends upon the validity of subjectification. He is therefore committed to discovering and describing the transcendental structures of personal or subjective experience, and of bringing these to full evidence before the intellectual vision or intuition of the individual phenomenologist. The process is transcendental but the act of verifying what is evident can only be personal: it can only be *mine*.

Since transcendental constituting takes place within historical persons, the historical person must validate that constituting. Husserlian descriptions are thus not arguments employed to persuade us by showing what must be the case, given that we have the experience that we have. They are rather descriptions designed to bring to full evidence so that each of us can intuit them, can intuit the structures that are latent in each of our subjective existences. No one can "see" the operations of the Kantian transcendental ego; one can only conceive them as necessary presuppositions of the phenomenal objects that we not only see but also understand. I believe that for Husserl it is necessary for us actually to *see* the operations of his transcendental ego. We thus have a situation in Husserl something like that in Fichte: There are two egos, the transcendental and the immanent, and *Wissenschaft* occurs only when the two coincide, when, in other words, the immanent ego sees fully the transcendental ego as the root or source of validity for himself or herself but also for every other immanent ego.

To summarize this line of analysis: inner perception is for Husserl not fundamentally psychological in the sense of personal subjectivity, but transcendental. As such, inner perception is the apodictic, final ground of experience, the "source of ultimate concepts of knowledge" (115). For Kant, on the other hand, as Husserl sees him, transcendental concepts are constituted within inner or psychological experience (the "intuitive *Umwelt*" of the life-world); therefore the transcendental concepts cannot achieve immediate intuitive evidence, since this would psychologize them, reduce or derive them from the temporality of inner experience. For Kant, inner subjective temporal experience is scientifically irrelevant; for Husserl, it is the ground or source of transcendental objectivity and therefore must itself be validated or brought to full evidence as the final ground of "theoretico-logical *Seinsgeltung*" (129). Carr translates this as "the theoretical-logical ontic validity." By "validating," Husserl means bringing to evidence, i.e., seeing with apodictic certitude the universal structure of the life-world: "the life-world does have, in all its relative features, a *general structure*" (138). And the universal a priori structure of the life-world precedes that of the objective mathematical sciences (141). "All natural questions, all theoretical and practical ends . . . occur somewhere within the world-horizon" (145).

All this being so, we require the development of an entirely new science—the science of the life-world—"a science of the universal *how* of the pregivenness of the world" (146). At the beginning of section 39, Husserl asks: "Now, how can the pregivenness of the life-world become a universal subject of investigation in its own right?" He replies immediately to his own question: "Clearly, only through a *total change* of the natural attitude [*Einstellung*], such that we no longer live, as heretofore, as human beings within natural existence, constantly effecting the validity of the pregiven world." In other words, we do not "validate" or "bring to evidence" for *this* kind of investigation in the same way that we bring evidence forward in our everyday existence. When we undertake the activity of validating, we stop being immersed in life, we no longer live life straightforwardly. Instead, our everyday existence is "neutralized." All our acts of intending, valuing, undergoing kinaesthetic modifications, using the entities of our spatiotemporal experience to carry out projects that are themselves expressions of rank-orderings, and so on—all this becomes a play for us to describe theoretically; we are no longer the engaged and fully situated selves of everyday existence.

In the natural attitude, we live in the world; in the new *epoche,* we watch ourselves living in the world. "Only in this way can we arrive at the transformed and novel subject of investigation, 'pregivenness of the world as such': the world purely and exclusively as—and in respect to *how*—it has meaning and ontic validity [*Sinn* and *Seinsgeltung*], and continually attains these in new forms, in our conscious life" (148). Again I emphasize that sense and Being are transcendentally constituted within the root of subjectivity. They are not contingent historical products of personal subjectivity, but neither are they pure visions of how beings appear when they are separate from, yet present to, intellect understood as the capacity to contemplate pure forms. Finally, they are not Fregean concepts or semantic meanings that mediate between us and the "objects" of experience to which we refer. On the contrary, they *are* the truth and being of the objects of experience. I think that we have to attribute to Husserl a distinction between brute existence and Being-as-a-validation, a distinction that certainly resembles the Kantian distinction between things in themselves and objects of experience. The distinction holds in the sense that we do not produce or constitute brute existences. In order, however, to know the brute existences, to evaluate them, or in any way to appropriate them to self-conscious intentionality, we must embed them within the structure of intelligibility that is in the last analysis the activity of transcendental subjectivity. This embedding is not accomplished by discursive thinking, as in Kant; it is not simply the transcendental application of rules, categories, concepts, Ideals, and schemata: it is the actual seeing of these applications. I do not "refer" to a cow by the mediation of a discursive concept of the cow; on the contrary, I see the look of the cow as validated by the functions of looking. I do not look at a cow through concepts, but neither do I view the cow by means of a neutral pure intelligence that has nothing to do with my own subjectivity.

Husserl's question is thus not: Are there any cows, or anything else, external to consciousness? He asks rather: How does consciousness validate the pure intentional objects of everyday intersubjective experience? It does not make sense from a Husserlian perspective to ask: "*Is* there anything outside our consciousness?" We can't ask this, we can't identify anything outside our consciousness except by projecting it outward as an external object from within the interior of intentional subjectivity. Traditional efforts to establish realism all founder on the rock of subjectivity; it is the self-conscious agent of transcendental subjectivity, I, who attempt to establish realism. And in fact, reality *is* established by this attempt, where "attempt" is understood here transcendentally, as a *Seinsgeltungsvollzug* or something of the sort.

Let me underline this point. As soon as I ask, "Does this cow truly exist independent of my cognition?" I have "intended," i.e., located or pointed out the external object, the cow before me, which acquires its structure as an element of experience and all the validations of its role in the life-world. To say this in another way, all cognition, sensory or conceptual, and all reflection on cognition, occurs as the projection of the world of cognition. We cannot move from the inside to the outside except as a transition within the inside. The outside *is* the outside of the inside.

In my opinion, there is no way whatsoever by which Husserl can avoid the problem of solipsism. The fundamental dilemma of all doctrines of transcendental subjectivity emerges in the following two questions. First, how can we move from my subjectivity to intersubjectivity? Second, how can we move from intersubjectivity to an external world, when "world" is a project of the very activity of subjectivity? This however is not my main theme.

I want instead to establish that the transcendental bracketing or neutralization of our validating situatedness within the flow of everyday life is, for Husserl, the necessary prerequisite for the pursuit of scientific knowledge of the life-world. He says: "Only thus can we study what the world is as the ground-validity for natural life, with all its projects and undertakings, and correlatively, what natural life and its subjectivity *ultimately* are, i.e., purely as the subjectivity which functions here in effecting validity. The life which effects world-validity in natural world-life does not permit of being studied from within the attitude of natural world-life. What is required, then, is a *total* transformation of attitude, a *completely unique, universal epoche*" (148).

This being so, it is obvious that Husserl does not provide us with a view of the life-world from within, that is to say, as lived. No doubt he would reply that such an account would be entirely unphilosophical. But this is because he conceives of philosophy as a science, whereas I contend that there is no scientific account of the life-world. Instead, the perspectives or judgments of the life-world are embedded within, and thus distorted by, the structures of the scientific world-view. Oddly enough, Husserl understands this point very well, but he employs the method of desedimentation to arrive at a scientific view of the life-world. This is not to return to the life-world, but rather to deprive it of life.

In section 41 of the *Crisis,* Husserl describes the transcendental bracketing (*epoche*) of the natural attitude, the disconnection of the phenomenologist from participation within and as a member of the life-world. This step, which is necessary for the acquisition of scientific knowledge of the life-world, involves a "turning-off" or neutralizing of the acts of validation by which we live. Husserl claims that everything goes on as before, except that we are now detached from the ongoing existence and have become a dispassionate and neutral observer of our phantom experience. We do not live except as transcendental beings who watch, and describe, the perceptible stages of life.

It is worth asking whether the phenomenological shift, from residence within the life-world to the transcendental lookout point of the scientist who describes the structures of the life-world, is itself a step taken within the life-world or a step to get outside of it. In one sense, it is obvious that we start within the life-world, move into the theoretical reflection that is an extension of, and still takes place within, the natural attitude, and then discover the need to perform the phenomenological bracketing or detachment from the natural attitude, and so from all worldly (i.e., inner-worldly) science. This discovery, of course, is first made by Husserl, but our own progress toward phenomenology is essentially a reduplication of his itinerary.

In short, we do not begin "outside" the life-world. Rather, we arrive there by a series of reductions or purifications of conscious experience. In other words, as living beings, we are always already within the life-world. But as philosophers or pure theoreticians, we can remove ourselves from fully engaged residence within the life-world and thereby transform it into a contemplative show. But it seems entirely unreasonable to say that the "shutting off" of life affects, of value, and so on, is itself an expression of life affect or valuation. As members of the life-world, we experience the desire to know, as Aristotle puts it, by our very nature. As the context makes clear, Aristotle means that we naturally enjoy perceiving the different beings and forms in the world, and that this is the basis of our desire for pure scientific or philosophical knowledge. But the basis is not the same as scientific knowledge itself. Acts of empirical perception or cognition are immersed in the ongoing flow of life. Even if we conceive of them as intervals in or disruptions of that flow, they do not stand alone but are incorporated by us into the stream of ongoing experience as a kind of enrichment.

In the crucial case, we decide that the pleasure of pure knowledge is sufficiently great that we plan to continue pursuing it. This plan to modify everyday life is itself a feature or expression of everyday life. It is not a decision from above, not an expression of the transcendental domain imposed onto the immanent life-world below. Quite the contrary. The occupant of the transcendental domain is not a historical person, not a participating resident of the life-world. Strictly speaking, no decisions are made at the transcendental level. Nothing takes place there but pure description. And this occurs in accord with the intentions of the scientist, who, as someone who is seeking pure knowledge, is still within, even if partly detached from, the life-world. In sum, the decision to turn off the life-world takes place within the life-world, or at least within an extension of it, just as the decision to commit suicide takes place within life, not within death. In order to avoid this inference, Husserl would have to postulate a world in between the life-world on the one hand and the plane of phenomenological vision on the other. But this leads to an infinite regress, since we would now be required to explain how we leave the life-world in order to enter into the intermediate world. In slightly different terms, Husserl has not validated phenomenology itself. He establishes it by cutting it off from the source of its value. And in so doing, he commits the very fault for which he condemns the modern scientist-philosopher or, as we might be inclined to say, the positivist.

Here are some simple examples of what Husserl means. In the life-world, I make moral and political decisions, act on the basis of my estimation of the characters of my neighbors, respond physically to the changing positions of spatiotemporal entities by altering my own physical behavior, and so on. All of these performances are undertaken within the world and presuppose its existence. The world is the horizon of human activity that is always given in advance of any anticipated action. In the natural attitude, I am engaged by my intentions within the world through the mediation of innerworldly entities. In slightly different language, life is a matter of existential concern for me; it is not a neutral object of theoretical contemplation. I am living, not observing life. And even if I observe this or that aspect of "the human scene," I do so as engaged by it, responding to the motives and fates of other people on the basis of my own values. Thus the kinaesthetic motions of my body are not the pure objective consequences of the laws of physics but intentionally directed expressions of a complex if partly tacit life plan. In the life-world I am not the object of the science of neurophysiology, but the person who plans to make the study of neurophysiology a way of life. Or again, when I evaluate some person or action, I (so to speak) lay my life on the line; I define myself in expressing that value.

By "the pregivenness of the world," Husserl means to designate the process of actually living in a situated and engaged manner. If we neutralize the assumption of the pregivenness of the world, we do not abolish that world but instead transform ourselves from engaged participants within it to phenomenological viewers of the world as process. Stated crudely, the bracketing process puts us into the position of watching a motion picture. As watchers of it, we cannot be said to be one of the characters within the story portrayed by the film, even if the story is that of our own lives. By detaching ourselves from inner, evaluating participation in the story of our lives, we thereby free ourselves from the restrictions of the personal or immanent ego and rise to the "discovery of the universal, absolutely self-enclosed and absolutely self-sufficient correlation between the world itself and world consciousness." That is, we discover the last ground of world-constitution within the universality of the subjective world-process that is the same for every historical person. Husserl calls this "die Weltgeltung leistende Subjektivität" (151).

Let us note carefully: there is no world without a correlative "I." This is a sign of the Kantian origin of Husserl's concept of "world" that we studied in the first section of this chapter. From the pre-Kantian standpoint, in particular from the standpoint of the ancient Greeks, the cosmos is not dependent upon the ego. Modern philosophy is solipsistically inclined from the outset because it takes its bearing by the perceiving and cognizing ego. In the natural attitude, this ego or "I" is my historical identity. After the bracketing or neutralizing of the world, the "I" is the transcendental subjectivity that is the world-source common to every historical ego. At this level, there is a kind of connection between Aristotle and modern transcendental philosophy. The transcendental ego is Husserl's version of the divine active intellect in Aristotle, which does not create but rather perpetually constitutes the cosmos. It does so not by thinking the things or forms in the world but rather by thinking itself. This process of thought thinking itself, when combined with the transcendent self-consciousness of the biblical God, is the paradigm of the absolute ego of German Idealism. Strictly speaking, Aristotle's god does not think itself as a determinate form or nature. It is itself pure thinking, which thinks nothing but pure thinking.

For Husserl, the immanent world is thinkable only as "my" world." There is no such act as the thinking of a world that is not mine or that is a world precisely as given (or pregiven) to me. By the act of bracketing, Husserl shifts from personal subjectivity to the universal, world-constituting subjectivity, but he does not shift from the standpoint of the "I" to some entirely neutral, non-self-conscious standpoint. The standpoint of transcendental subjectivity is as much mine as is the standpoint of personal subjectivity. The difference between the two is that, at the transcendental level, the "I" in question is that of each and every immanent or personal "I," for all of whom the world-constituting processes of transcendental subjectivity are one and the same. This is not at all the pure "thinking of thinking" that defines the Aristotelian divine intellect.

We have previously met with Husserl's next point. "And there results, finally, taken in the broadest sense, the absolute correlation between beings of each sort and every meaning [*Sinn*], on the one hand, and absolute subjectivity, as constituting meaning and ontic validity in this broadest manner, on the other hand" (151f.). Being and meaning are constituted by subjectivity, not discovered or viewed by pure intellect. Being and meaning are transcendental, not contingent or historical or personal. Nevertheless, without an intentional ego or "I," there is no world, hence no being and no meaning. To be is to be something, but to be something is to be something *for* an intending self-conscious subjectivity. I have no access to the "something" of the entity except by thinking it, and to think it is to constitute it as my object (for the time being). Absolute, apodictic, scientific knowledge of the object must therefore be knowledge of the process by which I constitute it. There is no ontology independent of egology.

Husserl goes on to emphasize that, in the transcendental attitude of the philosopher, none of the being or objective truth of the world is lost, nor is any of the spiritual accomplishment of one's worldly, historical existence lost. What happens is simply that the philosopher *qua* philosopher, in the singularity of his or her philosophical interest, renounces the carrying out of "the whole natural performance of his world-life; that is, he forbids himself to ask questions which rest upon the ground of the world at hand, questions of being, questions of value, practical questions, questions about being or not-being, about being valuable, being useful, being beautiful, being good, etc. All natural interests are put out of play" (152). This is what I call Husserl's attempt to achieve a state of objective subjectivity. It is not objective in the sense of occurring "outside" of subjectivity. But it is not subjective in the sense of playing a situated role within subjective activity in the everyday world. We are within subjectivity, but transcendentally, as divine observers.

When I phenomenologize, the world remains just as it is, except that I am not effectively plugged into it as participating in the validation processes, evaluations, end-fulfilling actions, and so on. After the act of bracketing, the world "is under our gaze purely as the correlate of the subjectivity which gives it ontic meaning, through whose validities the world 'is' at all" (152). Husserl goes on to emphasize that this is not an interpretation or conception of the world. Every grasping of or opinion about the world has its basis in the pregiven world. It is exactly this basis that I have removed through the bracketing or neutralizing act. "I stand *above* the world, which has now become for me, in a quite peculiar sense, a *phenomenon*" (152).

This passage makes it explicit that phenomenology is not a scientific, metaphysical, or ontological theory or interpretation of the world. All traditional philosophical doctrines about the world presuppose the world as in act (as the context of existence), and so such doctrines presuppose that I am still embedded in the natural attitude. This was Husserl's critique of Kant, that transcendental constituting takes place within the inner experience of the natural attitude, which has not itself been transcendentally thematized by an appropriate neutralizing. The transcendental bracketing by which we neutralize the life-world enables us for the first time to behold the life-world as fully present. The life-world, thanks to the bracketing, shows itself as it is. Phenomenology is the *logos* in the sense of the pure description of what shows itself as it is, and of what is as it shows itself. The world, we may say, is transparent to the phenomenological gaze. And this confirms my previous point that the decision to neutralize the life-world cannot itself be made *within* the life-world. Husserl owes us an explanation of how philosophers leave the life-world to gaze phenomenologically. He says simply that this departure is a decision of the philosopher. If this is true, then philosophers dwell somewhere in between immanence and transcendence. They cannot dwell in (i.e., make the defining decision within) either the immanent or the transcendental world.

I want to emphasize my questioning the internal coherence of Husserl's doctrine. As phenomenologists, we do not simply stand outside or beyond the world, which is now a phenomenon or pure presence for us. We activate the transcendental bracketing with the intention of studying, or let us say describing, the life-world, and this in order to uncover the last source of being and sense. The motivation for, the sense-bestowal upon, the attribution of being to, the transcendental bracketing, and what stands revealed to it: all these must themselves come from the life-world. I as potential philosopher must desire to know the truth about the life-world, about being and sense. But I as potential philosopher am a full resident of the life-world, not a divine phantom above and beyond it. It is innerworldly philosophical eros that drives me to phenomenology. But phenomenology depends upon the neutralization of innerworldly eros.

Husserl might be defended in the following manner. The desire to possess wisdom is indeed innerworldly. But in order to be wise, we must see the pure activity of this desire; and in order to see it, we must neutralize it or (in the properly qualified sense of the term) "objectify" it. I do not think that this defense works. Once we neutralize eros, we have disconnected it: it no longer motivates us to philosophize. Hence, our description of the pure, neutralized phenomenon of eros is no longer a description of eros. And this is a general problem. The neutralization of the life-world turns it into something else, denatures it, transforms it from life into a motion-picture about life as seen by a solitary and disinterested observer. An exact description of a film about life is not a description of life as lived, because there are no neutral descriptions of lived life. When I sit in a darkened theater and watch a film, I am participating empathically in the scenes, identifying with the hero, and so on. If I did not do this, I could not understand the film.

One might suggest that by watching a film I could see more objectively the processes by which acts of daily life are validated. But what I would actually be seeing is how a film is made about people who are living. The only reasons for my understanding the acts and speeches of the people who are acting in the film are that I am also a person, and that I have *not* detached myself from the life-world. If I were not myself in the life-world even as I watch the film, how could I know that the film is about people in the life-world? And as to the theoretical knowledge required for the satisfaction of the philosophical eros, a desire can only be satisfied when it is felt. At the level of the transcendental epoche, the "I" of the phenomenologist has no desires. There is no question of satisfaction at this level; the activity of viewing the film or of describing it ceases to have a point.

Husserl could still claim that I desire to possess apodictic knowledge in the life-world and *that* is a reason for performing the bracketing; after I acquire scientific knowledge of the life-world, I can then return to it. But I claim that an affectless description of human existence is not *for that reason* a scientific, i.e., true, description of existence itself. A correct description of the life-world is accessible only within the life-world itself. Husserl refers to the phenomenological description of the life-world as knowledge of transcendental subjectivity, but I insist that it would be more accurate to refer to this as knowledge of the objectification of subjectivity. The events of the life-world are transformed into structures and neutralized processes. The inside is seen from the outside. Husserl refers to this result of the bracketing as a theoretical approach to *doksa* (belief), understood as the foundation for *episteme* (knowledge, 158). But such a theoretical approach is itself outside of *doksa* and cannot be motivated by it. Furthermore, and even more important, the animating eros of the life-world is not a *doksa* but an existential fact about which we formulate opinions and beliefs. It is not the beliefs that generate science but the erotic desire or psychic motivation to acquire science or wisdom. By speaking of a science of *doksa*, Husserl has epistemologized the life-world from the outset. There can be a science of opinions, or at least an objective taxonomy of them, and there can even be a scientific description of someone who experiences erotic desire. But there is no science of the actual experience itself. So too there can be a science of values, but there is nothing scientific about evaluating even though that may be done systematically. It is the "accomplishment" of evaluation, the attributing of value, that gives value to speeches, to deeds, and to things, not the description of the value that is attributed.

As Husserl continuously emphasizes, the phenomenologist has no interest whatsoever in the being or nonbeing, the value or valuelessness, of anything that occurs in the life-world. In Husserl's eyes, this neutrality is desirable because his model of knowledge is science, and the paradigm of scientific truth is mathematics. But on my view this is precisely the wrong step to take with respect to what Husserl calls the life-world. My goal as a philosopher is not to acquire a scientific or apodictic knowledge of the structures of the life-world and of the processes of consciousness by which these structures are constituted. My goal is rather to show how the unstructured desire for knowledge in ordinary experience leads to the establishment of the sciences. Still more precisely, my goal is to show how the erotic desire of the soul transforms everyday desire into philosophy. There is no science of the life-world, because there is no life-world. Life is not a world and does not take place within a world. To the contrary, worlds are projects of life.

I thus deny the central Husserlian thesis that life transpires within the horizon of a pregiven world. This conception is derived from Kant. Husserl is right to say with reference to Kant that the world-constituting processes take place within inner experience, but he is wrong to attribute the horizon of a world to inner experience. In fact, Kant does not do this; he is interested exclusively in the world of objectivity. For Kant, inner experience or personal subjectivity is pretheoretical and prephilosophical; it is the domain of empirical psychology, not of scientific knowledge. In what amounts to a misunderstanding of Kant's doctrine of the transcendental, Husserl assumes that the medium of inner experience itself plays a constitutive role in effectuating transcendental cognition. For Kant, however, this would be to destroy the transcendental, to transform it into immanent temporal consciousness. Husserl is closer to Fichte than to Kant on this point; one could describe Husserl as attempting to avoid the dualism of immanent and transcendental consciousness by deriving the former from the latter, but also by arguing that both levels of consciousness possess a common structure and power, namely, the structure of intentionality and the power of an apodictic intuition of the intended object. This emendation of what Husserl says is required in order for the transcendental description of the life-world to be possible. In short, whereas Kant says that we cannot know the common root of the powers of the mind (in particular, of understanding, sensibility, and imagination), Husserl insists that phenomenology is precisely the science of the common source of all subjective activity, and so of all subjective constitutings of intelligible structure.

Even if Husserl were right on this point, the results are disastrous for an apodictic science. Let us assume that transcendental cognition depends on the medium of inner experience, and so that apodictic knowledge of transcendental cognition depends upon apodictic knowledge of inner experience. Since the life-world remains intact after the bracketing, the task of describing it is indefinitely long. The task requires the phenomenologist to assume as many points of view as there are existential, perceptual, or doxastic standpoints. But if the phenomenological description of the life-world is indefinitely long, how can such a description serve to ground objective knowledge? There cannot be any equivalent to the Kantian table of categories, regulative Ideals, rules, and so on, in the life-world. The life-world is *historical,* and so it brings forth a continuous stream of philosophical standpoints and scientific theories. But even if there were only two opposing tables of categories or philosophical theories, how could the phenomenologist adjudicate between them? He or she could only describe them. What looks to the phenomenologist of one epoch like the foundation of conscious activity could look to a phenomenologist in the next generation like a penultimate level of eidetic analysis.

Husserl assumes that the level of the transcendental ego reached by bracketing the life-world is valid for all human beings, but also that the task of describing the flow of subjectivity that originates from, and is accessible to, the transcendental ego, is unending. He claims that no conceivable human being could experience the world in any way other than as he has just described it

(165). This statement depends upon the assumption that he has articulated the conditions for the possibility of experiencing a world, i.e., the equivalent to the Kantian transcendental ego. If that is his assumption, he must distinguish between the apodictic account of world-experience and the infinitely large range of experiences themselves.

On this point, Husserl resembles Hegel, who claims that his *Logic* fully describes the process by which history occurs, but it does not of course describe the contingent events of an unending future. But Hegel is a Kantian in the following crucial sense. Although transcendental structure is revealed in contingent temporality, that structure does not depend upon temporality to actualize it. History is explained by logic, not vice versa. So too in Kant, objective cognition occurs within, but does not depend upon, inner subjective experience of this or that personal ego. Kant is here also a non-Hegelian, because inner subjective experience is *not* explained by objective cognition; it could not be so explained since objective cognition is precisely sensation without objective structuring. But Husserl says that we cannot acquire apodictic science of objectification without apodictic science of inner subjective experience. He thereby doubles inner experience: it consists of apodictic structure, accessible finally to the phenomenologist, and indefinitely large content, accessible only from this or that perspective and so never altogether. Why then does Husserl's own argument about objectification not apply to the structure of inner experience? If knowledge of objectification (of the nature of objects in the external world) depends upon knowledge of the inner experience of the life-world, why does not knowledge of the quasi-objectifying powers of the inner or life-world depend upon transcendental knowledge of the content, upon the stream of historicity within which objectification occurs? In fact, the problem is even more pressing, because there are not two separate processes of objectification, one for the outside and the other for the inside. The objectification of the outside is precisely the work of transcendental subjectivity, which produces the outside by constituting its objective structure.

In short, the grounding of the life-world is precisely the grounding of the objectivity of nature. Objectification is the work of transcendental subjectivity, which is accessible to the phenomenologist only through an exact description of the life-world as rendered neutral by having been bracketed. Phenomenology gives us *ex hypothesi* apodictic knowledge of the world-constitutive powers of transcendental subjectivity. But how can transcendental subjectivity do this without acquiring an apodictic grasp of the content of these structures, especially since such content is nothing other than the medium within which objectification occurs? This medium, however, is temporality; even worse, it is historicity: the unending flow of the life-world.

I conclude that, if an apodictic science of objectification is accessible, it cannot depend upon a correlative science of subjectivity in the sense of the phenomenologically purified description of the flow of inner temporal (and so contingent or personal) subjective experience. The transcendental must be accessible altogether independently of the mode of accessibility of the immanent. If knowledge of the contingent everyday experiences of the personal ego is unnecessary for knowledge of the world-constituting acts of transcendental subjectivity, then there is no second science of subjectivity (i.e., of the life-world) that is the correlate to the science of objectivity. The step from Kant to Husserl is therefore unnecessary and in fact illusory. Husserl's endless descriptions of the life-world do not provide us with the ultimate basis for the formation of the objective world. They lead us deeper and deeper into historicity, not ontological but immanent historicity, the Sisyphean task of acquiring a complete description of perceptual objects, among which forms, values, and senses are included.

As I see it, this brings us back to dualism: Plato versus Kant. In the first case, the forms (Platonic Ideas) that bestow thinghood (or what Husserl calls objectivity) are separate from the intellect (or what Husserl calls self-consciousness or subjectivity). In the second case, the forms of objectification are embedded within and activated by the operations of cognition. But this second case generates another alternative. We may say that the empirical subject produces the objective world or we may distinguish between the transcendental or absolute ego on the one hand and the empirical ego on the other. The choice of the absolute carries its own difficulties, and for the most part it has been evaded in favor of the empiricist option, even by those who still call themselves Kantians, Hegelians, or phenomenologists. Unfortunately, empiricism is unable to live up to its name, that is, to sustain the everyday distinction between the subject and its objects. As a result, it becomes impossible to say whether the mind is reduced to the body or the body is not itself still permeated with the subjectivity of objectification. The life-world soon disappears in the ensuing dialectic of chaos. Validation and evaluation are desubjectified by being converted into formal structure, but formal structure loses its objectivity by being conceived as the products of transcendental subjectivity. Apart from the largely rhetorical term "transcendental," I see no difference in the outcomes of phenomenology and empiricism. Very much as in the case of Montesquieu, the attempt to establish a scientific basis for the analysis and validation of experience, whether that basis be transcendental or empirical, leads to historicism, understood either as the flow of inner subjectivity or more directly as the latest stage in the progress of science.

In the first two chapters of this book, I have studied two paradigmatic versions of the attempt to produce a scientific account of everyday human life. Montesquieu's attempt concerned everyday life in its social and political sense; Husserl's attempt construed everyday life in the more general sense of pretheoretical activity.

With all due caution, one can fairly say that Montesquieu's procedure remains within the Aristotelian orbit on two main points. He does not move from everyday life to an ontological or transcendental doctrine of the structure of human action, and he assigns the fundamental role in political understanding and action to prudence. These two points can be summarized as an Aristotelian devotion to moderation. I have tried to show that this commonsense, practical tendency in Montesquieu's thought does not sit well with his scientific aspirations. One might almost suspect that this is because those aspirations are themselves too moderate. In any case, the lack of fit between the two tendencies opens a fissure through which history enters, at first as the ally of science and moderation, but eventually as their rival for primacy.

It would not be easy to accuse Husserl of moderation. He sees his role as that of prophet and revolutionary in an age of radical crisis, a crisis that can be overcome only by a return to the roots of the meaning and value of human life. This return is to be accomplished by means of the new science of phenomenology, a science that is not only new but universal and fundamental; it is the science that grounds all other sciences in the sources of meaning and value that it alone can uncover from the sediment of history. As we have seen, Husserl's science is transcendental, and so Kantian, in the sense that it is devoted to the processes by which consciousness constitutes the intelligible world. On the other hand, Husserl's science is as it were too transcendental to be genuinely Kantian, since it applies not merely to the forms of ordinary experience but to the particular content as well. Whereas Kant restricts science in order to preserve morality and freedom, or what one could call the integrity of everyday, pretheoretical life, Husserl, for all his talk of meaning and value, extends science to encompass the everyday and the pretheoretical. Husserl thereby comes dangerously close to, if he is not in fact indistinguishable from, the positivism that he believes himself to be combating.

Chapter 3 Kant and Heidegger: Transcendental Alternatives to Aristotle

I turn now to two different ways of responding to the incompatibility between modern natural science and an account of human life that is true to the manner in which we actually live it. The first way is that of Kant himself; the second is that of Kant's most idiosyncratic student: Heidegger. Rather than attempt a direct comparison between these two thinkers, however, I propose to contrast each with Aristotle. This will allow us to see the difference between approaches to everyday life that are entirely free of transcendental or ontological intentions, and those that are not. I shall begin with an analysis of the Kantian critique of eudaimonism which, although it is not directly addressed to Aristotle, certainly applies to the Aristotelian tradition. I then turn to Heidegger's use of Aristotle's practical philosophy, and in particular to his notorious interpretation of *phronesis*. I want to show, among other things, that whereas there is a genuine argument between Kant and Aristotle that turns upon a different assessment of human life as it is directly experienced by all normal persons, no such genuine encounter takes place between Heidegger and Aristotle because Heidegger replaces practical reasoning with fundamental ontology.

I preface my analyses with a general observation. Aristotle and his followers were centrally concerned with happiness or blessedness as the highest fulfilment of human striving. In Kant, happiness is replaced by the worthiness to be happy. This modification does not destroy an intrinsic agreement between the two philosophers. Contrary to some of the more dour passages in his writings, Kant recognizes happiness as an essential goal of human striving.[1] If we look at the British and French social and political thinkers of the seventeenth and eighteenth centuries, we shall find, if I am not mistaken, a de-emphasis upon happiness in favor of comfortable self-preservation or *douceur de vivre*. Kant's attack on eudaimonism, despite its recognition of the importance of happiness, nevertheless contributes to the rise to prominence in the nineteenth century of notions like satisfaction (Hegel) and work (Nietzsche). We can be satisfied that we have done our best to be worthy of happiness, even if we cannot be certain and therefore are not yet genuinely happy. Satisfaction is surely lower than happiness, and work implies satisfaction in the limited sense of ceaseless labor. In the twentieth century, happiness is replaced by anxiety (discussed already by Kierkegaard, who subordinates it to religious salvation or blessedness) and authenticity (Heidegger).

This highly condensed history of the decline of happiness is obviously related in some intimate way to the steady deterioration of practical philosophy, or let us say its transformation in the image of the modern mathematical and experimental sciences. But the decline of happiness is also accelerated by the rise of ontology and epistemology, not to mention theories of action and, more recently, the philosophy of artificial intelligence. The notion of happiness becomes an eccentricity or expression of private irony in the presence of a theoretical dissolution of our living experience, or conversely, in the reconstituting of ethics, especially when it is from a Kantian perspective, into theory of a systematic and rule-governed type.[2] In chapter 4, I will consider the role of happiness (or the absence of such a role) in two major attempts to repudiate the modern theoretical approach to practice, as represented by Wittgenstein and Leo Strauss.

One last preliminary remark: the contrast between Aristotle and Kant turns upon the way in which morality emerges from everyday or pretheoretical life. The contrast between Aristotle and Heidegger, on the other hand, illustrates the transformation of everyday life into ontology. Ethics and politics are thus eliminated from the consideration of "everydayness." The result is a peculiar isolation of the individual human being that is totally uncharacteristic of what Heidegger's view is supposed to explain. The Heideggerian resident of average everydayness thus becomes more like the plain speaker of ordinary language in the analytical tradition than like the citizen of a political community. It is true that the ordinary human being is a member of a linguistic community, but the inner function of language is ontological, not political.

KANT'S CRITIQUE OF EUDAIMONISM

Kant addressed himself in all of his major works to the relation between morality and happiness. As is well known, he protests strongly against what is often called "eudaimonism," the doctrine that we are good because it makes us happy. For example, in the *Groundwork of the Metaphysics of Morals,* Kant says that the principle of private happiness makes it impossible for us to distinguish between virtue and vice: "Making someone happy is quite different from making him good, or making him prudent and sharp-sighted for his own advantage is quite different from making him virtuous."[3] That is, the pursuit of happiness is the pursuit of our personal advantage, not of what is objectively good. Again, in the second *Critique,* Kant holds that the principle of private happiness is the direct opposite of the principle of morality. The former is concerned with the empirical circumstances that gratify our natural inclinations, and so they vary from person to person and case to case. "The moral law, however, is conceived as objectively necessary, because it must hold [*gelten soll*] for everyone who has reason and will" (40–43).[4] The same distinction between happiness as empirically conditioned by nature, and the possibility of morality as established a priori and dogmatically because free from natural effects, is made in paragraph 88 of the third *Critique*. Finally, in the *Metaphysics of Morals,* Kant notes that there are no a priori principles for happiness or joy; experience teaches us what causes these. "But it is different with the teachings of morality. They command for everyone, without taking account of his inclinations, merely because and insofar as he is free and has practical reason. He does not derive instruction in its laws from observing himself and his animal nature, or from perceiving the ways of the world, what happens and how we behave (although the German word *Sitten,* like the Latin *mores,* means only manners and customs)."[5]

Goodness is for Kant a matter of duty; to regard happiness as the goal of, or a reward for, moral goodness is to obscure the fact that morality is obligatory upon us regardless of the personal consequences. It should be emphasized that for Kant, duty and happiness are not opposed; one might be made happy by doing one's duty, but the latter supervenes over, and is not done for the sake of, the former.[6] Furthermore, although it is false that a virtuous disposition (*Tu-*

gendgesinnung) necessarily produces happiness in the sensible world, it is not impossible that this should occur in the noumenal world.[7] The gratification of our natural inclinations is a species of obligation, but it carries no moral value. Nothing exercises Kant's scorn more forcefully than the failure to distinguish between the obligation to duty and the pursuit of pleasure, and, in his analysis, it is difficult if not impossible to distinguish between natural happiness and pleasure. We must act morally even if it should be painful; and indeed, in some extreme passages, Kant seems to prefer that it be painful, lest we be tempted into acting for pleasure. As he says in the Second Critique, moral man "lives only out of duty, and not because he finds the slightest pleasure [*Geschmack*] in life."[8] In other words, Kant distinguishes, often implicitly, but in the *Metaphysics of Morals* explicitly, between physical and moral happiness. The former is derived from what nature bestows, and is enjoyed like a gift from a stranger; the second lies in "satisfaction with one's Person [=personhood] and in his own moral conduct." Only the second constitutes a legitimate use of the term "happiness." "For he who shall feel happy in the mere consciousness of his righteousness, possesses already that perfection that in the previous section was explained to be duty."[9]

Natural happiness, as dependent upon empirical contingency, is not obtained through pure reason, and obviously not by a grasp of the universal and a priori form of the moral law, but rather through prudence or cleverness (*Klugheit*), the ability to calculate the consequences of particular acts for the aforementioned purpose of satisfaction.[10] We are allowed, however, to strive for the worthiness to be happy, which depends upon our obedience to duty for its own sake; as we shall see, we must so strive. Since genuine or morally deserving happiness is available only in a future world (as Kant normally argues), it can have nothing to do with the gratifications of our natural inclinations. Kant does not discuss the precise nature of genuine happiness; one has the impression that it is always out of reach, a goal that somehow motivates our striving, without presenting itself as merited or accessible for any other reason or in any other way than through the possession and exercise of a good will and respect for the law.

Kant says that the ancients tried to identify virtue and happiness, and so succumbed to eudaimonism.[11] He has in mind the Epicureans and Stoics rather than Aristotle, who is scarcely mentioned in the second *Critique,* and only in passing, in a somewhat later footnote (p. 147), in which *Klugheit* is once more associated with happiness (*Glückseligkeit*) of the egoistic type. It seems clear that Kant did not have an accurate picture of Aristotle's teaching. Nevertheless, it is helpful to contrast Kant's approach to the question with Aristotle's own argument. Aristotle's treatment of the connection between virtue and happiness is the most detailed and subtle presentation of this topic in the history of philosophy. A comparison between the two thinkers helps us to see the main points in Kant's often obscure presentation of his doctrine of morality and, in particular, of his treatment of happiness.

It would not be possible, nor is it necessary, to present an exhaustive analysis of the practical philosophy of Aristotle and Kant. My aims are much more limited. I want to show the difference between an account of ordinary experience that begins with common sense and prudence, and one that takes its bearings by the joint influence of the biblical tradition and modern scientific rationalism. One crucial consequence is that Kant drops, or radically modifies, Aristotle's link between ethics and politics. In so doing, he sets the stage for the post-Kantian treatment of ethics, just as his critique of pure reason sets the stage for Idealism and phenomenology. In both cases, an essential goal is to preserve the integrity of ordinary human experience from scientific reductionism. And in both cases, the underlying conception of rationality raises insuperable obstacles to the achievement of that goal.

I shall begin with an introductory summary of the major points of difference between Aristotle's and Kant's moral teaching. The main feature of this contrast is not merely that the two philosophers seem to be in diametrical opposition on the relation of morality and happiness. Even more important is the fact that both start with an observation based upon common sense or the pretheoretical reasoning of everyday life. And yet the observations from which they begin are themselves incompatible. This is not to say that both are not justified by an important aspect of ordinary experience. But we learn something fundamental about common sense and ordinary experience when we see that it leads two of the greatest philosophers to views on moral virtue and happiness that are mutually incompatible.[12]

For Aristotle, it is plain that all human beings seek happiness as the highest good.[13] Equally obvious for Kant is the fact that, as all would agree, happiness is only part of the highest good, of which the other part is morality or the worthiness to be happy.[14] Aristotle proceeds to articulate his commonsense understanding of the highest good into a doctrine of virtue as a mean between two extremes that is calculated by prudence or practical intelligence. Such intelligence is itself possessed only by the person of perfect virtue.[15] It is not clear whether Aristotle holds consistently to his claim in book 1 of the *EN* that every normal person can be blessed (*makarion*) through virtue (1099b18 ff.). He more frequently emphasizes the great difficulty of achieving genuine virtue (e.g.,

2.1109a24), and says that the truly virtuous person (the *spoudaios*) judges each case correctly and so serves as a canon and a measure because he possesses practical judgment (*phronesis*), which never errs (3.1113 29a ff.; 6.1142b31 ff.). Whereas everyone seeks happiness, and although, according to Aristotle, genuine happiness is virtuous activity, it does not follow that everyone is virtuous or perceives the connection between virtue and happiness.

Finally, Aristotle refers to the views on the link between virtue and happiness both of the many (the ordinary person) and of the few distinguished persons (*endoksoi*); he says somewhat puzzlingly that both sets of views are likely to be largely right (1.1098b27 ff.). In sum, Aristotle often seems to be making an analysis of common sense in his study of ethical virtue, or of what all sensible people know in general; yet the actual ability to determine and practice what is virtuous in each case seems equally often to be reserved for the few. This is by no means incompatible in all respects with Kant's own procedure. He too starts with common moral judgment, as for example in section 1 of the *Groundwork,* and he often emphasizes the fact that morality must be easy to understand: Everyone knows and can do his duty (second *Critique* (41); in this passage, cleverness or prudence (*Klugheit*) is once more distinguished from morality and defined as self-love). Yet the full justification of the connection between duty or worthiness to be happy, and genuine moral happiness itself, requires a philosophical argument of extraordinary complexity. On the whole, Aristotle does not provide us with a full statement of the link between practice on the one hand, and a theoretical account of the natural context or substructure of practice on the other. One could say that there are three stages in Aristotle's ethical philosophy. The first stage is that of the citizen, who requires no theoretical explanations of any kind but only a good, i.e., properly habituated character (I here omit consideration of the complications introduced by the type of regime under which the individual lives). The second stage is that of the lawgiver, educator, or statesman, who needs to know only the simplified theoretical account provided by Aristotle of the nature of the virtues, justice, friendship, and pleasure, and to a still lesser extent, of theory, as well as of the faculties of the soul as sketched in book 6 of the *EN*. The third stage is that of the philosopher, and here it is entirely unclear how much of a theoretical knowledge of nature is required for a full grounding of ethics.[16] Certainly there is nothing comparable to Kant's philosophical justification of duty, goodness, and the possibility of genuinely deserved happiness. On the contrary, we are told explicitly that our present inquiry is not for the sake of theory, but is designed to make men good.[17]

We should also note that what is for Kant admitted by "everyone" is quite different from the commonsense views of the few (*endoksoi,* those of good repute)—or the many—as identified by Aristotle. Kant starts from the perception of the lawlike character of moral principles and their subsequent rejection of prudence or any reference to the contingencies of personal gratification. Incidentally, there is an ambiguity in Aristotle as to whether we are virtuous for the sake of happiness, or whether virtue simply is happiness. I cite two passages from the *EN.* Toward the end of book 1 (1101b25 f.), Aristotle says that *eudaimonia* is beyond praise, unlike justice. Much later, in book 10, Aristotle says that *eudaimonia* in the primary sense is identical with theoretical contemplation (1177a16–18). The practically virtuous life is *eudaimon* only secondarily (1178a9). For Kant, of course, moral virtue is higher than theoretical contemplation; the latter does not make us worthy of happiness, as does the former.

This will suffice as an introductory overview of the difference between Kant and Aristotle. The main point for us is that the two disagree on the testimony of ordinary experience. Both hold that this testimony is obedient to practical reason, but for Kant, practical reason remains under the influence of the connection between rationality and universality. Kant thus makes the notion of a rule central to his doctrine, which is tantamount to the demotion of prudence. It is of course also true that Kant's interpretation of everyday moral understanding is influenced by the biblical tradition, and in particular by the Protestant teaching, which is different from the Hebrew emphasis upon laws, but which Kant interprets in such a way as to unite conscience with duty as expressed in rules. In short, Kant's conception of everyday understanding is affected by his scientific and religious judgments. Some would say that Aristotle's analysis is closer to nature than Kant's. This thesis is open to the objection that Aristotle reflects the views of educated pagans who are partisans of aristocracy, but that is not decisive. What counts is whether the adherence to the spirit of noble behavior is verified by our experience and common sense. The question is then whether there can be a conception of everyday life that is theoretically neutral, or expressive of human nature as it is and must be, regardless of prevailing religious and scientific views.

Let us now study the details of Kant's account of happiness in the first *Critique* (A800–B828). I have selected this passage because it contains a convenient and reasonably concise statement of the essential elements in Kant's position with respect to the difference between morality and happiness. So far as I can see, nothing that Kant says in this passage is rejected in his later treatments of the topic, nor is anything radically essential added afterwards, on the topic that concerns us, namely, the connection between everyday life and morality.[18] It will be a valuable introductory exercise to analyze closely the position taken in the first *Critique,* especially because the last part of this work is seldom studied with the care that is devoted to the earlier sections.

The immediate context is the introduction of three topics that concern all human beings: God, freedom, and immortality. The nature of our concern in these cases, or let us say the way in which to reflect upon them, is practical, not theoretical. "Everything is practical that is possible through freedom. But if the conditions for the exercise of our free choice [*Willkür*] are empirical, then in that case reason can have none but a regulative use, and can only serve to produce the unity of empirical laws, as e.g., in the doctrine of prudence [*Klugheit*] the unification of all ends that are given to us by our inclinations [*Neigungen*] into the single end of happiness [*Glückseligkeit*] and the harmony of means for attaining that end constitute the entire business of reason, which can therefore provide none but pragmatic laws of free conduct for reaching the ends recommended to us by the senses, and therefore can provide no pure laws that are determined completely *a priori*" (A800–B828).

The word *Willkür* suggests the arbitrariness of inclinations that are determined by our senses rather than the freedom characteristic of the will. On this point, see A534–B562: "*Freedom in the practical sense* is the independence of the power of choice from *necessitation* by impulses of sensibility." In other words, the impulses of sensibility, or our natural inclinations, are not free but given; we are "free" to employ prudence or cleverness (*Klugheit*) to obtain the ends we desire. The ends themselves are natural, and so compelled. They have nothing to do with morality. "Happiness" means here the "satisfaction" of all our inclinations (*Befriedigung,* A806–B834). This passage, incidentally, bears upon my earlier observation as to the link between Kant and the subsequent replacement of happiness by satisfaction. Strictly speaking, for Kant, satisfaction has nothing to do with morality, which is rather associated with the *worthiness to be happy.* We see already that Kant distinguishes between empirical happiness and moral blessedness; we are about to see that the latter is postponed to the next world or is given the shape of a hope for the future rather than a condition of life.

Since morality depends upon free choice, a proposition that Kant accepts without argument as undisputed, it cannot depend upon sensual inclination, which determines choices relative to its satisfaction. But why must moral choice be a priori? The implication is that empirical laws will all be infected by the senses, that is, by nature. In other words, we have to remember the main thesis of Kant's philosophy: the distinction between the phenomenal domain, in which freedom is impossible because it is ruled by physical determinism, and the noumenal domain, in which pure practical reason acts spontaneously and autonomously to give laws to itself. That is, the laws are not imposed upon us from outside ourselves, and so neither by God nor nature. In order to be free, we must be able to choose. If, however, we choose a particular action on the basis of our analysis of the particular circumstances, we fall back into the domain of experience, that is, of the senses and their inclinations, and so of nature.

This shows very clearly the influence of Christianity on Kant's moral doctrine, and so too his rejection of the Aristotelian notion of human nature. What one could call "natural" ordinary experience is for Kant not decisive. Otherwise put, he takes it more or less for granted that the biblical interpretation of everyday and so too moral life is decisive, with one major exception. The biblical account of morality is secularized or revised in such a way as to give practical reason primacy over revelation and religious faith. Practice, and so freedom, upon which morality depends, require a rational choice. The choice must not be of the individual action so much as of a pure practical law that we give to ourselves, and that itself obligates us to perform the act in question.

As we shall see later, the obligatory or regulative role of the law comes from its universality. We are to act in such a way that we could will to live in a society in which everyone would be required to act in the same manner. Let us note that it makes no difference to Kant whether the pure practical laws of reason are "practical" in the empirical sense. He assumes that the individual person can always will correctly, that is, correctly understand the possibility of making universal the requirement to act in such-and-such a manner. The point is not discussed here, but the assumption is that morality, and hence the worthiness to be happy, is equivalent to a good will rather than to a life of good actions. Since good actions take place in the phenomenal world, whereas pure practical laws are invoked or formulated in the noumenal domain, it would seem that Kant is required by his own theory to give precedence to willing over acting. This is of course entirely non-Aristotelian.

The universality of the moral law does away with the danger of selfishness or the identification of one's own inclinations with what ought to be done. Making the same point in another way, the law must be a priori, because for Kant, all universal laws are spontaneous productions of pure reason; that is, they constitute the form of empirical experience rather than an induction from experience itself. Kant makes this very point: "Pure practical laws, on the contrary, whose end is given by reason completely *a priori,* and which do not command under empirical conditions but absolutely, would be products of pure reason. Of this sort, however, are the moral laws; thus these alone belong to the practical use of reason and permit a canon" (A800–B828).

I turn now to A804–B832 ff. The immediate context is the formulation of the three questions of interest to both speculative and practical reason. I note in passing that Kant says here *spekulative,* not "theoretical." The distinction is explained at A634–B662 f. "A theoretical cognition is *speculative* if it pertains to an object or concepts of an object to which one cannot attain in any experience. It is opposed to the *cognition of nature,* which pertains to no objects, or their predicates, except those that can be given in a possible experience." In other words, we can speculate about things that we cannot know. The point here is that we speculate about certain questions that are of decisive importance to human life but we cannot know their answers theoretically. Kant sometimes uses "speculative" as an apparent synonym for "theoretical," as for example at Bxxvi, where he says that speculative cognition is restricted to objects of experience; that is, it is identical with theoretical knowledge of nature.[19]

But this point of terminology is not essential to our purposes. What counts for us is Kant's claim that there is evidence in the domain of the practical that allows speculative reason to believe, and on that basis, to hope, that certain answers to the aforementioned questions are true. The first question is: What can I know? This is "purely speculative." That is, it has nothing to do with morality. The second question, on the other hand, is "What should I do?" This contains an "ought," and therefore invokes free will. It thus lies entirely outside the sphere of cognition or science, and is "purely practical." There is no possible knowledge of objects that may be brought to bear upon the answering of this question. The third question is as follows: "If I do what I should, what may I then hope?" This question, Kant says, is "both practical and theoretical, so that the practical leads like a clue to a reply to the theoretical question and, in its highest form, the speculative question." But this does not of course mean that the practical clue leads us to objects, the cognition of which provides us with theoretical knowledge of the conditions of hope. The practical clue uncovers a dimension within which our hope is enabled to stand as a surrogate for theoretical knowledge. "For all *hope* concerns happiness, and with respect to the practical and the moral law it is the very same as what knowledge and the natural law are with regard to theoretical cognition of things. The former finally comes down to the inference that something *is* (which determines the ultimate final end) *because something ought to happen;* the latter, that something *is* (which acts as the supreme cause) *because something does happen*" (A805–B833).

Allow me to expand this crucial statement. The domain of practice furnishes us with grounds for the assertion that it is the case that my good will makes me worthy of happiness. But I will not actually achieve this happiness except for the fulfillment of certain conditions that may be summarized for the moment as the existence of God and personal immortality. I ought to be justified in my hope for happiness; therefore I believe that God exists and that I am immortal. It is essential to grasp that there is no "reason" in the theoretical sense for such an inference. In his fullest statement on this point, at the outset of the second *Critique,* Kant says that we know the moral law, which in turn requires for its validity that we are free (4). Note that the authority of the moral law is autonomous; i.e., it is not dependent upon beliefs in God and immortality. These beliefs are required in order that the good will may obtain its highest good, namely, the coincidence of worthiness to be happy and actual happiness. But moral law is obligatory in itself, regardless of whether we are or become happy thanks to our obedience to it.

In the next segment of the passage on which I am commenting, Kant introduces the distinction between happiness and the worthiness of happiness. So doing, he prepares the way for a distinction between two senses of happiness, which are referred to in the *Metaphysics of Morals* as physical happiness on the one hand and moral happiness on the other. Speaking of the former, Kant says in the first *Critique* (A806–B834): "Happiness is the satisfaction [*Befriedigung*] of all our inclinations. . . . The practical law from the motive of *happiness* I call pragmatic (rule of prudence) but that which is such that it has no other motive than *the worthiness to be happy* I call moral (moral law)." The happiness that derives from satisfaction of the inclinations is in one sense determined and in another contingent. It is determined in the sense that we must act in accord with the laws of our empirical nature, but it is contingent in the sense that prudence or cleverness is required in order to calculate correctly what acts will achieve the aforementioned satisfaction. We are as it were "free" only to choose the means to the naturally determined end. But the laws associated with this end are not autonomous or legislated by us; hence we are not free and therefore morality is not involved. Finally, when worthiness, which depends upon hope for a future life, is replaced by secular doctrines that exclude personal immortality, we are left with what could be called the vulgar conception of happiness as empirical satisfaction of natural drives.

To continue: "The first [i.e., the practical law] advises us what to do if we want to partake of happiness; the second [i.e., the moral law] commands how we should behave in order even to be worthy of happiness. The first is grounded on empirical principles; for except by means of experience I can know neither which inclinations there are that would be satisfied nor what the natural causes are that could satisfy them. The second abstracts from inclinations and natural means of satisfying them, and considers only the freedom of a rational being in general and the necessary conditions under which alone it is in agreement with the distribution of happiness in accord with principles, and thus it at least *can* rest on mere ideas of pure reason and be cognized a priori" (ibid.).

Once again I emphasize that, according to Kant, I can know that I am acting morally through obeying the moral law, and so that I am worthy of happiness. In what is certainly one of the weaker passages in his exposition, he says: "I assume that there are really pure moral laws, which determine completely *a priori* (without regard to empirical motives, i.e. happiness)." He appeals to "the proofs of the most enlightened moralists" and to "the moral judgment of every human being, if he will distinctly think such a law" (A807–B835). The argument in the second *Critique* is in my opinion no stronger, since it takes for granted what needs to be proved, namely, that every person has a clear idea of a moral law, and further, that this idea is accurate and reliable. It looks very much as though Kant is grounding transcendental necessity in empirical contingency. Otherwise put, the perception of moral laws is made a part of everyday life, but a part that can be intuited as emanating from the transcendental domain. However peculiar this may be from Kant's own standpoint, it is not entirely dissimilar to Aristotle's claim that the *phronimos* always knows what is virtuous. The major difference from a practical point of view (and so putting to one side knowledge of the transcendental domain) is that Kant extends to all normal people what Aristotle reserves for a few.

But I am here concerned to make a different point. To be worthy of happiness is not the same as to be happy. Even if we accept Kant's assurance with respect to the existence of pure a priori moral laws that are evident to all, and the freedom of choice that is required if we are to acquire the worthiness to be happy, we need some further reason to hope that this worthiness will be rewarded. Differently stated, we need some reason (since we are in the domain of moral or practical *reason*) to make our hope plausible.

In the next section of our passage (A807–B835), Kant turns to the task of establishing this plausibility. Having assumed that there are pure moral laws that command a priori and absolutely, he goes on to say: "Pure reason thus contains—not in its speculative use, to be sure, but yet in a certain practical use, namely the moral use—principles of the *possibility of experience,* namely of those actions in conformity with moral precepts which *could* be encountered in the *history* of humankind. For since they command that these actions ought to happen, they must also be able to happen, and there must therefore be possible a special kind of systematic unity, namely the moral," as is not the case, for reasons irrelevant to our present concern, with the speculative principles of reason (that is, the unity of nature). Kant's reasoning is as follows. We know that there are moral laws, to which we are absolutely obligated. Therefore we must be free to obey these laws; otherwise they would not be moral but natural or theoretical. But if we are free to obey them, then this obedience is possible. Furthermore, the possibility extends to every human being. But Kant is of course not claiming that universal morality is possible in the empirical, pragmatic, or natural domain. That would in fact be impossible, not merely because most people are selfish or evil, but because even the exercise of a good will depends upon the freedom of the noumenal or transcendental domain. We thus have the following curious consequence. Actions that could be in conformity with moral precepts are to be discovered as situated within human history. But the free choice of such acts, and so our very existence as moral agents, cannot be situated within history. I mention in passing that when Kant addresses the question of historical progress toward political virtue (an expression I use in the Machiavellian sense), he puts universal peace at an asymptotic distance. This is equivalent to placing it outside of history.

Kant continues: "I call the world as it would be if it were in conformity with all moral laws (as it *can* be in accordance with the *freedom* of rational beings and *should* be in accordance with the necessary laws of *morality*) a *moral world*" (A808–B836). This is not the empirical or phenomenal world. It "is conceived thus far merely as an intelligible world, since abstraction is made therein from all conditions (ends) and even from all hindrances to morality in it (weakness or impurity of human nature)." Kant does not say so, but the implication is that the empirical world can never coincide with the intelligible world; otherwise put, such a coincidence would be tantamount to the destruction of the empirical world as it exists now, and in particular of human nature, that is, sensual desires or inclinations. To refer to the moral world as "intelligible" is thus the same as to say that it exists in our thoughts only, whether these thoughts be called speculations, beliefs, or hopes. The intelligible world is "thus far" (implying that it could become something else) "a mere, yet practical, idea, which really can and should have its influence on the sensible world, in order to make it agree as far as possible with this idea."

One way to read this passage is to infer that in the perhaps distant future, yet somewhere within historical existence, human beings may be brought to coincide in their behavior with the idea of the intelligible world of complete and systematic morality. Such a notion may perhaps be found in Kant's essays on history and world politics, but it does not seem to be what he has in mind here. "The idea of a moral world thus has objective reality, not as if it pertained to an object of an intelligible intuition (for we cannot even think of such a thing), but as pertaining to the sensible world, although as an object of pure reason in its practical use and a *corpus mysticum* of the rational beings in it, insofar as their free choice under moral laws has thoroughgoing systematic unity in itself as well as with the freedom of everyone else" (A808–B836). In other words, even if everyone in this world were to become completely moral, we would all still be bound by the nature of the phenomenal world within which we actually exist; hence freedom, and so goodness or the worthiness to be happy, would remain in the intelligible world as a *corpus mysticum* of rational beings. The split between the sensible and the intelligible world is not one of morality alone, and not even fundamentally, but rather it is one of phenomena and noumena. So long as there are human beings, there will be a dualism of the sensible and the intelligible worlds. But this means that the dream of complete morality is impossible, since it depends upon the disappearance of the body, that is, on the appearance of a *mystical* body as the replacement for its corporeal imitation.

On the other hand, if we believe in God and immortality, then we can assign the power to grant moral happiness to God, and the worthiness of the recipient to its incorporeal nature. Kant now turns to this final step in the argument by providing an answer to the third question: "If I behave so as not to be unworthy of happiness, how may I hope thereby to partake of it?" (A809–B837). The answer to this question, Kant says, depends upon "whether the principles of pure reason that prescribe the law *a priori* also necessarily connect this hope with it." The key word here is "connect." The implicit assumption at this point is that since I am compelled by my knowledge of the moral law to strive to be worthy of happiness, it would be absurd if there were no possibility that my striving should be rewarded. But this possibility does not follow from the moral law itself, since as Kant regularly stresses, we are obligated to it independently of any consideration of reward or personal happiness. The most Kant can show is that the hope for reward is not absurd, or in other words, that it is possible for me to be rewarded. This is why Kant refers to such a possibility as a hope. Morality is binding in its own right, or as this could also be expressed, it is intrinsically good. But it is not by itself the *summum bonum,* which also includes the actual achievement of happiness, and this means, of course, the achievement of blessedness, not of physical or empirical happiness.

Kant, despite his moral severity, does not attempt to persuade us that human life is justified by a good will alone. The good have a right to be happy, if not in this world, then in the next, or in the intelligible kingdom of the *corpus mysticum*. If this right is not fulfilled, then life is unjust, or rather, it is neither just nor unjust but absurd. To see this, we have only to imagine a world in which those who act morally are never rewarded and indeed, are miserable in this world without receiving recompense in the next. Aristotle avoids this possibility by identifying happiness as virtuous activity. This line is unavailable to Kant, since it raises the danger of eudaimonism, namely, that we act virtuously in order to be happy, and not for the sake of virtue itself. It is also not a thesis that can be easily sustained by distinguishing between physical and moral happiness. Aristotle admits that virtue requires luck as well as external equipment, but such an admission would be fatal to Kant's moral doctrine. In short, if morality does not in itself guarantee happiness, then this happiness must be supplied by an external agent, namely, God. For without God, that is, without the possibility of being rewarded for our worthiness, it is not simply the case that we cannot achieve the *summum bonum*. We are committed to hold that the world is amoral, or in other words that goodness does not make us happy. And even worse, we can be good and miserable at the same time. I said a moment ago that in this case, life would be neither just nor unjust but absurd. But it could be argued that on Kantian grounds, we are required to say that life is in this case unjust, since we understand ourselves to be obligated to justice rather than to injustice. If the just are punished with misery and the unjust rewarded with happiness, of however worldly or empirical a kind, then this is surely injustice. But whether we call it absurd or unjust, it is obvious that the *summum bonum* is not merely a welcome bonus to minimal but sufficient goodness. Without the guarantee that goodness will be rewarded with happiness, the goodness of the good becomes ambiguous and therefore questionable. This reward cannot come simply from being good, because moral goodness is an obligation, not a reward. It must therefore come from God. A belief in the existence of God is required in order to exclude the possibility that life is unjust or absurd, or both.

Thus far it is reasonably clear why we might hope that God exists. But why should we believe it? Kant's first assertion in defense of this belief is not very helpful. "I say, accordingly, that just as the moral principles are necessary in accordance with reason in its *practical* use, it is equally necessary to assume in accordance with reason in its *theoretical* use that everyone has cause to hope for happiness in the same measure as he has made himself worthy of it in his conduct, and that the system of morality is therefore inseparably combined with the system of happiness, though only in the idea of pure reason" (A809–B837). The necessity of the moral principles rests upon "the moral judgment of every human being" who thinks clearly moral laws. This ostensible necessity arises from the universal form of a moral law. But that we have cause to hope for happiness if we are worthy of it does not follow from the universal form of moral law. Neither does it follow from the act of being moral, i.e., of willing in accord with such a law. From where, then, does this hope arise? It must be from the desire to acquire the happiness of which we deem ourselves worthy. This desire, although it is not the cause of our being moral, is nevertheless justified. That is to say, it is just, and therefore moral, to hope for what one deserves. But the belief that we will obtain our deserts is something else again. Hope that transforms itself into belief without reason is tautologously unreasonable, and Kant is engaging in moral philosophy, not Christian homiletics. What is not yet clear is why a cause to hope for happiness, that is, a cause that transforms hope into belief, has anything to do with the *theoretical* use of reason.

With this question in mind, let us proceed to the next paragraph of Kant's text. "Now in an intelligible world, i.e., in the moral world, in the concept of which we have abstracted from all hindrances to morality (of the inclinations), such a system of happiness proportionately combined with morality can also be thought as necessary, since freedom, partly moved and partly restricted by moral laws, would itself be the cause of the general happiness, and rational beings, under the guidance of such principles, would themselves be the authors of their own enduring welfare and at the same time that of others" (A809–B837). It is worth emphasizing that in the empirical or natural world, there are hindrances to morality that cannot be overcome; in other words, the moral kingdom is always, and always will be, an intelligible rather than a natural kingdom. But this is almost trivial compared to the major claim of the passage. If we abstract from the hindrances of actual human life and consider the intelligible world of freedom to will the moral law, and further, if we populate this world with rational beings, namely, those who in fact obey, that is, will, the moral law, then we can say that freedom "would itself be the cause of the general happiness." But this is a non sequitur. Or rather, it assumes what is to be proven, namely, that a good will in fact makes us happy. And if it does, is this not to contradict entirely the previously asserted separation between morality and happiness? It is also far from obvious that the rational residents of the intelligible world are identical with the residents, some "rational" (in the sense of moral) and many more not, who populate the natural world. In other words,

Kant assumes that since everyone can think a moral law, once the hindrances of the inclinations or nature are removed, we will all do what we ought to do, namely, will the moral law. Finally, in the intelligible world as described by Kant, freedom, not God, awards happiness. Since the intelligible world is the result of human abstraction or rational power, it would seem that God is unnecessary.

Let us see if the immediate sequel clarifies these ambiguities or removes the contradictions just noted. "But this system of self-rewarding morality is only an idea, the realization of which rests on the condition that *everyone* do as he should, i.e., that all actions of rational beings occur as if they arose from a highest will that comprehends all private choice in or under itself." If all persons had good wills, happiness for everyone would be the result of universally moral behavior. In other words, each of us would rejoice in the knowledge of our perfect goodness. We would collectively constitute the deity (the "highest will") from which all actions arise. But there remains one problem. Why should knowledge of our goodness make us happy? Now as a matter of fact, I am prepared to grant this as an empirical observation; human being are so constituted as to be happy about their own goodness. If we abstract from all hindrances to goodness, we will also abstract from all sources of pain or sadness that might impinge upon this happiness. But I see no reason to infer from a consideration of the pure moral will, as described by Kant, that we are made happy by its activity. Neither do I see any reason to agree that every free will (i.e., every will freed from the hindrances of the natural world) will be a good one. If this were so, then moral good would be necessitated by the freedom of the will alone. But this would contradict its freedom, and thus destroy morality.

To continue: "But since the obligation from the moral law remains valid for each particular use of freedom even if others do not conduct themselves in accord with this law, how their consequences will be related to happiness is determined neither by the nature of the things in the world, nor by the causality of actions themselves and their relation to morality" (A810–B838). That is, the moral law is always binding, regardless of whether it is obeyed by all. Otherwise put, although I am free to disobey, I am obligated to obey. Neither the nature of things nor the causality of actions in the phenomenal world determines the relation of things or causes to happiness in the genuine or moral sense. My choice, whether to obey or not to obey, is independent of these empirical circumstances, and so too is the act of obedience or disobedience. This is what it means to be free. Therefore "the necessary connection of the hope of being happy with the unremitting effort to make oneself worthy of happiness that has been adduced cannot be cognized through reason if it is grounded merely in nature, but may be hoped for only if it is at the same time grounded on a *highest reason,* which commands in accordance with moral laws, as at the same time the cause of nature."

In this passage, Kant almost but not quite makes the desired shift from hoping to believing. My hope for happiness is unreasonable, and also immoral, if it is based upon the prospects for the gratification of my natural inclinations. I may hope for happiness, however, if there exists a *highest reason,* that is to say, "the highest will," which does not obey but rather commands. There is still no reason to believe in such a highest will, nor has any reason been given to assume that the source of the moral laws desires our happiness or is prepared to grant it. What I have now, assuming that the highest reason exists, is a reason for hoping, but not yet for believing, that I will be happy. But why should I accept the grounding of the hope of being happy in a highest reason? There seems to be a reason for *not* doing this, namely, that it cancels our autonomy and makes God the ground of moral law. One could reply that "highest reason" refers to something like transcendental moral reason, but this has the consequence that we are divided in half within the moral world: into wills that are free to obey or disobey, and a transcendental will (the same in all) that is free to command. I note that such a line attributes the practice of esotericism to Kant, or the use of popular (exoteric) speech to veil his meaning from the orthodox, something that Kant denies doing.

I must quote one more paragraph at length. "I call the idea of such an intelligence [namely, the highest reason] in which the morally most perfect will, combined with the highest blessedness, is the cause of all happiness in the world, insofar as it stands in exact relation with morality (as the worthiness to be happy), *the ideal of the highest good*" (A810–B838). An "idea is a concept made up of notions, which goes beyond the possibility of experience" (A320–B377). An "ideal" is "the idea not merely *in concreto* but *in individuo,* i.e., as an individual thing which is determinable, or even determined, through the idea alone" (A568–B596). Kant also says in this passage that "what is an ideal to us, was to *Plato* an *idea in the divine understanding.*" Suffice it to say that the ideal of the highest good is in the first instance the purely intelligible concept of the unity of perfect morality and blessedness as the cause of all happiness in the world. The last phrase is a bit confusing, since it cannot refer to natural happiness; it would in a way have been better to say "all happiness not in the world" or, perhaps still better, "all happiness in the intelligible world alone." This to one side, the ideal tells us that perfect morality and blessedness together cause happiness. But what is the connection between the two? No reason is given to justify such a connection; instead, the ideal expresses precisely what we hope for. It cannot therefore serve as the ground of belief.

Is this ideal the concept of God? One would surely think so from the expression "cause of all happiness," and Kant is about to introduce God in the continuation of the paragraph. "Thus only in the ideal of the highest *original* good can pure reason find the ground of the practically necessary connection of both elements of the highest derived good, namely of an intelligible, i.e., *moral* world." I interrupt the citation to note that we find this necessary connection only because we put it there. To continue: "Now since we must necessarily represent ourselves through reason as belonging to such a world, although the senses do not present us with anything except a world of appearances, we must assume the moral world to be a consequence of our conduct in the sensible world; and since the latter does not offer such a connection to us, we must assume the former to be a world that is future for us. Thus God and a future life are two presuppositions that are not to be separated from the obligation that pure reason imposes on us in accordance with principles of that very same reason" (A811–B839).

Why must we necessarily represent ourselves as belonging to such a world? Because of the acceptance of the nature of moral laws, and the corollary necessity that we be free if we are to carry out our obligations to those laws. But what guarantees that morality and happiness are connected in this world? Only, I suggest, our conviction that if morality is not rewarded with happiness, then it becomes absurd. In other words, a connection between morality and happiness is assumed from the outset, but this is obscured by the explicit denial that moral action is for the sake of happiness. Kant insists that we act out of duty, but he admits that in so doing, we assume that we have the right to be rewarded with happiness. I must do my duty even if it deprives me of worldly happiness, but I am made happy in another sense by the hope that I will be rewarded with genuine or moral happiness in a future world. The highest possible good is for me, as for every human being, the unity of worthiness to be happy and actual happiness. But the cause of this unity is God, and furthermore, a God whom I assume to be just or morally good, namely, a God who will indeed reward me as I deserve. The belief in God, and so in a future life, is necessary because I cannot reward myself. One might suppose that I could derive happiness from thinking of myself as a resident in the *corpus mysticum* of the intelligible world, but as we have already seen, this is enough to give meaning to moral choice but not to the reward of happiness, since I continue to exist as a sensible creature in the natural world, and thus to be subject to the hindrances to virtue that my inclinations impose. It is all very well to say that, appearances to the contrary notwithstanding, my will is free to obey the moral law because I dwell in both the natural and the intelligible world. But my residence in the natural world is enough to deprive me of moral happiness, not only by setting up hindrances to virtue but by actively directing me toward the happiness of fulfilling my natural inclinations. I must, in fine, believe in God if I am to have any hope of happiness, and in immortality, since not even God could make me genuinely or morally happy in the physical world.[20]

What reason, then, do I have to believe rather than to hope? So far as I can see, Kant never answers this question at any point in his argument. The real reason is finally made apparent at A811–B839. "Morality in itself constitutes a system, but happiness does not, except insofar as it is distributed precisely in accordance with morality." By "system," Kant means a rational structure or interconnection of elements based upon one principle (A645–B673). We can deduce what it is to be moral from the principle of obedience to a universally valid and a priori law, and therefore, we can also identify those who are worthy of happiness. Otherwise put, morality is entirely autonomous; it is a consequence of the self-regulation of the human will, independent of empirical circumstances or divine rewards. Morality is within our own grasp, and so we can enter into the intelligible world through the exercise of the will, even though we remain residents of the natural or phenomenal world.

The same is not true of happiness. We cannot achieve happiness simply through the exercise of our own will. There is no necessary connection between morality and happiness in this world; physical happiness is a matter of cleverness and corporeal inclinations. But neither is it sufficient to claim that we achieve the moral happiness that we deserve as residents of the intelligible world, simply through being good. The requisite systematicity of happiness, that is, its distribution in strict coordination with the deserts of the recipient, "is possible only in the intelligible world, under a wise author and regent. Reason sees itself as compelled either to assume such a thing, together with life in such a world, which we must regard as a future one, or else to regard the moral laws as empty figments of the brain, since without that presupposition their necessary success, which the same reason connects with them, would have to disappear" (A811–B839). Human beings do not have the power by themselves to achieve the happiness that is the just reward of a good will. We can will to be good, but not to be happy. Kant makes this latter point with respect to nature at some length in paragraph 83 of the third *Critique*. Since our concept of empirical happiness is tied to the imagination and senses, we formulate it so diversely and change the concept of happiness so often "that nature, even if it were subjected completely to man's choice, still could not possibly adopt a definite and fixed universal law that would [keep] it in harmony with that wavering concept and so with the purpose that each person chooses to set himself."[21] In other words, Kant rejects the Aristotelian notion of an activity that provides happiness by our very nature.

We can restate this last conclusion as follows. In order for moral goodness to overcome the deficiencies of nature and to provide us with happiness, we require a ground that is systematic in the sense that the correct consequences always follow from the operation of the first principle. This ground or principle must be entirely superior to nature and thus able to overcome every natural hindrance to genuine happiness. Only God possesses this power. But furthermore, it is clear after a moment's thought that this divine power can be exercised only in another, future world, namely, the genuine intelligible world of immortal and so disembodied souls. In order for God to reward us with moral happiness, he would have to destroy the natural world by changing it into the intelligible world, or what is traditionally called "heaven."

This is why, unless God exists and we are immortal, we would have "to regard the moral laws as empty figments of the brain." But this must be made much more explicit than even Kant makes it. Not only is it the case that a God is required in order to guarantee the proper distribution of happiness, but the God must himself be a moral agent. We must not forget that morality is autonomous; in other words, it depends upon ourselves, not on God. The morality of God lies in his *justice;* that is to say, in his desire to reward the worthy. How does Kant know that God is just? He may hope this to be true, but why does he believe it (if indeed he does believe it)? Certainly this belief cannot be based upon any thesis of steady progress in history, for that would be to naturalize both morality and happiness. The answer that Kant gives in the passage under analysis is that, if we were not rewarded with happiness, the necessary success that reason connects with the moral laws would have to disappear. But this can mean only that reason connects the necessary achievement of happiness with the possession of a good will. Either we are justified in expecting happiness as the reward for our goodness, or morality is a figment of the imagination. And in this case, of course, life is reduced to absurdity.

"Hence everyone also regards the moral laws as *commands,* which, however, they could not be if they did not connect appropriate consequences with their rule *a priori,* and thus carry with them *promises* and *threats.* This, however, they could not do if they did not lie in a necessary being, as the highest good, which alone can make possible such a purposive unity" (A811–12/B839–40). It thus turns out that the core of the purposive unity is not morality but happiness. Absent the just reward of happiness, morality becomes a figment of the imagination.[22] We thus pay a very high price for the autonomy of morality. By separating morality from the desire for happiness, Kant believed himself to be safeguarding the former from eudaimonism, or corruption through the selfishness that is an inevitable consequence of the natural, i.e., sensuous, inclinations. But he could not and did not separate morality from the desire for a justified or merited happiness. Having taken the capacity to satisfy this desire away from both human hands and the power of nature, he had no choice but to entrust it to God. By the same token, he was unable to find a more satisfactory basis for belief than hope.

Once we work our way through Kant's endless hypotheses, counterfactual conditionals, and obscure and often inconsistently employed terminology, the suspicion may occur to us that his self-styled preservation of the possibility of freedom, morality, and happiness is no more substantial, and indeed, no more rational, than traditional biblical religion. The latter requires us to believe in a just God, exactly as does Kant, but with radically less intellectual baggage. Kant claims to have shown the aforementioned possibility by distinguishing a realm of freedom from the determinist domain of nature. But if nature is incorrectly or inadequately described by his generalization of Newtonian mechanics, then the distinction seems to be unnecessary. Moreover, even if it were necessary in order to preserve freedom, it is open to the charge of unintelligibility. How can acts that are determined as we perform them express our free choice with respect to our ostensible residency in an intelligible world that Kant himself calls a *corpus mysticum?* To say that we dwell in two mutually exclusive worlds simultaneously is to offer us what looks suspiciously like a miracle. And of course, Kant does not say that we do in fact dwell in these two worlds, simultaneously or otherwise, but only that we might. Some (myself included) would say that we cannot. But let us assert only the minimum that follows from Kant's own claim: We might not. The justification (in moral terms) for assuming that we do is to rescue a conception of morality that is itself highly questionable, namely, the conception of morality as obedience to universal laws. And as if this were not bad enough, Kant deprives us of access to happiness through natural or supernatural means. Happiness depends not upon our actions but the justice and mercy of a God who is the *summum bonum.* Perhaps it would be more reasonable, and certainly less tedious, to accept this God in advance, and to explain his agency in this world as one of divine intervention. Kant, like so many other rationalists (a term I use here in an extended sense), wished to do away with miracles in this world, but he was unable to preserve the significance of human life except through a miracle, namely, the hypothesis of the intelligible world or the state of grace. I conclude that the desire to preserve freedom and morality was enacted in such a way as to accelerate the advent of antirationalism, or of spontaneity severed from law, and so the destruction of morality.

I want to add a point from the second *Critique* that supplements what we have already learned. In the first *Critique,* the emphasis is upon the noumenal domain as a possible world of freedom. In the second *Critique,* this is modified in such a way as to meet part of the difficulty of simultaneous human residence in two distinct worlds. In the section "On the Typic of the Pure Practical Judgment," Kant says: "The subsumption of an act that is possible for me within the sense-world under a *pure practical law* has nothing to do with the possibility of the action as something given in the sense-world; for this belongs to the judgment of the theoretical use of reason in accord with the law of causality, which is a pure concept of the understanding, for which reason has a schema in the sensible intuition. The physical causality or the condition under which it takes place, belongs under the natural concept, the schema of which is projected [or "sketched"] by transcendental imagination. Here, however, there is no question of a schema of something that falls under laws, but of the schema (if this word is here appropriate) of a law itself; because the determination of the will (not of the action with reference to its effect), binds through the law alone, without any other ground of determination, the concept of causality to altogether different conditions than those which constitute the natural connection."[23] In other words, obedience to the moral law has no consequences within the world of nature (the domain of phenomena). "The rule of judgment under laws of pure practical reason is this: Ask yourself if the action you propose, if it were to occur in accord with a law of nature, of which you yourself were a part, could you regard it as possible by your own will?" This makes it clear that morality is not a question of an action within the natural world but rather of the willingness to assume responsibility for such an act, were it to occur. And this responsibility would of course be universal, i.e., binding for anyone willing to take on the same responsibility, because that is the nature of a law. But a willingness to take responsibility for an act is not the same as actually causing that act. In order to establish this, Kant would have to show that the free will has a causal power within the determinist world of nature, and this, as I argued previously, is a contradiction. In this passage, he instead holds to the weaker case that the good will exhibits itself by stating what it would do if it could and were required to take a stand. The result is that the will does not know how it could be causally efficacious, or whether it ever is, even in those cases when it affirms an action that takes place thanks in part to its own deeds. The net result is to weaken radically the moral significance of actions themselves, with a correlative strengthening of the importance of a good will.

I come now to the conclusion of this line of investigation. Kant appeals to everyday life or the moral experience of ordinary persons, but with three limitations. First, he accepts without critical discussion the general moral horizon of the biblical tradition, and employs this as though it were equivalent to the general pretheoretical understanding of human practice. Second, he suppresses or demotes prudence, which deals with the particular circumstances of practical life, in favor of a conception of practical reason as hypothetical universality. Practical reason thus shares the link to rules or laws that characterizes theoretical reason. Third, his complex argument makes it impossible for happiness to be acquired in this life; instead, we are left with the hope of happiness in the next life. I suggest that the net result of these three limitations is to cut Kant off from the common moral understanding to which he initially appeals. Ordinary experience is thus transformed, and indeed, limited in its capacity to guide us in practice, by the consequences of Kant's scientific rationalism. The shadow of Newtonian mechanics falls across the life-world and thereby excludes any sense of practical reason that takes its bearings by everyday experience.

PHRONESIS OR ONTOLOGY?

Let us now see how practical intelligence fares at the hands of Heidegger, who replaces Kant's epistemology with ontology in his interpretation of "average everydayness." Once again we will see the influence of the biblical tradition, this time in its Christian version. Heidegger, of course, was also influenced by Aristotle, as has often been pointed out; but the blending of Aristotelian practice, Christian theology, and Husserlian phenomenology into existential ontology results, as I hope to show, in a narrow and desiccated version of everydayness.

The influence of Aristotle's practical philosophy on Heidegger's existential ontology has been much discussed by specialists, among whom I mention Franco Volpi, Jacques Taminiaux, Theodore Kisiel, and H. G. Gadamer. Many years before the works of these thinkers were published, those who, like my own teacher, Leo Strauss, had attended Heidegger's lectures in Marburg, spoke of a seminar on Aristotle's *Rhetoric* that contained an ontology of the human passions.[24] As of this writing, the seminar was never published. But we now possess, in addition to the master text, *Sein und Zeit*, Heidegger's remarkable lectures of 1924/25 on Plato's *Sophist*.[25] The first 225 pages of the published text are devoted to Aristotle, and in particular to the treatment of the intellectual faculties in *EN* 6 as well as in related texts from other works. The focus of this section of Heidegger's lectures is on practical intelligence, and the main topic is *phronesis*. The entire analysis culminates in Heidegger's account of why wisdom (*sophia*) or *theoria* is higher for Aristotle than *phronesis* (sound practical judgment) or *praxis*.

There seems to be widespread agreement that Heidegger appropriates Aristotle's practical philosophy as part of an attempt to overcome Husserl's exclusive emphasis on theory.[26] Theodore Kisiel goes so far as to say that, in the 1924–25 lectures, Heidegger "will time and again look for ways, both in and out of the Aristotelian opus, in which phronetic insight asserts its potential superiority over contemplative wisdom."[27] In what follows, I take my bearings by Heidegger's continuous attempt in the *Sophist* lectures to transform *phronesis* into a crucial element in the ontology of human existence. For my part, I regard this attempt as a mistake. It leads to a distortion in Heidegger's often penetrating account of the Aristotelian doctrine. But even more important, the consequences for ethics of the ontological temptation are disastrous. Here as elsewhere, Aristotle saw things more clearly than Heidegger.

For introductory purposes, we can say that the task of *phronesis* in Aristotle is to calculate the means to the fulfilment of the ends of practice. Prudence does not calculate about the ends; these are given by *nous* or intellectual intuition. The aforementioned calculations culminate in the restatement of an end in the form of a particular command, a command that accommodates the end to the particular circumstances under deliberation. The calculations will not be good unless the calculator is good; thus prudence is not like theoretical calculation, say, in mathematics, nor is it like the pure contemplation of the eternal beings, which is neither good nor evil since it has no practical consequences. In short, prudence is connected to ethics and politics, and it is dependent upon the perception of ends as well as the calculative capacity to engage in sound deliberations that culminate in the right choice. This little sketch of prudence is based upon *EN* 6, and in particular chapter 6 at 1144a–b.[28] To it I add a crucial point, noted previously in the discussion of Kant, that runs throughout the entire work. Prudence, which is instrumental to virtuous activity, is a means to the achievement of the highest human good, happiness. As book 10 of *EN* makes explicit, but as was already indicated in book 1, the happiness derived from ethical virtue or praxis is not the most perfect that is available to humankind. This rank is reserved for the happiness or blessedness (*eudaimonia*) of the life of theoretical contemplation.

I pause for an interpretive comment. Aristotle separates practice from both theory and production, thereby introducing a radical modification into the Platonic classification of the arts and sciences. I note in passing that it would be possible to argue that for Plato, "demotic" virtue (the artifact of philosophical demiurgy, as it is called in the *Republic,* 6. 504d4–9) is intrinsically unsatisfactory, not simply for philosophers but for all citizens, and that happiness or blessedness is available, if at all, only to the philosopher by way of a pure intellectual vision of the hyperuranian beings or Ideas. This view, which is implicit in the Socratic thesis that virtue is knowledge, is modified as follows by Aristotle. Strictly speaking, the thesis is not wrong (see for example *EN* 7.1147b12–19). But there are two kinds of knowledge. Theoretical knowledge provides us with the highest form of happiness, but theoretical activity as such has nothing to do with ethical virtue. Its excellence is quite distinct from the human good as embodied in noble and just deeds. The second form of knowledge is neither "scientific" nor "theoretical" in the strict sense of the terms. But it is knowledge of how to adapt the ends into a correct command of the calculative reason concerning the correct act to perform under the relevant circumstances of the situation about which we deliberate now. This type of knowledge is closely connected to sense perception, both as a perception of the particular and as concerned with pleasure and pain.

Let me make a clarifying remark about this second kind of knowledge. I am not confusing the act of judgment itself with an epistemic process. But the act of judgment, in which is expressed the characteristic skill of *phronesis,* is itself dependent upon practical knowledge of human affairs. As Aristotle says over and over again, *phronesis* is assisted by and is in accord with *orthos logos* (correct reason). The significance of this point can be expressed as follows. Aristotle's distinction of practice from both theory and production, together with his contention that man is by nature the political animal, connects nature with rationality in a way that is separate from philosophy and *episteme* (knowledge) in the purest sense of the term. The correctness of the *logos* of praxis is not dependent upon the theoretical vision of the philosopher. Plato of course refers to human nature and to the nature of the city, but he never says that man is by nature the political animal. That is, he never attributes to the non-philosopher the possibility of achieving a practical perfection. This is possible, if at all, only through the philosopher-king.

The situation in Aristotle is complex but nevertheless distinguishable from that in Plato. There are for Aristotle two kinds of happiness, theoretical and practical. In principle, happiness through ethical virtue is accessible to a large number of persons, as theoretical happiness is not. "It would seem to be common to many [*polukoinon*]. For it is capable of belonging by some kind of learning and care to all those who have not been incapacitated with respect to [ethical] virtue" (*EN* 1.1099b18–20). One might support this statement by noting that *eudaimonia* is by nature the highest human good; if it were extremely rare or unusually difficult to attain, this would suggest that nature has worked in vain. Unfortunately, Aristotle emphasizes regularly the rareness and difficulty of attaining to prudence and thus to the status of the *spoudaios* or perfectly virtuous gentleman (e.g., 2.1109a28). This is also evident from the nature of *phronesis* or practical intelligence, which never makes a mistake and is a requirement for being virtuous. It is perhaps even more evident from the virtue of *megalopsuchia* or greatness of soul, which Aristotle describes as the ornament (*kosmos*) of the ethical virtues: "It makes them greater and cannot be achieved without them. It is therefore hard to be truly great-souled" (4.1124a1 ff.). To this I add that since one cannot be *spoudaios* or a perfect *kalos kagathos* (gentleman) unless one possesses all the virtues, such a person is extremely rare. Everything therefore depends upon the degree to which one can approximate to the paradigm and still be virtuous in Aristotle's sense.

Suffice it to say that the extent of the possibility of practical happiness seems to be threatened. But Aristotle's general approach remains dedicated to the distinction between theory and practice, and his analysis of practice remains wedded to a grasp of everyday or pretheoretical life. In sum: happiness is accessible, to one degree or another, to human beings through ethical virtue, and so in effect apart from all theoretical reflection. Heidegger is more like Plato than Aristotle to the extent that he transforms practice into ontology. At least in the period culminating in *Sein und Zeit* (hereafter *SZ*), Heidegger is of course unlike Plato, and in fact very much like the Plato he criticizes, in advocating a quasi-theory that is practico-productive. I mean by this expression that in *SZ*, the acts of illumination and uncovering are also acts by which human existence (*Dasein*) produces from within its own concern (*Sorge*) for itself (*jemeinigkeit*) the structure of the world. The transformation of *phronesis* into fundamental ontology is based upon the transformation of Aristotelian ethical virtue into authenticity and the transformation of happiness into anxiety in the face of death.

On the basis of this simple summary, we are now ready to cite Heidegger's famous, indeed, notorious definition of *phronesis* in the 1924–25 lectures. The general context is a discussion of *phronesis* as *a-letheuin*, that is, a mode of uncovering of something that is hidden by pleasure or pain. This type of uncovering is not experimental, like *techne*, nor can it be forgotten, like *doksa* (opinion) and *mathesis*, (knowledge) because it is always new (i.e., appropriate to the circumstances, not a universal rule). Heidegger says that *phronesis* is no more nor less than "den Ernst der bestimmten Entscheidung," or "the seriousness of determinate decision" (54). I call attention to the word *Ernst*, which could of course be justified as a translation of *spoudaios*, "serious" or "good," a term that Aristotle uses with great frequency. *Entscheidung* reminds us of *Entschlossenheit* (resoluteness). These two terms will take on greater importance for us in a moment.

In the continuation of the passage just quoted, Heidegger is interpreting Aristotle's statement that whereas we can forget a piece of knowledge, *phronesis* is a capacity to arrive each time at something new, namely, the correct *logos* for the current situation. Whereas knowledge can be forgotten, *phronesis* cannot. Aristotle does not mean by this simply that we cannot forget our intellectual faculties, for this point would apply to all forms of cognitive activity. Heidegger is right to concentrate upon the impossibility of forgetting the content of the exercise of *phronesis*. Heidegger says: "The ability to forget is a specific possibility of *aletheuein* [to speak the truth] which has the character of *theorein*. For the *heksis meta logou* [the habit that functions in common with reason] is a habit of *aletheuein*, into which *Dasein* expressly brings itself. The situation with *phronesis* is different. This shows itself in the fact that I can experience, observe, learn what is already experienced, observed, learned, whereas *phronesis* is each time new."

This interpretation is misleading because it gives the impression that theoretical truth is associated with *logos* as *phronesis* is not. Equally important, Heidegger overinterprets Aristotle's very succinct remark about the novelty of *phronesis*. What is new is the decision with respect to the immediately desirable course of action. But this decision is itself dependent upon the general knowledge of human nature, and so of human affairs. This is surely why Aristotle regularly says that *phronesis* acts in accord with the "correct *logos*" (*EN* 6.1138b24, 5.1140b4–6; 6.1144b21–23 et seq.). After all, *phronesis* is the virtue of the logistical, that is, the calculative or deliberative part of the soul. It is not like the logistical skills of the mathematician, who uses them to arrive at the correct answer to a technical problem. Prudential deliberation must establish the good in each case, and the ability to do this is not purely formal or empty of knowledge about life. *Phronesis* is no more *logos* than virtues are principles in the Socratic sense of forms of knowledge. But *phronesis* is based upon *logos*, just as the virtues or principles are both *meta logou*, that is, function with the aid of *logos*, and *kata ton orthon logon*, "in accord with correct reason" (*EN* 6.1145a18–30). Heidegger, on the other hand, tries to weaken the significance of *logos* in these passages by identifying it with "discussion [*Durchsprechen*], not reason." He is right to interpret *orthos* here as *orthotes boules* (correctness of counsel), but neither this nor the correct discussion of a practical issue requiring a judgment can exist apart from reason.

To continue with my translation from Heidegger, "There is thus with respect to *phronesis* no *lethe* [forgetting]... In *phronesis*, there is no *Verfallensmöglichkeit des Vergessens* [the possibility of fallenness that is forgetting]." In *SZ*, *Verfallen* refers to the "fallenness" or "dissipation" by which *Dasein* turns away from itself. It is marked by "the three dynamical characters of temptation, tranquilization, and self-alienation [*Versuchung, Beruhung,* and *Entfremdung*]," as Kisiel (257) glosses *SZ* (177f.). In other words, we see in 1924–25 the tendency to elevate *phronesis* from a moral status to the ontological level of authenticity. This also separates *phronesis* from the mode of uncovering that is typical of theoretical reason. "Indeed, the explanation that Aristotle gives here [i.e., of the fact that *phronesis* does not forget because it is always new] is very concise. But it is nevertheless evident from the context that one does not go too far in the interpretation if one says that Aristotle has here bumped into *das Phänomen des Gewissens* [the phenomenon of conscience]. *Phronesis* is nothing other than conscience thrust into movement, that makes activity transparent. One cannot forget the conscience. One can, however, allow what conscience uncovers to be blocked and rendered ineffective through pleasure and pain, through passions. Conscience announces itself always anew," and so forth (56).

Stated concisely: Heidegger interprets *phronesis* as the silent call of conscience, hence as something *aneu logou* (without reason) rather than in accord with *ho orthos logos* (the correct reason), through which *Dasein* calls to itself to return from fallenness to an authentic resoluteness (*Entschlossenheit*) in the face of *Angst vor dem Tode* (anxiety before death). This *Angst* opens up all possibilities for *Dasein*, and in that way it delineates the whole *Dasein* (*SZ*, 264). This corresponds, incidentally, to Aristotle's statement that *phronesis* is not about this or that aspect of human activity, but about the whole of life. *Phronesis* functions in accord with the correct *logos* as well as the intellectual intuition of the end in order to arrive at the recommendation that will contribute in this particular case to the agent's goodness, and hence to his happiness. Heidegger's conscience, on the other hand, "reveals itself as the call of care: the caller is *Dasein,* anxious within thrownness (already-being-in) with respect to its possibilities for being" (*SZ,* 277). And again: "the fact of *Gewissensangst* [pangs of conscience] is a phenomenal verification for the fact that *Dasein* is itself brought, in the understanding of the call, before uneasiness [*Unheimlichkeit*]. *Das Gewissenhabenwollen* becomes readiness for anxiety" (296).

As is so often the case in Heidegger's interpretations of Plato, Aristotle, Kant, and Nietzsche (to restrict ourselves to these), it is often unclear whether he is refuting his predecessors or assimilating them into his own doctrines. In the particular case, this means something considerably more than that, as Kisiel puts it, Heidegger is always looking for ways to raise *phronesis* above *sophia* in the theoretical sense. More important is the fact that Heidegger radically revises the flexibility or "newness" of *phronesis* by detaching it from its specifically ethical and political context. In shifting *phronesis* to ontology, more specifically, to *Gewissen* (conscience), Heidegger empties it of all specific content. In Aristotle, *phronesis* is "new" but not empty. For example, Heidegger in my opinion overemphasizes the importance of the future in prudential deliberation. It is of course true that we do not deliberate about the past. But we *do* deliberate about the present: "the present emergency" or "the present situation." And we do this only on the basis of our knowledge of the past, that is to say, of the regularity of nature, of the stability of human motivation, of practical likelihoods, and so on, all of which define the practical present as the locus of prudential calculation.

In sum: we do not forget our cognitive intellectual faculties (although we may lose them). Rather, we forget something that has been discovered or uncovered by them. We forget something that we already possessed, and thus something that was true in the past and that would apply to the present situation or an anticipation of the future. We forget what applies generally. Heidegger emphasizes the fact that what *phronesis* uncovers is unique to the present moment, or more precisely, to the future moment as presently anticipated. But what is unique to this moment will not be applicable to the next moment. A new judgment is required *at each moment.* This is part of what Heidegger means by "das in Bewegung gesetzte Gewissen, das eine Handlung durchsichtig macht," that is, "conscience situated within movement, that makes an action transparent." This is, I think, to say something more than that *phronesis* has a temporal structure, a point that Heidegger could legitimately make. But the content of the temporal structure is not ontological; it is practical or "political" in the broad sense of the term. And above all, *phronesis* aims toward human happiness, not *Angst vor dem Tode*.

Heidegger might wish to say in his own voice that anxiety is ontological whereas happiness is ontic, but I do not find this very persuasive. It might even be true, but the consequence would not be to identify *phronesis* as conscience. On the contrary, it would serve to distinguish sharply between the ontological and the ontic, that is to say, between the theoretical and the practical, in Aristotelian language. Heidegger derives *Gewissen* from the ontological structure of human existence and assigns to it an ontological function; but Aristotelian *phronesis* is not derived from a theoretical or scientific analysis of the soul, and its function is not ontological but ontic.

Heidegger mentions in passing but does not develop the following point: that for Aristotle, the first principles of ethics are supplied by the *endoksa* (the sound views) of sensible or serious persons. To be somewhat more precise, the principles in the sense of the ends are furnished by intellectual intuition, but these are not derived from the ontological structure of the cosmos. As Heidegger of course knows, the principles are of changing things and they themselves change; even natural justice is changeable, as Aristotle states explicitly in *EN*, 5.7. The *endoxa* are not the ends or principles in this sense, which do not derive from *doksa* but *nous*. They can only be the general maxims concerning what constitutes prudent behavior under circumstances of such and such a sort (*EN*, 8.1.1145b5–7). And it is up to *phronesis* in its deliberative capacity further to specify these common opinions into a recommendation or command (Aristotle refers to the epitactic character of *phronesis* at 6.10.1143a8) for the immediate situation.

One is tempted to say that from a Heideggerian standpoint, the principles of ethics are derived from the inauthentic speeches of *das Man*. Aristotle regularly introduces a point with the verb *dokei* or a variant, "it seems," "it appears," or even "people say." If the first principles and ends of practice were actually categories or "existentials" in either the Aristotelian or Heideggerian senses, they would be useless for serving as the basis for a derivation by practical logistics of a prudential recommendation. We should not forget that Heidegger, speaking in *SZ* as an ontologist, explicitly distinguishes his doctrine of the conscience from the ethical concern with good and bad conscience. "The good conscience would have to announce the 'goodness' [*Gutsein*] of *Dasein*, and correspondingly, the bad conscience an 'evil' one [*ein Bösesein*]. One sees easily that thereby, conscience, previously the 'emanation of divine power,' now becomes the servant of Pharisaism. A man ought therefore to be allowed to say 'I am good. Who can say that, and who would want to affirm this less than the genuinely good person?" (SZ, p. 291).

Heidegger is here distinguishing ontology from the Bible, not Aristotle, but in this context, the difference extends to both. The main point of *SZ* is precisely not to furnish prudential recommendations for this or that practical situation, but to prepare us, through the acquisition of an understanding of the ontological structure of *Dasein,* to ask the question "what is Being?" One could add to this that the existential analysis describes the machinery thanks to which someone might make a "prudential" calculation, but it is not itself concerned with doing so (see *SZ,* 295). One could not say the same of Aristotle's *EN*. But this has the following surprising consequence. For Aristotle, practice is of course necessary for all persons, but it is inferior as a way of life to theory. For Heidegger, practice, and in a very abstract sense, *phronesis,* does not participate in the factic choice of an authentic existence; instead, it exhibits, i.e., explains, the underlying ontological structure of the epitactic dimension of human existence. In that sense, it is ultimately theoretical rather than practical. Let me make this more precise. Heidegger does not say that practice is higher than theory. If anything, he says that practice *is* theory, that is, the genuine theory of fundamental ontology; or at least, that it is the first stage in the pursuit of a genuine theory. Heidegger's ontology is practico-productive; as to theory, that is rejected along with the associated doctrine of Being as presence. Practice is the first stage of theory, where by "theory," I mean the answer to the question "what is Being?" or if not the answer, then the correct articulation of the question. In Aristotle, practice, and so of course *phronesis,* has nothing to do with the answer to the question "what is being?" or for that matter with the question itself.

It thus turns out that Heidegger's desire to avoid Pharisaism is an essential ingredient in a way of thinking that transforms all of philosophy into Pharisaism, because *sophia* is assimilated into *phronesis.* The question of Being is thus transformed into the quest for Being, or a kind of romantic mixture of fragments of Aristotle, Christian anthropology and the Gothic *Sturm und Drang* of Nietzsche. The self-righteousness of the feeling or habit of authenticity, or an empty and silent voice, replaces both greatness of soul and the calculative articulateness of *phronesis.* Thus the resolute *Dasein* cannot give reasons but, to adapt a famous expression from American politics, "in his heart, he knows that he is right."

Heidegger's analysis of *phronesis* is filled with interesting observations, but the most valuable aspect of that analysis is his attempt to show how the Aristotelian doctrine emerges from the ordinary reasoning processes of everyday life. For the most part, Heidegger is faithful to the great peculiarity of Aristotle's procedure; there is no deduction of the first principles of practice or grounding of them in a presumably deeper or more comprehensive ontological structure. But Heidegger deviates from this procedure toward the end of his analysis. He very reasonably observes that for Aristotle, the superiority of *sophia* to *phronesis* is grounded in the mode of being of the existents to which *sophia* gives access, namely, the *aei onta,* that which is always (170 f.). "Human *Dasein* is then authentic [*eigentlich*], when it is always in the manner in which it can be in the highest sense." He then makes the following general statement about the difference between Greek and modern ethics: "For the Greeks, reflection on human existence is purely oriented toward the meaning of Being itself, i.e., to this, to the extent to which human existence has the possibility of being always" (178). In other words, Heidegger assumes that the grounding of the superiority of theory to practice in the superiority of eternal to transient beings is the same as the ontological grounding of ethics. But this is false. Ethics is grounded in the *endoksa,* if it is grounded in anything; and that is to say that the ground of ethics is common sense, not the meaning of Being.

Another serious obstacle in the path of Heidegger's interpretation of *phronesis* is his use of the term "conscience," which, however he modifies it, is unmistakably derived from Christian anthropology. This is closely connected to the fact that neither piety nor shame is a virtue for Aristotle. The virtuous man cannot feel guilty because he is not tempted by vice and has nothing of which to be ashamed. Thus guilt, a crucial element in Heidegger's existential ontology, is entirely missing from the sphere of Aristotelian *phronesis.* I have one more comment in this series of remarks. So far as I can see, Heidegger makes no reference to an apparent similarity between what he calls *jemeinigkeit* (what is genuinely mine or me) and Aristotle's emphasis upon the fact that happiness or blessedness is the highest good, and that it is *my* happiness that I strive for. Of course, the centrality of *jemeinigkeit* or the orientation in terms of one's own existence, cannot be easily perceived in Aristotle's account of practice, because perfect ethical virtue, that is, general justice, is not simply for oneself but for the sake of others (*EN* 5.1129b31–33; 1130b18–20). One seems to find it, however, in the account of the theoretical life as higher than the human and indeed, divine, a life that is lived through the highest element in human beings, namely, pure intellect. "It would seem that this is the highest element in each person, since it is the dominant and better part. It would then be odd if one were not to choose one's own life but the life of someone else" (10.1178a2–4). The life of someone else, in the highest case, is the life of justice, that is, the life for another. One's own life is the life of pure theory, "the only activity that is loved for itself. For nothing comes into being from it apart from theorizing; whereas from practical activities we procure something, more or less, beyond the act" (10.1177b1).

Whereas the self-love of the good man could perhaps be confused with Pharisaism, the same cannot be said of the autarchy and consequent bliss of the theoretical life.[29] Furthermore, the happiness of pure theory is in Aristotle connected with completeness or perfection, but this in turn is very close to the notion of the priority of the unchanging to the changing and of the *aei onta* to the transient. The anxious man is placed before the totality of his existence as a sign of incompleteness, that is, as a warning that it is time now to act resolutely in an authentic manner. *Angst vor dem Tode* is a stimulus to action, which is itself a sign of recognition of incompleteness. Happiness, on the other hand, is a sign of completeness or perfection of one's natural capacity. It is an invitation to leisure.

To say this in another way, Heidegger's ontology seems to me to undergo an internal tension. On the one hand, it is dynamic and activist; on the other hand, despite its ontological assimilation of *phronesis*, it leaves practical activity very much to the determination by historical destiny of what I must do in the given circumstance. This looks superficially like Aristotelian *phronesis*, but it is more like historical determinism, and not less so when the activist element plays its role. Freedom is then identified with the assumption of responsibility for a determinate interpretation of historical destiny. In addition, there is a shift in Heidegger's publications from activism to passivity (not the same as pacificism) or *Gelassenheit* after the fiasco of the Nazi commitment. At the risk of being branded a Pharisee, I must add that nowhere in Heidegger's ontological writings, whether before, during, or after *SZ,* do I find any conception of ethical virtue or in still simpler language, the autonomy of decency from ontology.

My central thesis is that Heidegger makes the enormous mistake of attempting to overcome the split between theory and practice. He does this by transforming both into poetry. But without an independent theory, poetry becomes first ideology and then doggerel. And without an independent practice, ethics degenerates at first into existential ontology and then into action theory, not to mention neurophysiology.

To this I add a second enormous mistake. Heidegger regularly proceeds as though moods, feelings, passions, desires, and other "attunements" of the soul were ontologically prior to discursive reasoning. There is something here of the

Platonic doctrine of eros, which remains visible in Heidegger's conception of *Sorge*. But eros is itself defined by the rank-ordering of the objects of desire. The fact that we are "attuned" to the external world in a certain manner before we begin to reason about it in no way demonstrates that these attunements more truly or primordially "uncover" the truth of Being than does the discursive intelligence. Neither is it true that the initial or primordial feeling or attunement is intrinsically superior to or more illuminating than subsequent attunements. Heidegger tacitly accepts Nietzsche's genealogical approach to philosophy, an approach that is of course older than Nietzsche but no less dubious for that. Neither should one blur the distinction between such moods as guilt, anxiety, and resolution on the one hand, and the intellectual perception of principles, whether universal or particular, on the other. It is these mistakes, or let us say acts of hermeneutical *Entschlossenheit*, that permeate Heidegger's interpretation of Aristotelian *phronesis*.

I want next to make some remarks about the difference between the Aristotelian and the Heideggerian conception of the "wholeness" of life. In a passage that incidentally also illustrates the connection between *phronesis* and the *endoksa*, Aristotle says: "It seems" or "it is believed [*dokei*] that the prudent man [*phronimos*] is able to deliberate nobly [*kalos*] concerning what is good and beneficial for himself, not in a particular sense, such as matters that concern health or strength, but with respect to living well entirely" (*holos*:1140a25–28).

Aristotle means by this that *phronesis* does not aim at some one aspect of practical life nor at the arithmetical sum of individual aspects; instead, it aims to produce a habit of the soul that is expressed in every action in which human beings are called on to pass judgment on the noble and the good. There are two ways in which to speak of good acts as a whole. When the emphasis is upon the agent, we speak of nobility; when the act is directed primarily toward political and social relations, we refer to justice. These terms are intended as complementary, but there is a slight tension between them, to which I shall return shortly. In the present context, we may take them as coordinate predicates by which to designate the twin perfections of practical life. *Phronesis* addresses itself to the continuous expression in activity of a soul that is "whole," not because it has completed all of the actions that its life-span allows but because it is completely good, that is, perfect or *teleios*. A person of this sort we call "good," and we say that things are good if they appear to be so to the good man. Barring madness or some incapacitating misfortune, and granting the accomplishment of a reasonable stretch of life, the good man is whole while he lives, and something similar can be said of happiness. In short, "goodness" is not the property of an individual act but of the soul that initiates good acts; and this is the nobility of the soul that Aristotle associates with *phronesis.*

In his discussion of this passage, Heidegger correctly says that "the deliberation of *phronesis* affects the Being of *Dasein* itself, the *eu zen* (living well), i.e., that *Dasein* should be a righteous being" (*ein Rechtes:* 49). The *telos* of *phronesis* is thus not, as in *techne,* something beyond the deliberation. The object of this deliberation is life itself. This is excessively condensed, but basically sound. Let us now ask ourselves how Heidegger understands the wholeness of existence in his own terms. Consider the following assertion in paragraph 39 of *SZ,* "The question of the original totality [*Ganzheit*] of the total structure of *Dasein.*" On page 182, Heidegger says: "Anxiety furnishes as a possibility of Being of *Dasein,* in unison with the openness of *Dasein* itself in anxiety, the phenomenal ground for the explicit grasp of the original totality of Being of *Dasein.* This Being reveals itself as care" (*Sorge*).[30] In smoother English, anxiety is the capacity of *Dasein* to open or display itself as a whole. It is the self-activation of *Dasein's* certain knowledge of its death, thanks to anxiety, that is the prerequisite for the totalizing function to come into play (264). Heidegger says: "Conscience manifests itself as the call of *Sorge;* the caller is *Dasein,* anxious [or "rendering itself anxious"] in the thrownness . . . concerning its most intimate capacity to be" (277). In sum: totality depends upon *Sorge* (231), which in turn is *Schuldigsein,* "being guilty" (286). This engenders the resoluteness (*Entschlossenheit*) to project my anxiety-ridden self upon my guilt (285). And the fundamental truth of existence requires an equally fundamental *Gewisssein* [certitude of conscience] as oneself remaining in that which resolve makes manifest" (307).

Totality or wholeness is connected with anxiety before death on the one hand, and resoluteness on the other. These limit-points are moods that express the *jemeinigkeit* (my-ownness) of *Dasein*. I mean by this that the world is a project of the inner activity of the various modalities of *Dasein's* care. At this fundamental ontological level, it is fair to speak of the solipsism of *Dasein. Dasein* cares for itself; its wholeness lies in the wholly self-centered character of *Sorge.* "All being next to the object of care and all being together with others breaks down, when it is a matter of one's ownmost capacity to be. *Dasein* can only then be authentically itself when it makes that possible from within its own self" (263).

Next, we note that for Heidegger, it is not conscience that actually discloses the practical judgment (and of course, "practical" in Heidegger refers to ontological practico-production). Heidegger scarcely mentions the procedures by which *Dasein* engages in the discursive consideration of the details of the existential choice. One might almost assume, when reading this section of *SZ*, that no discursive thinking or "calculating," and so no *logos*, transpires at all. The silence of care, the silence of guilt, the silence of conscience, are all gathered together in the silence of resoluteness. Everything functions through the instrumentality of moods or passions that are themselves activated by fear of death, or in its ontological version, *Angst vor dem Tode*.

This selection of passages will have to suffice as evidence for my conclusion. The big difference between Aristotle and Heidegger on this point is as follows. "Whole" for Heidegger means finite and finished, with no further possibility to take us beyond the boundary. Furthermore, the condition for the structural totality of *Dasein* is not the quality of its acts but the terror of its obliteration. I express my wholeness by responding to anxiety with a resolute decision to act in an authentic manner. But conscience does not tell me what to do or, in other words, how to perform the analogue to the actual vision and articulation of the particular judgment. Instead, it is the silent signal of my guilt. In Aristotle, there is no conscience, but rather a good *heksis* or character, which, together with intuition and prudence, is an expression of perfection or completeness. This accounts for the central role of anxiety in Heidegger, as contrasted with that of happiness in Aristotle. There is for Heidegger always something more, even new, to be done; hence the anxiety or restlessness that characterizes even the resolution to live authentically. Heidegger celebrates work, whereas Aristotelian activity is more like leisure.

To say this in another way, Heidegger's conception of wholeness is inseparable from his interpretation of human existence as temporal. I do not mean by this to suggest that Aristotle treats the individual person as immortal. But for Heidegger, all meaning or significance of human existence is derived from within the free and resolute choice of one's own radical finitude. *Dasein* cannot appeal to separate entities, and above all it cannot appeal to eternal entities as the source for the authenticity of its own existence. Furthermore, since death is imminent, or literally intrinsic to the temporality of my own existence, resoluteness is not enough to liberate me from anxiety. It can serve only to allow me to take personal responsibility for the decisions with which I fill up the temporary openness of my life. For Aristotle, on the other hand, it is not necessary to be eternally in the presence of the eternal entities in order to achieve perfection. Theoretical contemplation is intrinsically pleasant and loved for its own sake, but not for any possible decision that will lead me to act in one way or another. In sum, it is precisely the freedom of theory from practical activity that makes possible the perfect happiness of a finite human life. By transforming theory into a kind of practice, Heidegger builds anxiety into existence. Leo Strauss once described John Locke's view of life as "the joyless quest for joy." I am inclined to think of Heidegger's account as the irresolute quest for resoluteness.

There is, however, a problem in Aristotle with respect to happiness. The "standard" position is to be found in Book Six in the assertion that "the end of production is separate from the act of making itself, whereas this is not true of practice. For doing well [*eupraksia*] is itself the end" (5. 1140b6–7). If this is true, then happiness is itself an element of doing well. Sometimes Aristotle seems to be saying just this, but at other times, as for example in Book One, he says clearly that happiness is the highest end, or that toward which all practice aims (1097a22–23 et seq.). But that at which something aims cannot be a part of what it is in itself. And as we saw previously, he says in book 10 that moral virtue is always sought for something in addition to itself, whereas theoretical contemplation is the only thing that is sought and loved for itself alone. The question is not merely one of the subordination of practical to theoretical happiness. It is rather that of the accessibility of happiness to practice apart from theory.

I leave this as an aporia to be investigated on another occasion and turn to the related difficulty of the changeability of practical truth. Once more, prudence is defined as a practical habit that acquires "truth in accord with *logos* concerning what is good and evil for human beings" (1140b4–6). As in the case of art or production, the truth is changeable in the following sense. What is good under one set of circumstances will not be good under other circumstances. But the judgment of the prudent man is true under *these* circumstances. In other words, there is a practical truth under each set of circumstances that bear upon acts leading toward or away from the good life altogether. Aristotle is not a relativist in this sense. And the truth is not accessible to formal intuition, the induction of principles, logical deduction, or any other method or technical procedure. It is accessible only to the judgment of the prudent man who judges *qua* prudent (and not as temporarily deranged).

Once again, there is a superficial resemblance to Heidegger. Just as Aristotle provides us with the definition of virtue as a mean between two extremes, but does not tell us what is virtuous under this or that circumstance, so too he leaves us to identify the good man by our assessment of the goodness of his judgments (see 10.5.1176a15 ff. for a hypothetical statement of the principle). Similarly, Heidegger provides us with the existential structure of authentic choice, but he does not elucidate what would be an authentic choice in particular instances. Both philosophers are entirely reasonable in their behavior, in view of their common recognition of the endless variability of particular circumstances. But the German ontologist gives us no basis for apprehending, deciphering, and evaluating the silent call of the silent voice of conscience, which is his surrogate for the calculations of prudence in accord with the correct *logos*.

In keeping with his ontological approach, Heidegger gives no historical examples of prudent individuals. But he does make it clear that conscience and resoluteness, the two ontological agents of authentic choice, are incarnated in the individual *as* individual. Those who act otherwise have sunk into the inauthentic existence of *das Man*. Aristotle's position is quite different. He gives Pericles as an example of persons we call prudent, because they are able to envision (as I translate *theorein* here) good things for themselves and for humankind. We regard people like Pericles as gifted in the management of his own household as well as in that of the polis (1140b7–11). In other words, prudence addresses itself to the two wholes of human life, the family and the city, and it does this by distinguishing good from evil and the beneficial from the harmful. In so doing, it must of course address individual acts, since it is persons who act, not households or cities. And it is Pericles who decides, not the Athenian assembly (except in the secondary sense that they are persuaded by him). But the decision of Pericles is itself a function of the collective wisdom of the Greeks, and by extension of the civilized world. This is precisely the significance of the *endoksa*. The crucial point is that the *phronimos* (man of prudent judgment) decides on the basis of his own judgment, but that judgment is an expression of what he judges to be good for others as well as for himself, and for himself precisely because and to the extent that it is good for others.

This brings me to a final difficulty for Aristotle that Heidegger overlooks. At the beginning of chapter 8 in book 6, Aristotle says that "politics and *phronesis* are the same habit, although their being [*einai*] is not the same" (1141b23–24). Both are concerned with what is good and beneficial to human beings, and in order to determine this, one must possess excellence in practical calculation. This in turn entails acquiring of the habits of the ethical virtues. But there is a difference between *phronesis* and politics in that the statesman must adapt his calculations about the good to his calculations about what benefits the city, and in actual cities these are rarely identical. Politics is divided into two parts, of which law giving refers to the city as a whole. The part that deals with individual acts is called "politics" (*politike*), although the name actually belongs to the two parts equally. So too, the name "prudence" (*phronesis*) is given to calculation with respect to oneself, whereas it actually belongs to all parts of politics. There is thus a certain confusion in Aristotle's divisions and names of the parts of politics, an ambiguity that is already visible in the two parts, ethics and politics, that presumably constitute one subject, namely, that of practice. So far as I can see, Heidegger is entirely silent on this point. He oversimplifies Aristotle's treatment of *phronesis* because he abstracts from the ethical and political per se, which he replaces by an ontology of action. But this has the odd consequence of making *phronesis* less useful, and perhaps even useless, for human action.

By reflecting a confusion that arises from the fundamental ambiguity of the relation between the individual person and the community or political association, Aristotle is much closer to the facts. In one sense, the interests of the person and the community are the same, but in another, they are divergent. They are the same, because a person's ethical acts depend upon the education and laws, written and unwritten, of the city to which the person belongs, as well as to one's family, friends, and the character of one's fellow citizens. But the interests of the person and the city diverge, because the highest end of the individual human being is happiness, but the highest end of the city, depending upon the circumstances, is to survive. Without their survival, virtuous acts are impossible; in order for them to survive, acts that are not virtuous may be required. It is pointless to pretend that the need for the survival of the city transforms a vicious deed into a virtuous one. In fact, it is worse than pointless, because it sets the precedent within the city for excusing vicious deeds that may be required for individual survival. For if the person does not survive, he or she cannot perform virtuous deeds.

Aristotle cannot suppress these tensions, but he attempts to camouflage them by not calling explicit attention to them. We have to discern them in the twists and turns of his analysis and terminology. The obvious reason for Aristotle's reticence is that full disclosure would mean disruption of the delicate balance between the individual person and the political association. Heidegger commits a different error; he assimilates ethics and politics into history, and thereby tends to trivialize the good and the just in terms of the successful. The closest Heidegger comes to Aristotle's concept of nobility is authenticity or genuineness, and this is not close enough. Heidegger himself insists that his term is ontological and has no "value" connotations whatsoever. But if this is so, then neither does human existence.

I restrict myself to one final textual contrast between Aristotle and Heidegger. Aristotle emphasizes throughout that *phronesis* is not the same as quickness. On the contrary, it takes time to arrive at a correct practical judgment.

Furthermore, to understand a situation is not the same as to arrive at a judgment about what to do. So *phronesis* is the same as judging nobly or well (*krinein kalos*); as such, it is epitactic, that is, it commands rather than merely explains (1143a8, 1143a14–16). He means that a judgment is not a statement of fact or the expression of an opinion but the command of practical reason to do something in particular.

This helps us to see that Heidegger is wrong to draw an analogy between *phronesis* and *Gewissen*. If any analogy of this sort were conceivable, it would be that between *phronesis* and *Entschlossenheit* (resoluteness). Whereas *Gewissen* is the anxious self-thrownness upon one's own guilt, the authentic consequence of conscience is resolution. "But upon what does *Dasein* resolve itself within *Entschlossenheit*? To what end [*Wozu*] ought it to resolve itself? Only resolve itself can give this answer" (*SZ*, 298). That is, "each factic possibility of *Dasein* is indeterminate; resoluteness is certain of itself only as resolution" (ibid.). Heidegger replaces the Aristotelian variability of practical affairs with their uncertainty, and he replaces the correctness of the judgment, that is, its accord with *orthos logos*, with resoluteness. One is tempted to say that stubbornness replaces reasonableness. But stated more moderately, for Aristotle, the calculation of the *phronimos* is not uncertain; it is always correct. For Heidegger, certitude has nothing to do with calculation; it is more like the determination to endorse a decision that, in itself, may or may not be confirmed by future events. Otherwise put, the decision is certified by my resolution, not by the "objective" facts of human affairs. At bottom, there is still no parallel to the Aristotelian *phronesis*.

It thus turns out that Heidegger's authentic individual is far more self-centered than the Aristotelian virtuous person correctly calculating and prudently acting upon the mean in specific circumstances. If Heidegger is right to say that Greek ethics is determined by the predominance it ascribes to what is forever, this may well be the basis for a more noble conception of ethics than one that is rooted in historical destiny masked as the free choice of authenticity. I conclude that *phronesis* is superior to ontology on its own grounds, that of everyday life, and that Heidegger's existential ontology, however brilliant, and perhaps because of its very brilliance, can bring nothing to human affairs but blindness. The attempt to extract the inner ontological depth of everyday human existence is a failure for the same reason that modern natural science fails to domesticate the unruliness of ordinary experience. In both cases, there are two different orders of being, and it is impossible to reduce one to the other. What looks like the root or the foundation turns out to be the grave of human significance.

Chapter 4 Wittgenstein, Strauss, and the Possibility of Philosophy

The two thinkers I discuss in this chapter can be initially described as two different but related responses to Kant. The most important sense in which they are related is that they share the intention of returning to the pretheoretical domain of ordinary language. The most important difference between them is that Wittgenstein's "return" is itself neo-Kantian, or let us say post-Kantian, in the sense that it derives from the nineteenth-century process by which transcendental philosophy was transformed into the philosophy of language. This process is itself decisively marked by the emergence of the historical ego, at first as a complement to the transcendental ego of pure reason and then as its replacement. Strauss on the other hand was decisively influenced by Plato and Aristotle. He once put it to his students that they inoculated him against Heidegger, against the phenomenological version of the consequences of the emergence of the historical ego and of the philosophy of language. This remark is of more than anecdotal importance. Readers should preserve it as an element in inoculating themselves against interpreting Strauss as a secret Nietzschean.

Strauss begins with Socrates, whereas Nietzsche and Heidegger begin characteristically with the pre-Socratics. This is not to deny that Nietzsche plays a role in Strauss's "deconstruction" of the philosophical tradition; but that deconstruction is intended to lay open the political nature of everyday human life, not its ontological roots. As to Wittgenstein, one almost has the impression that he furnished the Nietzschean element of deconstruction from his own personality. Wittgenstein did not take his bearings from history, but from his own direct understanding of the debilitating consequences of a scientific philosophy modeled after mathematical constructions. Unfortunately, his lack of interest in history facilitated the process by which he uncritically accepted the modern scientific understanding of nature. The inevitable result was that in his work human discourse is understood as the voice of history and convention rather than of nature. For Wittgenstein, ordinary language is the changing idiom of history; but as such, it is a theoretical construction. There is for Wittgenstein no discursive return to the origin, but only an acknowledgment of the rules invoked by local agreement.

Strauss and Wittgenstein were both charismatic personalities who produced a wide range of disciples. In both cases the disciples have engaged in endless disputes about the authentic teaching of the master. This disagreement is of considerable importance. It is obviously due in large part to the aesopic styles of the two thinkers, styles that succeeded in muffling the words of their author despite the ostensible attempt in each case to defend ordinary, commonsense language. Although Strauss frequently spoke out in what purported to be his own voice on behalf of positive philosophical theses, in particular those from the domain of political philosophy, he subordinated his views throughout his career to interpreting the great figures of the tradition: Greek, Hebrew, Arabic, Latin, and modern European, as well as those of the United States. Whereas this species of esotericism was absent from Wittgenstein's writings, the obliqueness with which he presented his linguistic therapy frequently made it difficult to distinguish the ailment from the remedy. Nevertheless, salient points emerge from the false lucidity generated by the two thinkers, and these points constitute the influential legacy of both.

What is of central importance is to reconstruct the main arguments propounded by Wittgenstein and Strauss that bear upon the connection of the need to return to pre-theoretical discourse with the possibility of philosophy. In his criticism of theory, Wittgenstein comes very close to the thesis that philosophy is impossible. It is a corollary, at least an inferred corollary, from this, that Jerusalem triumphs in her quarrel with Athens.[1] Strauss is both more explicit and more extensive in his discussions of the quarrel between reason and revelation, but also more ambiguous. It is not a simple task to set the record straight, since Strauss's understanding of the nature of philosophy is aporetic, and there is good reason to suppose that his very formulation of this aporia is itself aporetic.

As I hope to show, Strauss was no reactionary: he did not share the illusion that it is possible for the residents of late modernity to return to the past. But he did hold with great energy that it was both possible and necessary for us to learn from the past, with respect both to politics and philosophy. The difficulty in understanding his views on philosophy is, I believe, much more severe than the difficulty of understanding his political views. No doubt the former difficulty has long-range consequences that tend to exacerbate the latter difficulty. In general, however, Strauss was a classical liberal who appeared to be a reactionary only from the viewpoint of extreme progressivism, or what he himself called "historicism." There was no doubt something old-fashioned about Strauss's liberalism, but although he grasped the defects of the Enlightenment as these were delineated most eloquently by Nietzsche, he never drew Nietzsche's conclusions.

So far as I can see, it would be very difficult to attribute a political philosophy to Wittgenstein. He seems to follow Kant tacitly in regarding ethics as higher in importance than politics, although because of its very height, too deep to be articulated in discursive thought. I have the impression, based solely upon reading his major works, that Wittgenstein was rather conservative politically, in the sense that he saw very clearly the defects and vulgarity of late-modern European and American culture.[2] I see less difficulty in drawing the conclusion that Wittgenstein regarded philosophy to be impossible. The technical devices he introduced into his teaching (for example, language games) were solely for therapeutic use; they were designed to purge ordinary or usual language of theoretical detritus and distortion, rather than having any positive or constructive use. Of course, Wittgenstein's case against philosophy may be mistaken, and even contradicted by his own procedures, as some would claim. There is something to this last claim, because the abolition of philosophy can be conducted responsibly only by philosophy itself. But one does not find in Wittgenstein, as one does in Strauss, a case on behalf of philosophy that is a veiled statement of its aporetic nature.

For our purposes, then, the main questions are these. What is the connection between ordinary or pretheoretical language and the possibility of philosophy?

Is it possible to return to the pretheoretical context without engaging in theory, and if not, does this not transform the ordinary into a theoretical artifact, that is to say, the extraordinary?

The underlying difficulty can be stated as follows. The vigor derived from the return to the common roots of political life in the texts of Plato, Xenophon, and Aristotle, where these roots are presumably undistorted by twenty-five hundred years of theoretical construction, is obscured if not diminished by a stubborn theoretical problem. The pretheoretical experience to which Strauss returns in doing philosophy is the condition of ordinary Greek life before Greek, and so western European, theory emerged. If we think this through, the following dilemma arises. Either the truth of Greek pretheoretical experience is available in principle at any time, and so a return to the Greeks is superfluous; or else Strauss advocates the historicist thesis that our Greek heritage has predisposed us to search for the origin of philosophy in the pretheoretical understanding of the Greeks themselves.

There is one other point that should be mentioned in this context. Strauss also placed a very high value upon the testimony of Thucydides and Aristophanes on the nature of everyday life. Their testimony can be summarized as follows: Philosophy is either superfluous for politics or it is dangerous. In slightly different terms, philosophy is already a distortion of the nature of political life; one does not therefore find a pretheoretical account of that life in the writings of the Socratic school. This apparent conflict in Strauss's interpretation of pretheoretical Greek life might be resolved as follows. The portrait of political life is the same in the two sets of testimony; the difference lies in how they each assess the political consequences of philosophy. Strauss's work on the Greeks thus raises two questions. First, is there a theoretically neutral account of the nature of politics? And second, what is the connection between politics as understood in its own terms (if that is possible), and philosophy?

If then we put to one side for the moment all questions of political doctrine and scholarly interpretations, the central fact about the thought of Leo Strauss is his confrontation with Heidegger on the nature of philosophy. For the reasons I stated in chapter 3, Heidegger's "return" is too radical, because it directs us back to a time that is outside our history, and proposes in prophetic terms (the only terms suitable to the enterprise) that we make a different choice, not just a radically different choice but one that can be made only after we have pulled up our roots. I will not comment here upon the content of Heidegger's prophetic vision of "the other way," except to say that it is not as free of Western elements as he seems to believe. This to one side, the very attractiveness of the Heideggerian return must rest upon his interpretation of Western philosophy, and thus not only of its origins among the Greeks but its ostensible distortion by Platonism throughout its subsequent history.

For our purposes, the central fact about Wittgenstein's thought is encapsulated in the following remark from his manuscripts of 1931. After a reflection about the kinship between Brahms and Mendelssohn, Wittgenstein breaks off the comparison and says: "That must be the end of a theme which I cannot place. It came into my head today as I was thinking about my philosophical work and saying to myself: 'I destroy, I destroy, I destroy'—."[3] To put this in a slightly more positive way, Wittgenstein frequently emphasizes that "philosophy may in no way interfere with the real//actual// use of language . . . with what is really said. It can in the end only describe it. For it cannot give it any foundation either. It leaves everything as it is."[4]

To summarize these introductory remarks, Wittgenstein takes up the Nietzschean theme of the destruction (or deconstruction) of the philosophical traditions as it appears in Heidegger, but he does not at all do so for the sake of the creation or discovery of a new beginning. In fact, Wittgenstein's return to common speech is saturated with Kantian and post-Kantian themes. Even his claim that philosophy leaves everything as it is, is compatible with Kant's insistence upon grounding ethics in the conscience of the average human being. The difference between Kant and Wittgenstein arises from the fact that between Kant and the post-Kantians, the transcendental is replaced by the historical. More precisely, the transcendental is moved entirely out of the realm of discourse, which is thus occupied entirely by history. Strauss on the other hand rejects the clarion call, "Back to Kant!" but his adherence to the Greek *logos* is qualified by a keen recognition of the irreversibility of history as well as by a failure (or unwillingness) to resolve the quarrel between Athens and Jerusalem.

Wittgenstein and Strauss are two of the most important spokesmen for the contemporary effort to recapture the ordinary, pretheoretical context of philosophy without recourse to the methods and principles of *mathesis universalis,* on the one hand, and fundamental ontology, on the other. In Wittgenstein's *Remarks on the Philosophy of Psychology,* he says without comment: "In order to climb into the depths one does not need to travel very far; indeed, for this you do not need to abandon your immediate and accustomed environment."[5] On reading this passage, I was struck by its similarity to Strauss's frequently repeated observation that the depths are contained in the surface and only in the surface. In *Thoughts on Machiavelli,* Strauss says: "There is no surer protection against the understanding of anything than taking for granted or otherwise despising the obvious and the surface. The problem inherent in the surface of things, and only in the surface of things, is the heart of things."[6]

In these statements concerning the surface and the depth, I take both Strauss and Wittgenstein to be cautioning us against the tendency to replace the immediate context of experience with a theoretical artifact. Both disagree with the transcendental and ontological approaches to ordinary experience that Kant and Heidegger take. Finally, both reject the attempt to reconstitute philosophy in the image of mathematical and experimental science.[7] But this does not mean that both are opposed to theory in the same sense or to the same degree. For Wittgenstein, theory is erroneous or obfuscatory conceptual construction; "'Don't look for anything behind the phenomena; they themselves are the theory' (Goethe)."[8] And again: "Since everything lies open to view there is nothing to explain. For what is hidden, for example, is of no interest to us."[9] Wittgenstein is objecting primarily to recourse by philosophers to inner or subjective processes, as opposed to the publicity of the common language, and to semantical entities like meanings or Platonic forms, as opposed to the syntactic or grammatical rules of the common language. Strauss, on the other hand, is opposed to theories that are not grounded in our direct experience of the natural order of human affairs, an order that is not the product of grammatical rules but determines them.

Wittgenstein speaks inconsistently on the crucial point of the sense in which human nature regulates our behavior. In apparent harmony with Strauss are assertions like this: "The common behavior of mankind is the system of reference by means of which we interpret an unknown language."[10] In the same sense, we are told that language corresponds to how things actually are, or to what Wittgenstein calls "normal cases,"[11] and so to "ordinary" or "customary language" (*die gewöhnliche Sprache*).[12] He describes his work in the *Philosophical Investigations* as "remarks on the natural history of human beings; we are not contributing curiosities, however, but observations which no one has doubted, but which have escaped remark only because they are always before our eyes."[13]

But the expression "natural history" is compatible with a historicist view of human nature. Furthermore, according to Wittgenstein, "Essence is expressed by grammar."[14] Since grammars define families of language-games or constitute a "life-form,"[15] and life-forms are multiple as well as diverse (in other words, since there is no universal life-form, any more than there is a universal form of the proposition), it seems that human nature, and so what counts as ordinary or healthy use of language, is a function of history, that is to say, of chance. Wittgenstein says that his interests include the conformity of concepts to "very general facts of nature," but the latter are not invoked as causes of the former. We are instead instructed to imagine different facts of nature as producing different concepts. He is not asking us here to focus on the natural order but on the contingency of concepts.[16]

This point has to be emphasized. For Wittgenstein, the "surface" or familiar environment of everyday life is conceptually defined by linguistic practice. What we call "the world" or "reality," and so the aforementioned facts of nature themselves, is a function of how we carve up the conceptual and so discursive space of ordinary experience.[17] But this does not mean that ordinary experience is available to us as a standard that exists prior to the act of carving up. Wittgenstein's emphasis upon ordinary language is at best only ambiguously accompanied by an appeal to human nature, to the nature of discourse or *logos*, let alone to a natural order that is accessible to contemplation. The ambiguity arises from the fact that Wittgenstein excludes the possibility of theorizing on questions of this sort. He begins from the conventional or historical fact of the linguistic community whose members speak in more or less the same way.[18] It is as a member of this community that the philosopher or speech-therapist has access to standard idioms and rules of linguistic use by which to eliminate mistakes arising from misuse of those idioms and rules.[19]

For Wittgenstein, as I understand him, nature is itself a theoretical construction. This is to say that he takes for granted the sense of nature that derives from seventeenth-century philosophy and the then new physics. And this includes the sense of the expression "natural history," as it is used in the eighteenth and nineteenth centuries. By rejecting nature in the sense of *phusis,* that is to say, of an order external to human linguistic invention, Wittgenstein is left with *nomos* or custom. His analysis of the "ordinary" use of language is thus endless; it has no beginning and no end. Otherwise stated, it has no bottom and no top. There is no "theory" of correct linguistic use in either of the two senses of "theory." We cannot "intellectually perceive" something about human nature or experience that is regulative of discursive practice, nor can we construct a unique and comprehensive conceptual framework for the rank-ordering of this practice. Ordinary language is ordinal only in a local or historical sense.

Nevertheless, I do not wish to suggest that Wittgenstein differs completely from the Socratic teaching that Leo Strauss defends. The Platonic dialogues illustrate two of Wittgenstein's own theses or assumptions. The first is that human discourse, and in particular, philosophical discourse, has no beginning and no end. We are always *in medias res.* Second, there are, therefore, no final or comprehensive discursive constructions, or "theories" in the sense deprecated by Wittgenstein. But for Plato, contrary to Wittgenstein, there is a top and a bottom to philosophical discourse, and this is represented by the Ideas on the one hand and the doctrine of eros on the other. In more prosaic terms, we are united by our desires, and these in turn are regulated by the natures of the objects of our desires. What one could call ordinary or ordinal discourse is thus defined pragmatically by the intelligibility of desire. This way of formulating the classical position may seem anachronistic. But there is a conceptual parallel, even a continuity, between eros and the Ideas on the one hand, and desire and its objects on the other.

There are of course also crucial differences. One such difference, especially important for us, is that the founders of modernity de-politicize desire and thereby reduce the difference between *thumos* (spiritedness) and *epithumia* (desire) to the homogeneous notion of "the passions of the soul," as Descartes expresses it. For Socrates and his students (including Leo Strauss), the question of the proper satisfaction of human desire is necessarily a political question, for the simple reason that we depend upon each other for that satisfaction. But it is also a question that takes us outside, or rather, above, the city, to natural differences in the nobility and baseness of desires. By rendering this dependence physiological, Descartes shifts the emphasis from the community to the isolated ego, from politics to psychology. Nobility and baseness do not quite disappear, but they are redefined as "*générosité*" or autonomous greatness of soul, that is, egotism. The subsequent shift back to the predominance of society and history, begun in the eighteenth and completed in the nineteenth centuries, while in one sense a re-politicizing of desire, retains its physiological foundations; that is, it retains the modern scientific conception of nature, which is incapable of sustaining the natural distinction between the noble and the base.

In short, the shift from the political to the physiological, that is to say, from the public to the private, initiates the materialist interpretation of the spirit, soul, or mind. Still more precisely, the soul-body problem is replaced by the mind-body problem, which makes possible the gradual redefinition of the mind as the faculty of analytical discourse that can be duplicated by machines. And the transformation of nature from politics to physiology is the necessary prerequisite for the rise of political science and sociology, that is, for the quantitative or descriptive study of human beings in their behavior toward one another. Wittgenstein, to repeat, starts with the modern scientific conception of nature and, if I understand him correctly, attempts to repair its defects through religion rather than through philosophical theory. In other words, the ordinal analysis of language turns out to be rooted in silence rather than in more language, since the latter can be correctly used only to describe or express facts (including experiences), and so relative values, but not the absolute values of ethics or religion.[20] Wittgenstein's linguistic therapy points to the triumph of Jerusalem over Athens. He is a Socrates without Platonic Ideas.

If the general picture I have presented thus far is accurate, the difference between Wittgenstein and Strauss in their approach to the surface is now obvious. Wittgenstein is very close to Nietzsche on the crucial point that nature in itself, that is, as effectively defined by the philosophers of modern science, is in the extreme case a discursive artifact, and that, in any case, its value for human existence is derived from the particular linguistic horizon or life-form of the community to which we the evaluators belong. It follows that the surface is a linguistic convention. There is no depth lying beneath the surface; thus we enter the depth only in the act of immersing ourselves within the surface. There is a multiplicity of surfaces, but no common depth. The attempt to penetrate the surface leads either to the malfunctioning of language, of which the outstanding example is the construction of metaphysical theories, or to silence. For Strauss, on the contrary, the surface is the manner in which the depth renders itself accessible to discourse. But this is to say that there is a depth. It is not, however, of a sort to lend itself to metaphysical theories.

One way to bring out the problem in Wittgenstein's later philosophy is to say that it addresses itself to a program that is never carried out. David Pears, in his study of Wittgenstein, presents the later philosophy as an attack against metaphysics, which is in effect identified as the attempt to model philosophy upon science. As an example, Pears cites the view, attributed to Plato, that the world imposes a fixed structure on our thought.[21] But the reader will look to Wittgenstein in vain for a detailed analysis of metaphysics or of Platonism (which is also the opponent of Heidegger, who does furnish such analyses). Even more striking, Wittgenstein does not support his constantly avowed dependence upon "ordinary language" (*die gewöhnliche Sprache*) with anything approximating to an explanation of the difference between ordinary and extraordinary discourse.

It is begging the question to identify ordinary language as that part of what we ordinarily say that is useful to Wittgenstein's teaching. Wittgenstein claims throughout the *Investigations* that philosophy leaves everything as it is, that "every sentence in our language 'is in order as it is'."[22] But this cannot apply to the theoretical sentences of philosophy, or at least to those of metaphysics. Wittgenstein is here referring to "ordinary" sentences. His claim is not merely that ordinary language provides us with a regulative criterion that assists us in the analysis of philosophical discourse, but that the philosophical discourse must be replaced in all nonformal cases by the ordinary language. Yet reasons for making this shift are assumed by the principles that underlie his blanket approval of ordinary or everyday discourse. There is already a philosophical doctrine concealed in the extreme endorsement of ordinary language. And the breadth of this endorsement is almost immediately contradicted by the fact that Wittgenstein regularly arrives at canonical usages of everyday expressions through the assistance of extremely nonordinary imaginary distortions and transformations of actual linguistic practice.[23] Finally, if every statement in our ordinary language is correct as it is, then, as others have pointed out, nothing new can ever be said. But this is too strong a limitation, since ordinary language, precisely on Wittgenstein's own terms, is historical and conventional; that is, it changes and so develops new canons of legitimate discourse.

According to Wittgenstein, "what *we* do is to bring words back from their metaphysical to their everyday use.[24] If this activity is successful, it leads to complete clarity, that is, to the complete disappearance of philosophical problems.[25] But why should this be desirable? Was it not the very extraordinariness of ordinary language that led to the philosophical problems in the first place? By assuming that what cannot give rise to complete clarity should be eliminated from our discourse, is not Wittgenstein tacitly retaining his loyalty to the scientific model of philosophical truth? I have no wish to cast aspersions on Wittgenstein's intelligence and seriousness, but this fundamental stratum of his teaching escapes the suspicion of philistinism only when one realizes the moral fervor with which he sought to rescue us from philosophy. Even so, a difficulty remains. By forbidding us to speak of that which cannot be completely clarified, Wittgenstein condemns us to silence about what is of the highest importance.

To summarize this portion of my argument, it looks as though Wittgenstein appeals to the ordinary in order to abolish philosophy, whereas Strauss makes a similar appeal in order to preserve philosophy. Wittgenstein's enterprise is flawed by the fact that the ordinary is for him already a theoretical artifact that presupposes a conception of philosophy that he wishes to repudiate. Wittgenstein inadvertently plunges us back into the depths, whereas Strauss, whether intentionally or not, bars our access to the depths. It is to this feature of Strauss's work that I now turn.

Leo Strauss devoted his life to the defense of philosophy in the grand tradition of Socratic rationalism. According to Strauss, the central characteristic of this tradition is the claim to knowledge of ignorance. The possibility of philosophy rests upon the coherence of this claim. The question is then whether Strauss provides us with a satisfactory argument for, or more modestly a plausible account of, that coherence. But before we can articulate the problem itself, we must first face the puzzle of Straussian rhetoric.

One can discern a prevailing dualism in the surface appearance of Strauss's teaching. On the one hand, Strauss's style, especially in his later publications, reminds us of two of his particular favorites among thinkers, Xenophon and Al Farabi. But there is an important difference between him and them. The exoteric teaching of the two ancient thinkers was in apparent conformity with the traditional doctrines of their time and place. By seeming to advocate a rehabilitation of this ancient tradition, Strauss adopted the posture of a man at odds with the predominant views of his own time and place. He was fond of saying that one is better positioned to understand Xenophon if one prefers the novels of Jane Austen to those of Dostoyevski.[26] But Strauss presents us with the curious figure of a revolutionary Jane Austen. His highly charged critique of the nihilism of late modernity is more reminiscent of Dostoevski than of Jane Austen. I believe that Strauss would have applied to the twentieth century Nietzsche's rhetorical question: "Is not the nineteenth century, especially in its commencement, simply a strengthened, brutalized eighteenth century, that is to say, a decadence-century?"[27] To answer this question in the affirmative about our own century is to commit oneself to certain rhetorical precautions. However, it is a complete misunderstanding of Strauss's views to associate him with Nietzsche's positive program.[28] Strauss was a strong and constant spokesman for liberal democracy whose political sympathies lay with Abraham Lincoln and Winston Churchill.

Strauss saw his task as that of contributing to the modification of contemporary liberalism by the moderate tendencies of the classical political thinkers as well as of the liberal rationalists of the seventeenth and eighteenth centuries. Strauss could be called a reactionary only by the most extreme partisans of the revolutionary left, but he shared an important trait with the intelligent among left-wing radicals: scorn for the version of liberalism that historical relativism has emptied of content.

But this was Strauss's political program. As I believe, and as he would have agreed, the highest political goal of the philosopher is the preservation of philosophy.[29] Suffice it to say that, for Strauss, this was in the best interests of the nonphilosopher as well. But this philosophical intention complicated Strauss's rhetorical task. For example, it sometimes obscures his own political liberalism, an obscurity I can immediately dissipate if not remove.

In his evaluation of Hermann Cohen's interpretation of Spinoza's treatment of Judaism, Strauss writes: "One may say that in his critique of Spinoza Cohen commits the typical mistake of the conservative, which consists in concealing the fact that the continuous and changing tradition which he cherishes so greatly would never have come into being through conservatism, or without discontinuities, revolutions, and sacrileges committed at the beginning of the cherished tradition and at least silently repeated in its course."[30] Strauss frequently stated that thought should be daring, even mad, whereas action should be moderate.[31] Rhetoric, as the public presentation of thought, is an action, and even when Strauss was daring, he never exercised the exaggerated idiom of Nietzsche. Nevertheless, he had his own mode of daring. There are Straussian texts for the few, and there are other texts for the many. Strauss's rediscovery and extensive presentation of esotericism falls into both categories.

I say this in part because it is easy to see that Strauss's revelations were in proportion to the urgency with which whatever author he interpreted requested discretion. As Strauss pointed out, modern esotericism is easier to penetrate than are its ancient and medieval predecessors. Strauss is accordingly quite explicit in the case of Machiavelli, Spinoza, Hobbes, and Locke, but he is extremely obscure when he discusses the ancient and especially the medieval philosophers or sages. As Strauss himself often pointed out, how much one can say in public about esoteric doctrines is in part a function of the particular historical circumstances.[32] He also held that, in a time when the older teaching is in danger of being lost entirely, it is permissible to be slightly more daring or frank than were the authors themselves. But not too daring! Thus, in the very act of what seems to be an exposition of Maimonides' hidden teaching, Strauss says that the position of Maimonides' interpreter (namely, Strauss) is "to some extent identical with that of Maimonides himself." He clarifies this as follows: "Since the *Guide* contains an esoteric interpretation of an esoteric teaching, an adequate interpretation of the *Guide* would thus have to take the form of an esoteric interpretation of an esoteric interpretation of an esoteric teaching." Although Strauss adds that "this suggestion may sound paradoxical and even ridiculous" to us, it is, I suggest, the procedure that he himself follows when writing about Maimonides, and not only about Maimonides.[33]

Strauss observes, with respect to the extreme caution of Jehudah Halevi, "the line of demarcation between timidity and responsibility is drawn differently in different ages."[34] There is a radical difference between our age and that of Xenophon, Farabi, or Halevi, and even of Jane Austen. In a fragment from the *Nachlass* of 1885–86, Nietzsche explains that "it is today necessary to speak temporarily in a coarse [*grob*] manner and to act coarsely. What is fine and concealed is no longer understood, not even by those who are related to us. *That of which one does not speak loudly and cry out, is not there.*"[35] To this, one should add that "coarseness" is a relative term; coarse Straussian rhetoric is much closer to that of Winston Churchill than to the rhetoric of Nietzsche.

Strauss often asserts that a careful reader is also a careful writer.[36] The careful reader should pay close attention to the possible relation between frankness and concealment. Nietzsche is once again helpful here. In the *Nachlass* to 1882, he says: "To speak much of oneself is also a way of hiding oneself."[37] I would modify this statement as follows. To make many heterodox pronouncements is a way of speaking of oneself, even if the pronouncements are partially concealed by rhetorical disavowals of one's own gifts and are often couched in hypothetical statements or ambiguous parenthetical clauses.

In sum, Strauss combines, or alternates between, classical esotericism and modern daring. He shifts back and forth from the subtle flirtation of Jane Austen to the relative frankness of Nietzsche, and then at last into the darkness that might remind us of the late Henry James. Strauss's last works on Xenophon and on Plato's *Laws* bring to my mind James's *The Sacred Fount*. This denseness may partially explain why his defense of modern liberal democracy is often overlooked.

The main reason for Strauss's obscurity, however, is the ambiguity of his portrait of philosophy. It is worth noting that Strauss, so far as I am aware, never referred to himself as a philosopher. He insisted that only a very few human beings in the recorded history of humankind could be regarded as genuine philosophers. Strauss gave no exact tally, as did his friend Jacob Klein, according to whom the number was somewhere between twelve and fifteen.[38] I believe that Strauss was a bit more generous; he occasionally observed that there were normally only one or two philosophers in each generation. As to himself, he told some of his students in private that he regarded his own accomplishments to be on a level with those of Lessing, who was instrumental in Strauss's discovery of the art of esotericism.[39]

The serious question here is how the nonphilosopher is able to penetrate the exoteric surface of the genuine philosopher's esoteric depths. In this crucial case, the maxim that the depths are accessible in the surface seems to be implausible. It is Strauss himself who points out this implausibility. I must quote the following passage about Heidegger in its entirety:

> The same effect which Heidegger produced in the late twenties and early thirties in Germany, he produced very soon in continental Europe as a whole. There is no

> longer in existence a philosophic position, apart from neo-Thomism and Marxism crude or refined. All rational liberal philosophic positions have lost their significance and power. One may deplore this, but I for one cannot bring myself to clinging to philosophical positions which have been shown to be inadequate. I am afraid that we shall have to make a very great effort in order to find a solid basis for rational liberalism. Only a great thinker could help us in our intellectual plight. But here is the great trouble: the only great thinker in our time is Heidegger.
>
> The only question of importance, of course, is the question whether Heidegger's teaching is true or not. But the very question is deceptive because it is silent about the question of competence—of who is competent to judge. Perhaps only great thinkers are really competent to judge the thought of great thinkers. Heidegger made a distinction between philosophers and those for whom philosophy is identical with the history of philosophy. He made a distinction, in other words, between the thinker and the scholar. I know that I am only a scholar.[40]

If we were to take Strauss's modesty literally, it would seem to follow not only that philosophy disappeared, at least temporarily, from the face of the globe when Heidegger died, but also that neither Strauss nor we could understand Heidegger's writings. What precisely did the sage of the Schwartzwald mean when he said, "Only once or twice in my thirty to thirty-five years of teaching have I ever spoken about what really matters to me"?[41] Or, to ask essentially the same question, how did Strauss, as he claimed, find an antidote to the doctrines of Heidegger in the exoteric writings of Plato, who tells us that he never, let alone once or twice, wrote down his deepest thoughts?[42]

The first ambiguity in Strauss's account of philosophy is then the doctrine of esotericism, which seems to make philosophy inaccessible at the outset to more than the one or two genuine philosophers in each generation. On this basis, knowledge of ignorance is for the rest of us, including Strauss, too ignorant to count as knowledge. We must instead return to the maxim that the depths are contained in the surface. This is of course no guarantee that the surface will yield a consistent meaning.

I begin with a quotation from Strauss's most famous book, *Natural Right and History:* "The historicist contention can be reduced to the assertion that natural right is impossible because philosophy in the full sense of the term is impossible. Philosophy is possible only if there is an absolute horizon or natural horizon in contradistinction to the historically changing horizons or the caves. In other words, philosophy is possible only if man, while incapable of acquiring wisdom or full understanding of the whole, is capable of knowing what he does not know, that is to say, of grasping the fundamental problems and therewith the fundamental alternatives, which are, in principle, coeval with human thought."[43]

This is one of several passages in which Strauss states the hypothesis necessary for refuting Heidegger. The passage is peculiar because it can be read in two different ways. The first is to take Strauss to be saying that genuine philosophy is accessible to us through a return to the pretheoretical surface of political life, which, if not directly intelligible to everyone, is certainly intelligible to the *endoksoi* or persons of sound judgment, and through their mediation, to a wider audience. On the alternative reading, however, the species-term "man" must be understood as naming a class with one prominent member and one only: Socrates. For the most superficial inspection of the history of philosophy is enough to dispel the notion that philosophers, or those whom even Strauss regarded as philosophers, restricted themselves to posing the fundamental alternatives.

The first question to be addressed to Strauss is then: What is accessible in pretheoretical life, and to whom is it accessible? What are we to make of the maxim that the depth is contained in the surface? For Wittgenstein, the meaning is, in effect, that philosophy is replaced by the wisdom appropriate to surfaces. This is not always acceptable to his readers, but it is quite clear, despite Wittgenstein's frequent obscurity. For Strauss, the meaning seems to be that knowledge of ignorance is what is accessible, or knowledge of the fundamental alternatives, but not knowledge of the foundation or fundament. But is this not the practical equivalent of saying that there is no depth? It would seem better to say that the fundamental alternatives are given to us prior to philosophical theory in the structure of ordinary experience. In order to verify this assertion, a kind of "desedimentation" or "deconstruction" of the philosophical tradition is then required. But this raises the great difficulty that every deconstruction of philosophy is itself philosophical, or let us say, theoretical. It looks as though ordinary experience is and is not accessible to us.

Without leaving this point entirely, I turn now to the development of a second question for Leo Strauss concerning the possibility of philosophy. One of the main themes of Strauss's work, from the beginning to the end, is the quarrel between Jerusalem and Athens. It is of extreme interest that a number of careful students of Strauss's work have arrived at the conclusion that he was himself a believing Jew. Strauss has made ambiguous remarks on this point. The ambiguity is a consequence of two sets of statements that are clear in themselves, but their net effect is to blur if not quite contradict each other. On the one hand, Strauss notes frequently that our Western tradition consists of two antagonistic and ultimately incompatible answers to the question of which—faith or philosophy—is the one thing needful.[44] He makes the same point with respect to the case of Judaism in particular: "Jews of the philosophic competence of Halevi and Maimonides took it for granted that being a Jew and being a philosopher are mutually exclusive."[45] As this expression makes clear, one may be a Jew and possess philosophical competence, but this is not the same as to be a philosopher. What is the difference? The philosopher denies miracles, or rejects the creation *ex nihilo,* and so on. In general, the philosopher rejects the authority of revelation and relies on unassisted human reason for the pursuit of truth and happiness.[46]

On the other hand, Strauss says with equal regularity that philosophy is not in a position to refute the possibility of revelation. A representative passage is to be found in *Natural Right and History:*

> Philosophy has to grant that revelation is possible. But to grant that revelation is possible means to grant that philosophy is perhaps not the one thing needful, that philosophy is perhaps something infinitely unimportant. To grant that revelation is possible means to grant that the philosophic life is not necessarily, not evidently, *the* right life. Philosophy, the life devoted to the quest for evident knowledge available to man as man, would itself rest on an unevident, arbitrary, or blind decision. This would merely confirm the thesis of faith, that there is no possibility of consistency, of a consistent and thoroughly sincere life, without belief in revelation. The mere fact that philosophy and revelation cannot refute each other would constitute the refutation of philosophy by revelation.[47]

This is an extremely important passage. Notice at the outset that the passage is written in the subjunctive. This was a favorite device Strauss employed to express his own views, and there is no evidence in the context of the passage that he does not intend it seriously, but I find the reasoning far from persuasive. There are many beliefs that reason cannot prove; this in itself does not make them more plausible than our relying on reason, nor does it even, perhaps, make them unreasonable. Part of being reasonable is to know what cannot be proved. Furthermore, one need not prove that philosophy is necessarily the best life: one must only show that it is plausible to say that philosophy is the best life; in other words, the philosopher need only show that the choice of philosophy as the best life is more plausible than the choice of religion. More generally, either reason can refute revelation, or it cannot. If it can, this will in no way impress the partisan of revelation. But if it cannot, this will not in itself transform the person of reason into a person of faith or a partisan of revelation.

The main point for us is that I know of no Straussian text, published or unpublished, in which Strauss shows, or even claims, that philosophy can refute revelation. The written evidence is all to the effect that no such refutation is possible. This being so, it must follow on Straussian grounds that philosophy has been refuted, and indeed, that it was impossible from the outset. If this is too strong, I can make the same point in a more moderate manner. The passage in question, along with others, shows us that Strauss wished to persuade a certain audience that philosophy cannot refute religion, but even further, that it is as arbitrary as it accuses religion of being. At the same time, it is at least one of the two or three main themes in Strauss's work that philosophy, understood as knowledge of ignorance, is exemplified in Socrates, who therefore represents for us the possibility of philosophy. Nor could anyone seriously deny that Strauss regularly praises philosophy as the highest form of human existence, or, to make a more modest claim, that philosophy is necessary in order for natural right to be possible, and with it, the basis for a just and rational political life.

This point has to be stressed. Regardless of the cogency of the argument, Strauss never deviates in his writings from his youthful assertion about religion in *Philosophy and Law* that "there can be no question of a refutation of the 'externally' understood basic tenets of the tradition. For all of these tenets rest on the irrefutable premise that God is omnipotent and His will unfathomable."[48] In a very late essay, Strauss writes that "the genuine refutation of orthodoxy" depends upon the systematic proof of the intelligibility of the world and life without the assumption of a mysterious God. And this in turn requires the success of the Cartesian project to replace the "merely given world . . . by the world created by man theoretically and practically."[49]

Please note carefully that in these texts, either the quarrel between philosophy and religion has been resolved in favor of religion, or else philosophy is preserved by the solitary labors of Socrates in advancing and sustaining the thesis that philosophy is knowledge of ignorance. As we are about to see, the argument becomes more complicated, and in two ways. The portrait of Socratic wisdom shifts from one set of texts to another, and the quarrel between Athens and Jerusalem is replaced by what we can call the quarrel between Paris and Jerusalem, that is, between Descartes and his progeny on the one hand and Moses and his progeny on the other. As to Socrates, it is not quite clear in which camp he belongs. I mean by this that Strauss frequently redefines the Socratic or favored version of the Athenian position in such a way as to render tenuous if not invisible the difference between it and revelation.

Consider the following text from the essay "What is Political Philosophy?"

Strauss asserts that the question of the nature of man points to the problem of nature in general, and so to cosmology, and then says: "Whatever the significance of modern science may be, it cannot affect our understanding of what is human in man. To understand man in the light of the whole means for modern natural science to understand man in the light of the sub-human. But in that light man as man is wholly unintelligible. Classical political philosophy viewed man in a different light. It was originated by Socrates. And Socrates was so far from being committed to a specific cosmology that his knowledge was knowledge of ignorance. Knowledge of ignorance is not ignorance. It is knowledge of the elusive character of the truth, of the whole. Socrates, then, viewed man in the light of the mysterious character of the whole."[50]

Classical philosophy now defends itself against the moderns by adapting elements of the language of revelation. Whereas revelation says that the intelligibility of the world and of human life depends upon belief in a mysterious God, the philosophical thesis as Strauss sees it depends upon "the light of the mysterious character of the whole." That these are not quite the same assertion is strongly suggested by a passage from the closing paragraph of Strauss's famous reply to Alexandre Kojève. Strauss observes that the idea of philosophy itself requires legitimation. He then contrasts his own "hypothesis" about philosophy with that held by Kojève: "I assume, then, that there is an eternal and immutable order within which history takes place, and which remains entirely unaffected by history."[51] A mystery is replaced by a hypothesis or assumption. But the shift is not strong enough to refute Kojève, let alone Heidegger. The superiority of rival hypotheses can be demonstrated only by deriving their consequences, and in philosophy this means something more than stating the fundamental alternatives. One could therefore defend modernity, or the replacement of knowledge of ignorance by knowledge of knowledge, by saying that we must wait for the *telos* or end of history, not return to the pretheoretical beginnings.

Strauss himself reminds us, with respect to Maimonides' discussion of Aristotle's physics, that one can hardly reconcile the creation *ex nihilo* with the belief in an eternal and immutable order. Still, this view is only an assumption. In short, "knowledge of ignorance" is at once the distinguishing characteristic of the genuinely philosophical life, a characteristic that separates Socrates from the believer, and it is defined in terms of hypotheses and mysteries that attenuate, if they do not dissolve altogether, the difference between philosophy and revelation. Differently stated, the life of the knowledge of ignorance is supported and guided by the pretheoretical or commonsensical accessibility of nature, whereas the life of faith in revelation is a direct rejection of common sense and a tacit denial of the notion of regulative nature, whether pre- or posttheoretical. Strauss both distinguishes and blends together these two distinct lives. The great riddle of his work is whether he does so intentionally or unintentionally. The riddle is what to make of Strauss's statements to the effect that "the whole as primarily known is an object of common sense,"[52] or that the discovery of human nature is as it were pre-cosmological and pre-ontological,[53] as opposed to his talk about hypotheses and assumptions.

Yet Strauss puzzles us further with a strange reference to Socratic piety in his most extensive published analysis of Aristotle's *Politics*. Strauss distinguishes between Socrates and Plato on the one hand and Aristotle on the other. For the former, "while the roots of the whole are hidden, the whole manifestly consists of heterogeneous parts." Nothing is said here about knowledge of these parts. Instead, Strauss speaks of the Socratic turn to common sense and "the highest opinions," which are the pronouncements of the law, in accord with which "a pious man will . . . not investigate the divine things but only the human things. It is the greatest proof of Socrates' piety that he limited himself to the study of the human things. His wisdom is knowledge of ignorance because it is pious and it is pious because it is knowledge of ignorance."[54] This passage blurs the distinction between the philosophical and the religious life on the decisive point.

As to Aristotle, in *Natural Right and History*, Strauss makes the validity of Aristotle's political philosophy contingent upon a solution to the problem posed by physics of whether modern science is teleological. In *The City and Man*, Strauss says that "Aristotle's cosmology, as distinguished from Plato's, is unqualifiedly separable from the quest for the best political order."[55] In unpublished lectures from the 1960s on the *Nicomachean Ethics*, Strauss says that Aristotle's apparently circular reliance upon the existence of virtuous persons to train others in genuine virtue depends upon the eternity of the cosmos, and so of human cities, and hence of political philosophers. But for Aristotle, we know that piety is not a virtue and his corpus does not sustain the thesis that he was an advocate of knowledge of ignorance. Strauss evidently leans upon Aristotle's authority in one set of texts and silently rejects him as un-Socratic in others. But even more confusingly, he presents us with contradictory statements about the crucial question of the relation between physics and politics in Aristotle's teaching.

Strauss pays very little attention to physics, or more broadly, to the inner nature of modern science, not because he denies its extraordinary power but because the problem of cosmology is for him relevant only as it illuminates the nature of human life. Modern science becomes defective to the degree that it obscures the whole, or let us say the place of human beings as human within the whole, and so as a heterogeneous element of nature that cannot be reduced to the super- or subhuman. Strauss does spend considerable time in tracing the influence of modern science on the history of philosophy. For our purposes we can summarize that influence as one that reduces the human to the subhuman. By rejecting the commonsense beginning of everyday political life, scientific philosophy replaced the concrete with abstractions, and thereby arrived at an abstract version of the concrete.[56] In short, philosophy is for Strauss primarily political, not scientific, although science of course plays an essential role within the economy of political life. The whole is the whole of common sense, not of Newton, Einstein, or quantum mechanics. It is the whole of noetic heterogeneity.

The question thus reduces to, or let us say intensifies into, the question of Strauss's understanding of Socratic philosophy. And this brings us to the doctrine of the Ideas. To employ the phrase I introduced a moment ago, Strauss endorses the Socratic beginning from "noetic heterogeneity," that is, Socrates begins from the recognition that the whole is articulated into distinct natural kinds. I cite the following pivotal statement:

> Only if there is essential heterogeneity can there be an essential difference between political things and things which are not political. The discovery of noetic heterogeneity permits one to let things be what they are and takes away the compulsion to reduce essential differences to something common. The discovery of noetic heterogeneity means the vindication of what one could call common sense. Socrates called it a return from madness to sanity or sobriety, or, to use the Greek term, *sophrosyne,* which I would translate as moderation. Socrates discovered the paradoxical fact that, in a way, the most important truth is the most obvious truth, or the truth of the surface.[57]

Here Strauss states explicitly the easy transition from the commonsensical approach to human things to the recognition and investigation of natural kinds. He is obviously implying that this Socratic discovery is the basis for the subsequent elaboration of the doctrine or hypothesis of the so-called Platonic Ideas. But there are two serious difficulties here. The first is that the principle of noetic heterogeneity seems to remove the difference between Plato and Aristotle, to disconnect politics from physics for Plato as well (or at least for the Platonic Socrates). Yet, we have just seen that Strauss distinguishes between Plato and Aristotle on this very point, and he even refers to the famous passage in the *Phaedrus* in which Socrates says that, in order to know the nature of the soul, one must understand divine nature.[58]

The second difficulty is perhaps even more important. Whereas the discovery of noetic heterogeneity is a mark of sanity, common sense, or moderation, the doctrine of Ideas is a product of philosophical madness or extreme daring. Strauss, when speaking of the *Republic,* says, "The doctrine which Socrates expounds to his interlocutors is very hard to understand; to begin with, it is utterly incredible, not to say that it appears to be fantastic. . . . No one has ever succeeded in giving a satisfactory or clear account of this doctrine of Ideas. It is possible however to define rather precisely the central difficulty." In the continuation, the difficulty seems to reside in two points, (1) the "separation" of the Idea from its particulars, and (2) the attribution of Ideas not only to mathematical forms and moral properties but to things of all kinds, including artifacts like beds.[59]

Please note that we have moved from Socratic piety to Socratic common sense and moderation and now to a daring and even fantastic philosophical hypothesis. Strauss seems to soften the fantastic quality of the hypothesis in other texts. For example, in a previously cited passage, Strauss is discussing the Socratic knowledge of ignorance and, contrary to his view in other texts, its detachment from any specific cosmology: "Knowledge of ignorance is not ignorance. It is knowledge of the elusive character of the truth, of the whole. Socrates, then, viewed man in the light of the mysterious character of the whole. He held therefore that we are more familiar with the situation of man as man than with the ultimate causes of that situation. We may also say he viewed man in the light of the unchangeable ideas, i.e. of the fundamental and permanent problems. For to articulate the situation of man means to articulate man's openness to the whole."[60]

I call attention once more to the apparent fluctuation in Strauss's understanding of the connection between nature, and so physics, on the one hand, and politics on the other. If noetic heterogeneity emerges from common sense but leads to the Ideas, does it bypass nature? This is obviously impossible. If politics is to be independent of physics, there must be two senses of "nature," one human and the other cosmic. But this would lead us away from Socrates and toward modern philosophy.

Otherwise stated, Aristotle's political philosophy is on this hypothesis no longer embarrassed by his erroneous cosmological physics. The quarrel between the ancients and the moderns can be reopened on the political front, regardless of the problems that exist at the deeper and concealed theoretical level. But this quarrel is soon transformed within modernity itself, not into the quarrel between Athens, or Paris, and Jerusalem, but between two different Cartesian descendants: let us say between England and Germany. This is the quarrel between two conceptions of politics, one as common sense and the other as metaphysics.

Even more pressing for the understanding of Strauss, however, is the question how Socrates is aware of the fundamental and permanent problems, given his ignorance of nature, or given his reliance upon common sense. There seems to be here a distinction between the sober and commonsensical recognition of the Ideas or noetic heterogeneity, and the elusive and mysterious notion of the whole. Strauss regularly states that philosophy is awareness of the fundamental problems. But he never tells us how we can discover or understand the foundation. Let me cite one more important text, taken from his extremely interesting reply to Kojève:

> Philosophy as such is nothing but genuine awareness of the problems, i.e. of the fundamental and comprehensive problems. It is impossible to think about these problems without becoming inclined toward a solution, toward one or the other of the very few typical solutions. Yet as long as there is no wisdom but only quest for wisdom, the evidence of all solutions is necessarily smaller than the evidence of the problems. Therefore the philosopher ceases to be a philosopher at the moment at which the 'subjective certainty' of a solution becomes stronger than his awareness of the problematic character of that solution. At that moment the sectarian is born. The danger of succumbing to the attraction of solutions is essential to philosophy which, without incurring this danger, would degenerate into playing with the problems. But the philosopher does not necessarily succumb to this danger, as is shown by Socrates, who never belonged to a sect and never founded one.[61]

Once more we catch a glimpse of a Socrates who is neither a system-builder or Cartesian nor an inadequate alternative to revelation. My point is not that Strauss is wrong, but that he owes us an account of how the Socratic path between Scylla and Charybdis can be maintained without shipwreck. And we need to know whether Socrates is or is not a genuine alternative to Moses and Abraham.

To summarize this line of reflections, academic philosophy, whether empiricist, phenomenological, or scientific, is marked by what Strauss called "the charm of competence"[62] or the construction of ingenious technical artifacts called "theories." I think that Strauss, like Wittgenstein, is right to scorn the excessively technical conception of philosophy, and to deny that artifactual originality or the ability to construct philosophical "systems" is by itself a sign of philosophical depth or genuine originality.[63] But the difficulty remains. If the Ideas are problems, then the foundation is problematic. Does it make sense to speak of problematic problems? Is this another instance of an esoteric interpretation of an esoteric interpretation of an esoteric teaching?

Thus far in my exposition, I have documented every point with citations from the Straussian corpus. In my conclusion, I put the texts to one side and indulge in speculation; whether mad or sober it is not for me to say.

Our study of Strauss's texts has terminated in an impasse or aporia. The quarrel between Athens and Jerusalem is formulated in terms of an equivocation on the nature of philosophy as fluctuating between Socrates and Descartes. The Socratic conception of philosophy is weakened to the point that it accepts at least part of the fundamental premise of Jerusalem. Philosophy remains within the camp of poetry; the quarrel between the two, if it occurs at all, is internecine or political rather than cosmic or philosophical.

There is good reason to infer from Strauss's texts that the truly secret teaching is the impossibility of philosophy, an impossibility that must be concealed from the human race for its own salvation. That is to say, philosophy, understood as the quest for universal knowledge, for the replacement of opinions by knowledge, for knowledge of the whole, is impossible. We are left with knowledge of ignorance. No wonder that philosophy, as Strauss conceives it, is incapable of refuting revelation. One could almost be persuaded to entertain the hypothesis that the main difference between Strauss and Wittgenstein is exoteric. That is, Strauss believes that philosophy is a noble lie, whereas Wittgenstein regards it as neither noble nor base but harmful. On this reading, both thinkers were psychiatrists whose therapies, sometimes similar and more often different, were directed to two different conceptions of spiritual health.

I leave this as a conjecture. Nor do I mean to imply in so doing that I know it to be true but am unwilling to affirm it. On the contrary, the conjecture may well be literally false while symbolically illuminating. In speaking about Strauss, we should understand fully the extraordinary benefits that are to be derived from a fruitful portrait of the ambiguous nature of philosophy. On the other hand, we do no honor to Strauss by refusing to attempt to clarify this ambiguity, and that is to say, we must accept the full significance of his maxim that the depths are contained in the surface, and only in the surface. This is precisely why the surface is itself ambiguous. And its value lies not in itself but in its ambiguous content.

In conclusion, I want to suggest that Wittgenstein and Strauss share the desire to free ordinary language of its theoretical sedimentation, but in two quite different ways. For Wittgenstein, ordinary language is local or historical, whereas Strauss argues that there is a natural dialect that corresponds to the original human character. For Wittgenstein, ordinary language replaces philosophy; for Strauss, ordinary language presents us with philosophy as the surface of depth. As it happens, neither thinker is in a position to demonstrate his characteristic thesis, because history is unintelligible if there is no common and therefore ahistorical language, whereas the common language always manifests itself within a particular set of historical presuppositions. Having demonstrated to his own satisfaction the impossibility of philosophy in the form of a complete or systematic speech, Wittgenstein lapsed into silence, that is, a silence in which he continued to say what could not be said at ever greater length, as embodied in a manuscript of ever increasing and contracting size. When all is said and done, this is not so different from the procedure of Leo Strauss, who multiplied his *Ur*-text in a stream of particular studies, but who never clearly identified the victors of his two signature quarrels: Athens versus Jerusalem, and the ancients versus the moderns.

Chapter 5 Moore on Common Sense

My intention in this chapter is to get clear on the relation between common sense and ordinary language, with special attention to the use of these terms in the approaches to philosophy that are characteristic of G. E. Moore, John Austin, and Paul Grice, to mention three important examples. I say "special attention," but I want to emphasize that my concern is with the theoretical issues and not with constructing an accurate historical account of this or that school, or set of schools, of philosophizing. I shall seek assistance from these eminent predecessors in clarifying the relation between common sense and ordinary language, but the last responsibility, as always in philosophy, is my own.

The topics of ordinary language and common sense are closely related in one way and quite different in another. A language is a set of procedures for constructing intelligible units of communication. Common sense, on the other hand, is a faculty of judgment. The terms "ordinary" and "common," however, suggest a deeper connection. It is a simple step to the inference that ordinary language is that which is spoken normally or usually within some specified linguistic community, as defined by some particular natural language or languages. An analogous step lets us infer that common sense belongs to the majority of a designated population, and perhaps to all of its members. But this inference is not quite so straightforward as the first. Whereas every normal member of a linguistic community speaks ordinary language by definition, it does not follow that every normal person in a given society possesses common sense. I will come back to this philosophically important point below.

Ordinary language is not what linguists call a "natural" language like English or French. It is a theoretical construction, an ideal representation of how we normally use our native tongue in nontechnical circumstances. Standard rules of grammar and dictionary meanings of words clearly play a large role in determining what the "plain man" or "ordinary speaker" would say in a given case. But these rules and meanings will not suffice to provide a rigorous definition of ordinary language. We need to know idiomatic expressions that are currently in widespread use, as well as unusual senses of common words, including expressions that are technically ungrammatical but that nevertheless regularly occur. In addition, the expression "nontechnical" is extremely vague. No one would call the terminology of quantum mechanics a part of ordinary language, but what about expressions taken from agriculture or carpentry? Nor is it easy to distinguish between poetry and prose in all cases, and the widespread use of figures of speech in everyday discourse makes it difficult to cite a standard by which expressions can be rigorously classified as ordinary or extraordinary. Then, too, ordinary language is continuously changing; what was correct in one time and place may not be so in another. Furthermore, the philosophical importance of ordinary language is not self-evident. A knowledge of, say, ordinary English does not tell us what to say but only how to say it.

Last, ordinary language "will often have become infected with the jargon of extant theories, and our own prejudices, too, as the upholders or imbibers of theoretical views, will be too readily, and often insensibly, engaged."[1] For this reason John Austin recommends that we prefer a field of ordinary language that is not too trodden down by traditional philosophy. This advice is reminiscent of Leo Strauss's thesis that, by returning to the pretheoretical political discourse of the ancient Greeks, we avoid contaminating our access to human nature by the philosophical and ideological language that has accumulated around it through the tradition. Both suggestions suffer from the same defect; they assume that ordinary or pretheoretical language has no philosophical or theoretical presuppositions of its own. Nevertheless, we have to start somewhere, and the suggestions are not entirely unreasonable. Everyday language has a certain priority, even if we are attempting to deviate from it.

Ordinary language philosophy is of course not restricted to the activity of collating normal usages. In his defense of ordinary language philosophy, Paul Grice cites G. E. Moore's distinction between knowing what an expression means and knowing its analysis. Grice builds on the distinction in order to explain the philosophical activity of conceptual analysis. According to him, I understand an expression E if I can use it correctly in particular cases. As a philosopher, however, "I am looking for a general characterization of the types of cases in which one would apply E rather than withhold it."[2] The pursuit of such a characterization is called "conceptual analysis." Although Grice notes that conceptual analysis can be applied outside of philosophy, we are primarily concerned with its philosophical use, and here it seems fair to say that, in Grice's account, there is an intimate connection between conceptual analysis and the knowledge of ordinary language.

In an immediately following passage (172), Grice states two propositions to which he subscribes. The first is that it is an important part of philosophy "to analyze, describe, or characterize (in as general terms as possible) the ordinary use or uses of certain expressions or classes of expressions. If I philosophize about the notion of cause, or about perception, or about knowledge and belief, I expect to find myself considering, among other things, in what sort of situations we should in our ordinary talk, be willing to speak (or again be unwilling to speak) of something as causing something else to happen; or again of someone as seeing a tree; or again of someone as knowing rather than merely believing that something is the case."

There is a second and less obvious sense in which Grice gives the palm to ordinary language. In the following passage Grice distinguishes between ordinary language philosophy and the conducting of polls to determine whether his analysis corresponds to that of others. "For one thing, I assume (justifiably, I think) that it does in general fit other people's use, for the expressions with which (as a philosopher) I am normally concerned are pretty commonly used ones; and if a particular expression E was given by some of the people with whom I talk in my daily life a substantially different use from the one which I gave to it, then I should almost certainly have discovered this; one does discover people's linguistic idiosyncrasies." Grice adds that, even if this assumption is mistaken, his analysis will be of use to himself and others who agree with him (175).

It is not entirely clear in this second passage whether Grice means by "commonly used [expressions]" those that are part of ordinary language, or whether he is referring to the technical discourse of his professional colleagues. In either case, Grice refers to people with whom he talks in his daily life. Taking this together with the previous citation, it seems fair to draw two inferences. First, Grice selects from the linguistic habits of his close associates topics that are worthy of conceptual analysis. Second, he inspects these topics in the light of what we ordinarily say about causes, perceptions, knowledge, and the like.

Grice says explicitly that he is not committed to banning nonordinary uses of language from the scrutiny of the philosopher. "The only restriction is that a philosopher who uses a technical term should recognize that it is a technical term and therefore stands in need of a special explanation" (172–73). This seems fair enough, but Grice does not make clear how we will decide that certain technical uses of an expression are acceptable whereas others are not. If the standard is that they can be rephrased in ordinary language, then the permission to employ nonordinary expressions has in effect been rescinded. We are left with our original problem of how to decide what constitutes ordinary usage. Since we have ruled out the conducting of polls, or even the relying upon a dictionary, it seems that we must fall back on the linguistic habits of those with whom we converse in everyday or professional life. If, on the other hand, it is acceptable for philosophers to provide technical (as Grice refers to nonordinary) expressions in the analysis of their technical terms, then we may bypass or jettison ordinary language entirely, once the definitions of our technical terms have been given.

That, or else we are permitted to define and restrict the authority of ordinary language in nonordinary, technical ways. Grice seems to rule out this alternative by his statement that the terms with which he as a philosopher is normally concerned are "pretty commonly used ones." Those who employ uncommon terms in nonordinary ways will presumably be left to their own devices, but the upshot of this generosity (if it is indeed extended) is to transform philosophy into a series of noncommunicating linguistic sects. No doubt Grice and others could argue plausibly that there is an ordinary language common to all members of philosophical sects, regardless of their professional idiom, but this does nothing to establish the philosophical authority of that common language. We may grant that the common or ordinary language is the linguistic stratum from which all technical idioms, philosophical or otherwise, are generated, while still holding that it is the task of the technical languages to analyze the conceptual coherence of ordinary language, not the reverse. Even the practice of ordinary language philosophy depends upon technical terms and procedures. Above all, that practice depends upon certain philosophical presuppositions as to what constitutes legitimate philosophical discourse. Austin in effect asserts this in the previously cited passage from his work.

These various problems are, however, in no way sufficient to lead us to repudiate the role of ordinary language in philosophical analysis. It is intrinsic to the nature of a language that it be capable of producing many standard utterances for a wide range of occurrences, and in particular for the most common occurrences of everyday life. In many cases, a disregard for ordinary language will lead to breakdowns in communication. But it is equally obvious that the attempt to restrict all speech within a community to ordinary language (assuming for the moment that we know what that is) would be intolerable. We should be unable to express any innovation; and science, art, and philosophy would soon come to a halt. No ordinary language philosopher would advocate such restrictions. Grice certainly is not such a philosopher. But the amorphousness of the concept of ordinary language leads even the best members of those who advocate it to paradoxical, circular, or incoherent formulations of the nature of their enterprise.

Reflections of this sort lead to my calling ordinary language "the standard idiom." Unless there is some good reason to shift to another idiom, or to introduce new terms for unusual experiences and concepts, this is the language we speak. Our mere discovery that someone is violating ordinary usage contributes nothing of philosophical interest. Philosophy begins (if at all) when we ask for the justification of this linguistic innovation. I have no reason to doubt that part of this justification will itself be constructed in ordinary language, since that is the basis for all our subsequent production of extraordinary discourse. When we wish to innovate in language, we say something like this: "By so and so, I shall mean such and such," where "so and so" is the new, technical, nonstandard expression, and "such and such" refers to the phenomena to which we now wish to refer. The phenomena in question require linguistic innovation because they strain at the leash of ordinary experience and discourse. They cannot be completely detached from ordinary language. If they were, there would be no way in which to express their novelty. But they cannot be reduced to ordinary language without diminishing our intellectual and spiritual life.

A tension exists between ordinary and extraordinary language that cannot be removed without dissolving human nature. The problem of sense perception is certainly illuminated by a close analysis of what we do and say when we see a tree or some other everyday object, as Grice suggests. I furthermore endorse

Grice's assertion that "it is almost certainly (perhaps quite certainly) wrong to reject as false, absurd, or linguistically incorrect some class of ordinary statements if this rejection is based merely on philosophical grounds. If for example a philosopher advances a philosophical argument to show that we do not in fact ever see trees and books and human bodies, despite the fact that in a variety of familiar situations we would ordinarily say that we do, then our philosopher is almost (perhaps quite) certainly wrong" (172).[3] As it stands, this proposition can be easily confirmed by the fact that the philosopher in question would have to appeal to our perception of trees, books, and bodies in order to deny that we see them; presumably he or she would mean that what we perceive are actually ideas or illusory manifestations of something else. No philosophical doctrine can be sound if it denies the very experience that produces philosophical inquiry.

But the more closely we analyze the process of sense perception, or the conceptual structure of intelligibility that underlies our capacity to identify anything at all as "this thing here of such-and-such a kind" (an Aristotelian expression), the more we pass from ordinary to nonordinary language. And this passage deepens our understanding of ordinary *experience*.

It is extremely important to distinguish between ordinary language and ordinary experience. Philosophical problems arise when we encounter aspects of ordinary experience that cannot be described or expressed in ordinary language. This is obvious in science, where technical expressions are introduced to refer to phenomena that cannot be explained by what was previously regarded as "ordinal" within the science itself. It makes no difference whether the "ordinal" in this context is the everyday experience from which science originates, or some technically advanced stage of knowledge that suddenly breaks down or requires supplementation. It is not what we ordinarily say that determines what can legitimately be said, but the adequacy of what we say to what we are now experiencing. And the same situation applies in philosophy. In general, linguistically oriented philosophies tend to give too much importance to language from the outset; despite occasional disclaimers, they tend to conceive of experience as itself a linguistic artifact. But that is a technical view, based upon complex and sophisticated philosophical arguments, which in turn must stand or fall on the basis of our experience. We do not "bespeak" experience, as a Heideggerian might put it.

Consider as an example the term "essence," which was much abused in the circles of ordinary language philosophy, until it received a kind of rehabilitation from modal logic. As soon as we notice that things present themselves as this or that (and whoever has not noticed this is not having any linguistic or conceptual experience at all), and that they retain this identity in such a way as to allow us to act and speak on the basis of their stability, we possess the framework for taking into account change and irregularity. Without that framework, there is no change, that is, no intelligible change but only chaos. This is the simple observation that underlies the introduction of philosophical terms like "essence," "form," and "nature." Stated with equal simplicity, essence is the way in which the thing holds itself together so as to allow it to present itself with sufficient stability to permit us to speak about it. This does not mean that we see the essence of, say, a cow, standing next to the cow, or better, inside it, and holding together its defining properties with some sort of magic grip. An essence is a theoretical entity that is introduced in order to explain something obvious about our experience. No clarity is achieved by saying that there are no essences but only things, because to be a thing is to be something, and something that is necessarily a thing of the sort it is; but this necessity is essential. One might object: "the thing could turn into something else." Perhaps so, but then the same story would have to be repeated about the newly manifested thing. Whether this elementary reasoning justifies a metaphysics of separate essences is another and infinitely longer story. But the story cannot be conducted entirely in the idiom of ordinary language, any more than can the story of quantum mechanics or cosmology. Ordinary language is a way of saying things, and it is tautologously the ordinary way of saying those things. But it is not a confirmation that the ordinary way of saying something is the best way. That will depend upon the circumstances, and in particular, upon what we want to say.

The situation of common sense is somewhat different. This can be illustrated in an introductory way as follows. It is appropriate to ask someone: "Don't you have any common sense?" if that person behaves in ways that are normally recognized to show poor judgment. But it would be odd to ask someone who had just made a grammatical error or misused a common word: "Don't you speak ordinary language?" In the first place, grammatical errors and misuses of words are a common aspect of ordinary language. They are excluded from the canonical or "textbook" variety of a language, say English, but that does not make them extraordinary. Instead, it makes them technically incorrect. Philosophers who are trying to discredit unusual speech, for example, that of traditional metaphysics, cite standard or textbook English to establish legitimate uses of expressions in that language. But in many cases, standard English may be less ordinary than colloquial English in which the textbook rules are broken. But if nonstandard or colloquial, and even incorrect, expressions are a legitimate part of ordinary language, then why should not metaphysical expressions be included as well? Is it true that ordinary language contains no metaphysical expressions? What about the language of myth, superstition, and religion?

Once again we see quite easily that whereas ordinary language exists, however amorphously, it entirely lacks the rigidly exclusive nature that is attributed to it by ordinary language analysts, including those who ostensibly celebrate the great number of subtle distinctions that the language incorporates. We might well say that "there are more things in ordinary language than are dreamt of in your philosophy" to these practitioners of linguistic purity.

There is one more remark that needs to be made in this connection. Despite their occasional fascination for humble sentences like "the cat is on the mat," ordinary language philosophers are not interested in all of ordinary language: they are primarily concerned with the standard uses of words that play a role in traditional philosophy, metaphysics, or some ostensibly impure sample of philosophical discourse that needs to be disinfected. Examples are the aforementioned "essence," "form," and "nature," a list that might be extended at length. Among the most discussed expressions of this sort are the various forms of the verb "to be," together with the mysterious set of words having "nothing" as their focal meaning.

The main purpose of ordinary language philosophy is to show that a traditional use of a term or expression in the philosophical literature violates ordinary usage and is therefore nonsense. But apart from the fact that the suspect terms often themselves appear as a part of ordinary usage ("Where did you go?" "Nowhere." "What did you do?" "Nothing."), the objectionable character of the traditional use cannot be established by its deviation from ordinary usage, since the terms in question are explicitly held to receive extraordinary senses. If this creation of senses is forbidden in philosophy, it must be equally illegitimate in all forms of technical discourse. In fact, the ban on traditionally nonordinary uses of certain words or expressions is rooted, not in a rigid adherence to the ordinary idiom but rather to complicated philosophical arguments, of varying degrees of cogency, that are themselves not at all parts of ordinary language. The appeal to ordinary language is bogus in this crucial sense: it is made after the fact, as a means of sustaining refutations that are not themselves based upon ordinary language. We require a technical philosophical justification for the claim that "substance" or "essence" is misused by metaphysicians like Aristotle or Aquinas, not the flippant reply that these uses would be nonsense for the plain man in the street.

The second point of difference between ordinary language and common sense is that it is much harder not to speak ordinary language than it is to act contrary to common sense. Let us look more closely at this expression. There are two senses of "sense"; one refers to the sensory powers of the living organism, including vision and hearing; the other refers to the meaning of an expression, or, as those who dislike meanings on metaphysical grounds would say, the expression's use. To the classical scholar, "common sense" strikes an immediate echo of Aristotle's *koine aisthesis,* or the grasping of the unified object of sense perception through the operation of the several sensory powers. But this is clearly a specialized sense of the term, very far removed from what we mean in English by "common sense." It would be interesting to investigate the ways in which natural languages express what we call in English "common sense," but the point is peripheral to our investigation, since it is not the expression but the concept that concerns us. One or two examples will suffice. The French have *le sens commun* as well as *le bon sens,* which bring out very well the ambiguity in the English equivalent (essentially the same distinction occurs in Italian). Common sense presumably belongs, or is at least accessible, to everyone, whereas not all sense is good. The German *gesunder Menschenverstand* (healthy human understanding) stands closer to *le bon sens* and thus leaves open the question of community.

The OED entry for "common sense" yields the following information. The first definition is the Aristotelian sense: the "common bond or center of the five senses." The second: "The endowment of natural intelligence possessed by rational beings; ordinary, normal, or average understanding; the plain wisdom which is every man's inheritance. (This is 'common sense' at its minimum, without which a man is foolish or insane)." More emphatically: "Good sound practical sense; combined tact and readiness in dealing with the everyday affairs of life; general sagacity."

Let us refer for convenience henceforth to the *minimal* and *maximal* senses of "common sense" (using English throughout as our example of a natural language). The minimal sense is possessed by every person of ordinary, normal, or average intelligence. The maximal sense comes closer to prudence or the special aptitude for dealing with practical affairs. "General sagacity" is not sagacity possessed by everyone but rather sagacity that functions generally, over the wide spectrum of practical circumstances. Even if we distinguish the maximal sense from prudence, it remains the case that general sagacity is not common to all human beings.

If we put to one side for a moment the distinction between minimal and maximal common sense, another point of extreme importance follows from the definitions just given. Common sense is a faculty, not a body of beliefs. We are often told that the propositions certified by common sense vary from one age to another. This is surely an exaggeration. Common sense (whether rightly or wrongly) has been certifying the existence of the external world and beings other than ourselves for a good many millennia, to mention no other examples. This certification rests upon an inference roughly as follows: The evidence for the existence of the world and its inhabitants is altogether greater than the evidence for solipsism, and it is sensible to draw the conclusion that is supported by the most compelling evidence.

If we suppose for the sake of argument that the case for solipsism is suddenly made in so compelling a manner that I immediately adopt that position, my inference cannot be called a result of common sense, since "common" implies "more than one." If I attribute my conversion to common sense, I am saying that all sensible persons, whether in the minimal or maximal sense, are or should be solipsists. And this is a self-contradiction. But it is unnecessary to examine more closely the ramifications of this line of argument. The serious point is that common sense holds to one view or another on the basis of a process of reasoning. That reasoning is sound if it is sustained by desirable results, or if it allows us to draw just that inference that is supported by the best facts now available. One can therefore draw up a list of propositions that we hold to be verified by common sense without being required to assert that these propositions are absolutely certain. Every proposition on the list could be refuted without impugning the excellence of common sense, provided that each of the propositions was the most warranted thesis at the time about the particular point at issue.

But this is not quite correct. I have to add a crucial qualification. The propositions held by common sense must fall within its jurisdiction. Common sense has no authority to pronounce upon black holes, anti-matter, or Fermat's last theorem. Why then should it be consulted on the question of the existence of the external world? It is perhaps a matter of common sense to trust the evidence of our senses. We do not reject these faculties because they occasionally err, any more than we discard our reason because we sometimes make mistakes in logic. But sense perception and reason do indeed err from time to time, and this leads us to be cautious in asserting that something is absolutely certain. Even greater caution is required to resist extending the application of common sense outside its sphere of competence.

No person of average intelligence is in a position to demonstrate that the external world exists, or for that matter that it does not exist. Nor would it occur to such a person to make the attempt. He or she might *believe* wholeheartedly in that existence, in the passive sense that it never occurred to them to question it. They might reject such a denial, should they be exposed to it, with incredulity, and perhaps say something like: "Can't you *see* that the world exists?" This is a minimalist argument to the effect that the perceptible existence of the world is its own certification. A person of general sagacity might take a few more steps in constructing a maximalist argument: "No sane person doubts the evidence of the senses" and so on. But maximal common sense has as its proper sphere questions of practice and everyday life. A maximal practical argument for the existence of the external world is not a philosophical argument, because philosophy goes beyond common sense, just as does science. I would not deny, but in fact assert, that philosophical arguments are often born in the musings of the person of maximal common sense. But this does not abolish the distinction between the two. It does not make the assertion "common sense tells me that the external world exists" into a philosophical argument. The argument becomes philosophical only when detailed reasons are given for relying upon the evidence of common sense.

It is of course true that there exist no rigorous criteria by which to distinguish between commonsense reasoning and philosophical argumentation. One is tempted to say that the distinction is itself a matter of common sense. But this is to say that philosophers require common sense, even though persons of common sense do not require philosophy. Just as ordinary language can be helpful in calling our attention to odd characteristics of philosophical speech that require further justification, so general sagacity is an important tool in the discrimination of general philosophical claims. But neither the one nor the other will perform the various technical tasks that their philosophical admirers have often set for them.

There is, however, a crucial difference between common sense and ordinary language that makes the former more philosophical than the latter. For common sense to work, it must understand not just how people use language but how they behave, and even further, how the world "works," regardless of the idiom in which we describe its processes. This being so, we can distinguish between sense and foolishness, whether in our own society or in that of others, by the criterion of success, regardless of whether we accept or reject for ourselves the particular conception of desirable outcomes. But we cannot say that one idiom of ordinary language is more successful than another, if our standard is merely what people in a given linguistic community say, or are very likely to say, under such-and-such circumstances.

With every allowance for variation in idiomatic discourse, every example of ordinary language is a correct exemplification of ordinary language. Some languages may strike us as more elegant or beautiful, others as more highly developed and capable of articulating an unusual number of distinctions. But this takes us beyond the express function of ordinary language as it is employed by its philosophical admirers. Otherwise put, there is a difference between "ordinary" and *standard* language, say English; and even standard English differs from England to America to Australia. The reference by philosophers to ordinary language creates the illusory impression that standard English (to continue with this example) is theoretically superior to its disheveled cousins of the ordinary persuasion. In fact, it creates the illusion that standard English just *is* ordinary English. But I am arguing that the actual situation is much more complex. Standard English is the idealization of ordinary English, which latter cannot be precisely codified in its own terms because, as a living tongue, it is continuously being modified and even misused without any radical discontinuity in intelligibility. I think this shows that it is not language that wears the trousers, to borrow an Oxonian expression, but understanding. Understanding cannot be the same as speaking, because we understand deviant speech-forms. We grasp linguistic novelty, and this requires that at some point, we do not simply translate one expression into another but (in an important sense of both words) *see* or grasp what is being said.

The point is that there is certainly a connection between ordinary language and its deviant dialect, philosophy. The latter emerges from the former, just as does standard English, but the two newcomers are not the same nor must one be reduced to or translated back into the other. Ordinary language, as the mother of us all, makes an indispensable gift to each, the gift of life. We do not repay this gift by extinguishing the new life within the maternal womb. In somewhat different terms, the attempt to show how traditional metaphysics differs from standard English is not itself an exercise in the reduction of metaphysics to ordinary language. But even if it were, the disappearance of philosophical language hardly counts as a demonstration of its nonsense or a clarification of its meaning. Whether clarity is enough, linguistic provincialism is not the same as clarity. What we want, then, is not the clarification of philosophy by means of standard or even ordinary language but rather the clarification of standard and ordinary languages by their philosophical offspring. This is already evident in the practices of the ordinary language philosopher, whose dialect is not ordinary but technical.

I can now draw together my points about the difference between ordinary language and common sense. Every example of ordinary language, the language by which human beings communicate with each other in the constant process of producing extraordinary modes of discourse, is correct by virtue of being ordinary. We can say with Wittgenstein, if not quite in his spirit, that ordinary language is all right. (It is essential to remember here the distinction between ordinary and standard language.) But not every example of ordinary language is also an example of common sense.

The statement "The cat is on the mat" is ordinary as well as standard, but it is neither sensible nor foolish. Instead, it is true or false. If I say, with respect to a particular cat and mat, that the cat is on the mat when the cat is not on the mat, then the statement is false. It would be going too far to say that all false statements are foolish; not all those who are mistaken are fools. But neither is it quite right to say that all those who utter true statements are sensible. Some fools can utter true statements. Rather than distinguishing between "being correct" and "not being part of ordinary language," I think it is better to distinguish between "sensible" and "foolish" as designating the possession or the lack of common sense. For perfectly understandable reasons, I may think that the cat is on the mat when it is not: a trick of the light, a movement to one side that distracts my attention, mistaking a raccoon for a cat, and so on. But once these mistakes have been identified, it then becomes foolish to insist that the cat is nevertheless on the mat. The example is an extreme one, but of a sort that enjoys a certain popularity in philosophical debates. It will also be helpful in preparing us to deal with G. E. Moore's defense of common sense, to which I shall turn shortly. Let us therefore take it one step farther. It shows a lack of common sense to doubt one's senses when there is no good reason to do so. But it does not follow that the evidence of our senses is indubitable. On the other hand, the form of common sense that expresses itself in judgments about alternative courses of action either issues a sensible judgment or it does not. If it does not, then the judgment was not one of common sense. If it does, then common sense is tautologously sensible. It cannot err in the sense of uttering a foolish judgment without ceasing to be what it is. That is why we say to people who disregard sensible advice: "You should have acted as he suggested."

To sum up, it is sensible to trust one's senses under the right conditions, but there is no absolute guarantee that the evidence the senses provide is sound. It is sensible to follow good advice, which is to say that only sensible people will make sound judgments about which viewpoint is sensible (although even a fool can make a lucky guess). But there is a difference between sensible advice and advice that obtains the desired end. The most we can say is that if we are sensible, we will never, or almost never, make bad decisions about matters of common sense. But we may still fail on occasion because of circumstances beyond our control. This is an important difference between truth and common sense. If it is true that the cat is on the mat, then it is simply or absolutely true (although we may not be absolutely certain for one reason or another). But a sound piece of advice can fail, despite the common sense of the advisor.

G. E. Moore begins his famous essay "A Defense of Common Sense," with a list of propositions, "every one of which (in my own opinion) I *know*, with certainty, to be true" (32).[4] The list need not be quoted in its entirety; each of the propositions expresses a fact about Moore's own existence at the time of writing the essay, or about the condition of the world before, during, and after his own life-span. Examples are: "There exists at present a living human body, which is *my* body," and "This body was born at a certain time in the past" (33). Moore's list is reminiscent of Husserl's various descriptions of the formal structure of the life-world, with the significant difference that he replaces transcendental description with the commonsensical knowledge of facts that he personally claims to know with certitude to be true. The structure of Moore's "life-world" is directly accessible to every normal person and requires no elaborate methodological purifications on our part. Nevertheless, the content of the propositions in his list is general or abstract in the sense that (according to Moore) each of us could draw up a similar list with statements that relativize the existence and properties of the world to the circumstances of our own historical life. I, and others like me, are born, grow, and exist on the surface of the earth, occupy dwellings, handle objects, know that the earth existed before we were born and that it will continue to do so after we are dead, and so on.

This general assertion is stated by Moore as follows: "each of *us* . . . has frequently *known*, with regard to *himself* or *his* body and the time at which he knew it, everything which, in writing down my list of propositions . . . , I was claiming to know about *myself* or *my* body and the time at which I wrote that proposition down" (34–35). The act of reflecting upon, and writing down, the relevant list of propositions, is Moore's version of what Husserl calls "transcendental *epoche*," a change in the natural attitude or Moore's world of common sense, a change that (to put it as simply as possible) detaches us from intimate, nontheoretical engagement with life, and so from what Husserl calls its "effective validities," that is, the acts of validation and sense making by which we enact our experience or live it through (for my fuller discussion, see chapter 2).

Suffice it to say here that the transcendental reduction (as Husserl also calls it) makes the world available as "the ground validity for natural life." This ground validity is the world of transcendental subjectivity, in which the individual rises to the level of the absolute ego and views the pure essences of natural or worldly things. The natural world, in sum, is "unthematic" and lived directly, whereas the transcendental world is the thematized object of phenomenological description.[5] In the second world, things, events, beliefs, institutions, and even sciences are all transformed into apodictically certain theoretical intuitions of the universal subjectivity in which each of us shares, and to which we have access thanks to the purifications developed by Husserl.[6]

Up to a point, Moore in effect assigns to the commonsense world alone the role that is played in Husserlian phenomenology by both the natural and the transcendental worlds. The commonsense world is indeed *common* to all human beings, not as a transcendental theme of universal apprehension but as the flow of diverse deeds and speeches of everyday life. There is in everyday life a minimal but necessary amount of prototheoretical abstraction in our recognition that it is the same world into which each of us has a peculiar view or point of access. This degree of abstraction is intensified by the philosophical exercise in which we attempt to characterize commonsense knowledge, but in this attempt we never shift completely from one world, that of common sense, to another, the world of science or philosophy.

Instead of appealing to a transcendental world as the ground of validity of the natural or commonsense world, Moore refers to the commonsense world as the ground of validity of absolutely certain truths (his version of apodictically certain intuitions). These are of course not the sum of all possible truths. Moore is making a point about the truths of common sense precisely in order to have a basis for repudiating nonsensical assertions by other philosophers, and the point is that the absolute status of the truths of common sense plays a role analogous to that which the next generation of linguistic philosophers assigned to ordinary language. Analogous, but not identical. As Austin and others acknowledge, it is appropriate to deviate from ordinary language under certain circumstances, of which the arts and sciences are obvious examples, provided that one states clearly the rationale for the new terms or expressions. No doubt Moore would grant a similar point, but what he calls commonsense propositions cannot by definition be invalidated or doubted. No expansion of knowledge is legitimate that contradicts the propositions in Moore's list. We can add to commonsense knowledge in Moore's sense but we cannot replace it, because to replace it would be to replace the very world in which we live and of which we attempt to acquire theoretical knowledge of its nature. It would be to transform ourselves into some other kind of being.

To sum up, in Moore's account, we are precisely the engaged and historically actual persons of everyday life who, according to Husserl, are not in a position to purify the structure of the life-world from its psychologistic and historical or relativized sedimentation. On the other hand, residents within the commonsense world do not engage in analytical exercises of the sort that currently occupies us. In order to philosophize about the commonsense world, we must partially detach ourselves from it. Part, and perhaps a large part, of our philosophizing about common sense may include the affirmation of the truths that it certifies, but our intention is not simply to reiterate what is obvious to the resident of common sense. Our intention as philosophers is to lay the foundation for the purification of anti-commonsensical philosophies.[7]

Moore goes on to insist at some length (and somewhat awkwardly) that he holds each of the propositions in his list to be wholly true as stated, and in no subtle sense: "I meant by each of them precisely what every reader, in reading them, will have understood me to mean." That is, Moore assumes "that there is some meaning which is *the* ordinary or popular meaning of such expressions as 'The earth has existed for many years past'" (36). And this makes explicit the link between common sense and ordinary language in Moore, a link that is to be found, I believe, in many if not all ordinary language philosophers. "Such an expression as 'The earth has existed for many years past' is the very type of an unambiguous expression, the meaning of which we all understand" (36).

It is important to emphasize that Moore provides no arguments to sustain his thesis about the universal intelligibility of the propositions asserting truths of common sense. Grice makes two general criticisms of Moore's treatment of common sense: "(1) he nowhere attempts to characterize for us the conditions which have to be satisfied by a generally held belief to make it part of a 'Common Sense view of the world'; (2) even if we overlook this complaint, there is the further complaint that nowhere, so far as I know, does Moore justify the claim that the Common Sense view of the world is at least in certain respects unquestionably correct."[8] I think that these criticisms, although correct in one sense, might be partially met by a defender of Moore. What Moore means by common sense is not a faculty but a body of propositions that are self-verifying because immediately given by conscious existence. In slightly different terms, these propositions cannot be denied except by referring to them as already affirmed. For the sake of brevity, I restrict myself to one example. No one can deny that I am holding up my hand despite the appearance that I am doing so, unless he or she sees that I am holding up my hand. Such a denial could not in fact be a denial so much as an interpretation; for example, someone can claim that I am an optical illusion. Moore could meet this objection by saying that the illusion is itself explained as my seeming to hold up my hand. That response is intelligible—i.e., the illusion is effective—if and only if we know immediately what it is to hold up one's hand.

It is not my contention that this defense is satisfactory. But it is worth making because it brings out something that cuts against all attempts to demonstrate the certitude of immediate experience. Moore cannot prove that the propositions of common sense are absolutely certain, since it is for him common sense that provides us with the basis or matrix for the intelligibility of nontrivial propositions. The absolute certitude of Moore's propositions depends entirely upon their immediate intelligibility to persons who have normal faculties and experience, and who speak some natural language. But if I may borrow a distinction from Moore himself, we may know something without being able to prove it. Moore's mistake lies in characterizing as "proofs" assertions like: here is one hand and here is another; therefore material objects exist. This is obviously not a proof since the premiss assumes that hands are material objects. Otherwise it would have been pointless to hold them up as evidence for the conclusion.

The difficulty, however, is not simply that Moore cannot "prove" his statements of common sense. It is rather that common sense is not a body of propositions, but a faculty by which we entertain propositions. I use "entertain" in order to convey that whereas we may be certain at one time of the truth of a proposition, thanks to common sense, we are prepared to give up the proposition in question when the circumstances change. Now in the case of many if not all of Moore's examples, the circumstances may never change; for example, it may never be true of me or anyone else that we can exist without a material body of three dimensions. But Moore's examples of commonsense propositions are all of statements of fact about the material world as relativized to the individual perceiver. There are however many more kinds of propositions endorsed by common sense, and most of them concern practical life. These statements may take for granted the existence and gross structure of the physical world, but they are judgments about how to act, not assertions of sense perception. Moore continues in the long tradition of British empiricism by giving pride of place to sense perception, and this skews his analysis of common sense, which is closer to Aristotle's *koine aisthesis* than to the senses of "common sense" in ordinary language.

Despite my attempt to give Moore partial support, I agree on balance with Grice. To the reasons I have now given, I may add another. It looks very much as though Moore ignores a distinction that I emphasized in the previous section of this chapter. The fact that a statement is intelligible to everyone does not mean that it is true or sensible. I do not mean to suggest that it would be foolish to assert the existence of the earth, but only that Moore's general procedure is unsatisfactory. The reason that it is sensible to affirm the existence of the earth is that the evidence is overwhelming in support of that proposition. I think that Moore assumes that this in itself is a sign of its indubitability on commonsense grounds. But common sense is a faculty, not a body of propositions. Moore might be justified in saying that we find it extremely difficult to doubt propositions that are endorsed by common sense, but this does not establish certitude.

This point comes up toward the end of Moore's essay "Proof of an External World" (149–50).[9] Moore claims that there are many proofs for the existence of external objects, which amount to the showing of the objects in the ordinary way, for example, by holding up one's hands and saying "here are two hands" or something of the sort. This proof turns upon the further (or prior) proof of the truth of the assertion "I did hold up my hands just now." Moore grants that there is no proof of the general statement as to how any propositions like the one just cited may be proved.[10] As the further example about dreaming shows, we can have conclusive reasons for holding that we are awake, or that we have just extended our two hands, but we cannot prove this. I think that this once more confuses plausibility with certitude. "Conclusive evidence" is evidence that leads us to a conclusion, but it does not verify the conclusion with certitude. But the entire difficulty can be avoided by giving up the attempt to prove the positions of common sense. This attempt is not, one is tempted to say, supported by the judgment of common sense itself.

Once again, I am not suggesting that Moore failed to hold up two hands, or that we have any reason to deny that the external world exists. I myself would not know how to describe evidence that would make me jettison belief in the existence of the external world. Suppose that the world were to disappear. Then I too would disappear, in which case, I should not be doubting, or still more strongly denying, the existence of anything. As to hypothetical assumptions, they all depend upon the present existence of someone who assumes them, and so the plausibility of the commonsensical belief in the existence of the external world is reestablished.

After admitting that he has not proved the propositions in question, Moore denies that this diminishes the conclusiveness of his proof by way of holding up his hands. "I can know things, which I cannot prove," among them that I have just held up two hands (150). In other words, he knows the truth of the premises of his argument, even though he cannot prove them. The whole line of reasoning comes down to this. What we know by common sense that we are now doing or have done in the past does not require proof; it is indubitable by the very act of doing (or saying).

With this in mind, let us return to "A Defense of Common Sense." After insisting upon the fact that we all know what it means to say something like "There is a body currently existing that is mine," and further, that we know this proposition (and others like it) to be true, Moore goes on to make a distinction between understanding the meaning of that expression ("which we all certainly do") and to "*know what it means,* in the sense that we are able to *give a correct analysis* of its meaning" (37). The presentation of an analysis, however, according to Moore, is necessary only in extraordinary cases. He says: "The question what is the correct analysis of *the* proposition meant *on any occasion* . . . by 'The earth has existed for many years past' is, it seems to me, a profoundly difficult question, and one to which, as I shall presently urge, no one knows the answer. But to hold that we do not know what, in certain respects, is the analysis of what we understand by such an expression, is an entirely different thing from holding that we do not understand the expression. It is obvious that we cannot even raise the question how what we do understand by it is to be analyzed, unless we do understand it. So soon, therefore, as we know that a person who uses such an expression is using it in its ordinary sense, we understand his meaning. So that in explaining that I was using the expressions . . . in their ordinary sense . . . , I have done all that is required to make my meaning clear" (37).

Since the propositions with which we are concerned are all certified by common sense, which in turn is identified as speaking in the ordinary or popular sense, and since propositions so asserted require no further analysis, the distinction in question between understanding and analysis need not be applied in the present investigation.[11] Whatever it may mean to give an analysis of "the earth has existed for many years past," such an analysis is unnecessary for the business at hand. It therefore cannot verify the claims on behalf of the popular assertions made by persons of common sense, namely, all of us. Instead, Moore's distinction serves to cast doubt on the certitude of commonsensical assertions. Who knows what such an assertion would look like if it were submitted to a proper analysis? But the situation is even worse. For Moore holds that no one knows the answer to the question of the correct analysis of popular assertions. This is an extraordinary admission, since it carries with it the consequence that we cannot, in any given case, distinguish correct from incorrect analyses with respect to the world of experience (formal or mathematical analyses would be in a different category). Philosophical analysis then becomes indistinguishable from poetic invention, and we would have been much better off remaining at the level of common sense.

On the other hand, I entirely agree with Moore that we must first understand an expression before we can analyze it. And this strongly suggests that the "immediate" (my own term) or popular grasp, and this is to say, commonsense understanding, must serve as the basis for discriminating between correct and incorrect analyses. Since common sense speaks ordinary language, we arrive at the conclusion that ordinary language is the criterion for sound philosophical (or properly analyzed) discourse. What we do not arrive at, however, is absolute certitude. In Moore's terms, we know commonsense or popular propositions but we cannot prove them. On the other hand, this knowledge serves as the basis for subsequent proofs, for example, of the existence of the external world. But our analyses of the meanings of these propositions cannot be absolutely verified. In sum: proofs in Moore's sense fall between knowable but unprovable popular or commonsensical knowledge (the axioms of demonstration, so to speak) and analyses of the meanings of propositions that have been proved on the basis of commonsense knowledge. These analyses are interminable; or at least no one knows what it means to say that a given analysis is correct. One can only assume that Moore's endlessly fastidious and involuted analyses are themselves examples of exercises in the unknown, to the extent that they go beyond listing propositions that everyone knows, in the "popular" sense of "knows."

A few pages later in the essay on common sense, Moore anticipates a point that we have already examined in his "A Proof of the External World." Someone may object that it is possible that Moore merely believes in such popular utterances of common sense as that the world currently exists. He replies: "I think I have nothing better to say than that it seems to me that I *do* know them, with certainty" (44). Moore's procedure is the same throughout the apparently complicated but actually quite simple structure of his essay. At each critical juncture, he gives examples of what he knows with certainty by citing a popular proposition of common sense or pointing out some physical body such as his hands, a mantelpiece in his room, and so on. In contrast to Husserl, who holds that absolute certitude about the world of common sense can be attained only through an elaborate methodology of the purification of our primary intuitions, Moore attributes absolute certitude to the intuitions themselves. Oddly enough, neither thinker claims to have arrived at final or definitive analyses or descriptions of the commonsense world or any of its contents.

For Husserl, an essence can apparently be known apodictically (certainly) but not completely. The endless viewpoints from which the essence can be regarded preclude completeness; but this makes it unclear what Husserl means by apodictic certitude, or the full self-presentation of the essence to the transcendental subjectivity of the phenomenologist. The situation is oddly similar in Moore, except that we begin with absolute certitude without the need for extensive purificatory analyses. There are no special or technical modes of purification in Moore analogous to those of Husserlian phenomenology, since for the British thinker, we are already in direct touch with the indubitable. There are, however, modes of proof that are based upon this indubitable knowledge, but these modes are standard logical argumentation. And finally, there are analyses of the correct meanings of propositions, but no one can say what these are.

Husserlian phenomenology seems to disappear into a stream of endlessly richer levels of subjectivity, each of which is further disturbed by the continuous shifts in perspective from which the objects of phenomenology are viewed. As I have tried to show, I do not believe that the situation is radically different in Moore. On one point, I regard Moore as superior to Husserl. Moore begins with common sense, and so with what everyone knows. The option of correctness or plausibility is thus open to us, but Moore unfortunately vitiates it by insisting upon certitude. Furthermore, the propositions that we understand are popular, not philosophical, and although they perform an essential role in the economy of our lives, they cannot cross the bar from common sense into philosophy. Moore implicitly grants this point with his distinction between popular understanding and meanings that require analysis.

I will not study in detail the example that Moore gives of the problem of analysis, but one or two words may be helpful. Moore does not concern himself with propositions such as "God exists" (except to say that he doubts it), or "Being is nothing," or with the terms "forms," "essences," "substances," and the like. Instead, he employs the propositions of common sense that have previously occupied us, and in particular, "Material things exist." This is no doubt because the theme of his essay is common sense, not traditional metaphysics.

But Moore shows that the act of analyzing even popular propositions soon leads us into traditional philosophy or metaphysics. "It seems to me quite evident that my knowledge that I am now perceiving a human hand is a deduction from a pair of propositions simpler still—propositions which I can only express in the form 'I am perceiving *this*' and '*This* is a human hand'" (53). I think that Moore conceals from himself a full awareness of the metaphysical nature of these simple propositions because he holds that there is always a sense-datum that the proposition in question is a proposition about, and that what he knows about the sense-datum is not that it is the object (a hand, a dog, etc.) that it is a sense-datum of.

Moore thus links himself to sense-data, and thereby renders it impossible to arrive at a plausible view on what it is to see *this*. The reason for this impossibility is that an object is not a sense-datum or a collection of sense-data, nor is it a synthesis of shifting streams of sense-data, but rather what Moore himself started out with as a man of common sense: a hand, a dog, a mantelpiece in the lecture room, and so on.[12] The next step is not to relate the sense-data to the hand or dog of common sense, but to see these "givens" to sense as abstractions from our direct perception of the hand or dog. We then ask for the conditions that make it possible for things to be visible, identifiable, and re-identifiable as what they are, which is certainly not sense-data. I have discussed this in an earlier passage and will not repeat the point here.

I take it as a residue of Moore's earlier Hegelianism that he still states the problem of philosophical analysis in the present example as that of what we mean by *this*. But the Hegelian analysis of "this" is an extreme version of a much simpler approach, namely, that of Aristotle. Hegel's analysis begins with the rejection of common sense and leads to what I may call here the demonstration of the identity within difference of "this" and "that." In other words, Hegel holds that all members of the commonsense world are interrelated by a process of the unfolding of formal structures, each of which can be "known" in Moore's sense, but which require to be analyzed in order for their "meaning" to emerge. The meaning of any single form cannot be stated in anything less than the bulk of Hegel's *Science of Logic*. And this seems to make the meaning the same in all cases. We cannot clarify this view of Hegel's here; suffice it to say that for Hegel, meaning is inaccessible at the level of common sense because the structures of common sense are dialectical. But Aristotle's approach is precisely that of common sense. One could even say, with all due qualification, that there are no "meanings" in Aristotle's ontology but only "knowings." We know men, women, dogs, trees, stones, and stars, and the central task of philosophy is to explain how common sense already supplies us with the basis for listing the formal properties that make the existence and cognition of these things possible.

This is not the place to present a detailed discussion of how Aristotle proceeds. My point is that Moore, if he is going to address seriously his question of the *this,* must engage himself with doctrines like those of Hegel and Aristotle. I can understand his repudiation of his earlier Hegelianism, but I think he made a serious mistake in disregarding Aristotle, because there are genuine points of contact between Moore's defense of common sense and Aristotelian metaphysics. I do not mean, of course, to say that Moore should have adopted Aristotelianism. What I do mean to say is that Moore asked the wrong questions. As a result, he moved away from common sense into a labyrinth of sense-data, and here his many minute distinctions disappeared.

This is as far as I want to go in my study of Moore. He has served us as a paradigm-case of what is in my opinion an extremely interesting procedure: the attempt to articulate the nature of a commonsense approach to ordinary experience in terms that are themselves validated by common sense. I hope to have shown that this procedure is impossible so long as we insist upon the criterion of absolute certainty. The spirit of modern metaphysics, which was deeply influenced by mathematics, continues to vivify Moore's antimetaphysical arguments. I have also tried to bring out some little-noticed similarities between Moore and Husserlian phenomenology. These similarities are rooted in the mathematicism of modern metaphysics, but also, and perhaps even more deeply, in the modern commitment, most characteristic of British philosophy, to sense perception. In sum: Husserlian Idealism is an extraordinary version of Moore's ordinary allegiance to the ostensible certitude of common sense.

Chapter 6 Austin and Ordinary Language

What is ordinary about ordinary language? I intend this as a question that is primarily but not exclusively inspired by the various doctrines or procedures of what used to be called "ordinary language philosophy." In raising this question, I shall take my bearings by some of the philosophical writings of John Austin. My intention is not at all to present a detailed study of Austin's philosophy, but to use passages from his texts as authoritative illustrations of the following problem. Despite the very frequent reference in Austin and many other thinkers to "ordinary language" or what we "ordinarily" say, there is virtually no effort to state in a detailed or even general way what is meant by the expression "ordinary language" and how it can be distinguished from the extraordinary variety. On the contrary, ordinary language is presumed to be directly intelligible and accessible, not only to the plain man, an important figure in Austin's often sophisticated exposition, but to the philosopher as well.

At first glance this seems quite reasonable, and I myself would agree that ordinary language provides us with "the first word" (Austin's expression) in our efforts to make sense out of philosophical discourse.

Furthermore, who could know what "we say" if not we ourselves, where "we" refers to the normal speaker of a particular natural language, say, English? It seems quite reasonable not to give a systematic account or formal definition of ordinary language in general; such procedures are appropriate in the case of formal or technical languages, but the main feature of ordinary language is that it is the comprehensive matrix for the production of all technical idioms. Austin's criticism of spurious philosophical generalization would seem to apply to the present case. Ordinary language is not a formal entity but a living process. We can identify what it says in the particular case by consulting our own speech as well as that of our friends and neighbors, and we supplement this knowledge by recourse to grammars and dictionaries. Finally, we make use of elementary logic, which is fundamental to any natural language and which is at least partly embodied in common sense; an example would be the widespread agreement by ordinary speakers that one must not contradict oneself, or that a counterexample invalidates a universal claim.

Someone may object that an appeal to logic already takes us outside the perimeter of ordinary language, or that Austin goes beyond the plain speaker not only in the refinement of his grammatical and semantical distinctions but in his introduction of technical terms and the precision of his analysis. To this we reply that Austin does not equate philosophy with the simple replacement of extraordinary by ordinary usage. He points out that "ordinary language breaks down in extraordinary cases. (In such cases, the cause of the breakdown is semantical)." It is thus not enough to be content with the facts of ordinary usage. "There may be extraordinary facts, even about our everyday experience, which plain men and plain language overlook" (68–69).[1] The expression "plain language" is evidently a synonym for "ordinary language." We shall see later that the speaker of plain language, namely, the "plain man," is not some person or persons distinct from unusual persons who speak obscurely or in an extraordinary manner. The plain man is each of us in a certain context that we can provisionally identify as that of "ordinary circumstances."

But this is to anticipate; let us return to the warning that philosophy is not simply a matter of replacing fancy or obscure language by plain or ordinary language. "Essential though it is as a preliminary to track down the detail of our ordinary uses of words, it seems that we shall in the end always be compelled to straighten them out to some extent" (134). In other words, there is a species of extraordinary language that has the legitimate function of "straightening out" the crooked parts of ordinary language. In order to distinguish this species from the part of extraordinary language that itself needs to be not simply straightened out but replaced, I will refer to it as the "analytical" or (sometimes) the "technical" part. This straightening by analysis is clearly not a job for the plain man, but neither is it a job for the philosopher who speaks obscurely. Analytical discourse is the proper idiom of the philosophical expert who, by means not yet explained, is in a position to complete the task that recourse to plain language cannot quite complete by itself. Austin's writings allow us to infer that the recourse to ordinary language for philosophical purposes (very much as in the case of Wittgenstein's linguistic therapy) is always, or virtually always, not just a matter of listing common uses of terms and expressions but a matter of employing analytical or technical language in order both to clarify those uses and to make a philosophical point. This is obvious from the fact that plain men do not engage in the systematic or analytical elimination of extraordinary discourse of the philosophically unacceptable kind; they simply speak plain English (or whatever their native tongue may be).

There is a difficulty inherent in this justification of Austin's philosophizing, to which I shall return shortly at greater length. The difficulty concerns the status of the analytical dialect of extraordinary language. This dialect (that is, Austin's view of philosophy) does not seem to be justified by ordinary language alone, of which it is an interpretation, and certainly not by the nonsensical part of extraordinary discourse (more precisely, of traditional philosophy). We shall have to ask after the source of its authority. But before we do this, let me present Austin's defense against another, commonly leveled charge against ordinary language philosophy.

Austin refers to this charge as an ostensible snag in "linguistic philosophy," namely, "the snag of Loose (or Divergent or Alternative) Usage" (183). It is objected that we do not all say "the same, and only the same, things in the same situation" and that usages differ. Finally, "Why should what we all ordinarily say be the only or the best or the final way of putting it? Why should it even be true?" (ibid.). Austin replies that sometimes we do disagree, but not as often we think. In a large number of cases, we merely imagine the situation being discussed slightly differently. "The more we imagine the situation in detail . . . the less we find we disagree about what we should say." When we do in fact disagree, and "must allow a usage to be, though appalling, nevertheless actual," all that is happening is not daunting but "entirely explicable. "If our usages disagree, then you use 'X' where I use 'Y'," or else our conceptual systems are different, although probably they are equally consistent and serviceable. "In short, we can find *why* we disagree—you choose to classify in one way, I in another." (183–84).

In this passage, the defects in what Austin calls "linguistic philosophy" emerge with surprising clarity. To begin with, his assertion that we disagree less than we think is probably true but it misses the point. We normally agree on the most obvious cases, or what could be called the most ordinary part of ordinary language. But this part is surely the least relevant to philosophy. Plain men do not disagree on the meaning of the sentence "the cat is on the mat." But neither do they debate the issue of whether "the cat is on the mat" is equivalent to "It is true that the cat is on the mat." In general, Austin calls the disagreement one that is usually due to the imagination. He advises us to imagine the situation in detail, and to stimulate our wretched imaginations with the most idiosyncratic or boring means as a way of discovering that we disagree less than we thought about what we should say. But this seems to assign the judgment of correct ordinary usage to the imagination; the person with the most ingenious imagination will establish the correct usage. And this is not going to happen in the obvious cases, but only in those that are sufficiently unusual (if still somehow within the penumbra of ordinary language) to be philosophically significant. Finally, if we determine at the conclusion of our exercises in the imagination that you choose to classify in one way and I in another, this seems to leave the ground open to traditional philosophy and thus to metaphysics. You choose to classify like Austin, but I prefer Aristotle.

This is enough to show the weakness of what looks initially like a reasonable defense against the snag of loose, divergent, or alternative usage. Nor am I familiar with any examples in Austin's corpus, or for that matter, in those of other "linguistic philosophers," of this recommended tolerance toward deviant usages. The cry "nonsense!" entirely drowns out the placatory "well, that's how you see it" when analytical philosophers respond in their discussions with traditional (or not so traditional) "metaphysicians."

The difficulty I first mentioned in Austin's views but postponed temporarily is a corollary to the difficulties we have just noticed. I infer from Austin's writings that the analytical language he employs is itself a product of a deep dissatisfaction with the extraordinary language that characterizes much of traditional philosophy, and presumably of metaphysics in particular. What is the source of this dissatisfaction? In part, of course, it rests upon the ostensible fact that philosophy of this sort violates important canons of ordinary language. But why is this important? It is far from true that plain men all dislike metaphysics, or for that matter that they concur with Austin's strictures on what may or may not be said. It is not the plain man who enforces the expulsion of traditional philosophers or metaphysicians from the precincts of professionally correct philosophy. And as we have just seen, Austinians at least have no grounds for repudiating those who classify differently from themselves. They can refuse to speak to such discursive deviates, but even this seems to violate Austin's occasional remark to the effect that "a genuinely loose or eccentric talker is a rare specimen to be prized" (184).

It seems reasonable to assume that Austin arrived at his conception of ordinary language philosophy as a result of dissatisfaction with the discourse of traditional philosophers, whose views he regularly caricatures and denounces as nonsense. This dissatisfaction takes the form of a conviction that correct philosophy must somehow accord with correct usage of the nonphilosophical or plain speaker of ordinary language. But this conviction is not itself a piece of ordinary discourse. No one would call "philosophical" a plain man who responded to the speech of a metaphysician with the cry "nonsense!" Austin's appeal to the common language is so to speak *metaordinary.*

Ordinary language itself requires from time to time to be straightened out.[2] It thus seems that we must already be in possession of analytical or technical discourse in order to be in a position to complete the task of eliminating obscure, and more generally, senseless extraordinary discourse. But this leaves us with a difficult question. How does the ordinary language philosopher arrive at the stage of analytical discourse? Since the latter straightens out ordinary language, and also tells us on occasion that ordinary language itself has broken down, or that we are in an extraordinary circumstance, it cannot be ordinary language that serves to produce the analytical discourse of ordinary language philosophy. But it cannot be the obscure or insignificant kind of extraordinary discourse that does the job, either. Whence comes the clarity and technical know-how that permits the ordinary language philosopher to move securely from the insignificant to the crooked and back again into the middle ground of analytical good sense?

The fullest statement byAustin on why we should turn to ordinary language is to be found in his essay, *A Plea for Excuses*.[3] It is interesting to note that Austin is apparently uneasy about such general characterizations of his philosophical program; he refers to the extended passage of his essay that contains the statement we will inspect as "cackle."[4] Ordinary usage attributes "cackle" to chickens, not to philosophers. Austin's little joke should not be subjected to psychoanalytical scrutiny; one cannot fight cackle with more cackle. But it is fair to note the discomfort with generalities that is certainly a pervasive feature of Austin's philosophical writing.

In the passage that we are considering, Austin has just finished examining the ambiguities of the expression "to do an action" as it is used in "an oversimplified metaphysics" of things and their qualities (178 f.). This metaphysics comes from Aristotle, incidentally, although Austin does not mention the fact. Instead, he refers favorably to Aristotle's discussion of excuses or pleas in connection with the problem of freedom. This is evidently a reference to the *Nicomachean Ethics,* a book that played a large role in the development of Oxford analytical philosophy of the ordinary-language type. The ambiguity that I noted at the beginning of this essay is also intrinsic to a consideration of Aristotle's practical writings. The *Nicomachean Ethics,* for example, is not a theoretical work in the strict sense; as Aristotle himself puts it, "the present study [*pragmateia* already echoes the "practical" nature of the book] is not for the sake of theory like other works, for we do not investigate virtue in order to know what it is, but that we may become good."[5] And yet it is obvious that Aristotle is "doing" theory in some sense of the term; he also refers to the work as part of his "philosophy of human affairs" (*ta anthropeia philosophia*).[6]

The exact nature of the Aristotelian investigation into human affairs is thus a matter of controversy. It is true that Aristotle begins from ordinary experience and its language, but it is also true that this substratum of commonsense reasoning is regularly modified by "theoretical" considerations about human nature. Aristotle "straightens out" the discourse of the plain man on the basis of his more general philosophical views. This is most obvious in Book 6, which deals with the faculties of the intellectual part of the soul, and Book 10, in which Aristotle states at length the superiority of the theoretical to the practical life. What is most like Aristotle's practical writings in Austin is the immersion in linguistic detail, as for example when he provides lists of different usages of the same term or expression in everyday language. But there are two important differences between Aristotle and Austin. Aristotle's linguistic distinctions are always rooted in the nature of things (in the present case, what we do, not what we say that we do). Austin, on the other hand, although he warns us that the purpose of linguistic analysis is to arrive at clarity about the phenomena, starts from, and normally remains within, the domain of what we say. Second, Aristotle engages in considerably more "cackle" than does Austin. Whereas the ambiguous nature of Aristotle's practical writings is at least mitigated by a study of his theoretical works, there are no theoretical works in the same sense in the Austinian canon. Even such theoretical questions as the types of linguistic expressions and the reference of terms of sense perception remain firmly oriented toward ordinary language: properly straightened out, to be sure, but by what ruler or criterion?

In the same extended passage, Austin introduces somewhat tentatively his decision to begin from what ordinary language has to say about excuses ("if ordinary language is to be our guide," 181): "But there are also reasons why it is an attractive subject methodologically, at least if we are to proceed from 'ordinary language', that is, by examining *what we should say when,* and so why and what we should mean by it" (ibid.). The reference to methodology suggests that the remarks to follow will clarify Austin's analytical language. The italicized expression, on the other hand, introduces an explanation of ordinary language. The recommended methodology is to examine "what we should say when." If this is to mean "under ordinary linguistic circumstances," then the recommendation is circular. If "should" refers to the canons of correct speech, it remains to be established that what is ordinarily said is correct. Austin does of course claim something very much like this, but as we have seen, with many qualifications. But for the moment I note that, if the claim is to carry weight, Austin must be in a position to list the canons of correct speech, and thereby to show that they in fact dictate what is actually ordinarily said.

As a second-best alternative, if the canons of correct speech are not available, Austin must show first what is ordinarily said, and next, that this is always or for the most part superior to the various extraordinary statements that might be made in each case. But this is clearly impossible, since, entirely apart from the difficulties I have already mentioned, such as the reliance upon the imagination, it requires a case-by-case analysis of everything that might be said, together with the demonstration that all nonordinary assertions are inferior to the ordinary one. And this cannot be done without the aforementioned criteria for the ordinary response. Austin gives a few examples in each of the cases he considers, but the entire exercise is arbitrary and incomplete. Even worse, as Austin himself admits, the inspection of ordinary responses to ordinary situations casts no immediate light whatsoever on extraordinary cases, that is, upon the adequacy of extraordinary assertions in response to, or as definitive of, something extraordinary. It is, for example, simple nonsense to pass judgment on the illegitimacy of a metaphysics of substance and properties on the basis of the ordinary use of the words "thing" and "quality," where "ordinary" is intended in advance to exclude extraordinary extensions of usage.

The reader should note that I have no objection at all to Austin's actual analysis of the vocabulary of excuses. Here as elsewhere, and perhaps even in most of his technical exercises, the sensitivity to nuances of meaning is admirable, and the method itself fruitful for unpacking the complexity of human language. As an example of Austin's good sense, I quote the first of the two main ways in which he says the study of excuses throws light on fundamental philosophical matters. "First, to examine excuses is to examine cases in which there has been some abnormality or failure; and as so often, the abnormal will throw light on the normal, will help us to penetrate the blinding veil of ease and obviousness that hides the mechanisms of the natural successful act" (179–80). This is well said, but Austin does not seem to notice that it says the reverse of what he is claiming for the virtues of the analysis of ordinary language. The examination of abnormal, that is, extraordinary discourse can indeed throw light on the normal or ordinary language of the plain man, and show that this ordinary language is philosophically defective, perhaps even irrelevant. In addition, scientific analysis of natural phenomena proceeds with the assistance of abnormal or extraordinary discourse, and penetrates the "blinding veil of ease and obviousness" that hides the mechanisms internal to natural acts of ordinary life.

Nevertheless, I do not reject outright his tentatively expressed, yet regularly pursued suggestion that we should begin from ordinary language. My point is that Austin does not simply begin from ordinary language as a guide to a deeper appreciation of extraordinary discourse; he pays only lip-service to his own principle that ordinary language is the first but not the last word. If this is too harsh, let us say that he does not explain the soundness of the tools that he employs to straighten out ordinary language when that should be necessary. He does not really give us a basis for deciding *when* that is necessary.

Austin's mixture of virtues and defects is clearly visible in the fuller statement of the methodological justification for starting with ordinary language. "First, words are our tools, and, as a minimum, we should use clean tools: we should know what we mean and what we do not, and we must forearm ourselves against the traps that language sets us" (181–82). I have no doubt that the traditional philosopher, and in particular, the metaphysician, would agree with this sensible statement. But to leave it at this would be naive. Why should we assume that our tools are statements in ordinary language? Is it not at least equally likely that these tools are dirty precisely because they are immersed in ordinary discourse, and that the way to clean them is by extricating them from their ordinary use and making them capable of engaging the extraordinary tasks of the philosopher? But Austin himself must know that the tools he employs do not come from ordinary language; they are technical and come from philosophy. In order for me to know what I mean, it is not necessary for me to check my assertions with what a plain man might say, unless I am speaking in my guise as a plain man. And if I am, then there is presumably nothing to check; I know what I mean precisely because I am saying what should be said, given Austin's account. What we actually require is not a clarification of ordinary usages of words like "excuses" or any other term that springs up from "working the dictionary" (187). We need a philosophical justification for the turn to ordinary language as the first word. And this in turn rests upon a philosophical refutation of traditional philosophy. To give only one example in passing, Hegel rejected ordinary language as philosophically irrelevant. Can Austin refute this contention?

In general, Austin clearly has a strong bias again theoretical justifications, which he regards as "cackle." On this point, he is very reminiscent of Wittgenstein. What is the cause of this repugnance? Austin never tells us, so far as I am aware, but in a way, the answer is obvious. Austin falls within the tradition of commonsense empiricism as supplemented with the bias toward philosophy of language that is typically Kantian, or let us rather say, neo-Kantian. Whereas he does not confuse philosophy with science, there is in his thinking an unmistakable commitment to the scientific rationalism of the Enlightenment; that is, underlying ordinary language philosophy is a tacit acceptance of the analytical component of the modern, mathematically influenced conception of rationality. Finally, Austin's considerable subtlety and the precision of his ear for verbal distinctions are both in the service of a penchant for simplicity and what can be verified by common sense supplemented with what used to be called "conceptual logic" or "philosophical logic." This component is paradoxically but traditionally a blend of English good sense and scholastic nominalism of the sort that goes back to the Middle Ages. In Austin's case, however, the good sense triumphs over excessively technical terminology; the linguistic *Spitzfindigkeit* serves to defend the plain man from the encroachment of obscure philosophy. But this by the way.

To continue with Austin's methodological justification: "Secondly, words are not (except in their own little corner) facts or things; we need therefore to prise them off the world, to hold them apart from and against it, so that we can realize their inadequacies and arbitrariness, and can re-look at the world without blinkers" (182). One cannot however prise words off the world unless one can see one's tools apart from the blinkers of language. In other words, this point contradicts the first, in which Austin claims that words are our tools. The techniques of analysis are not themselves derived from a view of the world as it is; instead, it is precisely these tools that Austin employs, in the good neo-Kantian manner, to determine the nature of the world, namely, the world as described by the plain man, properly straightened out when necessary. Furthermore, there is no guarantee that if we succeed in prising words off the world, what we will see is confirmation of the lack of significance of the extraordinary speech of traditional philosophers, and in particular, metaphysicians. Austin seems to know in advance that the world, freed of its linguistic corset, will verify (properly straightened out) ordinary discourse. But this is a philosophical prejudice. You cannot refute extraordinary language by citing ordinary language. You must validate the claim of your preferred version of extraordinary discourse to serve as the tool by which to prise off nonsensical extraordinary discourse from the sensible kind. Austin needs considerably more cackle than he provides us with.

To continue: "Thirdly, and more hopefully, our common stock of words embodies all the distinctions men have found worth drawing, and the connections they have found worth marking, in the lifetimes of many generations; these surely are likely to be more numerous, more sound, since they have stood up to the long test of the survival of the fittest, and more subtle, at least in all ordinary and reasonably practical matters, than any that you or I are likely to think up in our arm-chairs of an afternoon—the most favored alternative method" (182). This statement is especially revealing. To begin with, it assumes that traditional philosophy is something dreamed up in armchairs by a discontinuous stream of metaphysicians. Austin thereby overlooks the facts that the most important technical terms of traditional philosophy have a long history, going back to Plato and Aristotle in many cases, if not before, and that these terms have been subjected to the careful analysis of countless generations of highly intelligent persons. This is what it means to speak of *traditional* philosophy. The terms themselves may of course be defective, but this can hardly be established simply by checking them against nonphilosophical usage. Austin's irony fails to make a rational point against the use of armchairs.

No one, least of all the metaphysician, doubts that the plain man has produced a large stock of distinctions and connections that are sounder and more subtle with respect at least to "all ordinary and reasonably practical matters" than anything we philosophers could dream up of an afternoon in our armchairs. This is no doubt true with respect to ordinary and practical matters, but it is entirely irrelevant to the case of philosophy. Austin implies (no doubt unintentionally) that there is no legitimate difference between working up popular usages and engaging in the philosophical transformation of ordinary language. Furthermore, one would expect the body of plain senses to be more secure than that of metaphysics. The everyday senses are more secure precisely because they are everyday, that is, widely and uncritically used for situations that are accessible to us without philosophical analysis. Once again I note in passing that the statement is also deeply antiscientific. Surely Newton dreamed up distinctions and connections in an afternoon that are more subtle and sounder than everything said by the plain man on the subject of the motion of natural bodies. Equally absurd is the rhetorical allusion to "arm-chair philosophers," a category that presumably includes all those who do not take their bearings by ordinary language. It nevertheless looks from Austin's writings that he spent considerable time in his armchair, studying the dictionary and various grammars; in other words, his entire discourse is itself a deviation from the common stock of ordinary language. It is an *interpretation* of ordinary language, and it rests upon a failure to tell us the difference between the ordinary and the extraordinary. After all, dictionaries contain both kinds of expressions.

Austin's method makes it impossible for him to enter into the linguistic world of the traditional philosopher. As a result, his remarks on traditional philosophy are largely worthless, in contradistinction to his extremely interesting analyses of ordinary usage. Austin seems to have believed that these analyses are themselves an analysis and refutation of extraordinary and obscure statements by traditional philosophers. But he gives no reasons whatsoever for justifying this belief. He is himself a prisoner of the rules of grammar, despite his excellent observation that "when we examine what we should say when, what words we should use in what situations, we are looking again not *merely* at words (or 'meanings,' whatever they may be), but also at the realities we use the words to talk about: we are using a sharpened awareness of words to sharpen our perception of, though not as the final arbiter of, the phenomena" (182).

How can the reality of, say, an Aristotelian species-form present itself to someone who has undergone the Austinian training and acquired his sharpened awareness of words? What Austin does not seem to have appreciated once more is that Aristotelian "forms," or for that matter, Platonic "Ideas," are themselves derived from a sharpened awareness, not so much of words but of the phenomena about which we speak. To take a crucial example, neither Plato nor Aristotle has a doctrine of "meaning," and the question (however punctuated) "what is the meaning of a word?" is not the same as the question "what is a Platonic Idea or an Aristotelian species-form?" These are not meanings, for meanings, however we explain their ontological status, are properties of sentences, not of the natures of things. I will return to the topic of meaning in the next section of this chapter.

If every attempt to convey in words the perceived unity of the individual items in our everyday experience is obscure nonsense, then ordinary experience as well as ordinary language are equally nonsensical. Of course, as Austin well knew, we do not perceive sense-data or sensations but rather sticks and stones, rocks and stars, plants and persons, and so on. What would Austin call the unity of a cow or a human being? The plain man has no vocabulary that is adequate to the description of the most common stratum of his experience. Yet, in a deep sense, such speakers give us our clue precisely by speaking not of sensations or properties but initially of sticks and stones, in other words, of things. And things are identified by their properties. But the collection of predications that we use to describe any particular thing refers to what? Austin tells us: to the *phenomena*. Unfortunately, his preferred philosophical method leads to the dissolution of the phenomena, or at best to a silence in the face of questions like the traditional query, "How do we explain the unity of a multiplicity?" At this point, I find Austin's hearty common sense and donnish humor irritating, not illuminating.

"Certainly, then, ordinary language is *not* the last word: in principle it can everywhere be supplemented and improved upon and superseded. Only remember, it is the *first* word" (185). The problem is that the first word, as conceived and employed by Austin, is too often the last word; it excludes from the outset all philosophical discourse that deviates sharply from the ordinary. But we still have no clear basis for distinguishing between ordinary and extraordinary speech, and no way to tell when ordinary speech is pertinent to a philosophical problem and when it is not.

I want next to look more closely at a sample of Austin's method of eliminating obscure or insignificant speech from philosophical respectability. The sample is taken from "The Meaning of a Word," chapter 3 in *Philosophical Papers*. In the first section of this paper, Austin says, "I try to make it clear that the phrase 'the meaning of a word' is in general, if not always, a dangerous nonsense phrase" (56). Austin tells us that this section of his paper is trite; it should therefore provide us with a transparent example of his use of ordinary language. As we are about to see, the main point of his first section is to show the nonsense that arises in certain shifts from particular to general questions. Stated as simply as possible, and thus ignoring his peculiar notation, Austin will argue that although we can ask after the meaning of a particular word like "rat" or even "word," and also of the sentence "What is the meaning of (the phrase) 'What is the meaning of'?", it is nonsense to ask "What is the meaning of a word?" For Austin, words have meanings that are determined by our ability to use them correctly. But there is no entity called "meaning," neither in the particular case nor in general. As I have already suggested, Austin seems to be under the mistaken impression that meanings are a feature of classical metaphysics. The contrary is true; to ask after the ontological status of meanings is already to have entered into the domain of nominalism on the one hand or neo-Kantianism on the other. Meanings are the replacements for Platonic Ideas and Aristotelian species-forms provided by those who deny that we are in direct contact with things, and who interpose a domain of representations between the intellect and the objects of cognition, which thus become objects of subjects, and in particular, of discursive subjects.

The section that interests me and that will let me come more closely to grips with Austin's text is prefaced by seven specimens of questions that make sense and ten specimens of nonsensical questions. The first specimen of making sense is the question "What-is-the-meaning-of (the word) 'rat'?" The significance of the hyphens can be best brought out by quoting a nonsensical imitation of the proper question: "What is the-'meaning'-of-(the word)-'rat'?" We can legitimately ask for the sense of a word that refers to a particular type of entity, or to what Aristotle (but not Austin) calls a "this thing here of such-and-such a kind." The second sense, however, shifts from an inquiry into how we use a certain word, to an inquiry into the nature of the meaning of that word, in which the meaning is itself taken as a separate entity. And this error in turn leads to the spurious question "What is the-meaning-of-a-word?" "Meaning," in other words, is promoted to the level of an abstract entity or general property (55–57).

In ordinary discourse, Austin tells us, we determine whether someone understands a word, say "racy," by his ability to employ it in English sentences, or to distinguish between situations in which we should correctly and incorrectly use the English word "racy" (57). This sounds very much like what linguists do when they appeal to "the native speaker" in analyzing examples of grammatically correct or incorrect sentences. The expression "native speaker" is a pseudonym for the author of the paper in which the analysis appears. In both cases, in order to determine whether a sentence is a well-formed, sense-conveying example of a natural language, say, English, one must first know English. Strictly speaking, it is not necessary to be a native speaker; many foreigners learn English as well as, and in some cases (Vladimir Nabokov, for example) better than, native speakers. But this point is only peripherally important for the present inquiry. The foreign speaker is dependent upon the actual practice of native speakers, and so upon mimicking that practice. Foreign speakers do not depend just upon grammars and dictionaries. How the foreigner becomes fluent in English is as mysterious as how the native-born Englishman or Englishwoman becomes fluent in his or her own language. This becomes relevant to the present inquiry when we ask how it is determined that some sentences containing the word "racy" make sense and some do not.

Linguists attempt to avoid arbitrariness in ascertaining what the native speaker says, either by assuming that their own command of the natural language is exemplary, or, following the procedure of psychologists, by collecting the responses on various points of usage from a set of subjects, usually quite small. I am not sufficiently versed in linguistic procedure to know whether they also consult the unabridged *Oxford English Dictionary*. So far as I can see, Austin follows the first method most frequently, and next most frequently the third. The second is perhaps implied in his frequent use of "we say," which presumably refers on most occasions to what his friends and neighbors are saying on the relevant points.

Austin's example is an odd one, because the word "racy" is hardly a part of the average English speaker's vocabulary; it is a slang expression or an idiom likely to be employed at a certain historical period by a relatively restricted subset of English speakers. If Austin is asked "in ordinary life" how one might or might not use the word in English sentences, he is going to have to rely upon his own membership in a restricted community of speakers, very few of whom, for example, would be Americans. Austin might reply to this that American is not English, but this simply accentuates the difficulty. American is a dialect of English, but so too the meaning of the word "racy" depends upon how it is used, and it will be used differently by persons of differing dialects. All this to one side, if we shift to a philosophical word like "substance" or "essence," the plain man and the metaphysician are going to use this word differently. If the metaphysician uses the word in accord with the well-established rules laid down by, say, Aristotle, in such a way that his sentences make sense to other competent students of Aristotle, why should these speakers have the slightest interest in the perplexity felt by the plain man when he comes into contact with talk of the Aristotelian variety?

Austin's procedures themselves make sense only on the basis of three assumptions. First, despite all qualifications, it is philosophically correct to evaluate philosophical sentences on the basis of ordinary language. Second, ordinary language is directly accessible by appeal to the plain man, who is Austin's surrogate for the linguist's native speaker. Third, Austin is in adequate touch with the plain man; that is, he has not chosen too narrow a sample of subjects. I note that one cannot resolve these questions about correct uses of a specific word by appealing to a good dictionary, since the better the dictionary, the more extraordinary uses it will contain. If we then say that we will take only the most common uses (assuming that the dictionary indicates this statistic), we are still begging the original question, namely, why we want to consult common usage at all.

Austin illustrates the dangers of generalization by holding that, whereas it is legitimate to ask for the meaning of this or that word (and here the implicit model is that of someone consulting a dictionary or a native speaker), trouble ensues when we philosophers "try . . . to ask the further *general* question, 'What is the meaning of a word?'" (57). He calls attention to the difference between this and the legitimate sentence "what is the meaning of the word 'word'"?

Austin claims, somewhat quickly in my opinion, that the second sentence would be answered in precisely the way in which we might answer the question "what is the meaning of the word 'rat'"? But let us allow this claim. I will add only that we answer the question "what is the meaning of the word 'essence'" in the same way that we answer the parallel question about "rat," except that our explanation is necessarily extended, depending upon the linguistic context within which the question was itself posed. I mean by this that we can start from the ordinary language of the plain man, whether because he has stumbled upon a philosophical essay and asks us to explain a sentence about essence, or for some of the reasons that Austin has given us about the utility of taking our bearings by the common stock of connections and distinctions that is contained in the body of common speech. If we are required to rely completely upon common usage, then it is quite likely that we will never be able to explain the Aristotelian term "essence." But not even Austin requires us to be restricted by common usage; he acknowledges that ordinary language is the first word, not the last, and that it sometimes has to be straightened out.

So far as I can tell, Austin straightens out ordinary language in order to eliminate objectionable philosophical statements on the basis of his own technical or analytical idiom of extraordinary language, and not simply on the basis of the ordinary speech-habits of the plain man. Austin's own philosophical decisions are either employed without comment, as if they formed a part of what every competent reader knows, or they are justified by scholastic differentiations of what he tells us is ordinary usage. But these differentiations stop at the point where they might become interesting to the traditional philosopher or metaphysician. The latter can legitimately complain that Austin does not carry out his own program sufficiently; he stops at the point at which his own theoretical prejudices are confirmed.

Austin parses the spurious quality of the question "What is the meaning of a word?" by holding that philosophers who use it wish to ask "What is the meaning of a-word-in-general?" but of no particular word at all. Austin says that it is almost immediately obvious that this is an absurd question. "I can only answer a question of the form 'What is the meaning of "*x*"?' if "*x* is some *particular* word you are asking about. This supposed *general* question is really just a spurious question of a type which commonly arises in philosophy. We may call it the fallacy of asking about 'Nothing-in-particular,' which is a practice decried by the plain man, but by the philosopher called 'generalizing' and regarded with some complacency" (58).

I am tempted to call this statement by Austin mere sophistry. No metaphysician could possibly be moved to inquire after the meaning that is common to any and every word, except perhaps for some creatures who dwell upon the floating island of Laputa. But the question "What is the meaning of a word?" whereas it may exist on the margins of ordinary language, is directly licensed by the ordinary question "What is the meaning of (the word) 'word'?" endorsed by Austin on the preceding page (57). All we need do is rewrite the sentence as "What is the meaning of (the word) 'meaning'?" Austin, however, passes this version by, and instead attributes to the linguistically errant philosopher the variation "What is the-meaning-of-a-word?" or "What is the 'meaning' of a word?" (58–59). He wishes to convey thereby that the errant philosopher places the word "meaning" at the same level as the word "rat," namely, as the name of a particular object. This is what other philosophers refer to as the hypostasizing of meaning or the creation of an abstract term.

To recapitulate: Austin rules out as nonsense the question "What is a meaning?" But he does not explain how, if the word "meaning" has no general sense, he can use it in particular cases to refer to the meaning of such words as "rat" or "racy." Austin might try to avoid this question by referring to how we *use* words in ordinary language. "The meaning is the use," as some would say. But how can we use any word that does not have a meaning? The meaning of a particular word, let us grant, is particular (although this is itself an oversimplification). But each particular meaning is an example of the general conception of "meaning." Austin himself gives us a list of legitimate uses of the word "meaning," and this in turn entails that the word "meaning" has a meaning that encompasses or is common to all of the particular uses he lists. If that were denied, then the sentences themselves would be unintelligible. For we should be required, in each particular case, to explain what we *mean* by the word "meaning." If the sense of "mean" is different in each of Austin's examples, then what are they examples *of*? We use examples or specimens for general cases, not in order to represent more particulars, which would themselves depend for their meanings on still other particulars, and so on *ad infinitum.*

Austin quickly disposes of traditional philosophical responses to the question "What is the-meaning-of-a-word?" He does not examine the different but (according to him) equally nonsensical question "What is the 'meaning' of a word?" But this difference is extremely important. The query about "meaning" is entirely compatible with ordinary usage, as I have just shown. The sentence "Words have meanings" is unexceptionable and in fact indispensable for the intelligibility of ordinary (or any other kind of) language. If words had no meanings, they would be meaningless, and the entire debate about meaning would be reduced to gibberish, not just to nonsense. If they all had the same meaning, discourse of any kind would be impossible, since discourse depends upon differences of meaning as well as identities of meaning, or synonyms. But if each word had a different meaning, this would still require that each word have *a* meaning, and I see no way in which to explain what this means unless the particular meanings are all examples of the same sort of entity. *Austin's problem cannot even be posed unless the question "What is the 'meaning' of a word?" makes sense.* And the same is true of its surrogate, "What is the-meaning-of-a-word?" The different senses of the word "meaning" are tautologously senses of the word "meaning." They are not instances of different things. And none of this presupposes any "metaphysical" response to the question concerning the nature of meaning. We are not committed to the existence of hypostasized entities called "meanings" that are at the same ontological level as rats. But neither are we committed to a quasi-Platonic entity called "the Idea of Meaning." I would argue that it is as impossible to answer the question "What is meaning?" in a noncircular manner, without knowing in advance what we mean by "meaning," as it is impossible to answer in a noncircular way the question "What is the meaning of the word 'word'?" which bears Austin's seal of approval for making sense. But that is not an argument for claiming that the question "What is meaning?" (however hyphenated or punctuated) is nonsense.

To come back to Austin's rejection of "What is the-meaning-of (the word)-'rat'?" as spurious, which is tantamount to a cavalier and polemical dismissal of traditional philosophy, Austin demonstrates how "quaint" is the offensive reasoning by first offering the following example. (I paraphrase to avoid the intricacies of quotation marks and "scare" quotes.) Suppose that the plain man asks us "What is the meaning of the word 'muggy'?" If I were to answer, "The idea or concept of 'mugginess'" or "The class of sensa of which it is correct to say 'This is muggy'," Austin says that "the man would stare at me as at an imbecile"

(59). Presumably this is supposed to be analogous to the case in which someone asks "What is the meaning of 'meaning'?" and is told "The concept of 'meaningfulness' is what 'meaning' means." I would certainly agree that the answer is not acceptable. But who, outside of a play by Moliere, would give such a response? Let us assume that the correct answer to the query about the meaning of "muggy" is "hot and humid weather." The analogous reply to the question about the meaning of "meaning" could be something like "the sense of an expression as is agreed upon by members of a linguistic community." Now this reply is not nonsense, but it is circular, because the word "sense" can be understood only by someone who already understands the word "meaning." Nor can we avoid the difficulty by substituting "use" for "meaning," since we use words correctly when we are faithful to their meanings. There is no magic way to speak correctly without knowing what you are saying.

We can vary the suggested definition endlessly, but the problem of circularity will remain. However, this is no help to Austin, since circles are preferable to disintegration of the linguistic field. Furthermore, circles are intrinsic to the accumulation of ordinary language and the writing of dictionaries. How does anyone understand any sentence of ordinary language if not on the basis of something previously understood? To this I add: how do we understand any particular sentence, except on the basis of the general (i.e., dictionary) meanings of the words constituting that sentence? I say "on the basis of" and I mean this to be compatible with, but not identical to Austin's own principle that ordinary language is the first but not the last word. Ordinary language is of course not always identical with the current idiom of ordinary language, but this is to say only that extraordinary uses are continuously transforming ordinary language. These uses cannot be understood by consulting a dictionary, nor can we rely upon the testimony of the plain man, if he is not already conversant with the new idiom.

We do not need to examine the remaining examples in the first section of Austin's paper because they add nothing to our analysis. I will just cite the following brief passage, which makes clear Austin's underlying motive in this part of his essay. "Even those who see pretty clearly that 'concepts', 'abstract ideas', and so on are fictitious entities, which we owe in part to asking questions about 'the meaning of a word', nevertheless think that there is *something* which is 'the meaning of a word'" (60). Austin is opposed to the metaphysical notion of meanings that exist as independent abstract entities, something like Platonic Ideas.[7] When he says that meanings are "fictitious," he is saying that they do not exist. Rats, on the other hand, do exist. Unfortunately, if we accept Austin's analysis, rats will have to exist without the benefit of abstract properties, presumably including the property of existence. But if existence is a fictitious property, then surely all existing rats are fictitious. Try explaining that to the cat on the mat.

Who is "the plain man"? The first version of the presumably correct answer is "the speaker of ordinary language." But what is ordinary language? It is obvious that we are in the presence of the famous hermeneutical circle. In an idiom closer to Austin's, we could say that philosophers must jump through hoops in order to get started in their metier. Only after we have jumped does the hoop straighten itself out into a tightrope.

Austin at first contrasts ordinary language with extraordinary language. Presumably ordinary language is what we speak normally, under circumstances that are more or less common to all members of a linguistic community. But to put the point in this way is to run the risk of collapsing Austin into the late Wittgenstein. More generally, it leads us to ignore Austin's claim that the purpose of studying words is "to see the world without blinkers" (181), and this in turn implies that the world is independent of how we speak about it. If uses are established by a consensus of the local linguistic community, however, then we are immediately cut off by a veil of language from what we are talking about. Things become linguistic artifacts, or, to say the same thing in another way, we return to the primacy of representations that characterizes modern philosophy in both its empiricist and idealist branches.

Austin himself encourages this "Wittgensteinian" interpretation by identifying ordinary language with ordinary English. Furthermore, Austin does not use "ordinary" to mean what is usually said but what *ought* to be said on the basis of the rules of grammar and the "official" meanings of words as recorded in dictionaries. But people often use extraordinary language, as Austin himself points out. It might seem reasonable at first to subject extraordinary language to the standard of ordinary usage, but the two spheres are incompatible in all or most interesting cases. If the ordinary were always the standard, then nothing new could ever be correctly said. Finally, one can obey the rules of English grammar and remain true to the ordinary use of ordinary words while introducing new terms and procedures that either clarify or go beyond the ordinary senses.

Austin's doctrine suffers from the additional ambiguity that it seems to ignore the role of history in ordinary language. By tacitly accepting as normative the language spoken by the linguistic community of educated English speakers of the mid-twentieth century, Austin ignores, or encourages us to ignore, the linguistic procedures of the past, and of course to disregard the possible consequences of future changes. In other words, the dictionary and the grammar of our time become quasi-Platonic Ideas. But they are not eternal. In the course of time, they will be replaced by other grammars and dictionaries. And this leads to a series of discontinuous worlds, a series in which the shift from one world to another is camouflaged by continuous recourse to the standards of contemporary usage.

I therefore suggest that it is a mistake to make ordinary language be even the first word. Making that mistake will not lead us to the unblinkered vision of the world. Instead, we have to start with our vision of the world. The fact that we use language to report, to ourselves and others, what we have seen does not mean that that vision is itself the language we use. Austin's "plain man" is either too obtuse to serve as the standard against which we correct philosophical mistakes, or else he is transformed into a curious extension of Austin himself, or whoever is performing the linguistic analysis.

Austin can escape from historicism, from reducing the world to language, only by taking the plain man, that is, the speaker of ordinary language as ordinal, as setting standards for human nature. Ordinary language cannot be a historical phenomenon alone or altogether; it must make transparent in human existence the basis for its authority. To take this path, however, is to return directly to traditional metaphysics, something that the adherents of ordinary language analysis are (or were) eager to avoid. But there is no other way in which to prise language off the world and thus to see the world through unblinkered eyes. We need to determine not what people happen to say in this or that society or linguistic community but what they ought to say. And this "ought" is not and cannot be simply a matter of conventional agreement. We ought to say what the circumstances require.

But that is not the end of the matter. Human beings are naturally inclined to speak poetically, mythically, and metaphysically, not just scientifically or commonsensically, where "common sense" means "in accord with British empiricism." But is it not the case that human beings are naturally given to extraordinary speech, including myth, religion, poetry, and philosophy? Ordinary language, odd though it sounds at first, is saturated with extraordinary language. The term "ordinary" itself has two main senses; one is that of the common or usual, and the other is that of the ordinal or regulative. These senses are distinct even though they are often related. They should be separated in discussions of how to talk correctly. They are blurred in the expression "ordinary language" and this obscurity is compounded, not removed, by ordinary language analysis as Austin and his colleagues practiced it.

Similar considerations obtain if we try to distinguish plain or ordinary from technical or professional speech. The technical language of the electrician or the plumber is certainly ordinary in comparison with the discourse of a medieval scholastic philosopher or a contemporary cosmologist, yet Austin, in attempting to resolve various philosophical puzzles, does not consult the language of electricians or plumbers in their professional guise. Neither, of course, does he consult medieval metaphysicians, except to ridicule them as purveyors of nonsense.

Austin's enterprise rests upon the assumption that all of us possess a common language based upon our everyday activities that require no special expertise beyond our knowledge of the language itself. And yet, this assumption collapses the moment we consider how much technical knowledge the most ordinary circumstances require. If the plain man speaks the common tongue but is not "plain" *qua* electrician, plumber, poet, metaphysician, or ordinary language analyst, then he would seem to be incompetent to pronounce upon, and unqualified for adjudicating, subtle linguistic questions, philosophical questions in particular. But if the plain man has mastered the unabridged *Oxford English Dictionary*, he cannot be a plain man. Such a person spends very little time with a dictionary, and probably none with essays like those in which Austin draws his refined distinctions of usage. There begins to be something frivolous, not to say Laputan, in the spectacle of Oxford dons disputing about the speech habits of the plain man.

Part of the difficulty with Austin's essays is that he proceeds at two different levels without clearly distinguishing between them. He uses the "plain man" as a club with which to beat the traditional philosopher, while he also functions as an ostensibly "revolutionary" philosopher who is employing some subset of English usage to which he gives the appellation "ordinary." The function of this chunk of usage is to enable him to identify and reject "extraordinary" statements in the pejorative sense of the term. But Austin's plain man (unlike the "man in the street") is both indifferent and as such irrelevant to fundamental philosophical decisions. Austin himself makes these decisions as a representative of a certain way of philosophizing, as one who employs extraordinary or technical discourse. The very notion of "the plain man" is technical. The "plain man" normally means someone without pretension or sophistication, not someone whose linguistic preferences are determinative for philosophy.

The "plain" (e.g., on pages 51, 52, 58, 59, 67, and 69) or "ordinary" (94) man is Austin's name for the nonphilosopher. Why does Austin believe that the speech habits of nonphilosophers are regulative for philosophical discourse? Clearly it is because he believes on philosophical grounds that the themes of philosophical investigation are rooted in, and emerge or develop from, the soil of everyday experience. In this sense, Austin is an empiricist. He is a linguistic empiricist who believes that there are no separate philosophical entities that constitute the subject-matter of philosophy, but that philosophy is instead the clarification of ordinary experience. The sophisticated or empiricist side of Austin's construction, "the plain man," certifies this belief. Little wonder that this procedure obliterates the vocabulary of traditional philosophy, and in particular, of metaphysics.

Even metaphysicians can be impressed by the authority of ordinary language in its reports on our common human experience. But the purpose of philosophy (and not just of metaphysics) is to go beyond ordinary language, and to show how the ordinary develops into the extraordinary, not how the extraordinary collapses into the ordinary. Many of Austin's steps are illuminating, but, taken cumulatively, they are moving in the wrong direction.

Chapter 7 What Do We Talk About?

Bertrand Russell said that "the point of philosophy is to start with something so simple as not to seem worth stating, and to end with something so paradoxical that no one will believe it."[1] This amusing statement by Russell is at least fifty percent true. Russell, however, may not live up to his own good advice. In the series of lectures in which this passage is found, Russell begins the exposition of his chief thesis, the legitimacy of analysis (47), with a discussion of facts, propositions, symbols, and relations. He proceeds to a discussion of logically proper names, in the course of which he asserts that facts corresponding to statements about names like Piccadilly (a street in London) contain no constituent corresponding to Piccadilly, which latter can be reduced to a series of classes of material entities (50 ff.). This odd assertion is part of Russell's exposition of the view that the only logically proper name is one of an entity with which we are directly acquainted; all other proper names—"Piccadilly," "Rumania," or "Socrates"—are to be treated as descriptions of ostensibly complex entities that can be analyzed into statements about series of classes. Russell at that time believed that classes are logical fictions; accordingly he believed that ostensibly complex entities like Socrates or Rumania, and in addition chairs, tables, and the other baggage of everyday life, are also logical fictions. Since our ordinary experience consists largely if not exclusively of these so-called logical fictions, it is plain that, on Russell's view, logic and ordinary experience are in cognitive dissonance.

The upshot of this initial stage of Russell's account of the legitimacy of analysis is that the only logically proper names are demonstratives like "this" and "that." The referents of these demonstratives are, for example, dots made on a blackboard by a piece of chalk. We can retain our reference to these logical simples for a minute or two. Russell has arrived very rapidly at a thesis so paradoxical that "no one" will believe it. The reason for this, I believe, is that he actually starts from the desire to refute the Hegelianism of his youth, or what he refers to in this series of lectures as the philosophy of monism, which he defines as the view that "the universe as a whole is a single complex entity" (50). Russell on the contrary wants to assert that the universe is built up out of particulars, each of which stands entirely alone and is completely self-subsistent, although each lasts only a short time, seconds or minutes, so far as our experience is concerned (63). It is obvious that, in rejecting monism, Russell arrives at sense-datum particularism. There is then a disjunction between logically correct speech and ordinary discourse; logically correct or philosophical speech has nothing to do with ordinary speech. This is obvious from various standpoints, one of which holds that it is not the logician's job to give any examples of logically independent particulars or (as we may call them) atoms. Despite Russell's salutary and repeated admonition that philosophy must begin with the imprecise, he himself proceeds only briefly through the domain of the obvious, on his way from one metaphysical thesis to another.

I shall follow a different itinerary. My intention is to examine the obvious at my leisure, in order to determine how we emerge from it into the domain of metaphysical theses. It could be objected at this point that such a leisurely examination is possible only for those who have already emerged from the ordinary into the domain of philosophy. I grant this point, but it is not a serious objection to my procedure, because I do not regard philosophy as a thesis or doctrine but a style of inquiry. I am not going to ransack ordinary experience for evidence of some favored philosophical position but instead I shall allow it to regulate my retrospective search for the features that have launched philosophical inquiry. In other words, the only assumption I could be said to be making is that philosophy has already occurred; it is part of our experience. I want to find out how this happens, and what we can learn about philosophical procedure from studying how this happens. My ostensible assumption is thus not an assumption but an observation, and one that could not be denied except by confirming it, since the denial of philosophy is already a philosophical exercise.

To start again, it is not at all compatible with ordinary experience to say that facts corresponding to statements contain no proper names ("Socrates") of complex entities (Socrates), because from the simplest and most comprehensive standpoint, Socrates is not a complex entity. By "most comprehensive" I mean what most people accept and indeed, assume without discussion. It is obviously true that Socrates contains parts, and that these parts will vary depending upon the mode of analysis. One could say that Socrates is made up of a body and soul, or of a head, torso, and limbs, or of some other set of properties. It could also be maintained that our perception of Socrates consists of sensations. But none of these analyses is possible unless we have first identified the individual person named Socrates. Philosophical problems arise as soon as we turn from identifications of independent particulars to the question of how it is possible for us to make these identifications, and so to the question of how such particulars exist. But the fact of the presence of subsisting individuals is not in dispute. Even problems that arise with respect to identifying this or that particular are addressed on the basis of the identification of other particulars. No sane person doubts that human beings are independent particulars, although anyone may doubt whether this or that set of sense-perceptions is in fact a human being.

The simple starting point, so obvious that it seems hardly worth mentioning, is that Socrates, Plato, and Aristotle, or Frege, Russell, and Wittgenstein, or you and I, or the tables and chairs and the other items in our everyday experience, are each and all separate and independent particulars. This obvious fact is prior to all questions of whether what present themselves as independent are at some deeper level interdependent, or even, strange as it seems, aspects of one complex entity, the universe. We can restate this simple starting point in a more general but still uncontroversial way: our experience is always of heterogeneous particulars, each distinguishable from the others, either actually or potentially, and if potentially, by means of other particulars that are actually so distinguishable. It is also true, and obvious, although not quite in the same way as the previous point, that the heterogeneous particulars of our experience are not discontinuous but constitute some kind of continuum. Let us consider this continuum for a moment.

As I sit by my desk, I discern that I am separate from it, and that separate particulars—a computer, a lamp, a book, a telephone, and so on,—sit on my desk. What does it mean to say that any two of these entities is separate the one from the other? I am separate from my desk by virtue of the independence of my body from the body of the desk. But this independence is not simply spatial. Another person could perceive the separation between me and my desk because my look, form, or perceivable nature is distinct from that of the desk. I do not look like what the desk looks like. I am a person and the desk is not. Incidentally, suppose that there were two desks sitting side by side. We could still distinguish between them by the difference in their spatial location, to say nothing of differences in appearance, color, substance, the grain of the wood, and so on, as well as the very shape of each desk, a shape that cuts it off from its neighbor. Even if the two desks have the same shape, we are able to distinguish that there are two desks with one shape, not one desk. This is because the look of the desk, its nature, what a desk is at all, includes finitude of dimension, detachment from other surrounding entities by the edges and corners of the surface, the legs on which the desktop rests, and so on.

If there were not a multiplicity of separate particulars, further differentiated by heterogeneity of kind or look, then there would be no ordinary experience as we ordinarily understand it. Now it is possible (in the sense of logically conceivable) that there might not be any experience at all, or even that what look to us like separate particulars are actually aspects of one unique monad. But these possibilities are conceivable not simply because we know logic but because the actual situation is quite different. It is possible that the actual situation could be other than it is, but, actually, it is not. You may object that "actually" has two different senses: (i) the opposite of "potentially," and (ii) in truth or at a deeper level, and that the reference to the actual situation makes use of the second sense. But this changes nothing. If things are one at a deeper level, this means that we have to penetrate the surface, namely, ordinary experience, in order to arrive at the depth, namely, metaphysical or logical truth. And I claim that there are no metaphysical or logical truths that are entirely incompatible with the surface articulation of ordinary experience. On this point, I am in agreement with the so-called "ordinary-language" philosophers.

This again requires a more careful formulation. I do not doubt that there may be big surprises in store for anyone who makes a philosophical investigation of ordinary experience. I also grant that we may have to jettison this or that ordinary conviction about the truth of things. What I deny is that we shall arrive at a compelling reason for rejecting ordinary experience as a whole. It is possible that everything is one at some fundamental level. But that level does not interfere with or invalidate the multiplicity, heterogeneity, and distinguishability of particulars at a less fundamental level. I would reject any contention that things are not multiple, not heterogeneous, and not distinct, if that view is based upon the contention that at some fundamental level they are one. More precisely I would object to calling such a level of unity "fundamental." What is actually fundamental is the level of diversity or multiplicity. If it is true that all things are somehow one, that "somehow" must be from a certain point of view or set of assumptions, which viewpoint or set of assumptions is itself intelligible only from the level at which things are not one.

To come back to discontinuity and the continuum, I am distinct from my desk; it and I are each distinct from my telephone, and so on. Nevertheless, the desk, the telephone, and I are all three entities within my study, which is a room in my house, a house that stands on a street of houses, a street in Wellesley, a town in Massachusetts, and so on and so forth. By continuing with this series, we would eventually arrive at the boundaries of the universe. Furthermore, at each step in the series we would be able to establish some kind of continuity. Objects in a person's study cohere by virtue of the function of studies in human life. Studies cannot exist efficiently on the sidewalk; they must be part of a coherently designed house. And so it goes. Continua of various kinds may be established, but only because there are distinguishable elements to be included within them.

I believe that we can generalize at this point in our analysis. Not only are entities of distinct kinds continuous with other entities by virtue of local criteria like spatial proximity, temporal sequence, or participation in a set of human intentions. There is also a unity in our experience that encompasses all continua, such that things hang together, acts are coherent as well as sequential, space-time does not collapse into unexpected abysses. When the poet Yeats says that "things fall apart; the center cannot hold," he is not referring to the universe but to the events in an individual life, or perhaps the joint life of a community. But this dissolution occurs within the continuum of experience and is identified with respect to it. Is it possible that the universe could dissolve at any second? The honest answer is, of course, that no one knows. But the more we learn, the more unlikely it seems. Stars may die; planets may be destroyed by meteors; the galaxy may fly apart; perhaps eventually our universe will contract into a space-time singularity. But these events are all transformations of the continuum, not a sudden dissolution of the continuum itself. This, I think, is the most we can say.

Kant refers to the unity of experience as a synthetic unity of the manifold.

But this kind of language assumes that the continuum of experience is produced by the experiencing subject. That is certainly not the assumption we make in ordinary life; it is also not the philosophical conclusion to which I have been led and for which I shall argue. The conclusion for which I shall be arguing is that the continuum of experience is both given and produced. I would, however, accept the thesis that the human being is that part of the whole, that is, the continuum of experience, who is not only open to, but who constitutes the whole by thinking it. To think the whole, however, is not to think the entities that make it up or the continuum that is its mode of manifestation. I can ask you to think of the whole family of natural numbers, or as mathematicians would say, the set of natural numbers, and you can do this. But what you have constituted is the set, i.e., the concept of totality, as it obtains with respect to the numbers, but you have not constituted the numbers themselves. Similarly I can ask you to conceive of the universe or whole, and you can do this, but in so doing, you do not literally produce the entities that make up the universe.

This is, however, getting ahead of ourselves. I am in the process of defending the thesis that we ordinarily speak of entities like streets, towns, persons, animals, or whatever you like, not as complex objects requiring analysis but as individual things of such and such a kind. By "such and such a kind" I mean "belonging to a family that exhibits a look through which we may identify the family members." This can be expanded into a kind of ontological axiom that one finds in Plato and Aristotle: "to be is to be this something of such and such a kind." Such a formulation is the distant ancestor of the more recent statement that "to be is to be the value of a variable in an interpreted proposition of the first-order calculus." This sort of talk should not deflect us into difficult questions about being and existence; it is introduced here for a much more modest purpose, namely, to show the natural philosophical implication of ordinary experience and everyday discourse.

Underlying all talk of subjects and predicates, and by extension of propositional functions, is the notion of properties that belong to an owner or possessor, which we call a substance. A substance is that which stands underneath in the sense of supporting; by a slight extension of sense it is taken to mean the owner of its properties, that which it supports. There is a further ambiguity here, because some properties are essential to the existence of the substance and some are not. Hence we speak of essential and accidental properties. The ambiguity is due to the fact that we cannot distinguish the essential from the accidental properties until we know the essence, but unfortunately, the way in which we are said to know the essence is through the essential properties. The solution to the ambiguity does not look like a solution to those who insist upon analysis as the road to intelligibility. I am referring to the grasp or cognitive vision, sometimes called the "intuition," of the form or look of the individual entity or substance, which either occurs or does not occur, and which is the basis when it occurs of all subsequent analyses, including those into essential and accidental properties, but which itself, *qua* intuition of the look, cannot be analyzed.

I note in passing that the substance is not the same as the "subject" of grammatical and logical analysis. A substance simply stands beneath or sustains; a subject stands beneath as thrown or projected. There could be substances without conscious and intentional subjects, but the positing of a subject is necessarily a reflexive act, one that can be performed only by an already existing subject. This is why the problem of defining the origination or interior structure of subjectivity is so intractable. The subject so to speak appears as self-projected. The subject-predicate analysis of the structure of the proposition is of course the subsequent result of self-projection, not the analysis of its origination from simpler elements.

Back, however, to our main line of inquiry. I see a cow, and am able to distinguish it from all other things that I have hitherto encountered. I point to the cow and ask the farmer, "What is that?" He looks in the direction I am pointing, and replies "A cow." Note that despite all sophisticated analyses of the ambiguities inherent in this situation, which boil down to claims that it is impossible to know what we are referring to, and so how to translate not only from one language into another but from one idiom of a given language into another, and by extension, from one perspective into another, despite all these ambiguities, I repeat, this is how we communicate; and we do so quite successfully, although problems occasionally arise. I do not want to list all these difficulties here, together with my replies to them, because I am in the process of making a different point, one that is antecedent to those difficulties. So let me just say briefly that the difficulties can be formulated only on the basis of an apprehension of the situation that we claim to be ambiguous. We cannot be puzzled about how we refer to cows unless we have succeeded in referring to cows. I will come back to this below.

Meanwhile I call the reader's attention to the fact that every analysis begins with a whole. This is not the same as to say, as does Russell, for example, that analyses begin with complex entities, in other words, that things I am calling wholes are actually complex entities. I say that in order to count as a complex entity, something must first be a whole: this thing here, discernible as of such and such a kind, and so as not of some other kind or as some other thing there. Bessie the cow is no doubt a complex entity from a logical or conceptual standpoint. But the structure of complexity either belongs to, or simply is, the look of this particular entity, Bessie the cow. To say that, whereas from an ordinary standpoint Bessie and Socrates appear to be particular entities, from a logical standpoint they are complex, is just to grant my point. The existence of logical complexity is dependent upon the ontologically prior existence of unitary wholes that can be discerned or intuited as wholes not subject to analysis except relative to the antecedent apprehension of that whole *qua* whole.

I want to underline this point. The logical analyst who shares Russell's views speaks implicitly or explicitly as follows. "Do you see that thing over there, which we call a cow? Well, it is actually a series of classes of material events, each of which corresponds to our direct acquaintance with it." I say on the contrary: "Do you see that cow over there? Well, it is actually a cow (or the illusion of a cow, which we take to be a cow because we have actually seen actual cows), and the series of classes of material events that we can associate with the cow are all associable in that way by virtue of exhibiting the look that enables us to identify things as cows." This is a fundamental philosophical difference, because I take my bearings by ordinary experience, whereas the logical analyst only pretends to do so.

It will not have escaped the reader's attention that what I am calling "looks" has something to do with the so-called Platonic theory of Ideas or pure forms. I am not defending that theory in its traditional version, but I would like to say that the theory can best be understood as rooted in the sense of the look of a particular thing, a look that is a whole because it provides us with the being of the thing as a particular "this" of such-and-such a kind; and I maintain that this is the only way in which we can perceive particular things. There may be processes, relations, abstract concepts, values, and so on that are not particular things in the same sense as are persons, animals, or even streets and towns. But each of these entities, in order to be anything at all, and so to be identified as something, must be something in particular, something of such-and-such a kind: this process, this abstract concept, and so on. By and large we start the process of apprehension, and so of discourse, by way of wholes. This is so even if we start with perceptions, thoughts, or statements about complexes of particulars, because the complex is intelligible only with respect to its particulars, and these in turn can be identified as particulars only because they are themselves wholes in the sense of independent entities of such and such a kind.

It makes no sense to speak of a process unless we say of what it is a process, and so too with relations. We can say that there is such a thing as the relation of "greater than," but this is intelligible only because we know that one thing is greater than another, that is to say, in order for the relation to be manifested, there must be two identifiable existing particulars, one of which is greater than the other (and so the other is less than the first). In general I hold that there is no thinking at all, and hence no speaking, unless it is thinking about particulars as wholes. These wholes are apprehended as distinguishable from one another, e.g., as this cow, that man, Socrates, Piccadilly, Rumania, or what have you. Furthermore, the wholes in question are none other than the elements of ordinary experience. As such, they have a phenomenological, empirical, sensed, priority over products of logical analysis. They are not constructed out of series of sets or classes of properties. First we intuit the whole; then we analyze. If this were not so, we would not know what we were analyzing, which is absurd or leads directly to absurdities.

It is perhaps worth considering a simple example in somewhat greater detail. How do I perceive Commonwealth Avenue, the street in Boston upon which my office is located? To begin with, of course, I must have a certain body of previous experience that includes knowledge of what it is to be a street. So the question of how I perceive Commonwealth Avenue includes the prior question of how I come to know what it is to be a street. Now I would maintain that there is no rigorous analysis of how I come to know this, although one could of course describe in general terms how experience accumulates. But how does experience accumulate? Obviously on the basis of the apprehension of particulars, individual "this heres" of such-and-such a kind, one of them being a path, street, or road, identified as elements in local travel, places where people live, where I can find the candy store, places where autos move at rapid speeds, and so on.

Once I am in this situation, namely, at this level of experience, I am in a position to perceive some street or another in a new city, or in a neighborhood with which I am not familiar. But when I ask "What is that street onto which the philosophy department building faces?" I am not asking for a series of classes of sense-data constituting the background knowledge required to understand the answer to my question, nor am I asking for the series of classes of sense-perceptions making up the street, since there is no such series, or rather, since there are countless such series of various persons' direct experience of that street. Furthermore, assume that I make my first contact with Commonwealth Avenue by entering Kenmore Square from Beacon Street. I have no previous direct experience with Commonwealth Avenue. I don't know, even in theory, say by consulting a map, where it ends and where it begins. It is also possible, in the most absurd sense of "possible," that what I take to be a street or avenue is an illusion, or that it extends only for a few feet beyond the point at which I enter it, and then turns into a swamp, or that it is an illusion produced by Martians.

None of this affects in any way my ability to understand you if you tell me, "This is Commonwealth Avenue." My experience is such that I have grasped the concept of a street or avenue; by entering into a certain directed path, bounded by curbs, lawns, buildings, and so forth, with cars and streetcars passing by in opposite and regulated directions, I know that I am now not only cognitively in touch with, but physically on, a street or in this case, an avenue. I may never travel on more than a short stretch of Commonwealth Avenue, but this will not prevent me from grasping it as an avenue, as something that is a unified whole, a particular with a look of such and such a kind. And this in turn guarantees that any other stranger with experience comparable to mine who first asks "What is this street?" already knows what it is to be a street, and thus knows Commonwealth Avenue as a this-here of such-and-such a kind, as soon as he or she receives the answer, "Commonwealth Avenue."

Now of course, for a more detailed conceptualization of the avenue, one requires more information, such as "the street that runs from X to Y," where the variables stand for places, other streets, or what have you. As soon, however, as I know that this particular street is Commonwealth Avenue, I am in a position to connect particular experiences, or reports by others of their particular experience, with this particular street. I am then in a position to connect up series of classes of experiences and reports to Commonwealth Avenue. But if I did not grasp the identity, in the sense of "identity" appropriate to a street or avenue, of Commonwealth Avenue prior to learning the series, I would not know that the latter refers to Commonwealth Avenue. Russell's logical analysis of what we know by the name "Piccadilly" may or may not be a sound analysis of that knowledge, once we acquire it, but it is a false analysis of how we get to know a particular street and also of what it means to say that we know a certain street. If the analysis is sound, in other words, it must be for some purpose other than explaining what it is to know Piccadilly.

I suspect that Russell would be inclined to grant much if not all of what I have said here, except to insist upon the fact that ordinary speech is logically incoherent or conceptually muddled, and that the pursuit of philosophical knowledge demands an approach like his. I deny this. In the first place, ordinary speech is neither logically incoherent nor conceptually muddled. Ordinary speakers may of course become incoherent or muddled if they cease to speak in the ordinary way, that is, if they violate the ordinal rules of everyday discourse. But so long as we obey those rules we are all right.

I take it that on this point, I am in general agreement with the later Wittgenstein. I disagree with him when he characterizes intuition as "an unnecessary shuffle." On the contrary, I hold that it is precisely by the perception, that is, the intuition of subsisting particulars as wholes that we identify by their looks as a this-thing-here of such and such a kind, that we are put into the position of applying, consciously or otherwise, the rules of ordinary discourse. In my view, it would be nonsensical to say that we identify particulars of this sort by the application of rules of linguistic use. Wittgenstein reminds us here of Kant, according to whom perceptual identification takes place through a schema that mediates between sensation and a concept. This is in effect to say that there is a cognitive rule for the perceptual understanding of a sensed particular. One has only to study the relevant analyses of the first *Critique* to see that Kant is unable to explain what is the rule for distinguishing, say, a dog from an elephant. In fact, the rule for applying (in English) the name "dog" is patently based upon our prior intuition of dogs as creatures of such-and-such a kind. We have no real difficulty in speaking about streets, cities, animals, or persons as though they were separate and independent particulars, not because we start with a list of rules telling us how to use names, but because our intuitions allow us to formulate rules; and it is only thanks to this success that we are able to speak of parts of such particulars, such as sense-data.

Not only is ordinary language not muddled, but the series of classes to which Russell claims to be able to reduce the particulars of ordinary experience is clearly not the same as those ordinary particulars in any way. Bessie the cow or Socrates is not a series of classes but a particular cow or human being. When we eat a beefsteak, it is Bessie we are eating, not a class of material events; when we talk to Socrates, we are not talking to a series of classes. But I go beyond this and insist that, when we know what it is to be a cow or a person, it is Bessie and Socrates that we know, not series of classes.

I am now in a position to formulate some general remarks about how we talk, and so about what constitutes legitimate discourse. We talk about things, such as cows, persons, computers, streets, houses, and towns. We also talk about actions of living beings, relations of things of any kind, moral qualities, abstract ideas such as patriotism and virtue, and so on. Whatever we talk about is something or other, identifiable by virtue of a look that enables us to say what the thing exhibiting the look in question is like, to what it is related, what it is doing, or anything else we care to say about it. Talk is at least initially always *about* something, including itself (e.g., "That was a boring speech I gave yesterday"). If "aboutness" is the essence of intentionality, then all speech is intentional; there is no speech that is *about* nothing at all. The one possible exception to this rule is the case of nothing, and that case cannot even be formulated without slipping into paradoxes. Normally when we speak about nothing, we are negating something in particular: even the case of not-being is one in which we negate everything. It is only when we try to speak about nothing or what the Eleatic Stranger in Plato's *Sophist* calls "the altogether not" that we run into trouble. I have written on this limit-case elsewhere, and will not repeat myself here. It lies at the boundary of ordinary experience and is therefore not a helpful problem by which to take our bearings.

Although I claim that all speech is about something, I do not claim to be able to list all the somethings about which we do or could speak. Furthermore, I have claimed that it is the look of things that enables us to speak about them; but I have made no attempt to identify the nature or to give a deeper analysis of the inner structure of looks *qua* looks. Such an attempt would fall outside the perimeter of everyday discourse. The crucial point so far is that ordinary experience licenses us to move in that direction or to talk about the looks of things. To do this is not to engage in illegitimate, muddled, or meaningless speech. Claims that it does so are themselves absurd, although not quite meaningless, because we cannot speak of series or classes, let alone predicates or functions, unless we know what we are talking about. Since we obviously do not begin with logically and epistemologically perfect definitions of these things, but rather with an apprehension of the things themselves, such an apprehension is possible only thanks to the way in which things like series, classes, predicates, and functions exhibit themselves, namely, as stamped by a look of such-and-such a kind. In short, all talk about technical entities or logical analyses of everyday things is second-order discourse about the objects of ordinary experience, which themselves make up one class of what we primarily talk about (as do classes of emotions, actions, intentions, and so on).

The point about looks as the basic articulation constituting the continuum of experience carries with it another fundamental conclusion about speech. It cannot be the case that thought and speech are identical or even coordinate. Thought is antecedent to speech in the way that seeing something is the necessary presupposition for saying anything about it. It cannot be the case that things are constituted by our speaking about them, since then we could say and do anything we wished. And in this case, of course, we would not know what we are talking about, since there would be no "about," which always refers to something toward which speech is directed, and so which is independent of speech; it does not refer to something that emerges as we speak.

Neither does it make sense to refer to discursive constituting as transcendental; this would require every speaker to constitute things in the same way. But that is not how things work. We can, of course, try to discover the categorial structure that underlies speech about anything whatsoever, but this enterprise rests in turn upon our ability to speak about anything whatsoever, provided that "anything" means "anything of such-and-such a kind." I myself do not believe that we can state in advance what kinds of things we can speak about. A categorial structure of discourse, of course, claims to be something quite different, namely, the set of logical conditions that must be met in order for anything rational or intelligible to be said at all. I doubt whether such a structure could be determined. But let us assume that it could. It still tells us nothing about what to say next; this depends upon what happens, upon what things we encounter, and so what we see, not simply what we say or choose to say. The statements we utter will all be analyzable, once we have uttered them, in accord with the categorial structure (if it works). But the structure does not itself produce any statements; we do this, and not simply (or at all) by consulting the structure. We do it by responding to our experience, i.e., primarily to what we see, and secondarily to what we do on the basis of what we see. We should also note that even if we had to consult the categorial structure in order to speak, this would still give priority to seeing the looks of the structure, rather than to speaking.

To say that thinking is posterior to seeing looks is not to say that all thinking, and so all speaking, is just the description of previously existing looks. The priority of existing looks serves as the condition and so the license for the speech that produces new looks, for example, poetry, philosophy, or science. We recognize a look as new only by contrast with old looks. But we are certainly capable of doing so, just as we are capable of speaking in a new and original way. But novelty depends upon order. Perhaps we produce order transcendentally, but again, seeing it precedes speaking about it. We could hardly produce transcendental order simply by speaking about it, since then anyone could produce any transcendental order he or she happened to state. And there is another consideration. If thinking is talking, how could we understand the first sentence we utter or hear? Not by means of another previously existing assertion, since there aren't any, by hypothesis. At some point, and apparently at the first point, we have to see what is meant by what is said; and to see what is meant is not in turn to say something, although once having seen something, we can then say what we saw.

If I am right, then, there is no way in which to determine in advance what we can see, hence what we can say. And this is so both immanently and transcendentally. On the other hand, it is possible to identify the most pervasive features of everyday discourse within ordinary experience. I have just done this in my articulation of what it is to be anything at all, and why this is the basis for experience and so for thinking and speaking. Now from the standpoint of ordinary experience, of course, all talk about transcendental constituting makes no sense. Kant did not posit the transcendental as a result of his experience of cows and persons, but in order to validate causal connections and necessary truths. But this implies that ordinary experience is somehow in danger of falling apart unless it is glued together with a series of transcendental syntheses.

Kant was apparently persuaded by Hume's skeptical analysis of our inability to apprehend causal connections. But why should anyone be surprised at the impossibility of arriving at a necessary connection by way of the analysis of experience? Analysis takes apart; it does not connect. The only way in which we can grasp necessary connections is by intuiting them. Not even a synthesis will do the job, because there is no reason to attribute necessity to a synthesis. How do we know that it won't fall apart or in other words that its parts are not connected contingently? Nothing is changed by waving a wand and saying, "I christen thee a transcendental synthesis." We still have to see that the connection is necessary. And sometimes we are fooled. Therefore we could be fooled with respect to what we call transcendental syntheses.

There are two reasons for the rise of transcendental philosophy. One is a failure to appreciate the force of heterogeneity or the fact that things exhibit discernible and distinguishable looks. More precisely, there is a failure to see that the necessary connection between, say, a cause and an effect is not something separate from the behavior of the cause and the consequent appearance of the effect. Second, there is a failure to see that there could never be any question of "proving" that the sequence of cause and effect is literally necessary, i.e. that given the cause, the effect must follow. How could this be proved? What premiss serves as the first principle from which we derive the necessity of a causal connection? There isn't any. We can say that there is a principle called the law of causality and that when we perceive B following A, that perception is "synthesized" into the thinking of a causal connection; but that is just to say that we see or intuit a causal connection. We might be wrong, whether we call this perception transcendental or immanent. So I don't see that Kant has accomplished anything at all on this point, beyond raising the possibility that intuitions may be synthetic in some cases. But he has no method for proving which are the cases. Hence we have to fall back on intuition.

As a matter of fact, we establish causal connections without relying explicitly on either synthesis or intuition. We do this by observation and experiment. For example, if the sunlight falling on a stone for several hours heats that stone, and this process recurs frequently, we come to say that the sunlight causes the stone to heat. If someone asks us for a proof, we say: "watch what happens tomorrow when the sunlight falls on the stone. And note the temperature of the stone tonight, when there is no sunlight." This is a very simple example, indeed, one used by Kant himself. It may serve as a model for much more complicated examples, including those that involve highly sophisticated machines and elaborate controlled experiments. Nothing is added to the procedure by calling it a case of transcendental synthesis. In fact, the whole procedure reminds me of witch-doctors who pronounce magic formulae over ordinary acts in order to invest them with a special dignity.

The Kantian will of course be outraged at what I have said thus far about transcendental philosophy. Let me underline the fact that I am not denying the truth of claims that the cognitive process plays an essential role in the constituting of the whole. I am saying that we have to see what we are doing, in order to be able to state what is the meaning or sense or effect of what we are doing. We can see that there are certain connections that we take to be necessary. But we cannot see that they are in fact necessary because the cognitive process has glued them together. In fact, Kant never says that we can; instead, he says that his suggestion is a likely hypothesis, that is, it will solve the problems discovered by Hume if we adopt it as a working hypothesis. I claim that it does not solve those problems; it merely licenses us to ignore them by attributing connections to transcendental synthesis. Previous to Kant, we said that a certain sequence of events seems to exhibit a causal connection because, if we assume that it does, we can then account for a variety of experiences. Kant asks us to say that a certain sequence of events exhibits a causal connection because the transcendental ego has glued them together. Now how can we see that this is so? No one can see the transcendental ego. So we have to look at the sequence; and thus we are back to our starting point.

All Kant adds to the picture is the following argument. The causal connection seems to be necessary. But we can't see necessity unless we put it there by the very act of seeing it. So let's assume that we have put it there. Now we can be confident of our perception.

I reject this as absurd. Since we can't see the transcendental ego or any of its activities, all that we see is just what we saw before we invoked the hypothesis. The connection in question will be no more and no less necessary whether we invoke the hypothesis or not. Therefore I am not a Kantian. Needless to say, this is not the only reason I am not a Kantian. I think that on this important point, however, Kant instilled a false sense of confidence that began to dissipate almost immediately, thanks to the discovery of various truths that according to him were impossible. And this led in turn to the triumph of Humean skepticism, disguised in one form or another, e.g., as historicism, relativism, perspectivism, and now hermeneutics.

I suspect that we are in the same position with respect to causal necessity as we are with respect to the possibility of the universe dissolving suddenly. The possibility exists that some day a given causal law will not work, just as no one can prove that the universe will not some day disappear. But the appeal to transcendental synthesis is like going into a monastery or invoking the will of God in order to escape the horrible consequences. If the reader does not find persuasive what I have said here about Kant, I ask that he or she at least consider carefully my minimal claim, namely, that we have to see the categorial structure, and so too the operation of transcendental synthesis, in order to talk about it. This claim is all I need by way of repudiating the thesis that thought is entirely discursive, or that thinking is speaking.

Thus far I have argued that we talk about what the Aristotelian tradition calls "substances," and that these are nothing more or less than "things." Second, I have claimed that the things of ordinary experience are the primary referents of our discourse. And third, I have denied that we produce all things by the act of thinking or perceiving them. But this is in no way to deny that we do produce many things, and even that we modify or add to the properties of those things that we do not produce.

I want now to consider the role that construction plays in discursive thinking, as it functions within the ordinary experience that is the matrix of all philosophical speech. My argument in this section is based upon the assumption that the Aristotelian triple partition of the arts and sciences into theoretical, practical, and productive is validated by our pretheoretical experience of the distinctness of seeing, of making, and of performing an intentional act with a view to the acquisition of some good.

It seems initially that production is closer to theory than to practice because it depends upon specialized knowledge, and it has in each manifestation in the arts and sciences a particular intention rather than a concern with the totality of human life. Its intention is to produce a definite result rather than to evaluate the role of that result within common life. The closeness of production and theory seems to be a special feature of modern, and in particular, late-modern conceptions of theory, which tend to minimize the difference between discovery and invention. But even further, just as the meaning of theory has gradually shifted from "seeing" or discovering to making, so too has practice or "doing" come to be understood as a kind of self-production. It is a widely acknowledged characteristic of late modernity that these shifts in meaning have led to special prominence for *techne*. It is scarcely an exaggeration to say that life itself comes more and more to be regarded as a technical artifact. What used to be called "the soul" is now widely regarded as a product of history or society; as to the body, the extraordinary success of replacing its parts by artifacts lends support to the popular view (or revival of the eighteenth-century view) that the body is a machine.

There is, nevertheless, some kind of limit on this conception of total technology or let us say, of the combination of sociology and technology, with the former in process of being reduced to the latter. We still feel it necessary to argue the merits of a technical and constructive conception of practice, with its corollary that theory is productive or that it interprets rather than discovers. Even the greatest champions of technical proficiency find it necessary to speak of the love of truth, the glory of science, and the superiority for social and political reasons of a continuously improving, ever more powerful technology. These arguments will no doubt disappear if the tendencies intrinsic to contemporary philosophies of neuroscience and artificial intelligence should come to dominate totally. Very little can be said about the social and political life, and therefore the spiritual values, of parallel processing computers.

Meanwhile, the debate continues, and one must assume that, if truth is exclusively or essentially mathematical and technical, then the terms of the debate must be sheer rhetoric. It is not possible to transform the praise of technology into a mathematical equation. One could of course represent the syntax of the sentences of such praise in a formal calculus, but eventually the process of providing formal interpretations of the sentences must terminate in a human language that is no longer formal and that not only articulates the syntax of approving sentiments but itself approves. A formal representation of approval is not an act of approval by a sentient being. The assertion sign in logic is not itself an assertion, but a sign from one intelligent being to another that an assertion is called for.

A philosophy of machines is a human production, not a production by machines. The possibility of philosophy thus rests within the obscure region in which common sense and *techne* cooperate as distinguishable if not completely separate elements. The question is whether our primary sense of truth is more like *techne* than like common sense. Otherwise stated, is there a truth that expresses the totality of human experience without reducing theory to practice and practice to production or *techne*?

I begin my inquiry with the assistance once more of Aristotle. According to Aristotle, truth is a property of statements, namely, those that say of what is that it is, and of what is not that it is not. I believe that this is the simplest and most general sense of "truth," and I shall adopt it for introductory purposes. There is also a sense of "true" as "genuine" or "preeminent," but this sense is obviously derivative from the first. I cannot identify something as a genuine x without distinguishing between two or more instances of x, or more generally between those that are genuine and those that are not, and this in turn requires me to identify the kind x, or in other words to be able to say of x that it is x, and of not-x that it is not x.

This last point requires expansion. If we identify something as a genuine diamond, we mean to say that it is truly a diamond, and not a zircon, or a piece of glass. This is a way of saying of the diamond that it is a diamond, but one that rests upon a tacit comparison between diamonds and things that can be mistaken for diamonds. "Preeminent" carries a somewhat stronger meaning. We can compare genuine diamonds in order to determine which of them is preeminent of its kind, on the basis of whatever criteria are deemed apposite to the rank-ordering of diamonds, such as the number of carats. In this light, we say of one of a group of genuine diamonds that "this is a true diamond!" by which we do not mean that the others in the group are false, but that this one is superior to the rest. In general, words like "genuine," "preeminent," "authentic," and so on, are all implicit comparatives, and they invoke a judgment on the part of the speaker that is rooted in (at least) two poles: (1) the assertion that something is what he or she says that it is, and (2) that this correct identification serves as the basis to pass judgments on other items that either are or seem to be of the same kind as the identified item. When an expert says, "This is a genuine diamond," he or she is assuring me that it is indeed a diamond, and neither a natural nor an artificial simulacrum. It can be genuine without being preeminent, but it can be neither genuine nor preeminent unless it is a diamond. Hence the fundamental importance of the power to say of what is that it is, and of what is not, that it is not.

It should be plain that a similar analysis applies to actions, a term that I use here to refer to the intentional or purposive behavior of human beings. But there is a difference between actions and things. In order to identify a diamond,

I do not need to know the use to which it will be put or the value that is attached to it in society. If, however, I see a man who carries a leather ball and is running across a striped field with a number of other persons in hot pursuit, I cannot identify the motion of the runner as an action unless I know that he is playing (say) football. It is true that the diamond acquires a function or a group of functions when it enters into society that it does not have in the shaft or rock in which it is initially embedded. But a chemist can identify the diamond without knowing these functions. He must know these functions in order to identify the actions performed by human beings with diamonds, but not to know the chemical composition of the stone he is examining. The motion of the football player, on the other hand, when taken apart from the social institution of the game of football, has no particular meaning. We might be able to give a physiological or a physical description of the motion, but this would take us to a level different from that of social action. The chemical analysis of the diamond, on the other hand, remains correct (or incorrect) regardless of the social value of the diamond, and most important, it remains the same *within* society, as fulfilling its various social roles.

Action, in other words, is not the assertion of what is and what is not, but the investment of meaning in motions and objects, ranging from modifications of physiological desire to religious and philosophical rank-orderings of social and political institutions, laws, and customs in accord with our conceptions of the good life. Philosophy and science are themselves actions in the sense that we invest meaning in and attribute excellence to the pursuit of these inquiries. Whereas theory may not be practice, the life of theory is indeed a practice, because we choose to live this form of life rather than another, and we make this choice because we believe that it is the highest kind of life, at least for us and those like us.

It is of course true that the chemical identification of a diamond depends upon the activity of science, which is a social institution or essential dimension of our way of life. The identification of diamonds, or the discovery of planets circling some distant star, are actions that possess a special significance, which we normally call "the pursuit of truth," but the chemical composition of the diamond or the existence of the distant planet is independent of the value that society attributes to chemical or astronomical knowledge. The diamond and the planet must exist, and be identifiable, in order for the social value of truth to come into play. Otherwise, we could pretend that there are diamonds and planets, and science would become fantasy. I say "could" and "would," but this is already going too far, since the fantasy in question would depend upon the existence of stable simulacra of diamonds and planets, or in other words, things of which we can say truly that they are or are not, and of course, that they are or are not things of such-and-such a kind. Please note that this point holds good even upon the acceptance of philosophical doctrines according to which the cognitive process is itself an essential part in the formation of objects of experience.

In sum, we can say of actions that they are or are not things of such-and-such a kind: This is a touchdown run and that is a marriage ceremony. But actions are intentional in the sense that they are purposive. A diamond exists whether we encounter it or not, and certainly whether we employ it as a social entity or not. But the touchdown run and the marriage ceremony have no existence outside an intricate network of purposes that express human desires and aspirations.

There are then two different ways of talking about actions. The first way is to make true or false statements about them, just as we do in the case of diamonds, or the processes of human physiology. This first way includes factual statements about the function of things or processes within social and political action. In order to be in a position to make true statements of this sort, we must understand human motivation; that is, we cannot speak the truth about an action simply by describing it as a motion of bodies of such-and-such a kind. We must also state truly the intention underlying this concatenation of motions, and indeed, a purely kinetic account of the action, if such were possible, would be not only irrelevant but untrue. It would be a false description of characteristically human life.

The second way of talking about actions, and more generally, about the social and political institutions, customs, laws, and so on that produce these actions or give them their decisive significance, is to express our approval or disapproval, that is, to rank-order them as good, bad, rational, irrational, exalted, low, beautiful, ugly, and even healthy or decadent, to give some of the most salient examples. It is of course one thing to say that so-and-so approves of a certain action, and another to say that so-and-so is correct to approve of it. Social scientists, but also tourists, are likely to make assertions of the first kind, whereas members of a given society are likely to make assertions of the second kind. The social scientist and the tourist speak as observers, whereas members of a society speak on the basis of an intention shared with that of the actor.

Otherwise stated, there is a difference between explaining an action and performing it. And there are two different ways of approving an action. The first is the way of the observer, who distinguishes between acts that fulfil an intended purpose and those that do not. The second is the way of the performer, who intends through his action to carry out the purpose. Both the observer and the performer say, or may say, of the same action, that it is good. Yet they are making two different statements. The first statement can be reformulated as a hypothetical: "If you accept the intention of the agent, this is a good action." Note that members of a society can utter statements of this sort, which we call "detached," because the speaker is attempting to view the situation as a stranger, that is, as one who states the consequences of an action without endorsing them. The second statement cannot be accurately reformulated in this way, or rather, if it can, it requires a supplement. The supplement is of course that of endorsement, or the affirmation of the goodness of the action by someone who accepts the standards of the agent, or of the social context within which the action is to be performed.

On the basis of this simple sketch of what is more ostentatiously called theory and practice, it seems to be indisputable that we are constantly engaged in uttering truths. We also utter falsehoods, but the criterion for identifying and rejecting these assertions is the truth itself. Speaking the truth, in the sense of saying of what is that it is, and of what is not that it is not, is fundamental to human life. It is impossible to maintain coherently that the truth is entirely inaccessible to us. As Leibniz remarks somewhere, if life is a dream, what counts is the structure of the dream. We cannot express our lack of the truth except by describing, and so asserting it truly. And I believe that we can go one step farther. The "structure" of the dream cannot have been produced by the dreamer. In more prosaic terms, the various structures of life cannot all be "technical" in the sense of artifacts of the process of cognition. In order to buttress this step, we have to look more closely at the difference between ordinary and technical language.

I begin with a commonplace. The single most important fact about the modern age is the steadily increasing power of experimental science. This power manifests itself most clearly in the form of technology. I use this term to refer not simply to the complex procedures by which theoretical science is transformed into the mastery of nature, but also to what I shall call "technical discourse." The word *techne* can be most simply defined as a step-by-step procedure for accomplishing some intention, a procedure that follows an order that can be codified as a method, and so can be taught by one person to another. In this simple sense, of course, technical discourse, or as one could also say, technical thinking, is very widespread. It would not be easy, if it is even possible, to make a sharp distinction between technical discourse in the wide sense and what I shall call "ordinary discourse." But this distinction will at least allow us to begin the search for a more adequate analysis.

For introductory purposes, it will suffice to suggest that ordinary discourse cannot be reduced to a method, and that it consists of terms, expressions, and concepts that are readily available to every normal speaker of what linguists call a natural language. The expression "natural language" is itself a technical term, but this is not of decisive importance for the moment. A natural language is of course not natural but historical. It is called "natural" in order to indicate that its growth is not the result of an antecedent decision by a group of specialists, acting in accord with a well-defined method of syntactic and semantic construction. A language can be formalized once it has grown up, but the validity of this formalization is itself limited by changing usage within the natural language. And the changes cannot be rigorously defined in advance by a set of equations. I hardly need to emphasize the other differences between a natural language and its formalization, in particular, that we cannot carry out conversations appropriate to everyday thought and action in a formal language. One could not even state the point or utility of a formal language in a formal language.

Most of the sentences we utter in everyday life are instances of ordinary discourse. Examples range from platitudes ("Have a nice day") to the countless expressions of the desires and intentions that make up the web of communal existence. Sentences like "Please shut the door" or "I love you" can be easily understood within the linguistic horizon of human motivation that requires no special training beyond that provided by life itself. We shift from ordinary to technical discourse when we employ terms or expressions the meaning of which depends at least initially upon the decision of a subset of the speakers of the natural language. Special training is required in order to understand technical discourse. Words are taken out of their normal use or even invented, in order to express a procedure or entity that deviates from what is usually acquired or encountered. This is a very rudimentary definition, but I doubt that there is a technical definition of technical discourse.

It could perhaps be argued that all ordinary discourse is technical in the wide sense of the term, since we must learn how to use the elements of our language in order to express anything whatsoever. But this is implausible, since we cannot define technical discourse until we have mastered ordinary language. There must first be a common language before we can invent technical terms, which by definition deviate from what is ordinarily said. I do not doubt that this process begins at an early stage in our linguistic history. But it must be preceded by an understanding, however rudimentary, of the language, however primitive, within which the technical terms are to be defined. That preliminary understanding cannot possibly arise from the concatenation of elementary technical definitions.

It is important to note that the ordinary discourse of a natural language is historical and not simply natural. But this is not to say that it is entirely historical. The English spoken by residents of the seventeenth century contains many expressions that would not be immediately intelligible to the nonspecialist English speaker of the twentieth century, and this modification is greater, the further back we go into the linguistic past of each natural language. But the modification is not complete; if it is, then we have moved back from one language to another, as for example, from Italian to Latin. In sum: languages change with time, but in a manner that is intelligible. Each linguistic generation can learn how to read the version of its natural language that predominates in a previous generation. And, despite the fears of some philosophers, we can translate one natural language into another. This is enough to render entirely plausible the belief in some constancy of human nature that persists across linguistic change and serves as the basis for the intelligibility of translation, whether from an earlier to a later stage of the language or from one distinct language into another. It is thus not the language that is natural, but the speaker.

Natural language thus includes ordinary and technical discourse. I have already indicated that ordinary discourse is itself filled with technical expressions, in the widest sense of the term "technical." The vocabulary of ploughing the field, building a house, or producing a pair of shoes is already a mixture of ordinary and technical expressions. Although the instructions for making shoes are much simpler than those for programming a computer, we are not born with these instructions imprinted within our consciousness, or for that matter, in our DNA. Shoe making is not like breathing; we acquire the art through experience; we must learn how to make shoes. But the mastery of nature intrinsic to the discovery of shoe making requires a linguistic skill that is closer to breathing than are the various aspects of computer technology. I mean by this initially odd expression that walking is like breathing in the sense that we cannot carry out our lives without engaging in that activity. Whereas our parents assist us in the procedure of walking properly, they can do this only because we begin to walk spontaneously at a certain age. One could say that human beings employ computers because at an early stage of the life of all normal human beings, we begin to count. But the distance from primitive counting to the computer is enormously greater than the distance from walking to making shoes that can protect one's feet. In negotiating that distance, we have moved from technical discourse in the wide sense through one layer after another of progressively more technical discourse.

One of the great problems facing the philosopher is to understand the difference between "more" and "less" with respect to technical discourse. This problem can be restated as follows: What is natural and what is artificial about human beings? Let me press further the comparison between breathing and using a computer. The process of breathing can be described in ordinary, everyday terms as the inhalation and exhalation of air, or in a more complex way by a deeper uncovering of the relevant physiological mechanisms, which in turn requires a discussion of the chemical composition of what we ordinarily call "air." This last is part of the technical discourse of biologists, physicians, and chemists, to mention no others. The technical description of breathing differs from its ordinary counterpart in rendering more precise our understanding and ability to control the processes that constitute breathing. It is unnecessary if we want only to express a preference for fresh over foul air, or to grasp the connection between the cessation of breathing and the absence of life.

We could probably arrange examples involving the understanding of breathing in an order of approximately increasing technical knowledge. This increase in knowledge could conceivably result in the modification of human behavior, for example, through the invention of apparatus for the supply of oxygen below the surface of the ocean, or in outer space. But a refined knowledge of breathing would never result in the capacity of human beings to cease breathing altogether, however sophisticated the machinery upon which we might come to rely in order to avoid future limitations on our behavior. The more interesting question is whether the expansion of our technology, through which we are able to explore the depths of oceans and the reaches of outer space, has changed our minds, souls, spirits, or essential humanity. The attempt to answer this question would take us beyond our elementary reflection on breathing. It would require a profound analysis of what is meant by "mind," "soul," "spirit," and in particular, "essential humanity."

This brings us back to the computer. In my opinion, the first thing that needs to be said is that the whole question of whether the mind is a computer or computer software is itself based upon two assumptions that predispose many specialists to an affirmative answer. The first assumption is that the fundamental dualism in our reflection upon the nature of humanity is one between the body and the mind, and not, say, between the body and the soul. Think of how different philosophy of mind is from a discipline that asks whether the soul is erotic. The second assumption is that thinking is reducible to logical inference or calculation. These assumptions have not been verified by scientific discovery but are themselves the rhetorical consequences of a widespread confidence in the explanatory power of mathematical analysis and scientific experimentation. This confidence is rooted in, or let us say leads to, a narrowing in our conception of what it is to be a human being, a narrowing that is enforced for the sake of technical convenience. The two main forms of this narrowing are first, the mathematicizing of reason, and second, the shift in emphasis from virtue to passion. Both forms receive their exemplary expression in the works of Descartes.

My point here is that the present conflict about the philosophical, and so the human, consequences of computers and more broadly, neuroscience, is not going to be resolved at the technical level of engineering, computer programming, and cognitive science. This level has emerged as a result of philosophical arguments that themselves address human capacities having nothing to do with computers or neuroscience. And these arguments in turn are motivated by rhetorical expressions of enthusiasm for science and technology. I do not mean to say that these expressions are empty, any more than I advocate the smashing of machines and the suppression of science. But the task of evaluating their content depends upon a return to the wider context from which the terms of the present debate emerged. This return is justified by the fact that the rhetorical claims for computer technology and neuroscience have no scientific, mathematical, and so rational validity as philosophical recommendations. The conception of the human being that emerges from the logical extension of these claims is not self-evidently superior, to put it mildly, to alternative conceptions that preserve science and technology as instruments of rational agency.

In a different sense, one could say that poetic accounts of someone's breathing as passionate or stertorous or through the use of unique figures of speech, are also technical in that they reveal something about human emotion that would not normally be expressed in that way. The point that concerns me, however, is that both scientific and poetic speech about breathing depend for their intelligibility upon the antecedent intelligibility of our ordinary account of breathing.

The scientist and the poet both present us to ourselves in ways that go beyond what is ordinarily said or understood. But this does not mean that we can make a sharp break between ordinary and technical discourse. The roots of science and poetry are both contained within ordinary language; in addition, what counts as ordinary is itself modified by the steady influence of scientific and poetical language. As was implied in a previous remark about natural language, ordinary discourse is itself historical. Nor would it be plausible to contend that the modification of ordinary language, assuming that such a level of discourse could be identified, by technical terms and expressions, is inferior to ordinary language itself. It would be much more plausible to maintain that we ought to use different types of discourse, to the extent that we have some control over the selection process, in different contexts. There is a time for science and a time for poetry, but also a time for ordinary language. It remains to be seen whether there is also a time for philosophical language.

One point seems to be secure. Neither science nor poetry could exist if there were no accessible truths about what is and what is not. But this in turn requires at least a primitive level at which things have natures that permit us to identify them. Stated as simply as possible, science and poetry are about something. To take the most pertinent example, science and poetry are not autonomous processes but human actions, and therefore they are the expression of human intentions. If science and poetry themselves alter what it is to be human, they certainly do not create humanity ex nihilo. Intentions do not create themselves. In other words, science and poetry are abstractions; it is scientists and poets that intend. A total transformation in the intentional agent would result in actions that we cannot comprehend, or rather the cessation of action as currently understood.

No one can guarantee that this sort of transformation is impossible. My point is only that it is unintelligible. Therefore all attempts to explain human intentions and actions on the hypothesis of continuous self-transformation are equally unintelligible. In particular, the changing or historical character of ordinary discourse, whether in its technical or commonsensical idiom, is itself intelligible only if we possess a grasp of human intentions, purposes, and possibilities. Otherwise put, history must itself be intelligible, not in the grand Hegelian sense but in a way that accounts for our ability to understand change and to prefer one set of values or way of life to another.

I myself doubt whether epistemology, or the attempt to provide a quasi-scientific foundation to the knowledge of "knowledge," is itself possible. Formal accounts of knowledge restrict in advance what something must be to qualify as a kind of knowledge, and attempts of this sort have been historically unsuccessful. More reasonable are technical accounts of what it is to know in particular disciplines like mathematics, physics, and so on. Formal or technical epistemologies depend for their cogency upon our capacity to understand them and to assess their rival claims. This capacity cannot itself be explained by the epistemology of our preference. Nor is a biological, psychological, or sociological explanation of the mechanisms underlying pretheoretical understanding equivalent to that understanding itself. On the contrary, such technical explanations are themselves technical artifacts, and thus historical entities.

For the moment, I restrict myself to the following observation. Rather than try to provide a new theoretical account of intelligibility, it seems much more sensible to reconsider the commonsensical implications of the undeniable intelligibility of life, an intelligibility that allows us to recognize our ignorance and to perceive intractable difficulties as well as to argue for the relative merits of competing accounts of human experience. It is precisely this intelligibility that allows us to reject one standard and adopt another. And even if such changes are "unconscious" or historically induced, they can be understood once they have occurred. We know the difference between ourselves and our historical predecessors, even in the limit case in which we say that some ancient custom is no longer comprehensible to us. Even the prisoner of historical determinism is capable of preferring one cell in the prison to another.

I am therefore proceeding upon the basis of the inferred consequences of the fact of the intelligibility of human experience in the sense just stated. Human being is not constructed from a sequence of discontinuous historical moments, each of which is discursively inaccessible to the others. The modifications induced in our behavior by the accumulation of technical discourse are transmitted from one generation to the next by the ordinary discourse that preserves the meaning and value of the aforementioned modifications. This function cannot be performed by technical discourse itself, if the latter is by hypothesis the agent of continuous self-transformation.

Technical discourse, then, is necessarily incomplete for at least two reasons. First: whereas it raises the phantom of a radically historical process of continuous self-transformation, it possesses or expresses no historical or cultural memory. Human life is continuous within time, and each stage of technical progress is itself associated with a distinct stage of political, scientific, artistic, and social development. Precisely if it is true that technical change induces these developments, we require other modes of discourse in order to preserve the continuity of civilization, without which scientific and technological change are themselves impossible. A computer is no doubt technically more efficient than a typewriter, and both are more efficient than a fountain pen. But each of these artifacts is associated with a different style and tempo of human life; to speak succinctly, each is associated with a different cultural milieu. The computer does not "remember" the fountain pen. Less metaphorically, we who employ these devices must express their cultural significance in a dialect that is not just the technical discourse associated with the latest development of technology.

The second deficiency of technical discourse follows directly from the first. This kind of discourse tells us how to do something, but it does not tell us what to do. More broadly expressed, it tells us neither the value of what we have done nor the purpose of moving on to the next stage of technical development. Those who insist upon the continuous self-transformation of human being by scientific technology, and more generally, by technical construction in the wide as well as narrow sense, depreciate, no doubt unintentionally, the significance of technical construction itself, since that significance cannot be expressed in technical language alone. At the very least, there must be a rhetorical supplement that conveys the value of science and technology.

In fact, this supplement has in many cases replaced what we used to call "philosophy," but which is today understood most frequently as itself a form of technical discourse. This is true even of ethical and political philosophy, although in recent years there has been a concerted attempt to resist the assimilation of these branches of philosophy into epistemology. My inquiry, however, is not restricted to the questions of ethics and politics, important as these questions may be. I am concerned with something more fundamental, which could perhaps be referred to for introductory purposes as the question of the metalanguage, or better still, the *ordinal* language, that is, the language in which we take our bearings with respect to technical discourse in the wide and narrow senses.

I began with a distinction between technical and ordinary discourse, but the ambiguity of the expression "ordinary language" soon became apparent from the fact that such language is saturated with technical discourse. In other words, every definition of ordinary language is itself *technical*, because ordinary language is the background language within which such definitions are constructed. As I am about to argue, this means that we cannot return to the linguistic origin or ordinary discourse as the pure source of all technical speech. There is no systematic or transcendental or deductive foundation for the analysis of discursive idioms. But our inability to give an ordinary definition of ordinary language does not in the slightest mean that we do not understand or continuously employ ordinary language. In giving up a linguistic metaphysics, we do not surrender our capacity to understand what we are talking about.

The expression "ordinary language" becomes problematic, and even paradoxical, only when we attempt to transform it into a technical conception. I have discussed this attempt in previous chapters. Ordinary language itself is not reflective; it does not identify itself as ordinary. It simply transpires, until such time as we depart from it, for example by lapsing into poetry or shifting to a theoretical analysis of the difference between the ordinary and the extraordinary. This shift in registers is tantamount to the classification of two or more modes of discourse; as such, it is already a technical identification of the pretechnical. But this is to transform the pretechnical into a product of the technical operation. In other words, it is to engage in theory in the modern sense of constructive interpretation.

Very far from being entirely distinct, ordinary language is rather an anticipation of theoretical discourse. This is plain from both of its main components, the technical and the ordinal. For this reason, it is impossible to return to a natural stratum of discursive experience that is theoretically neutral, in the sense that, by grasping it accurately, we are able to determine a unique and correct standard for subsequent interpretations of the significance and value of human existence. Precisely if Socrates was right to refer to the human soul as philosophical by its very nature, ordinary or ostensibly pretheoretical speech contains the seeds of philosophical disputation, not the uniformly valid resolution of that dispute.

Philosophy originates in, but it does not take its final form as, ordinary discourse. The distinction between ordinary and technical discourse turns out to be at best an oversimplification, and at worst, one that is impossible to establish in a clear and coherent manner. There is considerable variation from one generation to another in the discourse that is readily available to the normal speaker of a natural language. Some of this discourse is technical in the wide sense that we modify the natural starting points in carrying out the simplest or most pervasive acts of everyday life. But it is also true that narrowly technical language enters frequently into ordinary language by a kind of informal osmosis. We become familiar with the use of machines, the principles of which we do not understand and cannot explain. Let us assume for the moment that it is possible to purify language of all technical or extraordinary elements. The remainder would be so primitive as to be useless as a criterion of philosophical theories. The idea of a return to the natural origin of human experience in some pretheoretical epoch is a misleading dream.

None of this is intended to suggest that reference to ordinary language is useless. There is an obvious difference between the technical formulation of a philosophical doctrine and the language that we use in everyday life. But the ordinal role of everyday language is a function, not merely of original nature but of the continuous technical or constructive modifications of original nature that constitute the structure of everyday life. Thus Wittgenstein's attempts to correct the errors of philosophical discourse by reference to what we ordinarily say is finally unsatisfactory. No one doubts that philosophical discourse in its technical dimension differs from ordinary language. So too does the language of modern physics. The question is why this deviation occurs, and how it can be justified.

In other words, we require a general account of ordinary discursive experience, and not a purification of philosophical theories by the criterion of ordinary language. Ordinary language is only illusorily accessible to us as prior to and independent of the technical speech of philosophy. But it is not an illusion in itself. It does illustrate something fundamental about human beings, for example, that we are the talking animal, and more precisely, that we are by nature philosophical. It should be obvious that we are not materialists or idealists or Platonists or Heideggerians by nature. But these technical discourses originate within and are a transformation of the everyday use of natural languages.

The fundamental premiss of this chapter is extremely simple: everyday experience provides us with the only reliable basis from which to begin our philosophical reflections. But it does so as the source of extraordinary or philosophical speech, not as a distinct and paradigmatic use of language. Our talk about the substances or things that occur within, or constitute, ordinary or everyday experience is therefore philosophical from the outset. Philosophy is accordingly the process of explaining how extraordinary modes of discourse are demanded for an adequate understanding of the ordinary. As that which is to be explained, however, ordinary experience is *ordinal.* This does not mean that extraordinary language is to be reduced to ordinary or everyday language, but that all deviations from the ordinary must be justified as superior to ordinary accounts.

Radical deviations from ordinary experience are indistinguishable from arbitrary constructions or even fantasies if they are not mediated by a careful exposition of their nature as responses to problems in everyday understanding. A construction having nothing to do with the everyday would of course be initially meaningless. Those who wish to begin their philosophical activity by an instantaneous departure from ordinary experience, as though they were shot from a pistol, as Hegel says of certain proponents of the absolute, must after all explain to us why and how they are justified in undergoing the immediate detachment in question. To take a prosaic example, the recommendation to employ a new technical language in order to clarify ordinary English is accomplished via a metalinguistic exposition that is largely ordinary. To go to the other extreme, even Heidegger prepares his readers for the new type of thinking with a few introductory pages on the origination of genuine problems from the everyday experience of things and the manner in which we speak about them.

I want once more to emphasize that by calling attention to ordinary experience as the basis of philosophy, I do not mean to imply that extraordinary experience and discourse are to be excluded. To the contrary, the ordinary demands that we speak in extraordinary ways. Everyday life is never self-sufficient, but it is impossible to depart from it entirely, nor would we understand what such a departure could mean. This may be illustrated indirectly by an example from literature. James Joyce's *Ulysses* presents a long excerpt from the stream of consciousness of a single person, Leopold Bloom, which looks initially like a radical departure from normal syntax and the relative semantical stability of everyday speech. Underneath the hyperbolical representation, however, is the point of the imitation itself; we take our bearings by the very fact that we know ourselves to be listening to the flow of Bloom's consciousness, a flow that is not homogeneous but that occurs at different levels and in different registers. Joyce, in other words, is making a point about human nature in its normal or everyday condition, which is itself the manifestation of the extraordinary. As an artist, Joyce explains indirectly by the act of representation, which is mimetic only in the sense that it presents the human soul by means of an artifact. The artifact distorts, exaggerates, adorns, and in countless ways transforms the ordinary original, but it does not deviate entirely from it or replace it with something uniquely other and entirely unintelligible.

Stated as simply as possible, an artistic construction is designed for two reasons: to enrich and also to illuminate our ordinary experience and understanding. The work of art assists us in experiencing more than we would be capable of by ourselves. But it also sheds light on experience and thereby helps us to understand what we already know about ourselves. It is essential to note that, whereas philosophical disquisitions may be inner elements in a work of art (as for example in Thomas Mann's *The Magic Mountain*), the art-work itself is not a philosophical disquisition. Marianne Moore says that a poem must not mean but be. In my opinion, this is not quite correct, but it points us in the right direction. Of course poems or novels have meanings; but they are presented indirectly as the silent penumbra of significance emanating from the illusion of direct experience, whether in word or deed. The long and brilliant reflection on art by the character Marcel in the last volume of Proust's *Remembrance of Things Past* can be read apart from its function within the novel, as though it were an essay in a philosophical periodical. But this would do violence to Proust's central intention, since the reflection emerges from the detailed experiences of his entire life, as transmuted by recollection within the soul of a person who is literally reconstructing himself by a long act of what one could call hermeneutical memory. The conclusions of this act are invalid apart from our own re-appropriation of the experiences from which they emerge, a re-appropriation that allows us to translate them into the terms of our own lives, precisely because at bottom, these terms are the same for every human being. They are the terms of ordinary experience. And they are not fully accessible except to the extraordinary speaker. But the extraordinary speech would be empty of genuine significance if it were not rooted in ordinary experience.

I have been trying to suggest a fundamental difference between art and philosophy. Art does not express discursively or conceptually its own function but instead fulfils it. To the extent that the artist shifts into philosophical discourse, he or she ceases to function as an artist, except in the cases just illustrated, in which the artist is representing a person as philosophizing. On the other hand, the artist may well be convinced of the superiority of art to philosophy and so (to employ my previous terms) of the superiority of illumination and enrichment to explanation. But we do not write poems or novels in order to explain the superiority of art to philosophy. In this case the "demonstration" of the artist is a pointing out or exhibiting of an instance of the ostensibly superior genre. But something is still missing here, even for the artist: an explanation of the superiority of one genre to the other. And the genre of explanation is philosophy.

Let no one take me to be on the way toward an attempted demonstration of the unqualified superiority of philosophy to art. I do not doubt that art, understood broadly, has an essential role to play within the philosophical activity. My intention is rather to identify that role. Stated somewhat more abstractly, I want to discuss the relation between seeing and making in everyday life, in the hope of casting light on the question of whether we construct, or play an active role in the constitution of, what we discover, and so, what we talk about. In slightly different terms, the question is whether "talking about" is also "making." In other words, I ask whether the world is an artifact of human perception and cognition, and therefore an art-work, or whether instead it possesses a nature independent of but accessible to our cognitive powers. And if it is an artifact, is it different for each of us or the same for all? This step in the investigation will require me to say something about a topic I touched on previously: the nature of truth.

If we cannot ascertain the difference between truth and falsehood, employing these terms in their broad, not their narrow or propositional senses, then there is no difference between a wise or informative artifact and an arbitrary simulacrum. But in this case, there is no difference between philosophy and art, and none between good and bad works of art. In short, if there is no philosophy, there is also no art, because at bottom the truth of an art-work depends upon its philosophical significance. A true work of art expands and illuminates our experience by its own devices, but the discursive appropriation of this expansion and illumination, upon which depends the identification of the truth or genuineness of the work in question, is philosophical. Without philosophy, it would make no sense to speak of a "good" as distinct from a "pleasant" artifact. If there is no valid distinction between good and bad pleasures, or what comes to the same thing, if pleasure is held to be the good, then goodness disappears into neurophysiology. As Socrates pointed out in the *Philebus,* one must reason correctly, and hence speak the truth, in order to establish the principle that the good is the pleasant. In sum: without the truth, art has nothing to teach us. The successful defense of truth by philosophy is therefore in the best interests of art as well.

The point toward which the following remarks are directed is this: the distinction between truth and falsehood depends in turn upon the distinction between seeing and making. Even if it should turn out that we constitute the world by our cognitive activities, the result must be visible in a way that is accessible in principle to everyone. To say that someone is "blind" to the beauty or meaning of a work of art is to imply that this beauty or meaning is genuinely present, but that the person in question lacks the intellectual or emotional attributes necessary to discern them. But it also implies that if the person were to undergo the proper training, his or her eyes might be opened to the manifest reality. Similarly, a tree is in principle accessible to all human beings, even though some are blind and therefore cannot see it. We must be in a position to see what we make, and hence to speak truly about it; and by "truly" is meant in a way that explains something about our common experience. Seeing in this sense is also possible for the blind. And it is in this sense that vision and truth are inseparable. Nevertheless, in keeping with my usual procedure, I do not believe it would be wise to begin with a strict definition of truth. In introducing the notion of truth, I have tacitly appealed to "what everyone knows," and in particular to the question of the difference between art and philosophy, something which perhaps not everyone knows but which can be ascertained without formal or rigorous definitions of the truth-predicate.

The truth-predicate applies to propositions within a formalized language. I am aware of attempts by philosophers to transfer the work of Tarski and others on the formal predicate of truth to the domain of ordinary language, but I cannot see any point to these ventures. To express myself with excessive brevity, the meta-statement that "'snow is white' is true if and only if snow is white" amounts to the assertion that the predicate "is true" adds nothing to the assertion of the statement itself, since obviously the expression on the right-hand side of "if and only if" is itself either an assertion or a discursive representation in thought of a perceived or assumed fact. In other words, the assertion "snow is white" has exactly the same meaning or force as the assertion "the statement 'snow is white' is true." I have no reason to doubt this. But as Tarski himself presumably granted, one must understand English in order to apply the general criterion to any particular English statement. And if we understand English, we know more about the word "true" than the very slender information conveyed by the criterion just noticed. It is correct that we use "is true" to characterize statements that we believe to convey a state of affairs. I note in passing that it looks very much as if Tarski is committed to a correspondence theory of truth here; if this is so, his criterion is subject to the further difficulty that we must know that snow is white, and so that it would be true to say that snow is white, prior to the enunciation of the criterion in this particular case. In other words, it looks as though we know what "true" is implicitly whenever we apprehend a state of affairs, and only because of this implicit or intuitive knowledge are we able to define the term.

More important for my purposes, however, is the fact that Tarksi's truth-definition is not a satisfactory basis for constructing a doctrine of truth for ordinary language. The sentence "snow is black" might be true in a poetic sense even though snow is white. Or to take another example, I might utter the statement "It is a beautiful day" ironically when I actually believe that the day is quite unpleasant. There are, in other words, other meanings of "true" than those illustrated by the meta-statement or paradigm. What for instance of "true" as "genuine"? It seems to me that in order to follow Tarski's procedure in the case of ordinary language, we would require a truth-criterion that corresponded to every use of "is true" in ordinary usage. But even if all these criteria could be formulated, how would we apply them? In other words, we could apply the correct criterion if and only if we knew which criterion actually applied in the given case. But if we know this, then the formulae are themselves redundant. We are using the language correctly on the basis of our understanding, not only of the language but of life, that is, of when it is appropriate to say something rather than something else. Someone could know all the rules and still not know how to apply them; there are no rules for the application of rules.

Examples like "snow is white" are especially misleading because it seems a simple matter to determine its truth. After all, either snow is white or it is not white but, say, blue or red; and everyone knows the colors as well as what snow is. But what about sentences like "Machiavelli is evil" or "the quality of mercy is not strained"? I dare say that the statement "the quality of mercy is not strained" is true if and only if the quality of mercy is not strained. But what is mercy, and what is it for mercy not to be strained? What is the point of this apparently tautologous procedure? We surely do not wish to say that sentences are true if and only if they correspond to the state of affairs that is their content. As I have already noted, we must first know that the correspondence in question obtains, in order to designate it by a true statement. But how do we know this? Not by uttering a statement that itself corresponds to the state of affairs, since again, we should first have to know that the state of affairs obtains in order to construct such a sentence. But this is trivial.

The interesting fact is that "true" is an equivocal term and none the worse for it. It has a range of meanings from which the normal speaker of a natural language is usually able to select the one that is appropriate to the linguistic situation. There are of course exceptions; sometimes we make a mistake. But the mistake is easily identified and corrected. And the mistakes cannot be legislated out of existence in advance, any more than the circumstances under which the individual meanings of "true" obtained can be defined in advance or codified by rules of correct usage. I am, however, very far from suggesting that we should not think as carefully as possible about truth. I believe that we can take at least one step toward a conceptual elaboration of the meaning of "true" in its everyday, as opposed to its formalist, uses. And we can do so in such a way as to bring out the relation between seeing and making. If this is so, then we shall at the same time be able to acquire a better understanding of the difference between art and philosophy.

Very frequently, if not always, we say that something is a true instance of a kind if it renders wholly visible the essential nature of that kind. By "wholly visible" I do not mean "in its entire structure" but rather "visible as a whole, and so identifiable as what it in fact is." A true believer is one who displays enough of the properties of a believer to allow us to pick out believers from nonbelievers with great accuracy. And this is so even if we are unable to define with complete rigor the "concept" of the believer. This incapacity is rooted in the ambiguous and equivocal nature of all or most concepts of everyday discourse, which we employ successfully, not thanks to rules but because of our linguistic tact. What I said a moment ago about the equivocity of "true" holds good for a wide range of other terms, perhaps for all of them. What is from a formalist's standpoint a terrible defect of natural language is from the standpoint of everyday life a tremendous advantage. It is absolutely false to say that, unless we employ formalist analyses of language, we do not know what we are talking about. The reverse is rather the case. We do know what we are talking about (and how to correct errors when we make them) in ordinary language; we cease to be talking about anything in particular when we shift to a purely formal language, and so it becomes literally true that we do not know what we are talking about, unless of course we are talking about the symbols and syntax of the formal language itself. But this, however impressive from a technical standpoint, is not very useful either to the average citizen or to the philosopher.

The ability to speak a natural language is not grounded in rules but rather in the innate mastery of equivocity. And this in turn is not grounded in the mastery of syntax but in the ability to see what needs to be said as well as to discern what it is that someone means when he or she says something. All rules are a posteriori or ad hoc. The philosophy of language, very far from explaining how we speak meaningfully, is itself a product of our ability to see what ought to be said. I would myself go one step further and say that there is in principle no explanation of how we see what we or others mean, if to explain is to analyze, that is, to break unities or syntheses into their component parts, and these again into simpler elements, until we arrive at something that resists analysis, and that exhibits easily intelligible properties that we believe can be transferred upward through the increasingly complex levels of structure until we arrive at the totality or whole. This entire procedure is a waste of time because the unity of our mastery of equivocity, that is, the living intelligence, is no more a property of some set of psychological or neurophysiological elements than the properties of mass, charge, motion, and direction that characterize atomic particles are properties of the activities of my lived body, that is, the episodes of my life.

To come back now to "true" in the sense of "genuine," I am proceeding by calling up examples before the mind's eye of my audience, not by formulating rules or defining configurations of symbols. When I spoke just now of a true believer, every reader of normal intelligence and experience understood what I meant; and this understanding, although of course impossible without our access to a common language and culture, is not explained by these but rather expresses itself, brings itself into actuality, by producing them. A true believer is not an arbitrary cultural artifact but a phenomenon of the human soul. In the last analysis, it is by the spontaneous light of the human soul that we understand what we mean by "true believer," and so by "true." If this is metaphysics, then so be it.

When I say that a kind is wholly visible in a true instance, I do not mean that every essential property of the kind is clearly and distinctly visible. In fact, I am hesitant to employ the term "essential" here because I regard it as possible that we are able to recognize true instances even if we should turn out to be incapable of defining essences, and even if there are no essences of an eternal or temporally unchanging nature. I know when I am in the presence of a true, that is, genuine, scoundrel, even though I cannot define the essence "scoundrel." It is probably more straightforward to define expressions like "a genuine diamond" or even "a genuine tiger" (despite old-fashioned worries about how Aristotle would respond to a three-legged tiger—the answer is that he would call it a defective or deformed tiger; tigers have four legs by nature, that is, always or for the most part). We run into special trouble when we try to explain exactly what we mean in describing persons or actions. Not to make too long a speech about it, let me just say that this is because Nietzsche was right to call man the not yet fully constructed animal. Not yet fully, but hence partly; animal, not vegetable or mineral. This extraordinary feature of our natures, that we are so to speak always "half-baked" or require further cooking, is closely connected to our mastery of equivocity. If univocity and determinateness were indispensable for meaning, then we could say nothing whatsoever about ourselves, and so by extension about our relations to other entities.

In general, there are no univocal terms in natural language; but this is essential to communication, because there are also no univocal experiences or uniquely valid interpretations of experience. The capacity to select the correct sense of a crucial word for a given context depends upon the aforementioned mastery of equivocation. Nor does it lead to a destructive regress of interpretations, because the equivocity of meanings allows us to select the appropriate interpretation, and the mastery of equivocity allows our discursive partner to see what is intended. Confusion and misunderstanding can of course arise from the equivocal nature of empirical sense, but it can also be corrected; in the language of traditional hermeneutics, to *subtilitas legendi* there corresponds *Einfühlung*.

To return to the main and narrower line of argument, my examples are intended to suggest that the wholeness of truth in its everyday sense is partly imagined or inferred from the appropriate presentation of properties. We can see an entity in its wholeness thanks to the ability of the speaker to pick out a property or set of properties that evokes in the auditor the correct picture. It is not even necessary for the property in question to be essential; successful communication frequently transpires on the basis of accidental predications. It is precisely *subtilitas legendi* that enables us to select the property that is appropriate to the given discursive situation. In some situations, reference to an essential property would not work, for example in technical contexts in which the auditor is ignorant of the official terminology. Rigid univocity would preclude the possibility of understanding in these cases.

This makes immediately evident a crucial point in the relation between philosophy and art. The perception of wholeness, or somewhat more precisely the success of identification, is not simply the discovery of what is given by nature, but depends upon the imaginative or productive capacity of the observer. On this point the advocates of hermeneutics are entirely correct. Philosophy no more records in language the rigid structure of beings than art photographs or rigidly copies the forms or natures of psychic states. "No more records": by this I do not mean "not at all." There is an element of recording or copying rooted in our apprehension of what we wish to interpret. We must see in order to make. The wholeness of intelligibility, the capacity to see a form or a formal structure or a pattern of events or the character of a human being, even if we cannot identify every element in these totalities, functions by our producing it as well as our discovering it.

If this is so, then discovery and production cannot be simply juxtaposed as the sources of philosophy and art respectively. Seeing and making function jointly in both philosophy and art, which, if they are to be distinguished at all, must be distinguished by some other criterion. I have been advocating the distinction between the explanation of the totality of experience on the one hand and the expansion and illumination (literally, lighting up or showing so as to be accessible to explanation) on the other. I claim further that the root of these two modes of productive discovery is one and the same. The root is the living intelligence, the most important sense of which I have represented here as the mastery of equivocation. We select the appropriate senses of the elements of our experience by an act of interpretation that in the case of artistic production can be likened to the telling of a story and in the case of philosophical discourse to an explanation of stories. A novel, a symphony, or a poem are distinct but related types of stories about some aspect of human existence. A philosophical speech spells out the significance of the story with respect to the wholeness of human life, and thus to the order of its defining aspects or dimensions. To this I add that something analogous, but not precisely the same, holds good of scientific theories. A theory of space and time is an articulated model or story about the inner structure of spatial and temporal phenomena. But the explanation of the significance of that inner structure for the totality of human life is philosophical discourse.

The last several paragraphs have been necessarily rather abstract; I want to get back to the everyday. In order to understand the distinction between seeing and making, or the relationship between philosophy and literature, we must begin, not with philosophy and literature themselves, but with the everyday experiences that give birth to these activities. I need, however, to make one more professorial remark. Despite the extensive criticism that I have directed elsewhere against such postmodernist movements as deconstruction, I do not reject outright the contention that the world is a text. This should have been evident from my discussion of hermeneutics as the mastery of equivocity. The world is a weaving together of discovering and making; we therefore participate in the process by which the "world" or "whole" emerges as a concrete determination of the horizon of intelligibility. Even what the Greeks called "cosmos" is an ordering suitable for human habitation. As such, it cannot be strictly synonymous with "nature" because neither in the Greek *phusis* nor in the modern senses of the term is nature suitable for human habitation without modification by human labor. The whole is an artifact to the extent that it is made to be visible by and for human beings only.

But this does not mean that the whole is unintelligible or that the task of understanding it is blocked by a vitiating equivocity of the discursively accessible senses of its elements. Equivocity is grounded in the unity of being. The different senses that one can attach to a horse in its relations to human beings do not succeed in transforming the horse into a dog. And the senses are themselves discernibly different because each preserves its own identity. I can make the same point in the language of textuality. A text cannot be woven together from subtexts that are themselves webs of subsubtexts, and so on indefinitely. To anticipate a later point, a text is a story or the content of a potential story, and stories are not about an infinite regression of other stories. At each level of story telling (and such a level is defined by the telling of an intelligible story) there are fixed points—things, persons, purposes, events, actions, values—the meaning of which within the given story may depend upon an integration of substories, but an integration culminating in a totality that functions as an element within the whole of the story of the particular world, or part of the world, under inspection.

A true account of the world would be one that tells the whole story. The whole story contains more or less detail. If we could tell no whole story about the world as a whole, however general, then we could never tell a whole story about a part. Many would say that this is precisely our fate, but this is because they adhere to an unnecessarily strict conception of wholeness. I remind the reader of my previous remark to the effect that we can see something as a whole, for example a thing or a person, thanks to the apprehension of appropriate properties, even when we cannot grasp the complete set of essential properties of the entity, assuming that such a set exists. In other words, we can identify a human being as distinct from a tree, a rock, a scarecrow, or an ape, as a fixed point of reference when we construct an interpretation or a story. There is nothing to argue about here; all arguments about the ambiguity of natures, the inaccessibility or nonexistence of essences, the puzzles of sense perception, and the endless variety of interpretations of sense, are arguments about individual beings of precisely this sort of fixed identity that we can say of them: the stories that can be told about this entity here—this man, this woman, this dog, this star—are endless and conflicting. If this were not true, there would be no experience, not even equivocal or ambiguous experience.

The demonstration of equivocity is rooted in the antecedent fixity of identifiable entities. As so identifiable, they are wholly accessible to a story about their role in our experience. I mean by "wholly accessible" that we can tell a story about a horse without fearing that it is actually a dog, or nothing at all. But to tell a story is to fit something into a larger context; in fact, it is the larger context of the world, or an ordering, however equivocal, of everything we come upon. Nor can the ordering be so equivocal as to prevent us from making reasonable selections, relative to our purposes, from among candidates to the whole story. To summarize: experience just is the identification of wholes as fixed units capable of identification and (as Strawson puts it) of re-identification. But it is the world or cosmos as context of the presentation of entities to be identified and interpreted that makes these fixed units accessible. We do not have experiences of a person or animal in a vacuum, devoid of all reference to anything else, but always within a horizon, the openness of which is again dependent upon a total ordering, even if the structure of this total ordering is not itself totally accessible.

The whole story, then, is the story of the world or cosmos within which human beings tell their tales. One could say that the whole story is itself a part of the whole, and the most important part, since it is as it were the last touch to the process by which the whole becomes a whole. But the whole is not simply or entirely an artifact of story-telling, because we cannot speak without seeing what we mean. Even if we produced every element of the whole by discursive cognition, we would still have to identify what we had produced in order to interpret it. Seeing would continue to play a coordinate role with making in the philosophical or artistic or scientific account of the world.

My qualified acceptance of the metaphor of the world as text is related to the thesis that the meaning of the world is elicited in, although it is not merely, a story. This in turn leads me to introduce the doctrine of authorial intentionality, as I shall call it. I mean by this that regardless of all subsequent modifications, a story is told by human beings to other human beings in order to accomplish an intention or to fulfil a purpose by the communication of meaning. The purpose is to achieve wholeness, in the sense of a correct ordering of activities or capacities to act; and by "correct" I mean conducive to the best life, which the Greeks described by the word *eudaimonia*. The stories that interest me primarily are those by which we attempt to complete our lives by rescuing them from meaninglessness. Nor am I concerned in the slightest by those who hold that only words have "meanings," or still more radically, that there are no meanings but only words. Since life as a whole is a text, that is to say, a whole that includes its own explanatory story, it is entirely appropriate to refer to the meaning of life, and so too to its equivocity.

Just as there are no meaningless experiences, so too there are no unintentional stories. What is meaningless cannot be experienced but only encountered; it remains external to the web of existence that we weave by incorporating meanings into stories. What is unintentional is not a story but meaningless chatter. Even the desire to entertain or to play is intentional. When these intentions extend to other persons, they become co-authors of the text. To speak of the text as having its own intentions is merely to animate it, that is, to take it as representing the author. Whereas texts like the world may exhibit divine intentions, these become meaningful for human beings only when incorporated into stories that we have ourselves composed. That a text has a multiplicity of possible readings follows from the equivocity of the senses of the words of which the text is composed; but the range of equivocity is narrowed by the intention of the author, which the reader's mastery of equivocity enables him or her to determine. Otherwise put, the multiplicity of readings is itself determined and regulated by a primary intention, without which no story can be told. Whereas stories can mean more than we intend, they cannot mean less; and if the minimal or regulative intention is indiscernible, then the story is incoherent, which is to say that it is no story at all. Finally, if one altogether denies intentions to the text, or rejects them as irrelevant to the task of interpretation, this is a covert way of replacing the author's intentions with those of the reader, or in other words it is to replace reading by writing. In this case there is no reading, and so there can be no verifiable way of referring to texts. There is then no writing but only scribbling, to which corresponds the chatter of meaningless interpretation.

What is it about our lives that causes us to weave together texts, whether these be subsequently identified as philosophy or literature? The answer I have suggested is as old as Plato, but I do not propose to defend it by textual exegesis of the orthodox or philological type. There is no point in reading a Platonic dialogue if it is not a true story (as opposed to a set of true propositions). Nor could we determine the truth of a Platonic story simply by reading or analyzing it. The reading must occur within the context of an ongoing inspection of the process of story telling. It is in this process that we are presently engaged. I am telling a story about story telling, but there is no danger of a vicious circle here, because this is how we learn what it is to tell a story, namely, by the activity itself. There are no rules or principles independent of the activity from which its nature is deducible. There are no a priori stories.

I begin with an expansion of my preliminary remark about intentionality. This is a much-discussed topic but we cannot avoid going over some familiar ground. Our goal is not originality but truth. The first point I want to make is simple and in a way obvious even though not easy to state. The difference between random or chaotic flux and identifiable change is that the latter is defined by a terminus. This point has nothing to do with metaphysical or theological doctrines of teleology; it bears upon the structure of intelligibility. A terminus is intrinsic to, and is the organizing principle of, the structurally constitutive elements of the change it defines. Termini are things, persons, events, relations, and so on: identifiable and re-identifiable elements of experience that serve as nodal points in stories. In a traditional vocabulary, we may call them subjects and predicates, or substances and properties. In the now familiar expression, each is a "this something" of "such-and-such a kind."

A change is identifiable to an observer at some stage in its development, a stage that may or may not be predictable in advance and which varies from observer to observer. Persons with different experiences and educations may recognize at different moments the identity of a process, as for example the blooming of a rose or the gestures of a mime. Often an observer is unable to identify precisely the terminus of the change, as for example, that a certain bloom is a hibiscus. But the identification of the process as a flower suffices for the terminus to be further specified in the varying contexts, scientific, aesthetic, and so on, of everyday life. We may look up the flower in an illustrated textbook or ask a specialist to identify it. And what is true of things is also true of events, as in the case of the mime's gestures. It may seem to my audience that one could speak directly of things and events rather than introducing the vocabulary of termini. But I wish to avoid basing my argument on the assumption that there are things or static substances independent of processes and multiple hermeneutical perspectives. A terminus is the fulfilment of a process in the sense just defined: We act with and speak about them. And thus we interpret them.

Each person is of course free to construct private variations on the public identities of things and events in the communal world of everyday life. But this freedom is not entirely spontaneous; it is grounded in the identities or termini themselves. And when we speak about a process rather than a terminus, we treat the process as a terminus. If we could not identify changes, there would be no improvisations, because to improvise is to say something new or unexpected about something that has already been, or could have been, identified in a customary manner. A story about a rose may differ sharply from the tale told by the horticulturist, but it is intelligible to an audience only because the rose has a public identity, one that is the same for all members of the audience and that serves as the basis for specialized identifications. This identity is the terminus of the change constituted for every normal speaker of English as a flower, and for many of these as a rose. One could say by a metaphorical extension of traditional terminology that the process of the change in question *intends* the rose as its shaping terminus; in doing so, of course, I do not mean to imply that the process is self-conscious.

Once again, traditional language is appropriate here, provided that one does not take umbrage at the ontological implications of substance terminology. Just as a conscious state is a state of a certain sort, and a thought is a thought of a more or less determinate content, so too a change is of the kind identified by its terminus (or that we identify by identifying the terminus). I have already referred to the Socratic maxim, common to both Plato and Aristotle, and intrinsic to our discursive intelligence, that to be is to be something of such-and-such a kind. Whereas I accept this maxim as indisputable, I have tried to arrive at the same result by honoring the anti-Platonist assumption that experience is constituted by change rather than formal structure. The anti-Platonist thesis cannot account for everyday life without smuggling the Platonist thesis back into the story, for the simple and obvious reason that change is of something. Formless changes play no role in our experience. Whether the forms that undergo change are ontologically separate will depend upon what we mean by "separate." Certainly the process known as a rose is, *qua* process, separate from the experienced rose. It really makes no sense to say that we are experiencing (nothing but) processes, when everyone knows that we are experiencing processes of such-and-such a kind. But the kind simply is not reducible to the process. We do not experience blurs. It is not my particular intention here to defend Platonism, but I did want to point out that there is an interpretation of the so-called doctrine of Platonic Ideas that is compatible with process-philosophy or the principle of comprehensive change. Changes have looks, and this allows them to look like other looks. But the Idea is the look.

By analogous reasoning, I think we can easily see that it is impossible to make sense of our experience, or even to have any, unless we refer to the "nature" of a look or terminus. First we must distinguish between two senses of "nature." In the first sense, it refers to the order of properties that make the look what it is. In the second sense, it is distinguished from "art" or "convention" and refers to what shows itself or comes into existence independently of human work. Even if we literally make every element in our experience, what we make must have a nature, just as even if everything in the world is a process or change, these processes or changes have looks. If I make a pear, it is not also a refrigerator. This is the technical sense in which we are required to employ the term "nature," and its validity is independent of the second sense of the term.

Nevertheless, a few words on the second sense are not out of place. What does it mean to say "I make the pear by perceiving it"? I might very well interpret the pear in a way that depends not only upon its identity but also upon my imagination or special scientific interests. But this interpretation depends upon the presence of a pear to my apprehension. I can imagine a pear, but this in turn amounts to the "re-presentation" in thought of something that previously presented itself to me directly. To a Kantian, the form of the cognized pear is a result of the functions of the transcendental ego; but this is a philosophical doctrine about ordinary experience, not an account immanent to ordinary experience itself. In our analysis of ordinary experience, we are looking for evidence that will enable us to decide whether to accept or to reject doctrines like Kantianism.

All theoretical accounts of perception, scientific or transcendental, start with the everyday perception of objects like pears, dogs, and trees. They must justify themselves by the properties of ordinary perception and the problems that these properties raise. I am not now contending that there are no problems associated with ordinary perception, but rather that perception is rooted in termini of processes, some of which we make and some of which we do not make but discover. The ordinary distinction between nature and art can be easily illustrated. A seed develops under the proper natural conditions into a flower. But a gardener can modify the result of germination by taking various steps, and a geneticist can make still more radical changes in the result of germination. The modifications imposed by the gardener and the geneticist onto the natural process of germination do not themselves make the seed, nor in a fundamental sense do they make the flower. In order for the modified flower to bloom, there must have been a seed to be modified. If the geneticist does not make the seed (we can ignore the gardener here) but finds it in the soil, then he is modifying nature but not replacing or creating it.

Is it possible for the geneticist to make the seed? I have no idea, but I am sure that if he could, he would have to employ natural materials at some early stage in order to produce it. In general, the identification of nature is altogether less problematic than in the example just given. We know what we do not make because making is intentional. One cannot make a seed simply by looking at the ground in order to admire the landscape or just to see what is there. I understand that sometimes our actions result unexpectedly or spontaneously in the production of something, but this is not making. In order to make something, we require a pattern or blueprint or what we call an idea of what we intend to make, as well as materials, instruments, training, and so on. To make is to employ all of these in such a way that, by directing our intelligence and skills toward the pattern or idea and the material, we can bring them together in a way that is a terminus of a process, a terminus that did not previously exist.

The terminus of a natural change, whether with respect to a particular instance or to nature as a whole, does not satisfy human intentionality merely by allowing things or processes to fulfil themselves. Nature compels us to provide additional discursively constructed termini beyond those which it produces by its own activity. There is then a disjunction within the continuity of nature, of which human being is the locus. Whereas humanity depends upon, and individual human beings exemplify, the integrity of natural change, something more is required. This requirement manifests itself in both deeds and speeches, but primarily in speeches. In order to survive, human beings must cultivate the soil, alter the course of streams and rivers, make clothing and build shelters, and thereby modify natural change by the productive arts. But deeds are not sufficient; the human animal is compelled by nature to talk, and in particular, to tell stories. As I am arguing, we cannot exist as human beings without telling, or attempting to tell, the whole story.

Most of our speeches are addressed to local ends, for example, to the acquisition of the necessities of existence; some few address generalized versions of these local ends, such as the need for survival. A still smaller but nevertheless significant number of speeches go beyond this, and are intended as justifications or evaluations of life as a totality. Such speeches attempt to tell the whole story, not in its every detail, but with sufficient detail to make the overall pattern evident. These stories are directed by termini not furnished by nature in the second of the two senses just distinguished. This is the main reason why students of nature so frequently regard the stories as empty or excessively vague. And yet, one cannot criticize stories of this sort for vagueness without implicitly telling another such story: in the present case, the story of what we may call the scientific world-view. The scientific world-view is not verified by the results of natural science; on the contrary, it is the former that directs us toward the pursuit of the latter by persuading us of the ultimate value of scientific truth. The difference between the story and the positive results of science is rooted in the fact that nature does not tell us how to live. On the contrary, we tell nature how we wish to live. Where nature seems to demur, we can devote ourselves to changing her through the mastery of scientific technique.

Within nature, termini are intrinsic to the processes of change. In the case of human action, termini are produced or projected, not spontaneously or ex nihilo but in response to a natural appetite, either in itself or as modified by custom and imagination, and so as naturally intended but not naturally furnished. To take an example, a cosmological myth is neither the direct fulfilment of a natural change, nor does it stand to the cosmos as an image to an original. The myth is intended to provide a supplementary or discursive completeness to the cosmos, a completeness that the cosmos, to the extent that it exists independently of human speech, does not itself require. The requirement comes from us, or from what Socrates calls our Eros. I should say here that the origin of Eros is somewhat ambiguous; although Eros is a function of the human soul, it comes from above and raises us up by taking possession of us. This is why Socrates calls it a god or a daimon. For our present purposes, it will suffice to say that Eros mediates between human desire and divine completeness. It is therefore an essential ingredient, even when it is not explicitly mentioned, in every attempt to tell the whole story.

Eros, one could say, is the artist who produces the variety of speeches elicited by our contemplation of the cosmos. This variety includes such types as myth, poetry, religion, science, and philosophy. Each element in the variety is subject to its own subvariations and improvisations. One speech elicits another. *Homo sapiens*, the talking animal, is also *homo faber*, who is in the process of constructing himself or herself as the hero in a cosmological drama. Such a drama is true if it displays the speech-telling nature as a whole. Philosophy is that form of speech whose stories are, or intend to be, self-reflexive or self-explanatory. That is, they intend not merely to display, but to bring to full articulateness, the speech-telling nature as a whole. This was the claim Hegel made on behalf of his own speeches, and his *Science of Logic* claims to provide the complete structure of the Concept, the speech of speeches.

Please note that to say that the world is intelligible in various ways is very far from saying that the world is unintelligible. Furthermore, the same problem is discernible at the heart of all interpretations, however diverse the one from the other. We are attempting to make sense of the totality of our experience, to reconcile the interpretations and perspectives with one another, to rise to a level of generality sufficiently great that what we see there illuminates the existence and nature of all perspectives; on this point, Hegel was undoubtedly right. But it is at the beginning rather than at the end of this process that we tell the same story. It is our ordinary experience that provides us with the common basis for subsequent diversity in our explanations of the totality of human existence. The more subtle and the deeper our accounts, the more they diverge. I would never say that there is no standpoint from which one cannot see the rank-ordering of these divergent accounts. My point is rather that there is no way in which to persuade those who do not see as we do that our vision is the best. Those who think otherwise have committed the error of identifying thought with speech. But even if everyone could understand the comprehensive and wholly true speech about the whole, one would still have to see the whole, one would have to see what the speech intends to say, what it means. And this vision is no longer a matter of speech; it is not a meta-discourse, a totally inappropriate notion that leads to an infinite regress or to mere chatter, and so, ironically, to a different kind of silence.

Every perspective, in order to do its work, must be determinate and intelligible. But the difference in each perspective, that which defines it as this perspective and not one of the others, is the produced or fictional element contributed by the artistic root of human nature in response to the work of the root of discovery. In a very general sense, at the level of what I am calling in this series of essays "ordinary experience" or "everyday life," all human beings see the same world and thus share the same perspective. Unfortunately, our attempts to grasp this communal perspective in conceptual speech result in the functioning of the productive element of cognition, and so in the steady replacement of the communal perspective by individual variations. I am attempting to articulate ordinary experience, not as the last stage in the process of telling the whole story, or in a vain effort to duplicate Hegelian science, but rather in order to make clear the *first* step in philosophy. And I do this, not because I believe that everyone will see the truth of my analysis, but because I regard it as in principle possible to achieve agreement sufficient to establish the self-founding of philosophy, and hence to rescue it from charges that it is dead, or that it never did and never could exist, or that we have finished with it and now dwell in a post-philosophical epoch. I have no pretensions of being able to tell the whole story; but I do wish to attempt to explain why we are forced to tell the whole story. And perhaps that in itself is the whole story.

Human existence is a delicate balance between communal and private experience. We live in the same world, yet our access to it differs not merely from person to person but from moment to moment in the life-span of the same person. The variations constitute a sometimes irresistible temptation to forget the common world, or to assume that we have become detached from it. I believe that this is an illusion. Variations are recognizable as such only with respect to the common world from which they deviate. In the extreme case, a transcendental world is not a human dwelling-place but a set of conditions that purport to define the necessary structure of the common world. As to fantasies or (as they are now called) possible worlds, they do not transport us from this world to another but allow us to consider this one as having undergone certain changes. We can of course pretend that our common world has undergone so many changes as to alter its present nature entirely. If the pretense goes too far, then I would claim that the act of imagination required to picture oneself as dwelling in the radically different world is beyond our powers. Instead we imagine some other being, speciously identified as oneself or our counterpart in the alternative world. What we actually understand is this world, the one in which we are engaging in the act of imagination.

There is a converse danger that the overpowering presence of the common world will induce us to underestimate the significance of perspectival variation. This temptation leads to the mathematicizing of experience in the extreme case, but more frequently to the thoughtless and unimaginative acceptance of public perception. Since there is no entirely neutral apprehension of the common world, the net result is unconscious adherence to a conventional interpretation of the public world. The imagination sinks comfortably into dogma and condemns all differences as "imaginative" in the pejorative sense of the term. Sometimes the operative conventional dogma is called "nature." This misuse of the term should not encourage us to assume that there is no legitimate sense in which one may (and must) speak of nature. The community of the common world is the exhibition of its nature, and so too are the perfections of the modalities of common existence. One must nevertheless conclude that, although the common view is the foundation of all others, it is not satisfactory unless we supplement it. It is no threat to a sensible rationalism to admit that we live much of the time in our imaginations, and that these imaginative revisions of the everyday are not simply imaginary in the sense of illusory or as empty of significance and value.

I shall refer to the interplay between the common and the private as a disjunction within nature that defines the structure of human existence. Up to a point, it is helpful to think of this disjunction as representing a different mixture or mode of regulation between reason and the imagination. Neither element is lacking in either branch of the disjunction, although each does its work differently in the two contexts. Reason is obviously not altogether different in the private world from its function in the communal or public, but it admits of more modifications and restrictions in the former than in the latter context. Conversely, the imagination is kept on a tighter rein in the common world than in its private variations. I also want to emphasize that the two branches of the disjunction of existence are not mutually exclusive. We live in both at the same time. The private is in fact a continuum of gradations moving from a point almost indistinguishable from the common world to increasingly different variations. Nor do we ever entirely detach ourselves from the common world, short of total madness or death; on the contrary, as I have noted already, we perceive the common as common from one of the nearby private perspectives, the privacy of which does not annul the common or our access to it.

We may consider the private access to the common as a story. The use of this term requires a preliminary clarification. I said previously that I do not entirely disagree with those who refer to the world as a text. Human existence is a web, of which the warp is the common world and the woof the private pattern that each of us weaves into the communal as an interpretation. This metaphor is not entirely satisfactory, since the individual or private patterns are all disjunct from one another even as they modify the warp. One should perhaps think of a magical Persian carpet in which the design is both always the same and continuously changing. I leave the metaphor for what it is worth and shift to a slightly more literal idiom. We tell stories about our view of the world, but "story" must be understood in its original sense as an inquiry (*historie*) and not simply as a "fiction" in the sense of an invention or creation.

Whereas each of us is the hero or heroine of our own stories, and although each storyteller is modified by antecedent stories, this is not the same as to say that each storyteller is a sheer figment of the imagination, a text in the sense of an invention or spontaneous result of a primordial weaving. We inherit the common world, and with it, the antecedent stories that define the horizon within which we contribute our own variations, which are thus not themselves spun from the whole cloth of imagination. In other words: I can tell a story about an actual person who is the hero of some other story, but this is not to say that I invent him; he is given by the common world as a natural unit of fabulation. Conversely, you may tell a story in which I figure as a character, but in so doing, you do not reduce me to the status of a fictional entity.

I am attempting to distinguish between human beings as instances of the story-telling animal, who are residents of the common world and accessible to philosophical investigation, *and* the stories that human beings tell. If philosophy is also a story, it is *the whole story.* As such it is subject to regulation by the common world, which is not itself a story. No private story is a whole story; at most it can be an interpretation of an individual life, or of the world as viewed from that individual point. The best examples of such stories are great novels like *War and Peace* or *Remembrance of Things Past.* However universal, novels require an adjustment of focus with reference to the common standard. This adjustment or reading necessarily dissolves the illusion of reality that the novelist seeks to project, but the purpose of the adjustment is not to enhance the aesthetic effect of the novel. It is instead to rectify the distortions of the fictional lens without sacrificing its revelations.

As resident in the common world of ordinary experience, I am a terminus already reached, and it is this degree of fixity that allows me to tell a story about myself, a story that will no doubt modify my own vision but will neither produce it ex nihilo nor transform it beyond recognition. It is furthermore only because I am a terminus already reached that I can function as the starting point for new destinations, or following Pindar, to become what I am through understanding. A terminus, the reader will recall, is the last stage of a motion or process that exhibits a pattern or look, by virtue of which we identify the motion or process as of such-and-such a kind. The look of the rose is the terminus that defines the process of its growth. We can tell different stories about roses, but only because roses exist and are identifiable in their common identity as subject to a more or less determinate range of kinds of stories. The same is true, and at a much deeper level, of human beings. I would never deny that we often learn important details about human nature from the telling and reading of stories. But human nature is not itself a story. Whatever we learn about ourselves from stories is not peculiar to the story; it is common property and belongs to the common world of ordinary experience.

My thesis, then, is that there is one comprehensive truth, the limit-case of stories because it is the whole story, but a whole story that is never wholly accessible to us, and therefore is in need of continuous reinterpretation. More controversially, however, I also contend that we must see the whole story somehow, in outline, as pre-given by the wholeness of everyday life, for otherwise our private stories would have no point beyond the mere telling. And in this case they would not be intelligible as particular stories about or interpretations of the common human world. The very fact that we understand a story is due to our recognition within it of the common world, and so of the added illumination that the story casts upon this world. It is impossible to understand a thoroughly private or unique story, which is not a story at all, because there is nothing to investigate if each act of story telling is a unique creation; nor would there be any reliable standard by which to determine what it means to understand.

I want to illustrate the preceding remarks with a very simple example. We tell a story, which may be a historical myth, about the young George Washington, who is said to have chopped down a cherry tree and subsequently to have confessed the deed with the assertion "I cannot tell a lie." None of the three main elements here, George Washington, his axe, or the cherry tree, is a story. There are of course stories intrinsic to what we mean by an axe, a cherry tree, and even the specific historical personage George Washington. One of them is the myth under inspection. George Washington has multiple significations for students of American history and so for Americans, the British, or other foreigners. But our story about the chopping down of the tree derives its meaning from the perceived unity of young man, axe, and tree as distinct termini.

It could be objected that these unities, and so too the unity of the particular story, arise in large measure from the integration of substories. One may grant this without compromising the integrity or common accessibility of George Washington or for that matter of his axe and the cherry tree. One can speak of the "integration" of substories only with respect to termini belonging to stories. Substories about George Washington are all precisely about George Washington, who is not "created" from an accumulation of fabulous detail but who exists independently of the stories, even if we come to an adequate recognition of his existence only through the hearing or reading of numerous tales, fictional and truthful alike. Even in a novel the character is held to exist prior to our becoming acquainted with him or her; the progressive information provided by the novelist about the character is intended to reveal that character to us in just the way that we become acquainted with actual persons in everyday life. Experimental techniques have exactly the same purpose, except that they are intended to convey these ways of discovery as extraordinary. We could not follow the progressive presentation of a character in a novel if this presentation did not mirror something fundamental to our experience of human beings. Things hang together in a novel in a way that we verify, even in the case of experimental techniques of fiction, by recourse to how things hang together (or for that matter fall apart) in everyday life.

The substories integrated into our understanding of George Washington may look from the standpoint of the novelist like the progressive creation of a character through the addition of one layer of meaning after another. But we connect these substories to the framework of Washington's historical identity. Regardless of how little we may have known of George Washington prior to the hearing of the story in question, there is a minimal core of historical meaning that we must grasp in order to see the point of the story. The point of the story is its terminus; it is a story that tells us something about our first president, and precisely as about the first president, the story does not pretend to have invented him. Those who have never heard of George Washington will not understand the story, but that has no bearing on the issue of Washington's antecedent existence.

A further objection could be made to the effect that we experience only fragments or spatiotemporal "slices" of persons, and that our understanding of the total person is in fact an inductive inference, or an interpretation of what it is like to be this particular person. After all, it is never the case that we experience anyone as a totality; our proximity to everyone is broken by sleep, to mention no other lacuna. By the same argument, we never experience ourselves as totalities; in addition to the lacunae of sleep or inattention, we are always in the process of living, a process that is completed only by our death, the final lacuna. This is an ingenious objection, but it misses the point. The unity of termini is intentional or formal, not spatiotemporal. I identify spatiotemporal slices of human beings by reference to the intellectual perception of the look or *eidos* that each exhibits as going beyond the immediate representation in such a way as to provide its terminus. I do not identify a slice of a human being as a fragment of a dog or a cow.

The argument from fragmentation, when it is carefully considered, leads not to chaos or radical hermeneutics but to something like the doctrine of Platonic Ideas or Aristotelian essences. There is no empirical reason for us to infer the identity of any fragment of spatiotemporal experience from the evidence of fragmented processes. As long as we concentrate upon the continuum of points of spatiotemporal appearance, rather than upon what appears, we shall never be able to assemble any heap of fragments into a stable identity. Even as infants, we identify processes by their looks, not by the direct perception of the continuity between two processes presented separately. The two processes are united as processes of the same look, not as fragments of multiple looks. And when we are misled by sensation into taking a multiplicity of processes for a unified entity, it is the common look that misleads, even if it is an illusion of a common look. Illusions of this sort are caused not merely by mistakes but by experience of successful identifications.

I do not refer to the presentation of looks as a version of Platonism because I wish to maintain the transcendent existence of looks apart from their spatiotemporal manifestations. The look of a person is ingredient within the processes constituting the spatiotemporal appearances of that person. But it is the same look in all persons. This does not mean, of course, that every person looks alike as a multiplicity of processes. Again, to infer this is to make the mistake of taking one's bearings by the processes rather than by the terminus. We must distinguish here between the *morphe* or perceptual *Gestalt* of an individual person, and the *eidos* of personhood. The distinctness of each person in no way interferes with our identifying them all as persons. On the contrary, if we could not make the general identification, we would be unable to explain what we mean by "distinct persons." There are no distinctions except with respect to differences of kind.

In glossing the simple example of the story about George Washington, I have moved from myth to metaphysics. And this is a perfect illustration of the sense in which philosophy is not a story, or at least not anything less than the whole story. The general structure of stories emerges from the attempt to understand assertions that stories are always particular, or that sameness is at bottom difference. I want now to restate my fundamental thesis. Existence is a text, and life is a story imprinted onto that text, in the following sense. As the cognitive animal, we contribute to the construction of our experience by acts of interpretation, at the level of perception and understanding. But the contribution is made possible by the presence of looks that serve as patterns of unification. In everyday life we cognize this as that by recognizing it as something of such-and-such a kind. We cannot make unified looks of such-and-such a kind except by antecedent acts of recognition of the kind that we are seeking to exemplify by means of our construction. This is why Plato and Aristotle are able to illustrate their doctrine of forms by the example of the demiurge or technician.

It is essential to note that the Kantian doctrine of transcendental construction is not different from Platonism on the crucial point. According to Kant, it is the object of perception that we construct, not the categories, concepts, rules, schemata, Ideas, forms of intuition, and sensations. It is impossible to create a unique individual that does not exhibit a look that could be instantiated by other individuals. This is because to be a spatiotemporal individual is to occupy a continuum of space-time that is not merely a series of points but that exhibits a determinate and identifiable look. The spatiotemporal continuum has a formal content, and it is this content that has location and admits of relations, whether internal or external. The look does its work because of its generality, which is both potential and actual. It is potential in the sense that there need be no end (in the sense of completion or fulfillment) of the actual generation of spatiotemporal instantiations of the look in question. It is actual in the sense that whatever individual of that kind is generated, is an individual of just that look. But the look does not come into existence with the individual in question any more than it perishes when the individual perishes. At this level of generality, there is no real difference between potentiality and actuality. The difference refers to material, not to form, to employ the old-fashioned but effective distinction.

But what of the difference between natural and artificial forms? Perhaps we do not invent the look of a person, but this leaves an infinite range of products of human invention, each possessing a determinate and general look in the sense just defined. Nevertheless, nothing needs to be retracted; invented forms are termini of processes that serve as foci for the integration of substories and as patterns for subsequent instantiations or productions of articles of that kind. As to the apparently endless multiplicity of produced forms, each creation fulfils an intention of the human soul, and can be understood only with respect to our understanding of human nature. This holds good for works of exalted or fine art as well as for the inventions of technology.

In sum, there is an element of construction or interpretation in experience. It is especially evident in sense perception, but it extends to the higher levels of cognition. Life is a web of diverse interpretations, but an interpretation has a plot and is like a story: it is about something. "Aboutness" refers not merely to the "somethings" of such-and-such a kind but also to the unity of the intention of the storyteller. And these intentions in turn depend upon the unity, regularity, and comprehensiveness of ordinary experience. The answer to the question "What do we talk about?" is therefore "Everything." But the precise articulation of the answer will depend upon whether we are talking about things or telling the whole story.

Chapter 8 The Attributes of Ordinary Experience

The stories that we tell about ourselves are made possible by certain pervasive traits of ordinary experience. I discuss four such features in the first half of this chapter: the inner connection between truth and goodness, the exemplification of a unified process, regularity, and comprehensiveness. The reader should not expect to find a general ontology of experience in what follows. My hope is rather to approach the traits as they show themselves within ordinary life. The description of the ordinary or common attributes of experience cannot be discussed entirely in the language of everyday life. I have emphasized throughout this book that the analysis of the ordinary is already a deviation from ordinary language. But a successful account of ordinary experience must actually save the phenomena rather than replace them from the outset with technical artifacts. In the second half of the chapter, I take up the question of how we ascertain the natures of the beings that we encounter within the continuum of experience.

I begin by defending the thesis of the goodness of reason. The good is what we esteem. Some might say that the good is what we desire, but this cannot be right, since we have a multitude of instinctual or involuntary desires, many of which we ourselves would condemn. It is also not enough to say that the good is that of which we approve, since under special circumstances we can approve of conduct that we do not esteem. If the conduct is in the service of an estimable cause, something of this esteem is transmitted down to the action, raising it upward, however unpleasant or regrettable the action may be in other ways. We recognize that esteem is higher than approval.

The estimable is that which compels our respect, not simply what benefits us personally. All other things being equal, however, personal benefit is more estimable than personal harm. We can estimate highly a speech or deed of ours that redounds to our personal disadvantage. That is, we can do so if we are ourselves of a noble rather than a base character. Most if not all of us can draw this distinction when judging the conduct of others, in whose actions we are not directly involved. I say that "we" can make these estimations and draw these distinctions. Someone might object that the "we" is arbitrary, and that many (if not most) people cannot judge the conduct of others, or that the manner in which they do so leads to heterogeneous and even mutually exclusive results. On this point, I am in the august company of Aristotle and Kant, who, as we saw in chapter 3, regard it as superfluous to demonstrate that moral standards are known to all normal persons. Those who deny this fact fly in the face of ordinary experience; their denial is a theoretical fantasy that commands no assent among sensible people. This denial really claims not that there is no common perception of good, evil, noble, base, and the like, but that we differ widely with respect to what constitutes the good, evil, and so on, in each case. This is true, but it is beside the point. These disagreements are themselves expressions of how to respond to common moral perceptions. Whether the disagreeing agents are aware of it, the perception of diversity is always amenable to a rank-ordering of better or worse, not with respect to an abstract philosophical ethics but rather, as I am about to argue, with respect to the very nature of rational activity.

I want to argue that the goodness of reason is directly visible at the level of ordinary experience. It is visible in such a way that depends upon no moral or political judgments, nor upon any theoretical presuppositions that are more complex than the most uncontroversial features of everyday life. It is this sense of goodness that validates or grounds the various derivative senses of "good" that are employed in practical reasoning. I want to say that life is intelligible, without implying the absurdity that it is completely intelligible. When I say that life is intelligible, I mean to include the fact that our problems and limitations are intelligible. This intelligibility is the obvious precondition for human experience, which in turn is possible because of the aforementioned structural elements: the distinction between seeing and making, on the one hand, and between praxis or intentional activity and making, on the other. Praxis is related to theory because it depends upon a kind of seeing, namely, a seeing what one is doing and why; the intersection or overlap between the two occurs at the locus of common sense. In short, it is the intelligibility of the common sense or everyday world that underwrites what we mean by "good" in all practical contexts.

I noted in my discussion of G. E. Moore (chapter 5) that appeals to common sense are challenged by the apparent variability of its judgments from one place or time to another. This challenge is partly met by the distinction between the faculty of common sense, which makes the best judgments available on the basis of local circumstances, and the judgments themselves. It is thus entirely compatible with common sense to know when it is time to replace one such judgment by another. But the difficulty remains that, whereas we all know "somehow" what is meant by common sense, we cannot articulate its structure. There is good reason to believe that common sense has no structure, since it serves as the horizon or cognitive context for all conceptual determinations. Furthermore, even though there is a difference between an erroneous judgment of common sense and a judgment that is merely foolish or unsound, we have no criterion by which to distinguish between common sense and specialized or technical ratiocination. The problem is like that of attempting to define the difference between the ordinary and the extraordinary. We appeal to common sense as protection against extreme or eccentric judgments, but, if we relied on nothing but common sense, there would be nothing but orthodox judgments. Otherwise put, common sense may delude us into thinking that it is self-certifying; something like this was visible in Moore's case.

For reasons of this sort, I think that it is inadvisable to begin with a rigorous definition of common sense, just as it would be not only inadvisable but impossible to philosophize reasonably in its total absence. The procedure I shall follow is to pick out from our rational activity a function that is fundamental to cognition and is directly visible to the "plain man." I shall contend that this function is not only an expression of common sense but that theoretical or conceptual analysis cannot invalidate it because it is the essential precondition for such analysis.

Let us therefore consider the activity that we call "formal analysis." This is a necessary corollary of, if not an intrinsic element within, practical judgment, since we have to discern the natures of the entities with which we are dealing in the effort to find the best line of conduct. Now from a practical standpoint, it is directly obvious that a correct identification of the formal components of the situation we are analyzing is better than an incorrect identification. But I want to claim further that, entirely apart from all practical considerations, human beings are so constituted that we regard accurate formal identifications as better than inaccurate ones. This is of course at least part of what Aristotle means when he says that all human beings desire to know, and that we take delight in the operation of the senses, in particular the sense of vision. At all levels of conscious activity, we prefer correctness or truth to incorrectness or falsehood. We prefer to be right rather than wrong. We estimate those who solve puzzles, not those who are defeated by them, although in a derivative sense, defeat can be admirable if the puzzle was unusually difficult and the effort to solve it intense. But the esteem paid to defeat is derived finally from the excellence of the truth for the sake of which the effort was expended.

Human activity is intrinsically a process of "trying to get it right." This is true even when it is our intention to deceive someone. Hitting the mark is virtually synonymous with success; we cannot imagine a way of life that functions by means of falsehoods and errors. Our beliefs are wrong, not when we cannot verify them rationally but when they fail to accomplish our intentions. And this is especially true in the case of calculation, whether perceptual or intellectual, which depends upon correctly identifying the entities to be calculated. Correctness is thus necessarily better than error. In sum, goodness is an essential ingredient in correct formal analysis. There is no way to function intentionally except by distinguishing between better and worse. We may do so erroneously, but the moment we discover this, we seek to rectify the mistake.

The goodness to which I refer is what human beings are compelled to esteem by the very structure of existence. There are moral consequences of this compulsion, but it is not in itself a moral postulate. Moral goodness must take into account what I shall call ontological goodness; no moral doctrine can command our allegiance if it requires us to disregard the consequences of our actions, or in other words, consciously to act on the basis of false distinctions and perceptions. We can of course attempt to change the world, but this in itself requires us to be right about the extent of our powers and the desirability of our intentions. And the same is true of nihilists, who attempt to deprive life, and the world itself, of any value whatsoever.

Even the nihilist assumes that his or her judgment is rooted in a true perception of human existence. The doctrine would be worthless if it were based upon erroneous reasoning. I do not see how the assertion could be proved, but it is my view that even the philosophical nihilist takes pride in, that is to say, esteems, the capacity to have arrived at the truth, however distressing, and so is not misled by illusion, however gratifying. Nietzsche is the classic example of this. When Nietzsche says that art is worth more for life than the truth, he means to be uttering a true statement that is based upon a correct analysis of human nature. He knows that he is a nihilist and he says so explicitly, but this does not prevent him from taking steps to purge his fellow human beings of the disease. Only Nietzsche (he believes) knows the steps that are required to heal us of nihilism, or even of decadence. Only Nietzsche has arrived at the truth about the nature of values in a universe of fundamental chaos, and he esteems himself accordingly.

Let me try one last formulation of my main thesis. When examining a philosophical doctrine, we should always ask whether it is less plausible than what we already believe. But degrees of plausibility here can be established only by some criterion that is not itself a theorem of a philosophical theory. We have to take our bearings by what all philosophers are compelled to believe. It is easy to say that there is no such object of belief, but it is not so easy to defend that assertion, since it amounts to the claim that there is no criterion for the rank-ordering of philosophical doctrines, and so to the assertion that philosophy, and in particular, practical philosophy, is impossible. But this is a philosophical claim.

In sum, it is a fundamental condition of human existence that we intend to respond correctly to things, experiences, events, and so on, as they actually are. A life devoted to getting things wrong is inconceivable, since if it succeeded, it would destroy itself. And this, I suggest, is not only a deep theoretical truth, but an obvious judgment of common sense.

The argument for the goodness of reason is extremely simple, and some may find it simplistic. I cannot agree with this latter criticism; the simplicity of the argument corresponds to the obviousness of the rank-ordering implicit in all intentional activity, including that of the identification and study of formal structure. On the other hand, the argument says nothing about the properties of formal structure through which we are able to pursue, and often to arrive at, correct identifications and analyses. I want to address this question in two steps. The first step considers the most general properties through which experience is a coherent unity of differences. In the second step, I turn from the continuum of experience to the unity of differences that constitute the look or identity of the elements of that continuum.

Throughout this book, I have been defending the thesis that human experience is the result of the intentional structure of consciousness, that is, the inclination to ascertain how things are, and to act on the basis of that knowledge in such a way as to carry out our purposes and to satisfy our desires. In the previous section, I identified as a general attribute of ordinary experience the intention to choose the better as opposed to the worse alternative in speech and deed. In other words, experience exhibits a structural connection between truth and goodness. We intend to determine the truth because it is normally better for us to know than to be ignorant. This is not a metaphysical doctrine but a description of what I take to be the defining characteristic of human activity. The pursuit of what is true and good for us begins with and is grounded in the act of carrying out the processes of conscious life. I have also argued throughout this volume that there are no determinate structures of ordinary experience in a sense that is amenable to systematic formal analysis, and that such an analysis, in order to be useful, must itself be controlled by participating in the process of rank-ordering. In other words, we cannot understand life by detaching ourselves from its flow. But neither does the "origin" of experience become reflexively accessible through metaphysical or ontological interpretations.

It must be noted at the outset that what I am calling properties of ordinary experience do not disappear when we shift to some extraordinary modification of experience. No one can philosophize, discover scientific laws, or create a work of art in a discontinuous, disordered, and so chaotic environment. This is to say that ordinary experience continues as the context within which the extraordinary occurs. If this were not so, the extraordinary would lose the basis upon which it is distinguished *as* extraordinary. We do not designate experiences as extraordinary because they negate or totally separate themselves from what usually occurs. If such a negation of the ordinary or the isolation of a disruptive moment were possible, it would have to furnish its own sense or value, since the ordinary would no longer be accessible, and the resulting discontinuity would also isolate each disruptive episode from all the others. But how can the continuous disruption of antecedent states, or the radically discontinuous production of the entirely new, provide a basis for rank-ordering, or for the identification of the ordinary? Conversely, if there is a common dimension to the discontinuous series of disruptions, then this will qualify as ordinary experience. And in fact, this is how we have any experience at all.

In short, the properties of which we are now speaking belong to all of human experience. But they are not in themselves sufficient to characterize an experience as extraordinary. Something more is required, but not something less. The adjective "ordinary" does not therefore designate a part or type of experience that we undergo, or produce, independently of extraordinary experience. It rather refers to the ongoing continuity of experience to which we appeal, often without noticing or calling attention to it, when we engage in theoretical efforts to discover or construct the structure of intelligibility, or to transform or modify it in the light of a religious or aesthetic vision.

To continue now with the aforementioned properties, the ordinary is what happens usually. "Usually" is of course ambiguous; it might include "always" as the limit-case. But one thing is clear: the unique or the rare is not the ordinary. Let us note that frequency of occurrence is not in itself a sufficient definition of "ordinary." If we attempt to count a set of natural numbers, we are going to arrive at each of the n members of the set just once. But this is not extraordinary; on the contrary, it is the ordinary result of obeying the rules of arithmetic. It would be silly to say that, in counting, it is extraordinary that we do not arrive more frequently at the number 2. The rules of arithmetic dictate that, in counting, say, seven apples, we arrive at each number in the sum just once, if our intention is to find out how many apples there are in the collection at hand.

In the case of counting, the laws of arithmetic determine what is ordinary. These laws are "ordinal" in the sense that they give priority to the result that follows from obedience to the law. This is not the same sense as that in which we say that the number 7 comes before 8 and after 6 in the series of natural numbers. The order in question is not numerical but refers to degrees of excellence. In adding two apples and three apples, the answer "five" to the question "how many" is better than the answer "four." In general, we can say that, wherever there is a rule or a law that governs some portion of experience, the ordinary is that which follows from the correct application of the rule. At the same time, it is obvious that rules or laws are formulated on the basis of antecedent experience. Life does not begin with a metaphysical reflection on the regularity of nature, nor do we initiate experience with acts of generative legislation. To take the most notorious example, the problem of the justification of induction itself depends on a coherence and order of experience that is much more immediate and secure than any proof could possibly be.

This is why I agree with those who hold that there is no solution to the problem of induction. My reason is that, in a sense, there is no problem, because the ability to formulate the problem depends upon the reliability of inductive reason. Stated somewhat differently, we apply inductive reasoning when we ask for the likelihood that a certain event will occur in the future. But that likelihood is based upon the frequency with which the event has occurred under a given set of circumstances in the past. By "future," we mean a state of the world that functions in the same way as those past states from which we have learned of the given frequency. If the world were to stop tomorrow, that would eliminate the regularity within which inductive reasoning is applicable. When someone asks us to estimate the likelihood that the sun will come up tomorrow, an answer is possible on the basis of our estimate of the age of the sun and the earth, or in other words on the knowledge we possess about the life of these two heavenly bodies. But to the question whether the world will exist tomorrow, or in the next instant, there is no answer that does not depend upon the assumption of the continuing existence of the world, for whatever the span of years allotted to it by the current theories of cosmologists. But this assumption is none other than that of the regularity of nature, or the repudiation of miracles or their practical equivalents, the totally unexpected. This assumption is not based upon scientific results, but rather upon the belief that there are no results in this domain other than those of scientific investigation. The assertion that science is better than religion, for example, is not itself a scientific statement. It is an evaluation of science by our pretheoretical judgment of what constitutes a reliable explanation.

We have no certainty that the initial order of things will continue, but this is not the same as to provide a calculation of the probability of such a catastrophe. In sum: induction functions within the horizon of the regularity of existence, and so too of human experience; but it cannot provide a rational estimate of how long, or whether, the regularity of existence will endure. What we can say is that regularity is a precondition for experience. Indeed, "regular" is a virtual synonym for "ordinary." The ordinal function of ordinary experience depends upon the rules that govern it. What one means by "rules" in the case of natural processes is not quite the same, however, as the meaning of "rules" with respect to praxis. Nature possesses intentionality in a metaphorical sense only, as when we speak of the purposes or ends of organisms. Natural processes may be thwarted, whether by human intervention or because of other natural processes. But there is no voluntarism in the following of the rules or laws of nature. Human beings, on the other hand, may disobey the rules that apply to praxis.

We can therefore make the following distinction. The unity and regularity of praxis, the domain of intentional human activity through speeches and deeds, is itself dependent upon the unity and regularity of existence, to which we sometimes refer, not with complete accuracy, as the order of nature. "Nature" is perhaps too weak a term to use here, unless we expand it to include ontological unity and regularity. But that is a terminological point. The substance of the point is that experience is a continuum that cannot be constructed out of antecedently existing or occurring smaller elements, but is the regular manifestation of a self-differentiating unity. It is within this self-differentiating unity that we choose the deeds and speeches that provide us with the opportunity to unify or dissolve the meaning and value of our individual lives.

In sum: experience depends upon the coherence of space-time and the regularity of the natural order. This cosmological or natural unity and regularity is expressed in our lives as the conditions upon which action is predicated, but they are not themselves praxis or intentional action. I am therefore always unified and orderly or regular in my natural existence, and this plays a large role in the unity and regularity of ordinary experience. But within ordinary experience there are many variations upon the intentional expression of cosmological or natural unity and regularity. These variations themselves follow general patterns of conduct, but the patterns can be violated. What makes life possible, and gives us the kind of experience that we actually have, is that the violations are infrequent. Ordinary experience is what usually happens. It is what we count upon, and "what everyone knows." As to the idiosyncratic behavior of the individual person, to the extent that it does not fall under the aforementioned general patterns of conduct, but is too trivial to qualify as extraordinary, we are free to disregard it. But we can also enjoy it, in the way that we enjoy novels about eccentrics, or for that matter about ordinary persons.

This series of remarks allows me to refine somewhat my previous remark about the nonconstructed nature of the unity of experience. In other words, it is impossible that human beings constitute the continuum of our ordinary experience out of simpler elements. It is this continuum that makes possible our discrimination of elements such as objects, actions, or events as distinct elements of experience. Drawing such distinctions does not dissolve the continuum but rather depends upon it. The simpler elements are abstractions from ordinary experience. To come back to an earlier point, it is not quite correct to say that ordinary experience is what "usually" obtains, because this is compatible with the inference that the appearance of ordinary experience is somehow episodic or that its appearances are enumerable. We have to make the following distinction. In the most general sense of the term, ordinary experience does not appear "usually" because it is always present. In the particular sense, however, and in keeping with the earlier remark about rules or laws, ordinary experience is what we are used to, what we expect, or what we can readily understand on the basis of what has gone before.

As that which is always present in its full nature or identity, ordinary experience is not built up ex nihilo out of simpler elements. Of course, as time goes on, we gain in familiarity with and knowledge of this or that particular manifestation of experience, for example, the behavior of physical bodies, efficient political arrangements, felicitous social customs, and so on. But we are not in these cases learning something radically new; that would be *extraordinary*.

Ordinary experience can become deeper and richer, but it does not come into being out of these depths and riches. Otherwise stated, at the most general level, which is represented by the properties I am now discussing, ordinary experience is everywhere essentially the same. The differences from one age or society to another are all contingent. When viewed from above, these particular differences can be classified under general properties that are common to every version of ordinary experience.

What has been variously called the cosmological, ontological, or natural unity of experience may be illustrated with an example from mathematics. One of the main problems faced by the philosopher of mathematics is to explain the relation between continuity and discreteness. This problem is also addressed by Hegel in his *Science of Logic*. In a Hegelian analysis, continuity is shown to transform itself into discreteness, and discreteness into continuity, by the very attempt to think either term in and by itself. Let me try to restate this in my own words.

That which is truly continuous has no discrete parts, and the discrete is not continuous. We can of course mark off parts on a line, but this depends upon the notion of segments or points, and so of discontinuity. Neither addition nor division will solve our problem. Let us therefore shift our perspective and ask: what must be the case in order for us to be able to conceive of continuity? The answer is not discreteness but difference. It is impossible to think of a monadic continuum, since there would be no opposition of what Hegel calls subject and object. In other words, even if the act of thinking is the constituting agent of consciousness, and further, even if it is impossible that one should exist without the other, they are distinguishable moments in a unified totality. But they are not discrete. Hegel calls this relation the identity of identity and difference.

A similar argument can be given in the case of discreteness. The key premise is the assertion that we cannot hold together two discrete elements in a relation of separation except through the unity of consciousness. To say that x is detached from y assumes an antecedent connection between the two items, which is not the same as their mere juxtaposition or contiguity, but which permits us to distinguish them. Hegel frequently calls this "negation," by which he means that to be something or another is also not to be everything else. This claim sounds absurd if we take it literally, that is, if we tacitly assume that it applies to elements or objects of perception and cognition rather than to the continuity of experience that is the precondition for the presence of elements of perception or cognition.

Hegel, of course, is attempting to provide a dialectical analysis of what Kant calls the "synthetic unity of apperception." But his central point is illuminating for our own investigation. No one, and certainly not Hegel, would say that a tree, for example, is a tree by virtue of not being a stone. But if we take our bearings by trees and stones, or in other words by elements of perception or cognition, then we shall begin directly with discreteness, and the sense that we give to "continuity" will invariably be that of an assemblage or synthesis of discrete elements. Our everyday experience shows us something quite different. When I perceive a stone, I do not sunder it from the spatiotemporal matrix within which it is part of a continuum of individually discernible properties, relations, or things. I see the stone as distinct from the tree next to which it lies, but I also "see," albeit in another sense of the term, the unity of which the stone and the tree, and I myself, are "differences."

It is much easier to notice the tree or the stone than it is to apprehend the unity of difference in which the tree and the stone are ingredients. Kant, of course, makes this apprehension central to his philosophy. He refers to it as "apperception" because it is a kind of awareness of awareness, that is, the immediate "opening" of consciousness as ego-centered and the dimension within which all perceptions belonging to a particular ego are manifested. Apperception is thus the unity of perception. It is also one of the most obscure elements in Kant's philosophy. But this is unavoidable, because the synthetic unity of apperception, as the ground of cognition, cannot itself be deduced from anything else. It is either there or not there. Hegel's apparently sophistical concept of the identity of identity and difference is intended to exhibit the dialectical properties of the synthetic unity of apperception, not its "logical" properties in the traditional rationalist sense of that term.

One defect in Kant's doctrine of the unity of apperception is his use of the term "synthetic." Kant does not mean by this term that apperception is the result of the adding together or blending of simpler elements, which, as prior to apperception, must themselves lack that property. What he wants to convey is the notion that apperception is not the result of the antecedent analysis of some more complex condition. It is synthetic in the sense that it serves as the ground for all subsequent syntheses. If this were a scholarly study of Kant, we would also have to investigate the connection between Kantian apperception and what he calls the "I think" on the one hand, and consciousness on the other. Apperception seems to be a logical condition for the possibility of consciousness, not consciousness itself. It is a condition marked by the fact that every act of consciousness must be predicated of a thinking subject that manifests itself as "I think" (the thought in question). Whether this is the correct reading of Kant or not, I am calling attention to the imperviousness to analysis of the unity of experience that initiates and preserves it. This imperviousness makes the expression "synthetic" inappropriate.

The same objection could be made to Hegel's "identity of identity and difference," a difficulty that Hegel vainly hoped to avoid by his method of dialectic. Stated as simply as possible, the difficulty that Hegel could not surmount is that in order for human beings to express the dialectical properties of conceptual moments or categories, they must employ the analytical discourse of traditional rationalism. I cannot explain the peculiar sense in which "the identity of identity and difference" is supposed to elicit the unity of flowing or living moments of apperception, except by stating, one step at a time, each moment of the total dialectic. The statement of the elements of dialectic cannot itself consist in dialectical statements. Hegel's dialectico-speculative logic is thus a surrogate for the expression of the dialectical motion of actuality. It is a surrogate that makes use of analytical rationalism in order to evoke or suggest the unity of identity and difference. But we cannot think this unity except by stating its individual components. This is why philosophy cannot entirely supersede the evocativeness of rhetoric or the superiority of poetry to logical and conceptual analysis. And poetry, of course, cannot itself capture the flavor of the lived consciousness of the unity of experience.

The mathematical problem of the relation between continuity and discreteness is now evident as itself subordinate to the identity of identity and difference. In other words, the mathematical continuum, as a class of points, is already built up out of discreteness. But this is not the same as the unity of experience. We can place a conceptual grid over our immediate apprehension of the identity of identity and difference; but in so doing, we transform it into a constituted totality of discrete elements. In fact, the very expression "identity of identity and difference" can shift us away from the intended unity, because it seems to detach identity and difference. I say "seems," since for Hegel, neither can be thought without the other.

So much for this example. It was of course not intended as a criticism of mathematics but rather to show the difference between mathematical analysis and philosophy. This is not to say that I fully endorse the Hegelian dialectical account of continuity and difference. This account is, however, at least directed toward the actual philosophical problem, which is not that of mathematical continuity and discreteness. And this is why we cannot build up ordinary experience from a list of ingredients. At the same time, it is not at all my point that we must shift from traditional rationalism to Hegelian dialectic. I want rather to evoke the most general feature of ordinary experience in its most general sense. This feature does not render careful description or analysis superfluous. It is instead the precondition for all descriptions and analyses.

Since it is cumbersome to refer constantly to the identity of identity and difference, and because I do not want to accept all of the Hegelian variations on this theme, allow me to refer to the underlying concept henceforth as the unity of experience. This has a much simpler, and certainly a much more familiar sound. It has the possible defect that it mentions unity but not difference; I therefore stipulate that "unity" here refers to the unity of differences. And in my everyday persona, as opposed to that of the logician or metaphysician, I mean to say that a unity is in fact a unity of differences. The simple confirmation of this intention is the human ability to identify a unity as *this* unity thanks to the arrangement of its different properties or relations.

No one would dispute that we have different experiences, but it is not plausible to be told that we build experience in general out of these particular occurrences. On the other hand, we often talk of creating a life, by which expression we mean living out our life in accord with some plan or principle. The unity of experience is not itself the plan or the principle, but neither is it the life in progress. Nor could we say that the unity of experience is a part of that life, since the former is a totality, not a part. It is much better, if not entirely accurate, to say that every life in progress is embedded within the unity of experience. This expression is somehow too physical, as if experience were a cake stuffed with the raisins of individual lives. Perhaps it would be still better to say that each life in progress is an expression of the overarching unity as seen from a slightly different standpoint, as in the case of Leibniz's monads. But that too is defective, since the image seems to position each life as outside of, albeit open to, the unity of experience.

These formulations are intended as examples of the difficulty inherent in the attempt to capture discursively the most general sense of ordinary experience. The difficulty is not simply that of trying to differentiate a unity without replacing difference by discreteness, and thereby disrupting continuity. At a deeper level, the problem lies in the inadequacy of any logical or conceptual articulation to capture the sense of life itself, of consciousness, that permeates all experience, ordinary or particular. Epistemologists and psychologists, like neurophysiologists, tend to talk of experience as though it were a process of the registration of stimuli upon sensory and cognitive machinery. In so doing, they leave out everything that is characteristic of life itself, as opposed to the analysis of the substructures of life. And something similar can be said of phenomenologists.

It would certainly be going too far to say that these substructures are irrelevant to our own investigation. But they cannot be our primary concern. We have to start with life as it is actually lived. In "lived life" (a barbarous expression!), the unity of experience is not accessible to us as a logical or conceptual structure. In the strict formalist sense, therefore, it cannot be described or analyzed, but only exemplified. I am very sympathetic to the characterization of our experience of the unity of life as a *Stimmung* or determination of the soul, to borrow an appropriate term from Heidegger. Or, as Heidegger puts it, we find ourselves as "thrown" or "fallen" into life, as already along the way. In my terms, we are preceded by the unity that we try to constitute analytically as we move along within the lived present.

This allows me to introduce a third general property of experience, closely related to unity and regularity, which I call *comprehensiveness*. We are never about to enter into ordinary experience but are always already there. Heidegger saw this especially well. Unfortunately, his description is too abstract (I refer here to the analysis of the "ecstatic" structure of the three tenses of temporality) or too doctrinaire (it gives a narrow and biased interpretation of the everyday).

Let us see whether we can identify the main features of this attribute of comprehensiveness. To begin with, the unity and regularity of experience constitute a framework or horizon within which life holds together at each moment as a continuous and ongoing process. We do not consciously or intentionally step into this horizon from some anonymous external location, any more than we attend to the event called "death" by which we exit from life. Intending and attending are themselves possible only on the basis of our already being engaged in life, and this is to say, as already engaged in experience. Experience, as opposed to the physical or psychological functions of human existence, begins as something that we are already familiar with, something in which we are already immersed. There is no experience of the ostensibly first moment of experience; we cannot be aware of immediacy except on the basis of a memory of some antecedent content of consciousness that serves as the basis for our interpretation of what we are now experiencing. But there is a last moment; and at this moment, we depart from life, that is, from the experience of life, as when we lapse into a coma or simply expire. We can, in other words, watch ourselves dying, but we cannot, as alive, experience being dead.

This is all that we require of the Heideggerian account. It is against this background that talk about extraordinary experience first becomes intelligible. I may have a vision, or a prophetic dream, of some extraordinary mode of existence in which unity, regularity, and comprehensiveness are absent, but, as having the vision, I identify its content by contrasting it to ordinary experience; and this is enough to show that I have not totally dispensed with or liberated myself from it. In fact, one cannot have an intelligible vision of an extraordinary state of affairs except on the basis of the unity, regularity, and comprehensiveness that characterize ordinary experience. The moments of the vision must be unified in such a way as to render the vision intelligible, just as my consciousness must preserve the unity of cognitive and perceptual awareness; and this in turn is to say that the event of the vision is rendered manifest as the anticipation of a rupture in the regular environment of everyday life. I am thus, as having and subsequently as recounting the vision, firmly resident within the comprehensiveness of experience as it is ordinarily understood: that we are always already in ordinary experience.

I have said relatively little about the three related properties of unity, regularity, and comprehensiveness. My only claim is that what I have said is indispensable, and that it does not obligate us to excessively complex ontological interpretations of the particular life-stories that are enacted within the general matrix of experience. One can be a Platonist or a Heideggerian and still accept my account. In that sense, my account is trivial, and intentionally so. Philosophy, and in particular a philosophical consideration of ordinary experience, is obliged to state the trivial and in fact would be remiss to replace it at once with a more conceptually elaborate analysis.

To conclude this portion of my discussion, ordinary experience in its most general, inescapable, ordinal, and regulative sense, cannot be constituted, constructed, or even synthesized. All of these activities presuppose the disjunction of continuity and discreteness, or the production of continuity from the collecting or blending of discrete elements. The concern of the analyst of ordinary experience is necessarily with particular manifestations of this general condition. Experiences of disintegration, meaninglessness, the fallibility of deductive argumentation, are all made possible by the indubitability of those experiences themselves. This is an unstated corollary of the Cartesian *cogito*. But what cannot be described in the analytical language of Descartes is the unity of the motions of cogitation, and so of the *ego cogitans*. It is the insight that life as lived is inaccessible to conceptual analysis that motivates such apparently diverse philosophers as Hegel, Nietzsche, and Bergson.[1]

Unity, regularity, and comprehensiveness are representative examples of the general attributes of ordinary experience. It goes without saying that this road has been frequently traveled before. Indeed, it is my claim that one cannot travel at all except along this very road. The next step in my argument covers more controversial ground, but I believe that I can present my argument in relatively straightforward language. The goal is to clarify the characteristics of the intelligibility of the elements of the continuum of experience. As usual, I begin from the commonsense reasoning of everyday life.

I contend that this commonsensical reasoning is the core of the doctrine of intelligible form introduced by Plato and Aristotle. Platonic forms and Aristotelian essences, like Fregean concepts, express something fundamental and unmistakable about ordinary life. Let me emphasize that it is the core with which we are concerned, not the fully developed doctrine (in either version). I will reconsider the general approach taken by Aristotle and compare it with its Platonic antecedent as well as with the modern, conceptually oriented approach. My claim is that at the level of the core of each of these "ancient" and "modern" ways of stating the issue, there is little or no difference between them. Nor should this be surprising, since that core expresses the everyday phenomenon that each is attempting to explain. This phenomenon is the self-presentation of the unity of experience as a differentiated totality of distinct looks.

Why do we speak of form at all? The etymology of the term arises out of the simple visual sense of ordinary experience. The form of something in its "look." In this sense, a look is not a separately existing entity but simply the configuration of elements, whatever these may be, that constitute the identity of a thing. This can be most easily clarified by starting with a case that is derivative logically or conceptually, but is not derivative so far as our pre-philosophical or commonsense reflection on experience is concerned. I have in mind the cases in which we see something and say "that looks like X," where X is simply something other than "that." For Y to look like X, they must have something in common, something that affects our sensory, cognitive, and linguistic faculties in the same way.

I see John. John reminds me of his father. I say "John looks like his father, Joseph." This is about as simple an example of our sensory-cognitive experience as one can construct. What are we saying when we say that someone (or something) looks like someone (or something) else? I am saying that each of the two things has the same look. Now, a look does not look like another look; it is the same look. If two things have the same look, then there is some look that they both have or show. It cannot be meaningless to speak of the look of a thing. The question is not whether anything has a look; it is rather how the same look can appear in different locations or instances. The same look can appear in different degrees within different perceived individuals, but there is no precise criterion by which to establish the sameness of the look in a wide range of cases, other than our ability to recognize it. This is the reason that Wittgenstein's phrase "family resemblance" can also serve to express sameness.

Let me now develop the general point with a simple example. Suppose that I ask "What is that?" and you say: "It is a cow." You have not mentioned a look in answering my question: you have mentioned a thing, a cow; and indeed, you are referring to a particular cow. Does this mean, as some would say, that there are no looks, or that the term "look" is an empty expression, and that we identify things, not looks?

This objection to the use of "look" is misconceived. When I ask you "What is that?" I am not asking you for the name of a look, because "that" is not a look; it is a thing, say, a cow, with a look of a certain kind. I do not ask, however, "What is that look over there?" I ask rather for the name corresponding to the kind of being of which the one to which I am pointing is an instance. The "look" comes into play only when I ask "How did you identify that thing as a cow?" How are you able to identify a cow as the kind of thing that we correctly designate by that name? This is a question that the person objecting to my use of "look" must answer.

The simplest answer, which not only conforms with but is certified by ordinary language, is "Because it looks like a cow." You say that this looks like a cow, not because it is a look but because it *has* a look. Now you may have selected the name of the identity of the cow initially by virtue of its physical or pictorial look, but this is only the start of the explanatory analysis of what you mean by saying "that is a cow." You might go on to give a physiological or biological account of the kinds of things that have the pictorial look we associate with cows; or perhaps you will give some other kind of explanation. All such explanations will be directed to the conditions for the presence of things *like the one we are talking about*. If we are trying to explain what it is that we mean by the word "cow," it is in fact impossible to talk about the unique cow to which we initially referred. To talk "about" the cow is to talk, not about this cow but about the properties and relations that make up the presence and the nature of cows. We can of course say "That cow is mooing too loudly" or "I admire the complexion of that cow" or even "Hey, you, cow; get out of my way!" But all these statements are intelligible in the last analysis only because we know what it is to be a cow.

To be a cow is to be a cow and not another thing. But what does "another" mean? It certainly does not mean "another cow," because then the statement would mean that "to be a cow is to be a cow and not to be another cow." No one ever suggested that this cow is another cow. The point is rather that this cow is not something other than a cow: it is not a horse. In some vague and general sense, cows may look like horses, but not enough for them to be confused by anyone of normal perceptual powers under normal circumstances. But in saying that cows look *something* like horses, we already distinguish cows from horses. They look something like horses, but more like other cows. And in some decisive sense, cows look like nothing but cows. I mean by this that if cows were nothing but look-alikes for other animals, then there would be no cows, or at least none that we could identify.

However we construe the situation, cows have a look that belongs to them in the sense that to look like that is to be a cow and nothing else. Only people who deny that anything can be identified as a cow, or that indeed anything at all can be identified as anything, will dispute this. But to do so is too absurd to take seriously. Our success in making such identifications is not invalidated by our encountering problems in our analysis of how we identify things. The entire discussion could not take place if you did not know the difference between a cow and a horse. I mean "know" in some sense that is adequate to make correct identifications but not adequate enough to explain in a rigorous and coherent conceptual manner.

Now what many philosophers are worried about is not whether one cow looks like another, but whether this requires us to speak of "looks" as though they were independent of the individual cows or of anything whatsoever that possesses them. They are worrying lest we smuggle a metaphysical doctrine of essences into our discussion of what things look like, or even into our discussion of the fortuitous fact that things can be identified, i.e., classified into families or collections or sets or species by virtue of their common look, where "look" means primarily "pictorial" or "visual." More extensively, "look" can mean "conceptual," "discursive," or whatever is your favorite faculty for identifying and defining things.

I want now to show that it is impossible to identify anything *as* anything unless the look is in one sense separate and in another sense not separate from the instance bearing that look. My demonstration will be based upon features of experience that are accessible to every person of normal intelligence.

All individual cows have a certain configuration of elements, whether we call these elements their bodily parts or the underlying electromagnetic disturbances that produce a sensory entity that we identify as a cow when these disturbances register upon, or rather interfere in a certain way with, the separate set of electromagnetic disturbances constituting us, namely, human perceivers. I note in passing that the latter set of disturbances results in a perceptible human being if and only if it interferes in a certain way with another set of electromagnetic disturbances that is also a human being, if it in turn registers upon yet another set of electromagnetic disturbances that constitutes a human being, if and only if—but the general picture is plain. The real question is this: How does one set of electromagnetic disturbances collide with another in such a way as to produce a human being perceiving a cow? Certainly the disturbances that would be a cow if any person were there to perceive them, do not in themselves produce a human being. One set of disturbances is already a human being and the other is already a cow.

My question requires instead the following observation. The set of disturbances that we might call "cow-producing disturbances" is different from the set of disturbances that we might call "human-producing disturbances." Each set has its own "look," no doubt even in the pictorial sense that if there were eyes or instruments sharp enough to see them, each would have its own configuration. But we do not need to limit ourselves to the pictorial sense of "look." Let us say that the equation, or ratio of particles, or expression of the gravitational field, or the calculation of the oscillations of this field, is different in the two cases of "cow" and "human being." The initial difference, expressed by the Aristotelian formula that to be is to be this thing here of such and such a look, holds good from the macroscopic to the microscopic level. It also covers fuzzy sets and things upon which other things can act at a distance.

To continue with the main line of my demonstration about separation, each cow has the look of a cow. The look is the same in all cases, and by "same" I mean "minimal set of qualities that make something a cow." Now what is the same in all cases cannot be identical with each instance. If the look of a cow can occur in two separate cows, then the look is not only common to both, but it is common to both by virtue of the fact that it is separate from either. By "separate" we mean here not only "distinguishable from," as in the case of the two cows, but "different in manner of being."

If the look of the cow were identical with the cow, the look would disappear on the death of that cow. In that case, there could be exactly one cow, namely this one, and this one is now dead, so there aren't any. But the same look shows up in many things, and we call each and every one "cow." So the look is obviously the same in all cases only because it is separate from each case, *qua* each individual.

Please note that exactly the same reasoning holds with respect to modern, say Fregean, concepts. A concept is the same in all of its instances, yet other than and so separate from each and all of them. If we destroy the instances, we have not destroyed the concept. Those who dislike separate looks no doubt also dislike separate concepts, and they will have to repeat the whole argument about not cognizing concepts but rather this or that thing, a cow or a horse. But this won't work. We don't cognize individual cows or horses; we perceive them. What we cognize are general terms, properties or relations belonging to more than one thing. And no general property can be identical with some individual that possesses it.

It should be entirely clear that the concept, like its antecedent, the look, is not the same as the instance (or the thing that has that look), even though it is the same concept or look in a whole set of instances. The way in which the instance "has" the look or "is an instance of" the concept is different from the way in which it exists under a definite set of spatiotemporal coordinates as a unique individual. We often express this by saying that concepts are "abstract entities." Of course, many people today like to say that there are no abstract entities. I suppose they mean by this that abstract entities do not exist as though they were individual potatoes or peppermint sticks. But who ever said that they did?

Could we say that a concept is "just a name"? What is that supposed to mean? A concept *has* a name, and the name is no doubt conventional or peculiar to some language or another; but the name cannot be used properly by simply applying it to something. We can apply any name to anything we wish. For example, we can call a cow "Elsie." I suppose that we could also call a cow "equilateral triangle." But that would not make the cow an equilateral triangle. Names have to be used correctly. This means not that the English expression "equilateral triangle" is reserved by nature for the beings we call equilateral triangles. It just means that once we fix upon the meaning of a name, we have to use it for one kind of thing and not others (unless by metaphor, analogy, or some figure of speech, all of which depend upon the notion of a core or focal meaning, of which they are identifiable variations). In doing this, we recognize that things have different looks, or are instances of quite different concepts. That is to say: all things that instantiate the same concept have that same look or nature. We would not say that all things instantiating a certain concept are that certain concept, or that the concept is the same as some one of its instances, or that it is the same as all of its instances, or—what? What else could we say except that the concept is the same in all cases in which it is the same? This is after all what we are saying when we say that all concepts are the same in all cases of the same nature.

But "same" in what sense? I claim that our previous analysis shows this: The concept is the same in all cases in which the same concept holds. That sounds like an empty tautology, but it is a deep metaphysical truth. The same concept can hold only in a multiplicity of cases or instances or circumstances. We identify it as the same precisely because it makes multiple appearances. If there were just one instance, no one would say of it, "That is the same concept." If they did, someone else would then ask: "The same as what?" You could reply "The same as itself," but this means that if this concept were to appear in a plurality of cases, it would be the same in all these cases. So concepts can be multiplied. But I claim that instances cannot be.

This sounds entirely wrong at first hearing, but consider. Let "Elsie" be an instance of the concept *cow*. Now let "Dora" be the name of another cow. What is being multiplied here? Certainly not Elsie, who remains her unique self, nor Dora, about whom the same is true. It is the concept *cow* that is being multiplied. So when we say "there are a multitude of instances of things of that sort," what we mean to say is that there is a multitude of the same sort of thing, i.e., the concept, or the look, and so eventually the *eidos* or Platonic Idea. And this shows that the look, concept, and so on, is not the same as the instance. In other words, nominalism is unintelligible.

To summarize: in order for there to be anything at all, things must be something or another, and when they are another, they are other than when they are the initial something. That is, things come in kinds, and kinds are the same in the set of cases in which they occur, although they are, precisely as the same in all these cases, separate from each and all of them. Even if you wiped out every cow in the world, more could come into being in a billion years, and they would be the same as their predecessors. Now how can we explain the fact that something is the same in all cases yet different in every one of those cases? I don't see any way except by saying "in one sense they are the same, and in another, not." But this is mere word play unless the sense that is both the same and other itself possesses an actuality or being that is not the same as the actuality or being of the instances.

I repeat an earlier point: it is false that concepts do not exist, or that there are no concepts. What is true is that concepts are not their own instances. So they exist or are in a different manner from the existence or being of their instances. You cannot totally and permanently separate concepts from their instances, because then the concepts would not be the concepts *of* those instances; the instances would dissolve, or be something other than what they were when we started. But you cannot totally and permanently identify concepts and their instances, since then there would be only instances but no concepts. This means that *being is dual.* The sense of "to be" is not the same in the two expressions "to be a concept" and "to be an instance." We can now translate this into Aristotelian language. To be is to be both an essence and a substance. There is nothing intrinsically more mysterious about substances and essences than there is about instances and concepts. What I find entirely mysterious is the claim that there are no concepts, and of course no essences or looks, but only instances. I do not know how to make any sense out of this claim, and I have now shown why it cannot make sense.

All this having been said, we now know why Aristotle's investigation into *ousia* is a serious business, and why it has not been superseded by modern antisubstantialist and antiessentialist philosophies. I am afraid that these philosophies do not know what they are talking about, and I emphasize the word *what.* It is a mark of presumption of the highest order for representatives of this kind of doctrine to hold that Aristotelian metaphysics is nonsense or that those who explain it do not know what they are talking about.

But we do *not* know the complete, coherent discursive analysis of the separation and yet the sameness of the two senses of being. Is this a defect on our part? Not at all, if the nature of a dualism is that it cannot be taken apart into the same separately intelligible elements. Now of course we can distinguish "substance" from "essence." My entire argument rests upon our ability to do this. A substance is a thing bearing a certain look, or it is the instance of a concept, and so on. An essence is a look common to a family of individuals, and so on. That is intelligible and true, as far as it goes. But we would like to go further. We would like some basis from which we can explain how substance and essence can be reconciled into a single sense of "being." And that is impossible. This is why Aristotle refers to "first" and "second" *ousia* (although he does not use these terms consistently; but that is beyond the range of our interest).

Substance and essence are themselves two abstract entities that are reconciled within the individual thing "cow," by which I mean *this* cow, Elsie. Elsie is neither a substance nor an essence alone but a substance having a certain essence. This is partly concealed by the fact that the term "substance" is used as a general name for Elsie. We say "Elsie is a substance, namely, a sensible separate particular." But of course Elsie can't be a sensible separate particular except thanks to the essence that particularizes her by arranging her matter into a shape of a definite kind, a shape that "somehow" exhibits the form or provides us with a basis for arriving at the form via intellectual intuition. Let us put the question of intellectual intuition to one side for a moment.

The form (in the sense of the species-form, or essence) is certainly present within Elsie. It can't be present in her matter; no one says that bones, blood, flesh, intestines, and so on, are a cow. The form is not present in the form, except in the tautologous sense that it *is* the form. We want to know "where" it is. It must show itself in the shape, which is the result of the work of the form on the matter. But it can't be just the shape itself, since that is material and relative to the nature of our sensory apparatus.

Perhaps we should note that the same problem arises with concepts and instances. In which part of the instance is the concept located? If anything, this question is harder than Aristotle's, since concepts are presumably just form (unless you are a materialist, which makes you a nominalist, and hence outside the possibility of rational discourse). Concepts, we might want to say, are just where they are. But where is that, exactly? In the domain of pure forms? In some hyperuranian *topos?* Or are they products of discursive thinking? If the latter, then the problems of Idealism arise, but I will not rehearse them here.

To come back to Aristotelian forms. I am saying that they are ingredient in the substances (Elsie the cow and her sisters) precisely because they are separate from them. But they are not too separate. What is the right amount? Aristotle suggests, or I suggest on his behalf: the right amount is the degree to which form enters into matter in order to produce an individual of a definite shape, which shape is a projection of that form. Note that Aristotle has not forgotten about the matter; prime matter is a kind of limit case or logical necessity. Actually, matter is always this or that kind, wood, metal, flesh, and so on. To say that the form enters into the matter to produce a certain shape is to say tacitly that the form is able to enter into only this or that kind of matter, which is itself this or that kind by virtue of its own formal principle or ratio of organization. This means that expressions like "rational animal" must be abbreviations for "rational animal made of flesh, and so on, rather than tungsten and beechwood." Contemporary cognitive scientists who believe that the mind is software that can be run on computers made of anything at all are actually more metaphysical than Aristotle, since they do not believe that rational animals have bodies of any particular sort. Suffice it to say that "rational animal" can't be the essence of human beings unless we recall that animals are made of flesh and blood, muscle, and so on.

The right amount of separation is one that permits attachment. Does this sound odd? It shouldn't. You cannot attach something to a second thing if the something just *is* the second thing. And we have already seen that the form cannot possibly be the second thing *qua* instance or sensible separate substance. We can understand how to attach two separate pieces of matter—e.g., two grooved pieces of wood—to one another, perhaps by using glue to attach one piece of wood to the other. But how do you attach a form to matter? This is why people become materialists: It looks as though we perform the attachment just by shaping pieces of matter. To be more precise, the shaping is done either by nature or by us. But we don't go about glueing forms to matter.

The case of art is different from that of nature. In the case of art, we can look at a blueprint or imaginary model and use it as a guide to glue matter together. Let us call this "shaping matter." In the case of nature, the shaping of matter takes place apart from our efforts, on its own. It may help us to understand nature by thinking of her as an artist. Then we try to discover or duplicate the blueprints or models by which she shapes matter into the cosmos. To the extent that we can do this, we say that nature is intelligible. That means that we have discerned the conceptual, (i.e., the formal) structure of nature. In the case of art, the situation is the reverse: We discern the model and then produce the surrogate for nature, namely, the art-work. In both cases, however, the shaping of matter adheres to a blueprint. One could ask whether we have made the blueprint or discovered it. I will turn to this in a moment, but please notice first that it makes no difference so far as the present inquiry is concerned. In both cases, there is an *isomorphism* between the blueprint or model or original and the shaped matter, the separate sensible particular, the instance, the thing of such-and-such a look, but also of whole families or ordered sets of such separate particulars, and in the last instance, the cosmos.

The shaped matter is an image of an original, whether this latter is made or discovered. Suppose we make the blueprint. One cannot make blueprints in the same way that one makes material realizations of the formal structure in the blueprint. I might invent the sewing machine; to invent something is to devise a blueprint for building it, i.e., for realizing it in shaped matter. The blueprint is not the shaped matter; if it were, I would not have to build the sewing machine. I could sew with the blueprint. On the other hand, the sewing machine is isomorphic with the blueprint; it is not the realization of some other formal structure. In the word "isomorphism" or its informal equivalent "realization of a model," is the entire problem of the "combination" of form and matter, or of participation, separation, and imitation.

I repeat, the blueprint or model is not the shaped matter. Furthermore, it can exist independent of the shaped matter. For example, you can keep the blueprint of some invention, a sewing machine or a submarine, locked up in a desk drawer in your study. Nevertheless, the form is actively present in the sewing machine or submarine, once these are built. And you could even say, if you saw a sewing machine in the parlor, "that looks just like the blueprint in my uncle's desk drawer." Furthermore, the original formal structure of the sewing machine first exists in the intellect of the inventor, where it remains independently of whether he commits it to pen and ink, i.e., whether he makes a blueprint of it. We have three forms: the form in the intellect; the form on the blueprint, and the form in the shaped matter called "a sewing machine." Each is separate from the others, yet all three are the same. How is this possible?

This question is not difficult to answer. The intellect, the paper and ink, and the parts of metal that go into the making of a sewing machine, serve as different kinds of substrate or matter, in Aristotle's terms, *hupokeimenon* or *hule*. The form is the same in all cases; what differs is its realization. The next question, however, is far from easy. Is this an "explanation" of how form combines with matter? Not really; it is a rendering more precise of the assertion. We have three different combinations of one and the same form but in each case with a different kind of matter. Nor is it really clear in what sense we "make" the form by thinking it (and so realizing it in the *hule* of thought). But enough of artifacts. Aristotle is primarily interested in natural things, and his references to art are intended to illustrate the work of nature. I don't believe that this is finally justified, but I am going to limit myself, after this illustrative remark, to natural things.

In the case of natural things, the form is certainly present in the shaped matter. But I have already shown that it cannot be reduced to shaped matter. All instances of shaped matter *of the same kind* exhibit a form that is the same as theirs yet other than they. That I think the form, or that it is "actualized" in my intellect, is a secondary phenomenon with respect to the primary act by which the form and matter combine to produce this shaped particular hunk of matter. Yes, nature does the work here. But how? We have no more of an answer to this question than we did in the case of art, except for the following version of an answer. In order for matter to be shaped into an identifiable particular thing, it must be shaped in accord with a formula or ratio that gives the matter in question a certain look, which we call its shape (*morphe*). As we have seen at sufficient length: no look, no thing. The look is both outside and inside the thing. It is the same look as in all things of that look. But it *is* no one of those things.

The following conclusion suggests itself from our investigation thus far. The reference to looks or kinds is a direct consequence of the intelligibility of things. This is true at the level of ordinary language; it is not the consequence of a philosophical interpretation of ordinary language. The doctrine of form is a philosophical account of the nature of looks that attempts to determine the underlying basis for the sameness and difference of perceived shapes. The philosopher understands that the form is brought to our attention by the shaped matter, i.e., by the particular thing. But he or she also understands that the form, or principle of organization, cannot *be* that shape, which is rather an expression or realization of that principle. This raises the question: how can the principle be both separate from and exhibited within the particular thing? The simplest answer seems to be that the mode of being of the principle is different from that of the thing. This can be illustrated by means of the following analogy. Just as the same person can be reflected in many mirrors, so the same principle can be reflected in many things. This is one version of the Platonic doctrine of Ideas. Note that the person can walk away from the mirrors and cease to be reflected in them. But the reflections will not occur without the person.

The main difficulty here is the assertion of separate modes of existence. We go wrong if we think of looks, forms, or Platonic Ideas as superior instances of the kind of things that look like them, i.e., the kind of things of which they are the principle. This is an error because it reduces the mode of being to that of the instance, and it generates the third-man paradox. If the form is just a superior or purer version of the look of the particular copies, then it is a superior or purer copy of some other and higher form that is mirrored in all the instances, including the initially noted form. The doctrine of original and image requires us to say that the original is not an image of something else; if it were, it would not be an original. For example, my images in mirrors are images of me, but I am not an image of some superior human being called "Meta-Rosen." I am just myself, an original in the sense that no one else is me.

One is still tempted to ask: but isn't the formal ratio in the original the same as that in the images? And if so, aren't the images originals? The answer to this question is as follows. The original is realized in a variety of substrata or *hupokeimena*. The ratio is the same, but its degree of realization differs in completeness or purity from one substratum to another. An image is a realization of the original that makes use of, and is limited by, its substrate or *hule* or *hu-*

pokeimenon. It is not the copy of the original within the image that makes it an image, but the particular *hule* and the associated degree of realization. With respect to the example of the mirror-image, it is not an image of me as a human being in the same sense that I, as this human being, am an image of the original ratio, look, or form "human being." We could perhaps call it an image of an image, or a simulacrum.

Let us now return to the claim that human beings manufacture principles, ratios, looks, forms, and so on by thinking them. This still turns upon the previously established difference between the principle and its instances. And it has difficulties of its own. For example, how does a cow remain a cow when no one is perceiving or thinking it? Obviously we require a transcendental doctrine like Kant's in order to respond to this question. The cow is a thing in itself when we are not perceiving it, that is, we can't say what it is except as a *Gegenstand* or object constituted within experience by the operations of the necessary conditions of perceptual cognition. Note that modern science is "Kantian" (or vice versa): a cow is an electromagnetic field or disturbance or something of the sort, until someone perceives it. But to repeat a previously noted question, why is the perceiver a perceiver and not an electromagnetic field, if he or she is perceiving a cow but no one, not even the cow, is perceiving him or her? I inferred from this that the perceiver is an actual human being who can be understood from a certain theoretical standpoint as an electromagnetic field or disturbance—in Nietzsche's expression, a perturbation on the surface of chaos.

But the main point with respect to Kantianism is that the object is constituted in accord with a rule or rather a set of rules, one of which is a schema that gives us the rule for the perception of the object of this particular look. The schema is not the object of experience but the rule for its formation within the *hupokeimenon* of sensory-cognitive experience. A schema is something between sensation and cognition; it is closely connected to imagination. It must partake of the nature of both cognition and sensation in order to attach the one to the other. But it is certainly not the particular object of experience, nor is it the visual or sensed material shape. The schema-rule must come into play when we perceive, say, a cow. The Kantian doctrine is confusing because we cannot perceive a cow without cognizing it. In other words, the sensing of a cow is not the occasion for the intuiting of the *eidos*. Sensation alone is *Empfindung*, not the apprehension of objects; it is a rhapsody of psychological or purely subjective impressions, feelings, and so on. We must therefore be fully stocked with schemata or rules for perceiving any object of experience whatsoever. *Any?*

Does this include can openers, i.e., artifacts of all sorts, or only natural beings? In either case, the doctrine is odd. It makes perception simultaneous with cognition.

I see a similar problem in Aristotle. Instead of applying the schema in a certain sensory situation, namely, the perception of a cow, we intuit the form from the sense-perception of the cow. But the cow is not a sense-datum; it is a this thing here of such and such a kind, a cow, with the essence or form *cow* exhibited within it. I must therefore be intuiting the form *cow* simultaneously with my perceiving it sensorily. In other words, this intuition is not in itself epistemic or discursive. It is the foundation or principle of subsequent discursive knowledge concerning the cow. But what of simple epistemic statements like "This is a cow"? This statement is either true or false. First, of course, I must become acquainted with cows. Someone explains to me that the thing I am perceiving is a cow. My teacher can also explain that I am able to perceive this cow because of its form (*eidos*), which I was intuiting, although I didn't know it. So we have to distinguish between the intellectual intuition of the cow's essence and the discursive understanding of the ratio of that essence. But what does this mean? What is an intellectual intuition of an essence? Not a sensory viewing of a pictorial look. But apparently also not a discursive account of the ratio.

In other words, it is not the case that, while Aristotle is claiming that we can look at a cow, which we have never seen before, suddenly the statement "mammal of type x, y, z" flashes into our minds. Aristotle must mean that the essence is accessible to the intellect in a way analogous to the way that the shape of a cow is accessible to the senses. But if this is what he means, what do we call cognitive statements like "a cow is x,y,z" or "man is a rational animal"? How do I verify that a man is a rational animal? Do I perceive it in advance of encountering human beings; do I intuit or just plain grasp it at once and simultaneously with the act of perceiving a human being for the first time? Must I not first have encountered various human beings and come to some understanding of what they are? Is this "coming to an understanding" not a generalization or induction from experience? And is an induction *really* possible on the basis of a single instance?

Difficulties of this kind may be more or less summarized by saying that the intuition of the form depends upon the perception of the cow, whereas the perception of the cow as cow depends upon the intuition of the form. You might say that the perception of the cow as cow is not the same as the perception of the cow, and that is true. But how does Aristotle explain the perception of the cow? I say that he explains it *as* the perception of the cow as cow. We don't just happen upon a never-before-seen thing and say "That is a cow." We see something that we don't know. Then we are told what it is. Then we say, "Aha, I can identify what I perceived because the act of perception included the noting of an essence, the discursive account of which I did not grasp at the time, but have now understood."

Understood how? The intellectual intuition was like a sense perception, but it was even less informative, since I saw without seeing, as it were; I did not know what I was seeing but only that I was seeing a *what* as well as a *that*. Thanks to common human experience, including learning what is the difference between animals and nonanimals, rational and nonrational, and so on, I come to see that human beings are rational animals. Even if that is the essence of human beings, I come to see it. Now I myself have said on Aristotle's behalf that we recognize other human beings at once, by virtue of our own humanity. Let us assume that this is correct. It is still not the same as recognizing that human beings are rational animals. That recognition comes later. It has to be learned. We have to learn *what* we intuited. So intellectual intuition is cognitively empty. But this is an aporia, since it is certainly not what Aristotle is maintaining. Or is it?

If this is Aristotle's view, then the perception of a cow is at once the intuitive awareness of the discursive formula "$x, y, z \ldots$" But that is Kantianism. If this is not Aristotle's view, then the perception of a cow takes place thanks to the activity or work of the eidetic substrate or essence, but without our discursive understanding that this is so. We have to learn, i.e., "recollect," what we understood at once in the drawn-out form of sentences in a language. And this is Platonism.

Aristotle doesn't want the form or principle to be separate from its instances, as it is in Plato. But he doesn't want the form or principle to be always and everywhere just the shape of the material particular thing, as in modern nominalism. He wants the principle to be both separate from and the same as its particular realizations. He doesn't see, or doesn't say, that this is in fact Platonism. And he gives what I regard as an unsatisfactory account of Platonism. But the defectiveness of this account comes from the way he articulated it technically, not from its intrinsic unreasonableness or absurdity.

Aristotle is verging toward Kantianism because in order to secure scientific knowledge, he has to put the principle into thinking. I don't mean by this that he is a Hegelian. Kant is not a Hegelian on this crucial point but a Platonist or

Aristotelian, because the object is essentially a rule or set of rules that regulates thinking. Thinking does not produce these rules, although thinking actualizes them. But this just means that we have to think in obedience to them. I agree that, by making the actualization of the rules dependent upon thinking, Kant takes a decisive step away from Platonism and toward Hegel. But he is still an "Aristotelian" Platonist; the principle is not a *Gedankending* or conceptual artifact. And both Aristotle and Kant have trouble in explaining how we actually think the actual form, because, for both, this thinking is both dependent upon sense perception and at the same time veridical.

Plato does not face this problem because there is no epistemic ontology in Plato. There is also no intellectual intuition in the Aristotelian sense; instead, there is the recollecting of originals thanks to the stimulus of their images. All accounts in Plato of direct apprehension of Ideas are fantasies, i.e., they are images. This is why some of the best students of Plato hold that poetry wins its quarrel with philosophy. In holding this, however, they fail to notice that it is philosophical *logos* that makes use of poetry, not the reverse. It is not the Ideas that are poems but our descriptions of them. We can still arrive at the Ideas as required by the fact that we perceive and cognize this or that as this or that kind or instance of a *what*. Unfortunately, we cannot see the Ideas except through a glass darkly. They themselves are always just over the horizon.

Aristotle attempts to rectify the absence of a scientific ontology in Plato by devising "first philosophy" (*prote philosophia*) or the science of being *qua* being. The history of philosophy subsequent to Plato, and beginning with Aristotle, is in its main tradition (what we can call the rationalist tradition) an attempt to do away with the poetic exhibition of philosophy and to replace it with "science." As our conception of science changes, so too does our conception of philosophy. But each attempt to think through the inner structure of a new scientific philosophy returns us to the set of problems first disputed by Plato and Aristotle, with some assistance from Kant and Hegel who help us to understand this originative dispute by spelling out this or that aspect of the overall problem. And that problem is immediately accessible as the structure of ordinary experience. This concludes my discussion of the attributes of experience.

It is not a metaphysical principle, or a transcendental Ideal, but the nature of life that compels us to prefer truth to falsehood and correctness to error. We prefer the truth because it is better than falsehood; in this sense, Nietzsche was right to say that life is rank-ordering. If we accept "reason" as a portmanteau term for the faculties through which we discern the truth, then it follows that there is an intrinsic bond between reason and the good. But the rational pursuit of the good depends upon the unity, regularity, and comprehensiveness of experience, and the articulation of this continuum by the heterogeneity of looks. This is the general structure underlying the process by which we make sense of our lives through the telling of stories.

Chapter 9 Concluding Remarks

In these chapters I have argued both that philosophy begins as a disruption within ordinary experience, and that the expression "ordinary experience" is itself ambiguous. Normally we mean by "ordinary" that which usually happens, but there are important exceptions. An extraordinary pianist could give an ordinary performance of a piece of music. We could also say that such a performance from that pianist is extraordinary if the pianist almost always plays at the highest level. But neither of these cases, nor others that might be mentioned, alter the central issue: The local or special senses of "ordinary" and "extraordinary" are defined with respect to the paradigm of what usually or rarely happens. The reason we sometimes find it difficult to distinguish between the ordinary and the extraordinary is that in these cases we cannot easily determine what usually happens. Nevertheless, in order to use the expression "extraordinary" meaningfully, we must allude to a sense of the ordinary that either does, or ought to, or could hold in the circumstance under dispute.

Otherwise put, not every situation is extraordinary. The "extraordinary" would then be ordinary, and the consequent dislocation of experiences would make rational inquiry impossible because there would be no coherent experience about which to inquire. Friends of the extraordinary may go out of their way to repudiate the ordinary, but each extraordinary episode they initiate or discover draws its distinction from the contrast with the ongoing ordinary experience that serves as the backdrop for their pursuit of disruption. Someone who enjoys highly seasoned food does so in contrast to normally seasoned food, but not in such a way as to repudiate the latter for the former. On the contrary, we can enjoy powerful seasoning only in contrast to everyday blandness. A constant diet of pungent sauces would destroy the palate or else itself assume the identity of the ordinary, and so we would be required to seek still sharper tastes. Human physiology sets the standard of the ordinary; we are free to experiment with its range but not to reject it entirely.

Some parts of our experience are ordinary in a noncontroversial sense. We all ordinarily breathe oxygen, but this is philosophically uninteresting since there are no extraordinary, non-oxygen-breathing human beings. By the same token, we all exist in space and time, and the structure of our experience is defined by these dimensions. The discovery of the metrics of space and time might be extraordinary, either because of the extreme difficulty of the investigation or simply because no one had previously attempted to find them. But spatiotemporal existence is itself not only ordinary but mandatory. A possible exception would be a mystical experience of transcendence, but so far as we know, such experiences, if they occur at all, leave the body exactly where it was previously. Presumably the conscious intellect is elsewhere but the soul must remain within the body or it will die.

Let us now move to more interesting examples. Controversy arises with respect to claims about the regulative function of the ordinary, for example, that ordinary discourse is the standard of rational speech. There is inevitably disagreement as to what constitutes ordinary discourse, and why it is entitled to supervene over some kinds of extraordinary speech but not others. The problem seems to be that although there is obviously such a thing as ordinary discourse, which all competent speakers of a given language use to conduct their everyday affairs, this discourse serves as a shifting kind of medium from which various kinds of extraordinary discourse are continuously emerging and into which they recede. There are rules for English grammar, for logical systems, and for various kinds of technical discourse, not to mention colloquial deviations from standard syntax and the constant modification of customary usage, the invention of hitherto unintelligible idioms, and so on. But there are no rules that set the precise boundaries of ordinary discourse itself.

Most human beings can handle shifts from ordinary to extraordinary discourse without great difficulty, although some are obviously more skilled at this than others. It would be difficult to deny that ordinary discourse is the aforementioned medium within which we change dialects as the need arises; but it would also be impossible to specify a set of rules that regulate these changes. We cannot, in other words, define precisely what constitutes ordinary language. And yet, we all employ it constantly; it is the "metalanguage" within which we perform shifts into and out of extraordinary or technical languages, and it is the standard by which we define a speech or a language as suitable to specialized tasks that cannot be performed without narrowing and intensifying the precision in our discursive habits.

Languages defined by precise rules may present us with technical difficulties posed by learning or manipulating those rules, but they are in principle simple, just because we construct them for rigorously defined purposes. The situation in mathematics is especially complex because, whereas we can define rigorously branches of mathematics, there is no non-controversial and internally consistent definition of mathematics itself, taking the activity as a whole. (Note that this is quite different from the question of the possible axiomatization of a formal language capable of expressing every mathematical truth.) Nevertheless, no one has any difficulty in distinguishing between everyday speech and mathematical discourse. The case of poetry is much more interesting, because the boundary between poetry and ordinary language is entirely unclear; in addition, one could claim that ordinary language is essentially poetic because it employs all the figures of speech that are to be found in poetry, and we constantly use it in inventing new expressions.

The example of poetry brings us face to face with the absurdity of attempting to define ordinary language as though it were a formal calculus or technical dialect. It would be going too far to say that there are no rules that can regulate the shift from ordinary language to poetry. But these rules are entirely different from those that regulate the employment, say, of the first-order predicate calculus. In the latter case, once the rules are established, they must be obeyed if we are indeed to "speak" the calculus. In the case of poetry, there is no metarule governing the inviolability of this or that set of rules employed by one tradition or another to define the nature of poetic discourse. To speak of the "poetry of ordinary language," whether altogether or in some particular case, might be controversial but it would not be at all absurd. But even if we agree on some very general set of formal properties that a speech must exhibit in order to be classified as poetry, the content of many poems remains saturated with ordinary language. Much poetry (but not, of course, all) is dedicated precisely to the task of heightening our awareness of some ordinary experience, and it does this by employing, among other devices, patches of ordinary language.

Poetry and ordinary language not only intersect but are in some sense coextensive, not simply with respect to formal structure (as might be claimed of logic or mathematics) but with respect to content as well. Poetry is about the stuff of our daily lives, including the extraordinary disruptions by which these lives are periodically punctuated. Since there are no rules to determine what will happen next in life, or how we are to respond to what does happen, we are able to exist because we possess a certain spontaneity of behavior, and in particular of discursive behavior, that shares with poetry the generation of new forms of speech and the modification of syntactical rules. It is obvious that there can be no coherent discourse without a syntax or set of conventions for concatenating words into intelligible units. But these conventions change with use and the flow of experience. The talking animal is necessarily the poetic animal; under certain conditions, discursive artifacts achieve the status of poems. Once again, we see that the extraordinary emerges from, and so is a disruption within, the ordinary.

I should perhaps state that what I call the poetic nature of discourse is independent of the controversy among linguists about a universal tranformative or generative grammar. In the first place, rules can always be broken; we are free to contradict ourselves. But the more important point is that the generative function of discourse is substantive, not formal or syntactical. There may conceivably be natural rules that regulate the deep structure of language, but it is impossible that there are rules determining the content of what we say.

If there is such a thing as ordinary language, it is not something that can be precisely defined nor does it consist in a finite number of typical assertions. Ordinary language is as various as life itself. The question is, rather, what limits this variety must exhibit in order to be accessible to cognitive discourse. Despite certain extreme claims by late-modern thinkers, it is obvious that life is not pure flux. Even if we were to grant the priority of interpretation to explanation, chaos is not accessible to interpretation. Still more fundamentally, if life were chaos, there would be no one to interpret it. An interpretation is a perspective, but a perspective is a view *by* someone *of* something. A perspective is a standpoint: it stands still. I can step back from a given perspective and ask you to assume it; whatever differences we bring to the common standpoint can be negotiated by discussion. If you cannot see anything similar to what I see, then we cannot communicate divergent interpretations. If our interpretations diverge, this divergence must be intelligible, and the properties of divergence themselves become the basis of discursive community. One can found a philosophy on difference only because difference is co-ordinate with and dependent upon identity.

It is therefore no refutation of ordinary experience to call attention to variety, historical change, or hermeneutical difference. All technical arguments to one side, the refutation is invalidated by existential facts. Nietzsche, Heidegger, and Derrida all step forward from the same everyday world in order to assert the priority of difference; in fact, they never leave it, since they sit at their desks and employ pens, typewriters, or word-processors in order to compose testimonials to chaos, or, more modestly, to the infinite regression of interpretative standpoints. One could of course maintain that the pen or word-processor is a tool of modern scientific technology, itself the dominant modality of western European rationalism, and so an artifact of a dominant perspective that has only historical status, regardless of the fact that those whose perspectives it shapes accept it. But this simply shifts the argument to the level of the historical epoch. The contention, in other words, depends for its intelligibility on the visible difference between our historical tradition and that of others. We could not even imagine an alternative, or what Heidegger calls "a different beginning," if there were not some common basis for comparing traditions or for interpreting human existence. This is why it is possible for philosophical hermeneuts to publish thick volumes in which they support the priority of difference for the edification of large audiences, each member of which has common access to the perspectival nature of human existence.

I very much doubt that serious proponents of difference intend to deny the ongoing presence of ordinary experience. What they wish to do is rather to deny its philosophical relevance or stability. Nietzsche, by his doctrine of interpretation, does not mean that trees do not exist but rather that the significance of the tree, and so too the sense of the word "exists," is a matter of dominant interpretation. What we normally mean by "tree" is of course determined by a kind of average interpretation that is uninteresting precisely because it plays an entirely subordinate role in the doctrinal economy of our lives. The sense of "tree" becomes interesting as we move away from the everyday toward scientific or aesthetic interpretations: those of the botanist, the ecologist, the poet, or the painter. Even in so-called everyday life, trees mean different things to different persons, depending upon whether they live in our own gardens, or we wish to cut them down for timber, or we stand in their shade on a hot summer afternoon.

What distinguishes Nietzsche from the imaginative yet commonsensical resident of ordinary experience is his contention that the common structures of interpretation, on the basis of which we assign a variety of senses and values to individual objects, are all products of a dominant hermeneutical standpoint. Nietzsche dramatizes the play of forces that the hermeneutical dominates by the expression "will to power." In so doing, he quite consciously anthropomorphizes chaos. One result is that the accumulation and discharge of force as studied by modern physicists is, on a Nietzschean account, imposed onto intrinsically disordered excitation by the web of hypotheses, principles, doctrines, and methods that physicists themselves employ. Even the Nietzschean doctrine of intrinsic chaos and radical human perspectivism begins from everyday life, the world of physicists but also of mathematicians, poets, philosophers, and prophets, all of whom attempt to restructure their common experience, each in his or her own image.

Everyday life is the dimension from which Nietzsche begins, the fabric he seeks to dissolve, that to which he necessarily returns in his role as historico-political thinker who prophesies a new epoch of human (or superhuman) society. The everyday is for Nietzsche the decadent residue of worn-out world-historical epochs, the common denominator of reciprocally canceling creative forces that is the human equivalent of the heat-death of Newtonian physics. Things stand forth in a kind of neutral penumbra of receptivity, awaiting a new evaluation that will restore them to significance. The transvaluation of values is what I call the disruption within ordinary experience. Unlike Nietzsche, however, I give a positive determination to what is for him decadence. Ordinary experience is ordinal; it regulates the transformative disruptions because it continues to function as their matrix and womb. What Nietzsche suppresses is that "decadence" is not simply the last stage of a culture but is present within it at all stages, including the most virile or creative, in the institutions and customs by which we organize our daily activities.

It is, in short, impossible to burn continuously with a hard, gem-like flame, as Walter Pater urged us to do. The daily business of life continues while empires are being forged and an artistic renaissance is under way. One family rather than another will acquire political power; one school of artists will dominate as others assume subordinate positions. Human beings are born into ceremonial roles that shape the course of their lives and set the scene for their deaths. The will to power is itself a brutal alias for ambition, lust, greed, pride, and above all, the instinct by which we seek to impose our thoughts and values onto our fellow human beings. In countless small details, out of which the fabric of existence is spun, the variety of customs and doctrines does not change the uniformity of the weaver's design. Precisely as *homo faber*, itself the lens that brings to a focus the will to power, human beings possess a common nature. This alone enables us to engage in what Nietzsche describes as his most important concern: rank-ordering. The extraordinary cannot serve as the standard for rank-ordering, because by definition each manifestation places itself in the highest position. The common thread to the multiple outbursts of extraordinary spiritual activity is ordinary existence. This is what furnishes the creator with the desires and aspirations that he or she transposes into an ostensibly unique means for satisfaction.

The ordinary is that from which we make our approach to philosophy. It is not at all what Heidegger calls *durchschnittliche Alltäglichkeit* (average everydayness), which is already a denatured residue of the richness of ordinary existence, the mode of life of the anonymous *das Man*, "one" or "they" in English. Ordinary experience is a question of "I" and "thou." It is therefore also not the Husserlian *Lebenswelt*, a kind of Kantian transcendental structure occupied by ghosts whose speeches and deeds are described in a vocabulary that abstracts from the psychic affects of emotion, value, and doctrinal conviction by which everyday life is in fact characterized. In short, ordinary life is not a kind of pallid or denatured existence, set off against more luxuriant and virile modes of experience. It is human existence in all its richness and complexity, and so it is not a *Gedankending* or artificial construction of a philosophical or scientific theory.

Ordinary experience is spatiotemporal and so corporeal. It gives rise to mathematics, physics, physiology, and the other specialized studies of four-dimensional existence. But it is none of these disciplines; it is not the content of geometry or chronometry any more than human life is expressible in terms of descriptions of physiological processes. The human agent of ordinary experience counts, measures, moves from one place to another, breathes, digests, reproduces, and dies, but this agent is not a sum, a length, a vector, or a chemical structure. The human agent is the being who investigates the common conditions of his or her existence.

Those who like Socrates and his students hold that philosophy begins in wonder, or that human beings desire by nature to know, are making the point that the love of knowledge is not produced by political regimes or social institutions, nor by religious dogma or philosophical arguments. The contrary is closer to the truth; it is our desire to know that leads us to form the institutions required in order to sustain our inquiries. In contemporary terminology, the natural desire to know is both articulated and concealed by perspectival interpretations of the knowable, but difference in human conventions is itself intelligible with reference to the natural end. The same point holds good with respect to our political, social, or religious institutions; they vary from place to place and generation to generation, but the intentions they express are everywhere the same. Just as all human beings possess three spatial dimensions and are marked by temporality, just as they digest and excrete, reproduce and die, so they seek the truth, struggle to fulfil their ambitions, and are marked by pride and the love of victory. Underneath the endless diversity of particular expressions of these common motives is a regular pattern that sustains and is the point of reference for understanding and evaluating difference.

With all due respect for the fluctuations of history, there is a mode of understanding that apprehends the common web of human existence, and we call it common sense, or perhaps practical intelligence or sound judgment. Common sense discerns not a body of always true propositions but what it is most plausible to believe with respect to everyday life. Sound judgment perceives the pervasive motive beneath the institutional or behavioral idiosyncracy. Practical intelligence identifies the prerequisites for the good or blessed life. Each or all of these faculties (depending upon whether they are distinct or all the same) establishes a bench-mark of plausibility; by this we measure the various solutions that are proposed to the desires of everyday existence. Ordinary experience is then not the solution any more than it is the problem: it is the medium within which problems and solutions arise, but it is also the standard against which we determine the plausibility of the interpretations put forward by one extraordinary thinker or another, interpretations of the problems as well as of their presumed solutions.

I want to emphasize here the distinction between common sense as I use the term and maxims or doctrines that pass in one age as common sense, only to be exposed as historical prejudice in the next. Sound judgment is not based upon the present state of science or technology, but neither is it defined by religious, political, or philosophical doctrine. To say furthermore that judgment is sound is not the same as to say that it is infallible. We do the best we can in accord with the circumstances. Sound judgment includes the capacity to revise one's opinions on the basis of new experience. But this capacity is rooted in the more general ability to discern the contours of enduring experience. Common sense is thus not a body of doctrine but the ability to assess the merits of a solution to a problem on the basis of life as we currently know it. It therefore includes the indispensable capacity not to be frightened into jettisoning our experience of life because of the theoretical hypothesis that it is logically possible for anything and everything to be other than it is.

If we suffer from a shortage of food, someone who promises to teach us how to dispense with it altogether will not be able to persuade us. When attacked by our enemies, common sense warns us to defend ourselves rather than to turn the other cheek. Some persons who follow the latter proposal do so because of their religious faith, but they deviate from common sense on behalf of an extraordinary solution to an ordinary problem. Religious faith as such is a phenomenon of ordinary life, but the solutions it proposes to ordinary problems may not be. The force of religion resides precisely in its challenge to ordinary experience, or rather to the commonsense understanding of ordinary experience. We may bind ourselves to this challenge in the clear recognition that we repudiate the ordinary, but the very intelligibility of the religious commandment depends upon the antecedent intelligibility of ordinary sound judgment.

Human beings exhibit a wide diversity of burial customs, but all people recognize the need to dispose of the dead in one way or another. The diversity exhibits the truth of the maxim that custom is the king of all men, but by the same token it illustrates the truth of the corollary that all men must have kings. Just as science proceeds only thanks to the regularity of nature (the actual regularity, not supposed or believed regularity), so human beings diversify their behavior thanks to the regularity of human behavior. And just as there is no final description of the ways of nature, so there is no final account of human behavior. But there will always be an effort to achieve that account so long as there are human beings. Our desire to know ourselves can of course be thwarted by the force of dogma, but this is itself a response to the desire, not its contradiction.

The structure of ordinary life is inescapable; in choosing to turn the other cheek to our enemies, we accept that they will probably slaughter or enslave us. If we refuse to believe that human beings cannot fly, then wave our arms and leap off a mountain peak in imitation of Icarus, we will plunge to the ground and be crushed. We may also deny that there are a small number of common human desires, such as love of knowledge, ambition, pride, greed, and lust, but this has no effect on the evident uniformity of human behavior in all historical epochs known to us. The only test of this last assertion is to ask oneself whether it can seriously be denied; there is no demonstration of claims like these because they are themselves better known than any principles from which we might deduce them. The desire for evidence is not the same as the demand for proof. This is a fundamental maxim of common sense; without it, ordinary experience soon becomes unintelligible. The skeptic will always accuse us of having imposed our prejudices onto experience; we reply by assimilating skepticism into our common understanding of human motives. Sometimes actions speak louder than words. Can the skeptic fly to the moon by wiggling his ears? Can he produce a radically new motive for human behavior that has never before been identified by commonsense observation? In the presence of a skeptic, are we in the presence of a genuine love of knowledge or of a desire to show off and to triumph at any cost?

There is a difference between stating a novel hypothesis or doctrine and attempting to persuade us that it is true. We understand almost immediately the motives underlying the attempt as well as our own accessibility to them. Are we then at a loss with respect to understanding the hypothesis or doctrine itself? If we were truly in the presence of radical uniqueness or of a cognitive surd, then we would never prefer one doctrine to another by any criterion other than pure chance. But this is nonsense. Not perhaps quite so obviously nonsensical, yet nevertheless implausible, is the claim that we always accept a doctrine on the basis of previously accepted doctrines, and so that there is no objective evidence at any stage of the chain. If this contention were literally true, then all human decisions would be arbitrary or determined only by the chance concatenation of doctrines. But the contention is also patently false. I do not accept a new doctrine of diet on the basis of previous doctrines alone but also on the basis of common sense. If the propounder of the new diet tells me to eat nothing but grass, or to gorge myself with goose-liver three times a day, there are certainly medical reasons to ignore him; but in addition to these my everyday intelligence tells me that human beings cannot subsist on grass, and after a point, goose-liver nauseates us with its richness.

By the same token, if someone tells me that bodies do not exist and that we only imagine the external world, I do not consult metaphysicians to determine whether this is plausible nor do I respond to the doctrine on the basis of my own metaphysical presuppositions. My initial response is to reject the doctrine as absurd, because of my direct experience of the external world. I may well come to change my mind on this point, but the evidence will have to be overwhelming, more overwhelming than the testimony of my daily experience. In general, I am free to consider every theoretical doctrine on its merits, even if I am incapable of making a final determination on any of them. Those who insist that we are all slaves of our presuppositions seem to be blessed with absolute knowledge that transcends the subjectivity of prejudice.

It certainly does not follow from my claim for the reliability of my daily experience that I am entirely free of prejudice, or that previous theoretical decisions play no role in my subsequent theorizing. Prejudices are part of ordinary experience; philosophy arises when we test our prejudices against what regularly occurs and dispense with those that the regularity of our experience shows to be erroneous or misleading. As to previous theoretical decisions, some are corrigible and some are not. I am not very likely to decide at some future date that I am made of gold and silver rather than flesh and blood. But neither am I likely to reject the existence of the external world. I may some day be persuaded of a theoretical interpretation of the external world that goes sharply against common sense and ordinary experience, but such an interpretation will be *of* the external world, which is preserved as the explanandum and even more profoundly as the indispensable condition of human life.

Ordinary experience, then, is not a theory of the whole, or a metatheory that serves as a standard against which to measure the adequacy of more specialized subtheories. How could life be a theory? It might in some sense be an illusion, as for example if we were dreaming that we are awake, or under the influence of soporific rays being trained on us by malevolent creatures from outer space, like Descartes' evil genius. But the contention that life is an illusion is itself a theory; we test its plausibility on the basis not of a countertheory but of ordinary experience, because this is what all theories purport to explain. A theory of sense-perception is fundamentally an explanation of the experience of sense-perception, not of theories of sense-perception. A theory of justice is fundamentally an explanation of justice, not of theories of justice. And so in all cases: there is no basis peculiar to two rival theories for deciding between them other than the experience they purport to explain. Even if we appeal to coherence, simplicity, or intuitive soundness, to say nothing of such factors as beauty or profundity, these criteria are derived from our life experience; they are not technical definitions peculiar to a given theory.

It is an odd fact of twentieth-century philosophy that interest in ordinary experience developed as a result of technical philosophical doctrines and scientific discoveries. This development is marked by two important and closely related processes: the scientific and technological explosion, and the new emphasis on history or, as it is today called, historicity. Modern science led to the repudiation of traditional metaphysics but even more so to a curious dialectical process in which ordinary experience was rendered canonical and at the same time was dissolved into its constituent elements or substructures. We see this same process repeated in the twentieth-century movement called "ordinary language analysis," which both appeals to canons of everyday discourse and at the same time replaces the everyday with a pseudoscientific construction modeled upon grammar and logic. In all such movements, traditional access to eternal order is denied and the radically temporal character of life is asserted. The "laws of nature," originally conceived as eternal structures of temporal existence, are themselves redefined as historical products of the human cognitive activity. The turn to empiricism is thus counterbalanced by a priori modes of rational construction, themselves stimulated by ostensibly faithful attention to ordinary experience, which thus bifurcates into universal mathematical laws on the one hand and contingent content on the other. But as one formulation of universality or eternity after another is seen to fall short of its goal and to be replaced by some other candidate, the formal laws of experience are themselves reassimilated into experience, which now comes to be known everywhere as history.

On one point, contemporary skepticism about the regulative function of the ordinary is a repetition of classical skepticism, already encountered in the maxim that custom is the king of all men. There is, however, a fundamental difference between the ancients and the moderns: ancient proponents of custom were not advocates of hermeneutical ontology. The rule of custom was understood to be a permanent feature only of human nature, and not one that affects the natural order of the cosmos. In other words, the perspectival nature of human experience is intelligible in itself. The context of the non- or transhuman order within which human life transpires further sustains our perspectival experience.

As Hegel puts this point, Greek skeptics doubted sense-perception, not reason, whereas modern skeptics doubt reason. Those for whom *logismos* or *ratio* is the highest form of reason are as much antirationalists as are the most extreme champions of imagination. Since calculation can no more validate itself than analysis is capable of delivering a synthetic explanation of a totality, the champions of formalist thinking must themselves turn to the imagination in order to produce edifying ideologies. The ordinary experience and everyday sound judgment that initiated the empirical component of modern science is today replaced by fantasy on the one hand and the historical process of theory-construction on the other, neither of which is able to give enduring stability or meaning to a priori or transcendental arguments on the one hand and pure mathematical invention on the other.

The net result of this complex historical process is the triumph of chaos, at first as something to be deplored and then as an occasion for celebration. In more immediate terms we have lost touch with the everyday, and we are therefore compelled to laboriously reconstitute it by abstract methodologies that are intrinsically unsuited for the task. Or rather, the task is not to recover ordinary experience but to transform it into a theoretically sound phenomenological description, hence into a theoretical artifact. We live in an age that is at once satiated by and starved for theory; common sense is boring to an epoch saturated since childhood in increasingly accelerating change that is accompanied by hyperbolical exfoliations of the fantasy.

In setting myself apart from scientific construction on the one hand and postmodernist deconstruction on the other, I put myself in the awkward position of refusing to gratify the two most advanced appetites of the day. But my initial recommendation of moderation is not equivalent to a campaign to enforce death by starvation. The moment of initial moderation to which I refer is the space of sound judgment firmly rooted in the pretheoretical experience that may well demand a theoretical explanation but that cannot be reduced, or for that matter raised, to something other than itself without destroying our very basis for distinguishing between ascent and descent.

As a last point in this series of remarks, I want to distinguish my view from Leo Strauss's thesis that Greek political life provides us with the pretheoretical access to human nature. What I mean by ordinary experience is as accessible in late twentieth-century Paris as it was in classical Athens. Wittingly or unwittingly, Strauss historicizes human nature by attempting to rescue it from history. Greek political and social institutions are as much a historical perspective onto human nature as are the institutions of postmodern France. If we are capable of access to human nature, this is because it is available everywhere. Simply because appetites were less jaded in fifth-century B.C. Athens than in contemporary New York, it does not follow that the desires of classical Athenians were fundamentally different from those of contemporary New Yorkers. Furthermore, whereas some points may be clearer in their Athenian context, we may well be misled into assuming that simplicity is always preferable to complexity if we assume that nature was then visible in Athens as it is not now in New York.

The reader must not assume that I have undertaken to provide a precise and detailed account of the structure of ordinary experience in these chapters. My examples and remarks have all been designed to elicit a recognition of the obvious, and hence of something that is too encompassing and too fluid to be captured by theoretical models or by phenomenological descriptions. It is tempting to direct the reader to the everyday routine of life as it unfolds outside the seminar room, a routine that is not entirely *routinized* but that contains such disruptions as the one that led him or her to read this book. We have no choice but to take our bearings by ordinary experience, because every extraordinary step we take is one that is initiated within the ordinary and contrasts with it. Nor should it be feared that I want to trivialize the remarkable character of philosophy. Philosophy is extraordinary, but the meaning of "extra" is unintelligible in detachment from the word "ordinary" that it modifies.

Notes

INTRODUCTION

1. Oxford: Oxford University Press, 1964, p. 63.
2. His lectures on "sense and sensibilia" could just as easily have been called "sense and sensibility," as I am sure that he wished to imply. Jane Austen is a splendid example of the kind of subtlety it takes to be a John Austin.
3. Condorcet is the paradigm-figure here. See especially Keith Michael Baker, *Condorcet. From Natural Philosophy to Social Mathematics* (Chicago: University of Chicago Press, 1975), and, as a supplement, Lorraine Daston, *Classical Probability in the Enlightenment* (Princeton: Princeton University Press, 1988).
4. "Two Dogmas of Empiricism," in *From A Logical Point of View* (2d ed., rev.; New York: Harper and Row, 1963), p. 45. For a typical statement of this point in the language of Oxford linguistic philosophy, see P. F. Strawson, *Analysis and Metaphysics: An Introduction to Philosophy* (Oxford: Oxford University Press, 1992), p. 21: "The acquisition of the theoretical concepts of the special disciplines presupposes and rests upon the possession of the pre-theoretical concepts of ordinary life."
5. L. Wittgenstein, *Philosophical Investigations,* tr. G. E. M. Anscombe (Oxford: Blackwell, 1998), par. 98, p. 45.
6. This point is frequently denied, and I do not mean to exaggerate. But with all due acknowledgment of Wittgenstein's own occasional foray into technical innovation (e.g., "language games"), the spirit of allegiance to ordinary lan-

guage necessarily inclines us toward tradition, and so toward the past. One could almost liken the inconclusive process of deconstructing traditional philosophy to Nietzsche's eternal return of the same. The process is inconclusive because, in the absence of a contrary positive doctrine, no clearly certifiable "solution" to any problem is available.

7. I will discuss Austin in greater detail in chapter 6. For a debate about the purpose of Austinian distinctions, see the papers by G. J. Warnock, J. O. Urmson, Stuart Hampshire, and Stanley Cavell in *Symposium on J. L. Austin*, ed. K. T. Fann (London: Routledge and Kegan Paul, 1969). Cavell's modified defense of Hampshire's position holds that Austin investigated distinctions primarily to show up "the slovenliness, the grotesque crudity and fatuousness, of the usual distinctions philosophers have traditionally thrown up," and only secondarily to bring to attention and focus the salient features of individual distinctions (p. 64).

8. It is also not to say that all admirers of Austin are deaf to the creativity of ordinary language. Stanley Cavell is an outstanding counterexample, but despite his celebration of democratic figures like Emerson and Thoreau and his interest in popular as well as high culture, Cavell is not an ordinary language philosopher but a representative of highly sophisticated late-modernism that fuses aesthetics and ethics in a personal and original idiom. Cavell comes intriguingly close to part of my concerns in this book in his essay "The Uncanniness of the Ordinary" (in *In Quest of the Ordinary* [Chicago: University of Chicago Press, 1994]). He is deeply concerned with the "unearthly oscillation" between philosophy on the one hand and the trivial and the superficial on the other, or in other words, with the (oscillating?) identity of the ordinary and the extraordinary (pp. 167, 169–70). In contrasting himself with Heidegger, Cavell says: "Whereas for me the uncanniness of the ordinary is epitomized by the possibility or threat of what philosophy has called skepticism, understood . . . as the capacity, even desire, of ordinary language to repudiate itself, specifically to repudiate its power to word the world, to apply to the things we have in common, or to pass them by" (p. 154). I take this to mean that our perception of the uncanniness of the ordinary arises in conjunction with our search for a response to skepticism, or perhaps better, that the drift toward skepticism *is* the discovery of the everyday (a view attributed by Cavell to Wittgenstein: pp. 170–71). I would prefer to state the central point here as follows: it is very difficult, and perhaps impossible, to distinguish the ordinary from the extraordinary by any theoretical or analytical procedures. But the ordinary is accessible to us as the horizon within which the extraordinary presents itself, in a way comparable to that in which lightning announces the quick approach of a summer storm. By the same token, there is no theoretical response to skepticism that does not presuppose the more immediately accessible domain of ordinary experience. Incidentally, Cavell is right to associate ordinary-language philosophy with Kant (p. 170).

CHAPTER 1: POLITICS AND NATURE IN MONTESQUIEU

1. I cite from the Bibliothèque de la Pléiade edition in *Oeuvres complètes,* ed. Roger Caillois (Paris: NRF, 1951), vol. 1. Translations are either my own or taken from the edition of Anne Cohler, Basia Miller, and Harold Stone: *Montesquieu: The Spirit of the Laws* (Cambridge

Texts in the History of Political Philosophy, Cambridge: Cambridge University Press, 1989). Numbers in parentheses in the text refer to page numbers in the French edition.
2. "Je n'aime point les gens qui renversent les lois de leur patrie": *Défense de l'esprit des lois*, in *Oeuvres Complètes* (*OC*), vol. 2, p. 1129. Hereafter designated as *Défense*.
3. See Paul Rahe's brilliant article "Forms of Government: Structure, Principle, Object, and Aim," in *Montesquieu's Human Science,* ed. David Carruthers, Michael Mosher, and Paul Rahe (Lanham, Md.: Rowman Littlefield, 2000).
4. *Leviathan* (Oxford: Clarendon Press, 1947), p. 142.
5. *Politics* A2, 1253a15–19.
6. See *Défense*, pp. 1121 ff.
7. Leo Strauss, *Persecution and the Art of Writing* (Glencoe, Ill.: Free Press, 1952), pp. 33–34.
8. Cf. Thomas Pangle, *Montesquieu's Philosophy of Liberalism* (Chicago: University of Chicago Press, 1973), p. 28: "It is a necessary part of human nature to be capable of acting contrary to nature."
9. *Défense*, p. 1129.
10. *De la politique* in *OC*, vol. 1, p. 112.
11. *Ethics*, in *Opera*, ed. J. Van Vloten and J. P. N. Land (The Hague: M. Nijhoff, 1914), vol. 1, part 3, p. 121.
12. *Défense*, sixième objection, pp. 1130 ff.
13. *Two Treatises of Government*, ed. Peter Laslett (Cambridge: Cambridge University Press, 1988), book 1, p. 206; book 2, p. 278.
14. Ibid., book 1, p. 209.
15. Ibid., book 2, p. 271.
16. For Hobbes, see *Leviathan* (Oxford: Clarendon Press, 1947), pp. 98–100. Compare the remark on p. 43 that the desire for riches is not necessarily blameworthy. The desire and hope for "commodious" living leads to peace (98).
17. This is an anticipation of Rousseau's criticism of Hobbes. See also Locke's assertion (against Filmer) that empire and domination are not heritable by nature (*Two Treatises,* pp. 210–12).
18. In support of the first clause of this sentence, I note that despite the peaceful and indolent nature of man in the state of nature, he is forced to "surmount the obstacles of nature" in order to preserve himself within that state, and accordingly moves toward cooperation and association with his fellow humans. See J.-J. Rousseau, *Discours sur l'origine de l'inégalité*, in *Oeuvres complètes* (Paris: Gallimard, Biblothèque de la Pléiade, 1964), vol. 3, pp. 165–66. In support of the second clause, see *Discours,* p. 171: The best stage for human beings is the mean between primitive indolence and "la petulante activité de notre amour propre." This stage disappears with the advent of cooperation and property, and there is no life freer, healthier, or happier.
19. *Oeuvres complètes,* vol. 3, p. 351.
20. *Natural Right and History* (Chicago: University of Chicago Press, 1950), p. 251.
21. *Wissenschaft der Logik* (Leipzig: Verlag Felix Meiner, 1951), *Bd.* 1, p. 20.
22. Up to a point, it makes more sense to call Montesquieu a Cartesian than a Newtonian. The influence of Descartes is discussed by Robert Shackleton in his *Montesquieu: A Critical Biography* (Oxford: Oxford University Press, 1961), pp. 59, 258–60, and passim.

23. *Les étapes de la pensée sociologique* (Paris: Gallimard, Collection Tel, 1967), p. 45.
24. Many of the general remarks about Montesquieu could also be applied to Hume. But Hume is closer to the "ordinary language" philosophers than he is to the tradition of the scientific study of "common life." See Donald Livingston, *Hume's Philosophy of Common Life* (Chicago: University of Chicago Press, 1984), p. 248. For Hume, "the standards constituting common life have an authority that is *independent* of philosophy." See also p. 274: "The criticism of metaphysics in common life is the unifying theme of Hume's philosophical and historical writings."
25. There is a good description of the timorous and hesitant aspect of Montesquieu's assault on the tradition, and of his intermediate status in the contemporary quarrel between the ancients and the moderns, in Simone Goyard-Fabre, *La philosophie du droit de Montesquieu* (Paris: Librairie C. Klincksieck, 1973), pp. 39–41, but with no reference to Aristotle.
26. For an interesting discussion of this point, see Julia Annas, *The Morality of Happiness* (New York: Oxford University Press, 1993), pp. 135–58. Annas does not in my view give sufficient weight to the concern of the ancients with the natural order of types of human life.
27. As previously noted, Montesquieu was influenced directly by Descartes rather than by Newton. But the important point is the general conception of the world, that is, of natural science as the model for the political sciences, that derives from the common heritage of Descartes and Newton. Shackleton, in *Montesquieu,* points out that Montesquieu's natural laws are not those of Grotius, Pufendorf, and other writers on law. "They are closer to the scientific concept of a law of nature as a law of movement, as used by Descartes, by Montesquieu himself, and made famous by Pope in his epitaph on Newton" (251).
28. In *Montesquieu's Philosophy of Liberalism,* Thomas Pangle seems to me to go too far in holding that moral virtue is for Montesquieu simply a means to freedom. Strictly speaking, the following judgment is correct: "The goal of a republic is not so much virtue as freedom" (54). But it is not true that, in Montesquieu, insofar as moral virtue is not reduced to political virtue, it is silently forgotten (64). Moral virtue is from the beginning the foundation of political virtue, the goal of which is not only freedom but also a civilized *douceur* or comfortableness as well as sympathy with one's enemies. Otherwise put, Montesquieu regards modern moral virtue as superior to that of the ancients. See for example the identification of political virtue as moral virtue in the sense that it is directed to the general good (*SL*, book 3, chap. 5, p. 255n). This should be kept in mind when evaluating the ostensible superiority of ancient to modern virtue (e.g., pp. 252, 266). Equally important, moderation, the principle of aristocracy but also the most important faculty of the spirit of the legislator, has as its basis what is clearly moral virtue (254). This apart, Montesquieu is concerned to restrict freedom; it is extremely important to his assessment of the modern republic (or pseudomonarchical republic like England), but it is not the most important thing. Pierre Manent holds a thesis very similar to Pangle's: "The primary intent of the *Spirit of the Laws* is thus to weaken decisively the authority of the Ancients, of the idea of the 'best regime,' the idea of virtue, in order to replace it with the

authority of the present moment, of the modern experience, summed up in the notions of 'commerce' and 'liberty.'" *The City of Man*, tr. Marc A. Lepain (Princeton: Princeton University Press, 1998), p. 15. I think that this is only part of the story. It leaves out Montesquieu's praise of classical virtue in contrast to the modern emphasis upon commerce, not to mention Manent's own immediately following argument that political and moral virtue are difficult if not impossible to distinguish (pp. 22–23). It also strangely ignores the central role of moderation in Montesquieu's doctrine. In short, I think that Manent's very interesting essay understates the conflict between ancients and moderns within Montesquieu by making him too modern. Furthermore, like Pangle, Manent concentrates upon the political teaching to the exclusion of the scientific model of political thinking, with a consequent overemphasis upon the role of history in Montesquieu's thought. My own procedure is to emphasize the incoherence intrinsic to Montesquieu's theoretical analysis of nature and law, and to argue that this incoherence underlies the importance of history, but that this importance is not compatible with Montesquieu's obvious desire to be the Newton of the political world.
29. Pangle, *Montesquieu's Philosophy of Liberalism*, p. 45.

CHAPTER 2: HUSSERL'S CONCEPTION OF THE LIFE-WORLD

1. *Tractatus logico-philosophicus,* in *Schriften* I (Frankfurt am Main: Suhrkamp, 1969), 2.0121–2.0251.
2. *Kant's Transcendental Idealism* (New Haven: Yale University Press, 1983), p. 39.
3. All page references are to *The Crisis of European Sciences and Transcendental Phenomenology*, tr. David Carr (Evanston, Ill.: Northwestern University Press, 1970).
4. See Carr's note on p. 5.
5. One of the most interesting consequences of Husserl's influence is the study of the origin of modern mathematics. See especially Jacob Klein, *Greek Mathematical Thought and the Origin of Algebra,* tr. Eva Brann (Cambridge: MIT Press, 1968).
6. *Beilage* 1 is contained in the German text (The Hague: M. Nijhoff, 1954), pp. 349–56. These *Beilagen* are not translated by Carr.
7. There is now available in English a sympathetic and lucid introduction to the main themes of phenomenology that avoids technical jargon to the maximum degree possible: Robert Sokolowski, *Introduction to Phenomenology* (Cambridge: Cambridge University Press, 2000). Especially helpful for the analytical philosopher is Richard Cobb-Stevens, *Husserl and Analytic Philosophy* (Dordrecht: Kluwer, 1984).
8. My own remarks on Husserl's program make it clear that, despite his orientation to mathematics and the apprehension of pure formal structure, he was deeply interested in the problem of universal history. For a detailed study of the role of history in Husserl's thought, see David Carr, *Phenomenology and the Problem of History* (Evanston, Ill.: Northwestern University Press, 1974). I will return to the historical role in Husserl's thought shortly.
9. For documentation and discussion, see "The Lived Present" in my *Metaphysics in Ordinary Language* (New Haven: Yale University Press, 1999).

10. Cf. Descartes, *Regulae,* ed. Giovanni Crapulli (The Hague: M. Nijhoff, 1966), rules 6, 7, and especially 11 for the simultaneity of intuition and deduction (*adeo ut in unam videantur coalescere,* p. 38) .
11. I have modified Carr's translation.
12. *Beilage* 5, p. 394 (my translation).
13. Ibid., p. 399.
14. Ibid.

CHAPTER 3: KANT AND HEIDEGGER

1. See, for example, the valuable essay by Stephen Engstrom, "Happiness and the Highest Good in Aristotle and Kant," in *Aristotle, Kant, and the Stoics,* ed. Stephen Engstrom and Jennifer Whiting (Cambridge: Cambridge University Press, 1996), pp. 102–38.
2. Even the recent revival of "virtue ethics," which seems to be derived from an appreciation of Aristotle, takes on a systematic, "meta-ethical," or abstract form that reflects a spirit quite different from that which motivates Aristotle. The main point of difference is the conviction of contemporary ethicists that rigorous arguments must be presented in order to establish the priority of virtue. This is understandable, since Aristotle is proceeding from ordinary experience, whereas our contemporaries are forced to "desediment" Aristotelian themes from the accumulated theoretical detritus of the modern epoch.
3. *Practical Philosophy,* in *The Cambridge Edition of the Works of Immanuel Kant,* tr. M. J. Gregor (Cambridge: Cambridge University Press, 1996), p. 90.
4. Page references to the *Kritik der praktischen Vernunft* (cited as the second *Critique*) are from the *Philosophische Bibliothek* edition (Hamburg: Felix Meiner Verlag, 1952).
5. *Metaphysik der Sitten* (Hamburg: Felix Meiner Verlag, 1959), pp. 16–17. Cited in *Practical Philosophy,* tr. Gregor, pp. 370–71. With this passage, compare the section entitled "Remark. Fragment of a Moral Catechism," in *Practical Philosophy,* tr. Gregor, pp. 593–95.
6. Second *Critique,* p. 108.
7. Ibid., pp. 132–33.
8. Ibid., pp. 102–3.
9. *Metaphysik der Sitten,* p. 228.
10. Since Kant's *Anthropologie* has been cited recently as an important modification of the ethical doctrines of the *Groundwork* and the three *Critiques,* it is worth noting that in the first-named work, Kant identifies *Klugheit* as using others for one's own purposes: *Anthropologie,* in *Vermischte Schriften* (Leipzig: Im Insel Verlag, n.d.), p. 384. Cf. p. 466, where *Klugheit* (making use of fools) is contrasted with *Weisheit.* For Kant's early view on *Klugheit,* see the *Groundwork,* in *The Cambridge Edition of the Works of Immanuel Kant,* tr. M. J. Gregor (Cambridge: Cambridge University Press, 1996), p. 69n. Once again, self-advantage is the key sense of the term. For the connection between *Klugheit* and *Glückseligkeit,* see the second *Critique,* p. 145.
11. Second *Critique,* pp. 129–30.

12. It is now fashionable to attempt to mitigate the differences between Aristotle and Kant. That they share some common ground is the essential premise of this chapter. But the differences are too great to warrant a modification of the statement in the text.
13. *Nicomachean Ethics* (cited hereafter as *EN*) 1.1095a17 ff.
14. *Kritik der reinen Vernunft* (cited hereafter as the first *Critique;* Hamburg: Felix Meiner Verlag, 1956), A813–B831.] I will normally follow *The Critique of Pure Reason,* tr. Paul Guyer and Allen Wood (Cambridge: Cambridge University Press, 1998).
15. *EN* 6.1124a29–b1.
16. For two quite different defenses of the thesis that Aristotle's ethics rests upon a knowledge of his theoretical philosophy, see Andreas Kamp, *Die politische Philosophie des Aristoteles und ihre metaphysischen Grundlagen* (Freiburg: Verlag Karl Albert, 1985); and T. H. Irwin, *Aristotle's First Principles* (Oxford: Clarendon Press, 1988).
17. *EN* 2.1103b26; cf. 1.1094b11ff and 1.1095b6.
18. As to the connection—or distinction—between morality and happiness, I have already cited and discussed passages from crucial works of all periods of Kant's mature thought; these passages testify to the continuity in Kant's thought on the point under investigation.
19. Compare *Kritik der Urteilskraft* (Hamburg: Felix Meiner Verlag, 1954), p. 171 f.
20. The question arises whether Kant places the same emphasis upon God in late works like the *Metaphysics of Morals*. My reply is that Kant's basic argument is much the same in all of his treatments of ethics and happiness. If it is true that in the last-named work Kant holds that doing our duty makes us happy, it has to be objected that sometimes it does and sometimes it does not. This line of thought leads to the identification of happiness as empirical, which is impossible on Kantian grounds. Without God, the transition from being worthy of happiness, and actually being happy, cannot be grounded by anything but hope.
21. *Critique of Judgment,* tr. W. S. Pluhar (Indianapolis: Hackett, 1987), pp. 317 f.
22. Lewis White Beck sees a defect in Kant's argument at this point, which is not solved until after the completion of the first *Critique.* At B840–41, Kant says that without the hope for happiness promised by God in the future world for those who are worthy, "the glorious Ideas of morality" are admirable but not springs of purpose and action. A few paragraphs later, at B841, Kant notes that neither happiness alone nor only morality and the worthiness to be happy constitutes the complete good. Beck interprets the continuation as follows: "Yet almost immediately and with no obvious consistency, he denies that the prospect of future happiness makes the moral disposition possible." I cannot quite find Beck's inference in the text; Kant denies that worthiness to be happy is the complete good, and adds that it is not by itself the spring of morality. But that does not contradict the passage cited above from B839–40. In any case, even if Kant does not furnish an analysis of the desire to be worthy of happiness in the first *Critique,* the elements to his solution of the problem of morality and happiness are the same here as in later writings. See Lewis White Beck, *A Commentary on Kant's Critique of Practical Reason* (Chicago: University of Chicago Press, 1960), pp. 214–15.
23. I translate directly from the *Kritik der praktischen Vernunft,* p. 80 of the edition cited in note 4 above.

24. Franco Volpi, *Heidegger e Aristotele* (Padova: Daphne Editrice, 1984), p. 26.
25. *Platon: Sophistes* [*Gesamtausgabe*, Bd. 19 (Frankfurt: Vittorio Klostermann, 1992)].
26. Volpi, *Heidegger e Aristotele*, pp. 91–94; cf. Jacques Taminiaux, *Heidegger and the Project of Fundamental Ontology*, tr. Michael Gendre (Albany: SUNY Press, 1991), p. xx.
27. *The Genesis of Heidegger's Being and Time* (Berkeley and Los Angeles: University of California Press, 1995), p. 303.
28. As usual, *EN* abbreviates *Nicomachean Ethics*.
29. This is no doubt why recent interpreters of Aristotle have attempted to absolve him of the charge of egoism by emphasizing that happiness consists in doing good for others for their own sake. See for example Julia Annas, *The Morality of Happiness* (Oxford: Oxford University Press, 1993), p. 223, and the valuable corrections to this view offered by Nancy Sherman in *Making a Necessity of Virtue* (Cambridge: Cambridge University Press, 1997). I restrict myself to two remarks. First, theoretical contemplation, the highest form of happiness, is the one that is truly mine, and this has nothing to do with performing virtuous deeds for others. Second: it remains true that the performance of such deeds makes *me* happy; and this is why (according to Aristotle) I perform them.
30. *Sorge* means "care" or "concern," and is related to anxiety.

CHAPTER 4: WITTGENSTEIN, STRAUSS, AND THE POSSIBILITY OF PHILOSOPHY

1. The triumph, however, is silent. See "A Lecture on Ethics," in *Philosophical Occasions, 1912–1951*, ed. James C. Klagge and Alfred Nordmann (Indianapolis: Hackett, 1993), p. 44, and in the same volume, "Remarks on Frazer's *Golden Bough*, p. 119.
2. See for example L. Wittgenstein, "Sketch for a Foreword," in the collection *Culture and Value*, tr. Peter Winch (Chicago: University of Chicago Press, 1984), p. 6.
3. Wittgenstein, *Culture and Value*, p. 21.
4. Wittgenstein, "Big Manuscript," section on philosophy, in *Philosophical Occasions*, ed. Klagge and Norman, p. 177.
5. Wittgenstein, *Remarks on the Philosophy of Psychology*, tr. G. E. M. Anscombe (Chicago: University of Chicago Press, 1980), vol. 1, p. 71 (361). I have slightly modified the Anscombe translation. See also *Culture and Value*, p. 50 and, for a qualification, p. 73.
6. Glencoe, Ill.: Free Press, 1958, p. 13.
7. It should be apparent that throughout this chapter, I am referring (unless otherwise stated) to the so-called later Wittgenstein, whose most important text is the *Philosophical Investigations*, tr. G. E. M. Anscombe (Oxford: Blackwell, 1998).
8. *Remarks on the Philosophy of Psychology*, p. 157 (889). Cf. p. 117 (633): Simple language-games "are poles of a description, not the ground-floor of a theory."
9. *Philosophical Investigations*, p. 50, par. 126.
10. Ibid., p. 82, par. 206.
11. Ibid., p. 56, par. 142.
12. E.g., ibid., p. 129, par. 436. *Gewöhnlich* can be translated as "common," "ordinary," or "habitual." Wittgenstein is thinking of the everyday language of the nonphilosopher: of how we ordinarily or normally express ourselves. But this assumes in advance that extra-

ordinary modes of expression are somehow problematic. And the boundary between "ordinary" and "extraordinary" seems either too flexible or too rigid.

13. Ibid., p. 125, par. 415.
14. Ibid., p. 116, par. 371; cf. par. 373.
15. Ibid., p. 8, par. 19 et seq.
16. Ibid., p. 230, part 2, section 12. Compare *Culture and Value*, p. 37. Note the resemblance to Husserl's doctrine of eidetic variation via the imagination.
17. "The connection between 'language and reality' is made by definitions of words, and these belong to grammar, so that language remains self-contained and autonomous." *Philosophical Grammar*, tr. Anthony Kenny (Berkeley and Los Angeles: University of California Press, 1978), p. 97 (par. 55).
18. "What has to be accepted, the given, is—so one could say—*forms of life*." *Philosophical Investigations*, p. 226, part 2, section xi.
19. " . . . philosophical problems are misunderstandings which must be removed by clarification of the rules according to which we are inclined to use words." *Philosophical Grammar*, p. 68 (par. 32). The German, "nach denen wir die Worte gebrauchen wollen," brings out the notion of custom. In other words, the rules are determined by the linguistic community within which we happen to find ourselves, and not by an extralinguistic natural order.
20. See note 1 in this chapter.
21. David Pears, *The False Prison* (Oxford: Clarendon Press, 1988), vol. 2, p. 206.
22. *Philosophical Investigations*, p. 49, par. 124; p. 45, par. 98.
23. These devices should be compared with Husserl's imaginative variation.
24. *Philosophical Investigations*, p. 48, par. 116.
25. Ibid., p. 51, par. 133.
26. Leo Strauss, *On Tyranny* (New York: Free Press, 1991), p. 185.
27. F. Nietzsche, *Götzen-Dämmerung*, in *Kritische Studienausgabe*, ed. G. Colli and M. Montinari (Berlin: Walter de Gruyter, 1980), vol. 6, p. 152.
28. As has been done, in anger, by Shadia Drury in *The Political Ideas of Leo Strauss* (New York: St. Martin's, 1988), and, in praise, by Lawrence Lampert in *Strauss and Nietzsche* (Chicago: University of Chicago Press, 1996).
29. See Leo Strauss, "The Law of Reason in the *Kuzari*," in *Persecution and the Art of Writing* (Glencoe, Ill.: Free Press, 1958), pp. 8 and 18.
30. This passage appears in the preface to the English edition of Strauss's book *Spinoza's Critique of Religion* (New York: Schocken Books, 1965), p. 27.
31. See the title essay in Leo Strauss, *What Is Political Philosophy?* (Glencoe, Ill.: Free Press, 1959), p. 32.
32. *Persecution and the Art of Writing*, pp. 32 ff.
33. But not to Joseph Ibn Kaspi; *Ibid*, p. 56.
34. "The Law of Reason in the *Kuzari*," p. 110.
35. Nietzsche, *Werke*, in *Kritische Studienausgabe*, ed. Colli and Montinari, vol. 12, p. 41.
36. "How to Study Spinoza's *Theologico-Political Treatise*," in *Persecution and the Art of Writing*, p. 144. Cf. "On a Forgotten Kind of Writing," in *What Is Political Philosophy?* p. 230.

37. *Kritische Studienausgabe,* ed. Colli and Montinari, vol. 10, p. 95.
38. Klein made this statement in my presence in a public lecture given many years ago at Penn State University. He was reading a text that had been published in the *Saint John's Review,* a publication of the small liberal-arts college at which he taught, and to which I do not have access.
39. For a statement on Lessing, see, for example, Leo Strauss, "Exoteric Teaching," in *The Rebirth of Classical Political Rationalism* (Chicago: University of Chicago Press, 1989), p. 64.
40. "An Introduction to Heideggerian Existentialism," in *The Rebirth of Classical Political Rationalism,* p. 29.
41. Martin Heidegger, "Zürcher Seminar," in *Seminare, Gesamtausgabe* (Frankfurt am Main: Klosterman, 1986), p. 426.
42. Plato, *Epistulae,* 2.314b7ff; 7.341b5 ff.
43. *Natural Right and History* (Chicago: University of Chicago Press, 1950, 1953), p. 35.
44. "Thucydides: The Meaning of Political History," in *The Rebirth of Classical Political Rationalism,* p. 72.
45. Introduction to *Persecution and the Art of Writing,* p. 19.
46. See, for example, *Natural Right and History,* p. 74, for the contrast between "a life of obedient love versus a life of free insight."
47. Ibid., p. 75.
48. Tr. E. Adler (Albany: SUNY Press, 1995), p. 29.
49. Preface to *Spinoza's Critique of Religion,* p. 29.
50. In *What Is Political Philosophy?* pp. 38 f.
51. "Restatement," in *On Tyranny,* p. 212.
52. "Social Science and Humanism," in *The Rebirth of Classical Political Rationalism,* p. 4; introduction to *The City and Man* (Chicago: Rand McNally, 1964), p. 12.
53. For clear general statements of this component of Strauss's argument, see the essay "On Classical Political Philosophy," in *The Rebirth of Classical Political Rationalism* (previously printed in *What Is Political Philosophy?*).
54. "On Aristotle's *Politics,*" in *The City and Man,* pp. 19–20.
55. Cf. *Natural Right and History,* pp. 7–8, and *The City and Man,* p. 21.
56. See the title essay in *What Is Political Philosophy?* pp. 28 and 75 (in which Strauss makes his point with reference to Hegel's statement on the difference between ancient and modern philosophy).
57. "The Problem of Socrates" in *The Rebirth of Classical Political Rationalism,* p. 142.
58. See, for example, *Natural Right and History,* p. 122.
59. "On Plato's *Republic,*" in *The City and Man,* pp. 119–21. In the same passage, Strauss says that the interlocutors would have been helped in their attempt to understand Socrates by their experience with the Greek gods.
60. From the title essay in *What Is Political Philosophy?* pp. 38–39.
61. *On Tyranny,* p. 196. Cf. "Progress or Return?" in *The Rebirth of Classical Political Rationalism,* p. 240.
62. "What Is Political Philosophy?" p. 40.
63. "On a Forgotten Kind of Writing," in *What Is Political Philosophy?* p. 230.

CHAPTER 5: MOORE ON COMMON SENSE

1. J. L. Austin, "A Plea for Excuses," in *Philosophical Papers* (Oxford: Oxford University Press), pp. 182–83.
2. Paul Grice, "Postwar Oxford Philosophy," in *Studies in the Way of Words* (Cambridge: Harvard University Press, 1989), pp. 173–74. Numbers in parentheses refer to pages in this edition when Grice is cited.
3. The same point is obviously true of scientific theories. See Gilbert Ryle, *Dilemmas* (Cambridge: Cambridge University Press, 1962), chaps. 5 and 6, and in particular, p. 79.
4. G. E. Moore, "a Defense of Common Sense," in *Philosophical Papers* (London: Allen and Unwin, Muirhead Library of Philosophy; New York: Macmillan, 1959), pp. 32–59. Until otherwise stated, numbers in parentheses in the text will refer to pages in this edition.
5. For a very brief description of the transition from the natural to the transcendental standpoint, see paragraph 39 of E. Husserl, *The Crisis of European Sciences and Transcendental Phenomenology*, tr. David Carr (Evanston, Ill.: Northwestern Univeristy Press, 1970), p. 148.
6. The relation between the finite or natural and the universal or transcendental subjectivity in Husserl is something very like the relation between the finite or immanent human ego and the absolute ego in Fichte.
7. Compare the discussion of the passage cited from *Wittgenstein's Blue and Brown Books* by P. M. S. Hacker in his *Wittgenstein's Place in Twentieth Century Philosophy* (Oxford: Blackwell, 1996), p. 83. Hacker observes that "Wittgenstein dissociated his new style of philosophy from Moore's defense of 'common sense' and from the invocation of ordinary use in defense of allegedly common-sense views." But Wittgenstein meant by this that one must work through the philosophical problem in order to return to common sense (and so to ordinary usage).
8. Grice, "Retrospective Epilogue," in *Studies in the Way of Words*, p. 381.
9. In *Philosophical Papers;* see note 4.
10. Compare Grice, *Studies in the Way of Words*, pp. 157–59. Grice finds it hard to see the force of this distinction, but he notes that if Moore always appeals to ordinary language, the distinction cannot be preserved. And he suspects that a defense of Moore's position would lead after all to a defense of ordinary language. I agree with Grice on this point.
11. This passage militates against Grice's (qualified) claim that Moore does not always depend upon an appeal to ordinary language. See note 8.
12. See here Austin's brilliant lectures on *Sense and Sensibilia*, ed. G. J. Warnock (Oxford: Oxford University Press, 1962).

CHAPTER 6: AUSTIN AND ORDINARY LANGUAGE

1. Numbers in parentheses in the text refer to pages in Austin's *Philosophical Papers,* 3d ed. (Oxford: Oxford University Press, Clarendon Paperbacks, 1979).
2. See "How To Talk," in *Philosophical Papers,* p. 134.
3. In *Philosophical Papers,* pp. 175–204.
4. "So much for the cackle" (p. 189). The non-cackle consists in "a few remarks, not, I am afraid, in any very coherent order" about the nature of excuses in ordinary discourse.

5. 2.2.1103b26–28.
6. 10.9.1181b15.
7. "Are There A Priori Concepts?" in *Philosophical Papers,* pp. 42–43.

CHAPTER 7: WHAT DO WE TALK ABOUT?

1. *The Philosophy of Logical Atomism* (Lasalle, Ill.: Open Court, 1993), p. 53. Numbers in parentheses in the text refer to pages in this edition.

CHAPTER 8: THE ATTRIBUTES OF ORDINARY EXPERIENCE

1. For an interesting statement of the irreducibility of consciousness to physiological structures, written from the standpoint of contemporary analytical philosophy, see David Chalmers, *The Conscious Mind* (New York: Oxford University Press, 1996).

Index

Absolute ego, 85
Actions, 221–23, 229
Allison, Henry, 56
Analytical discourse, 183
Antibiblical views, 23
Anxiety, 95, 121, 123–24, 129, 130, 131
Apperception, 269–70
Aquinas, Thomas, 166
Aristophanes, 138
Aristotle: absence of scientific ontology, 288; "the altogether not," 215; Austin on, 187, 192; calculations, 118; cosmos, 49; delight in senses, 262; desire to know, 262; distinguished from Plato, 154–55; doctrine of intelligible form, 274; *endoksa,* 50; essences, 256, 274, 280; ethical and political writings, 50; *eudaimonia,* 120; "first philosophy," 288; and Heidegger, 94–96, 117–34; *hule,* 283–85; *hupokeimena,* 283–85; and Husserl, 67, 85; influence on Strauss, 135; intellectual intuition, 32; and Kant, 94–117, 286–87; knowledge, 119; *koine aisthesis,* 167, 176; misuse of essence, 166; and Montesquieu, 48–53, 93; and Moore, 176, 180–81; moral standards, 260; opinions, 50; *ousia,* 280; perception, 286–88; *phronesis,* 15, 60, 94, 117–34; political life, 14; political philosophy, 155–56; political virtue, 21; politics, 49–50; *Politics,* 14, 49, 153; practical judgment, 15; prudence, 49, 118–19, 131–33; rejection of philosopher-king, 50; science of being *qua* being, 288; substances, 280; such-and-such a kind, 164, 194, 246–47, 257–58, 277; thinking, 288; transcendental alternatives to, 94–134; triple partition of arts and sciences, 219; truth, 221; virtue, 49; wholeness, 128–30
Arithmetic, 66, 265
Aron, Raymond, 48

Art, 234–36, 241–42, 247–48, 282
Athens versus Jerusalem, 136, 139, 143, 149, 151, 153, 158
Ausschaltung, 57
Austen, Jane, 145, 146, 147
Austin, John, 182–203; analysis of linguistic distinctions, 6; analytical dialect, 184; analytical discourse, 183; and Aristotle, 187, 192; cackle, 186–87, 190; common sense, 183; conceptual logic, 190; contrast with extraordinary language, 200–201; deviation from ordinary language, 173; difficulties with views of, 184–86; distinguishing view, 12–13; and elusiveness of the ordinary, 12; empiricism, 190, 202; first word, 182, 193, 201; and historicism, 201; and Kant, 190; linguistic analysis, 182–203; meaning, 192–99; "The Meaning of a Word," 193; metaordinary, 186; native speaker, 194–95; neo-Kantian, 190; non-arbitrary character of ordinary words, 1; and ordinary language, 2, 159, 160, 182–203; *phenomena,* 193; philosophical logic, 190; *Philosophical Papers,* 193; plain language, 183; plain man, 2, 182–203; *A Plea for Excuses,* 186; *Sense and Sensibilia,* 1; snag of loose, divergent, or alternative usage, 184–85; study of excuses, 188–90; technical or professional speech, 163, 202; and Wittgenstein, 6, 184, 190, 200
Average everydayness, 4, 14, 95–96, 117, 296

Being: duality of, 280; science of being *qua* being, 288; and substance and essence, 280
Being and Time (Heidegger), 6, 69
Bergson, Henri, 274
Biology, 8
Body as machine, 220
Brutes, 33

Carr, David, 58, 80
Cartesian. *See* Descartes, René
Cartesian Meditations (Husserl), 58
Catholic church, 18, 19
Causal connection, 217–19
Censorship, 23
Chaos, 285, 301
Chomsky, Noam, 45
Christianity, 14, 17, 20, 22, 102
City and Man, The (Strauss), 153
Cohen, Hermann, 145–46
Common and private experience, 251–53
Common sense, 159–81, 297–98; challenges to, 261; defining, 159, 167; *doksa,* 14; erotic madness, 4; as faculty, 168; general sagacity, 167, 169; *koine aisthesis,* 167, 176; maximal and minimal, 167–69; Moore on, 159–81; and ordinary language, 159–81; process of reasoning, 68; role of, 12–13; self-certifying, 261; sense and foolishness, 169–70; and truth, 171
Commonsense reason, 4
Comprehensive change, 247
Comprehensiveness, 272–74
Computers, 220–21, 227–28, 230–31
Concepts, 274, 278, 279–80, 281
Conceptual analysis, 161–62
Conscience, 122, 124, 126, 129, 132
Consciousness, 68–69
Construction, 219
Continuity and discreteness, 273
Cosmological myth, 249
Cosmos, 49, 56, 85, 242
Crisis of the European Sciences (Husserl), 58–66, 74, 83
Critiques (Kant). *See* Kant, Immanuel

Deconstruction, 70, 136, 139, 242
"Defense of Common Sense, A" (Moore), 172, 177
Derrida, Jacques, 70, 294

Descartes, René: assumptions of, 60; *cogito,* 273; consciousness, 68–69; *ego cogitans,* 69, 75; egotism, 142; Enlightenment role of, 47–48; on God, 30; and Husserl, 62–64, 68–69, 73; limits, 273–74; *mathesis universalis,* 65, 68; method of doubt, 73; and Montesquieu, 27, 48; versus Moses, 151; narrowing conception of human being, 228; Paris and Jerusalem, 151; *Passions of the Soul,* 51, 142; shift to reason and passion, 228; soul, 51
Desire, 142
Desire to know, 296–98
Dialogues (Plato), 3
Discourses (Machiavelli), 20
Discovery, 241
Disintegration and meaninglessness, 273
Doctrine of original and image, 284–85
Doksa, 14, 64, 71, 89
Dostoyevski, Fyodor, 145
Douceur de vivre, 44, 95
Duality of being, 280

Eidos, 255–56, 279
Eleatic Stranger, 8, 215
Empiricism, 92, 190, 202
Endoksa, 14, 50
English, standard, 170
English grammar, 291
Enlightenment, 2, 45; Husserl's connection to, 6, 60, 63, 70; "moderate" Enlightenment, 16, 46–48
Episteme, 64, 71, 89
Epistemology, 229–30
Epoche, 72–73, 81–83, 172
Equivocity, 240, 242–43
Eros, 3, 128, 142, 249–50
Erotic madness, 4
Esotericism, 146–48
Essence: Aristotelian, 256, 274, 276; distinguished from Plato's Ideas, 55; essential properties, 209–10; of human beings, 287; Husserl on, 67–68, 73–75; intellectual intuition, 286; misuse of, 166; ordinary language philosophy, 164–65
Esteem, 260, 262
Eudaimonia, 244
Eudaimonism, critique of, 94–117
Experimental science, increasing power of, 224
Extraordinary: discourse and experience, 234; ordinary compared, 290–92; and ordinary experience, 8–9, 264–65, 273

Al Farabi, 146
Fichte, Johann Gottlieb, 80, 90
"First philosophy," 288
Folk psychology, 5, 7, 9
Form, 164–66, 274, 281–86
Formal analysis, 261–62
Formal and Transcendental Logic (Husserl), 58
Frege, Gottlob, 59, 274, 278
French Enlightenment, 47. *See also* Enlightenment

Gadamer, H. G., 117
Galileo Galilei, 21, 61, 66
General sagacity, 167, 169
German Idealism, 68, 85
Gestalt, 256
God: Descartes on, 30; Husserl on, 73; Kant on, 104, 107–9, 111–15; Montesquieu on, 30–31, 38; Strauss on, 151
Goodness of reason, 259–63
Grammar, 291
Grice, Paul, 159, 161–64, 176
Groundwork of the Metaphysics of Morals (Kant), 96, 97, 104

Halevi, Jehudah, 146, 150
Happiness, 95–117, 120
Hegel, Georg Wilhelm Friedrich: Concept, 250; continuity and discreteness, 268, 271; deviations, 233; dialectico-

Hegel, Georg Wilhelm Friedrich (*continued*)
speculative logic, 270; on Greeks, 301; and Husserl, 64, 65, 91; identity of identity and difference, 268–71; and Kant, 91, 95; life as lived, 274; manifestation of world-spirit, 65; and Montesquieu, 44, 49; and Moore, 180–81; negation, 268–69; satisfaction, 95; *Science of Logic,* 73, 91, 180, 268; speech of speeches, 250

Heidegger, Martin, 94–96, 117–34; anxiety, 121, 123–24, 129–31; and Aristotle, 94–96, 117–34; authentic choice, 131–32; average everydayness, 95–96, 117, 296; *Being and Time,* 6, 69; biblical tradition, 117; conscience, 122, 124, 126, 129, 132; cosmos, 56; destruction of Western philosophy, 69–70; "a different beginning," 294; eros, 128; everyday, 272–73; focus on past as way to future, 6; historical perspective, 55; and Husserl, 6, 59, 65, 69–70; manifestation of world-spirit, 65; mistakes of, 127–28; overview, 11; past, 6; Pharisaism, 125, 127; *phronesis* or ontology, 94, 117–34; and Plato, 118, 120; practical intelligence, 117; priority of difference, 294; resoluteness, 121–22, 132, 134; return, 138–39; *Sein and Zeit,* 118–34; and Strauss, 117–18, 135, 138–39, 147–49; technical or extraordinary language, 6; thrown or fallen into life, 272; transcendental alternatives to Aristotle, 94–96, 117–34; wholeness, 128–30; world-spirit, 65

Heracleitus, 2–3
Hermeneutics, 21, 23, 219, 241–42
Historicism, 51, 92, 137, 201
History: knowledge of, 17–18; new paradigm, 45; philosophy of, 15, 40
History of philosophy, 3–5, 288
Hobbes, Thomas: antibiblical views, 23; censorship, 23; foundation for analysis of behavior, 51; function of state, 39; and Montesquieu, 18, 20, 23, 35, 38–40; morality, 30; politics, 39–40; revolutionary shift, 23; state of nature, 39–40; Strauss on, 146; universal philosophy question, 63

Hule, 283–85
Hume, David, 47, 48, 69, 74, 75, 218
Hupokeimena, 283–85
Husserl, Edmund, 54–93; and Aristotle, 67, 85; assumptions, 55; basic component of phenomenology, 68; bracketing, 83, 90; brute existence, 81; Cartesian ego, 73; *Cartesian Meditations,* 58; commitment to scientific renaissance, 69; completeness of knowledge, 68; conception of the life-world, 11, 54–93; consciousness, 68–69; contingent particular, 73; *Crisis of the European Sciences,* 58–66, 74, 83; defending, 88; denying central thesis of, 89–90; and Descartes, 62–64, 68–69, 73; desedimentation, 69–70; difficulties of phenomenological method, 66; *doksa,* 64, 70, 89; dualism, 92; eidetic perception, 57–58; empiricism and phenomenology, 92; Enlightenment's role in thinking of, 6, 60, 63, 70; *episteme,* 64, 71, 89; *epoche,* 72–73, 81–83, 172; *Erkenntnisleben,* 78; essence, 67–68, 73–75; evolution from Montesquieu, 44–45; examples, 84–85; *Formal and Transcendental Logic,* 58; on God, 73; and Hegel, 64, 65, 91; and Heidegger, 6, 59, 65, 69–70; historical perspective, 55; human freedom and universal reason, 60–61; and Hume, 69, 74, 75; *Ideas,* 58, 247; intelligibility, 68, 73; intentional activity, 70; intentions, 67; intuition, 67, 69, 173; investigation, 72; and Kant, 55–57, 73–81, 85, 87, 89–93; knowledge of life-world, 70–72; manifestation of world-spirit, 65; mathematical artifact replacing life-world,

66; mathematical index, 66; mathematical model, 61; mathematical transformation of science, 66; *mathesis universalis,* 65, 68; meaning, 55; metaphysics, 64; modern mathematical science covering life-world, 65–66; and Montesquieu, 44–45; and Moore, 172–74, 179, 181; objectification, 90–92; overview, 11; paradigm of perception, 68–69; phenomenology, 57, 61, 65, 66, 70, 87; *phronesis,* 60; and Plato, 57–58, 62–63; Plato versus Kant, 92; Platonic Ideas, 55; positivism, 59, 61–63, 66, 70, 93; practical intelligence, 60; problem raised by historical dimension of, 69; product of transcendental subjectivity, 57; questioning internal coherence of doctrine, 87–88; rationalism, 62; on Renaissance, 62–63; replacement of everyday experience, 65–66; return to past, 6; and science, 58–63, 65–66; science of life-world, 80; scientific, 55; sedimented, 5; senses, 55, 57; *Sinn* as main assumption of, 55; state of objective subjectivity, 88–89; structures of, 57; subjectivity, 74–76, 76–83, 91–92; summary of main features, 73; summary of method, 68; technical or extraordinary language, 6; theoretical artifact, 57; transcendental bracketing of natural attitude, 85–88; transcendental consciousness, 72–73; transcendental ego, 85, 90; transcendental subjectivity, 76–83, 85, 86; unification of meaning and value, 69; universal knowledge, 65; universal philosophy of reason, 64; value, 70–71; world, 85

Ideas (Husserl), 58, 247
Ideas, Platonic, 24–25, 55, 72, 154–55; versus doctrine of eros, 142; essence distinguished from, 55, 75; humans striving for, 3; images and, 284, 288; "looks" and, 211, 256, 279

Idiom, standard, 163
Image and original, 284–85
Immediate, 177–78
Index of Forbidden Books, Montesquieu's work on, 19
Induction, 265–66
Instances, 278, 279–80, 281
Institutions, development of, 296–97
Intellectual intuition, 32, 67, 286–87
Intelligibility, 68, 73, 164, 230, 260–61
Intentional activity, 70, 261
Intentionality, 245
Intuition, 5, 210, 214, 217–18
Isomorphism, 282–83

James, Henry, 147
Jerusalem versus Athens, 136, 139, 143, 149, 151, 153, 158
Joyce, James, 234
Judaism, 145–46, 149–50

Kant, Immanuel, 94–117; apperception, 269–70; and Aristotle, 94–117, 286–87; and Austin, 190; biblical tradition, 100, 102; causal connection, 217–19; Christianity's influence on, 102; cleverness, 11; completeness of knowledge, 68; consciousness, 68; *corpus mysticum,* 107, 112, 115; critique of eudaimonism, 94–117; duty, 96–97; evaluation of doctrine, 247; first *Critique,* 55, 100–101, 104, 116, 214; freedom, 96–117; on God, 104, 107–9, 111–15; *Groundwork of the Metaphysics of Morals,* 96, 97, 104; happiness, 95–117; highest reason, 111; historical perspective, 54–55; hope, 109–11; and Hume, 218; and Husserl, 73–81, 85, 89–90, 92, 93; ideal of the highest good, 111; importance of, 2; inner experience, 76; intelligible intuition, 106–7; *Klugheit,* 11; limitations on, 117; miracles, 116; modern science, 285; morality, 96–117, 260; overview, 11; perception, 287–88; and Plato, 92,

Kant, Immanuel (*continued*)
257; practical reason, 102; pure practical law, 102–3, 116; rise of transcendental philosophy, 217–19; schema-rule, 285–86; second *Critique,* 96–97, 116; speculative, 103; state of grace, 116; *summum bonum,* 107–8, 115; synthetic, 269–70; synthetic unity of manifold, 208; thinking, 288; third *Critique,* 96, 113; three questions, 103; transcendental, 76; transcendental construction, 257; transcendental ego, 7, 55, 247; transcendental synthesis, 217–18; universality of moral law, 102; and Wittgenstein, 75, 137, 139; world, 55–57, 85; worthiness of happiness, 104–5, 107–8, 111
Kierkegaard, Søren, 95
Kinds, 240, 246, 257–58, 279, 284
Kisiel, Theodore, 117, 118, 123
Klein, Jacob, 147
Know, desire to, 262
Koine aisthesis, 167, 176
Kojève, Alexandre, 39, 152, 156

Language: Chomsky project, 45; defined, 159; formal, 225; metalanguage, 292; natural, 160, 225–26, 239; nonordinary expressions, 162; philosophical, 229; philosophy of, 239; and precise rules, 292; scientific and poetic, 228–29; standard English, 170; standard idiom, 163; technical, 162–64; technical or extraordinary language, 6, 162–64. *See also* Ordinary language
Law of politics, 21–22
Lebensgebilde, 75
Leibniz, Gottfried Wilhelm, 30, 49, 224, 271
Lessing, Gotthold Ephraim, 147
Life-world. *See* Husserl, Edmund
Literature and philosophy, 242
"Lived life," 272

Locke, John: function of state, 39; Montesquieu distinguished from, 35; morality, 30; natural law, 34–35; and Nietzsche, 44; politics, 39–40; revolutionary shift, 23; self-preservation , 34–35; Strauss on, 44
Logismos, 301
Looks, 211, 215, 255–57, 274–80, 284–85

Machiavelli, Niccolo, 18–21, 23, 49, 146
Machine, body as, 220
Magic Mountain, The (Mann), 234
Maimonides, Moses, 146, 150, 152
Mann, Thomas, 234
Mathematical continuum, 270–71
Mathematical index, 66
Mathematics, 268, 270–71
Mathesis universalis, 65, 68
Matter, 281–84
Metalanguage, 292
Mind as software, 281
Mind-body problem, 142
Moderation, 93
Modern scientific method, 2
Modern society, anonymity of, 15
Monads, 207, 271
Montesquieu, 14–53; aristocracies, 19–20; and Aristotle, 48–53, 93; atheism, 22, 34; *Avertissement,* 18, 19, 22; brutes, 33; and Cartesians, 23; Catholic church's authority and, 18, 19; censorship, 23; and Christianity, 17, 22; comfortable virtue, 45–46; comparison with Plato, 23–25; democracies, 19; and Descartes, 27, 48; despotisms, 19–20; diversity, 18; effect of modern mathematical and experimental science, 52; Enlightenment reflected by, 26–27; error of, 15; excellence, 18; external relations, 31–32; fear, 20, 39; feature of philosophy, 48–49; forgetfulness, 32–33; founder of sociology, 45; freedom, 42, 44, 53; French monarchy's authority over, 18; on God,

30–31, 38; grandfather of sociology, 15; and Hegel, 44, 49; historical perspective, 15, 55; historicism, 49; history, 17–18; and Hobbes, 18, 20, 23, 35, 38–40; honor, 19–21; human and nonhuman, 23, 52; and Husserl, 44–45; increasing comfort, 44; inspiration, 15; intelligent beings, 32; laws, 17–18, 23, 29–34; laws of nature, 24–25; and Leibniz, 30, 49; limitation of nature, 32; Locke distinguished from, 35; and Machiavelli, 18–21, 23, 49; mainspring, 19–20; meaning of "preface," 18, 22–23; moderation, 19, 93; modern study of, 44–45; monarchy, 19–20, 22; moral laws, 34; moral virtue, 22, 52–53; natural laws, 24–25, 29–30; nature, 17, 21, 23, 24, 45; and Nietzsche, 43, 44, 53; non-Aristotelian aspect, 31–32; overview, 11; partisan of new science, 21; peace, 40–41, 42; philosophy of history, 15, 40; *phronesis,* 15; political excellence, 18–19; political laws, 34; political philosophers, 24–25, 42; political virtue, 18–22, 52–53; politics, 39–40; politics and nature in, 14–53; positive laws, 29–30, 43; possible laws of possible beings, 31; practical judgment, 15; principles, 26–27, 32–33; problem with, 42; reason for studying, 53; reconciling aspects of doctrine, 43; regularity, 18; rejection of Locke-Hobbes thesis, 39; religion, 17; representative of moderate Enlightenment, 16, 46–48; republics, 19, 22, 41; restlessness, 44; revolutionary impact, 26; and Rousseau, 38–39, 43, 45, 47; science, 43; self-preservation, 34–35; society, 35, 37; sociology, 44, 53; and Spinoza, 22, 23, 27, 49; *Spirit of the Laws,* 15–19, 22, 28, 45, 48, 51, 53, 250; state of nature, 34–42; synthesis of ancients and moderns, 49; Virgil's *Aeneid,* 28; virtue, 18–19, 20, 21, 44, 48; war, 28–29, 39–40, 42–43

Moore, George Edward, 159–81; and Aristotle, 176, 180–81; common sense, 159–81, 261; criticism of, 174; defending, 174–76; "A Defense of Common Sense," 172, 177; distinction of knowing meaning and analysis, 176; distinguishing view, 12–13; and Hegel, 180–81; and Husserl, 172–74, 179, 181; list, 171–74; overview, 12; "Proof of an External World," 176, 178–79; propositions, 172–80, 178; self-certifying common sense, 261; sense-data, 180–81; summary of, 174
Moore, Marianne, 234
Morphe, 256, 283

Nachlass of *1882* (Nietzsche), 147
Nachlass of *1885–86* (Nietzsche), 146–47
Natural language, 160, 225–26, 239
Natural Right and History (Strauss), 44, 148–49, 150, 153
Natural sciences and philosophy, split between, 4
Nature: and art, 248, 282; growth and change in everyday use, 45; intentionality, 266; laws, 17; and look, 279; natural change, 247–49; philosophical term, 165–66; Wittgenstein on, 140–41; and world, 242
Neuroscience, 228
Nicomachean Ethics (Aristotle), 49, 153, 186
Nietzsche, Friedrich: doctrine of interpretation, 294–95; and everyday life, 294–96; and Kant, 95; life as lived, 274; and Locke, 44; and man, 240; and Montesquieu, 43, 44, 53; nihilism, 263; perturbation of the surface of chaos, 285; priority of difference, 294; rank-ordering, 296; self-overcoming, 44; and Strauss, 135–36, 137, 146–47; will to power, 295–96; work, 95
Nihilists, 262–63

Noema, 66
Noetic heterogeneity, 154–56
Novels, 234–35, 241, 253, 255

Ordinal, 164, 231, 233, 265
Ordinary: attempts at conceptual mastery of, 2; elusiveness of, 1–2, 12; scientific response, 2; split between natural sciences and philosophy, 4. *See also other entries beginning with "Ordinary"*
Ordinary discourse, 225–26, 232
Ordinary experience, 259–89; anonymity of modern society, 15; arithmetic, 265; attributes of, 259–89; Christianity's influence on, 14; common pretheoretical experience, 8–9; comprehensiveness, 272–74; continuum of experience, 207–9, 264–89; creation of theories of, 7–10; deviations, 233–34; disintegration and meaninglessness, 273; and extraordinary, 8–9, 264–65, 273; fundamental level of unity, 207–9; goodness of reason, 259–63; inner life of everyone, 15; ordinary language distinguished, 164; political life, 14; regularity, 266; revelation, 4; scientific theories, 7–8; separate particulars, 206–8; specialized studies, 296; speech, 215–17; talk, 215–17; twentieth-century philosophers, 4–5; unity and regularity, 266–68, 273–74; unity of experience, 207–9, 271; what we talk about, 204–58
Ordinary language: analysis, 300–301; Austin on, 2, 159, 160, 182–203; common sense, 159–81; defining, 293–94; expression of, 231–33; non-arbitrary character of words, 1–2; ordinary experience distinguished, 164; and philosophy, 170; and poetry, 293; Tarski's procedure, 237; twentieth-century philosophy, 4; Wittgenstein on, 6, 70, 137–44, 171, 233
Ordinary man, 15

Ordinary speaker, 15, 160
Original and image, doctrine of, 284–85
Ousia, 280

Pangle, Thomas, 53
Paris and Jerusalem, 151
Parmenides, 2–3
Passions of the Soul (Descartes), 51, 142
Pater, Walter, 295
Peace, 40–41, 42
Pears, David, 143
Pericles, 132
Phaedrus (Plato), 72, 155
Phenomena, 193
Phenomenology. *See* Husserl, Edmund
Philebus (Plato), 236
Philosopher-king, 24, 50, 120
Philosophical Investigations (Wittgenstein), 140, 143
Philosophical Papers (Austin), 193
Philosophy: and art, 235–36, 241; defined, 233; goal of philosopher, 89; historical perspective, 54–55; of history, 15, 40; history of, 3–5, 288; of language, 239; and literature, 242; and ordinary discourse, 232; ordinary language, 159–81, 170; plausibility, 263; and poetry, 270, 288; process, 247; and rhetoric, 270; science, 288; split with natural sciences, 4; as style of inquiry, 205–6; transcendental, 217–18; twentieth-century, 4–5. *See also specific philosophers*
Philosophy and Law (Strauss), 151
Phronesis, 15, 60, 94, 117–34
Physics, understanding of, 8
Plain man, 2, 14–15, 160, 182–203, 261
Plato: absence of scientific ontology, 288; comparison with Montesquieu, 23–24; "demotic" virtue, 119; *Dialogues,* 3; distinguished from Aristotle, 154–55; doctrine of intelligible form, 274; Eleatic Stranger, 8, 215; forms, 274, 281–86; happiness, 120; and Heidegger, 118; and Husserl, 57–58; influence on Strauss,

135; and Kant, 92, 257; perception, 287–88; philosopher-king, 24, 120; poetry and philosophy, 58; recollection of originals, 288; such-and-such a kind, 246–47, 257–58; well-ordered soul, 24; and Wittgenstein, 141–42. *See also* Ideas, Platonic; Socrates

Plea for Excuses, A (Austin), 186
Poetry, 228, 234–35, 241, 270, 288, 292–93
Political philosophers, 24, 42
Politics (Aristotle), 14, 49, 153
Positivism, 59, 61–63, 66, 70, 93
Postmodern movements, 242
Praxis, 44, 54, 118–19, 261, 266–67
Prime matter, 281
Prince, The, 20, 49. *See also* Machiavelli, Niccolo
Principles, 285
Private and common experience, 251–53
Process-philosophy, 247
Production, 219–20, 241
"Proof of an External World" (Moore), 176, 178–79
Proust, Marcel, 234–35
Psychologists, 57

Quine, Willard, 5

Rank-ordering, 260, 288, 296
Ratio, 301
Rational animal, 281, 286
Rationalism, 62, 70
Ratios, 285
Reason, goodness of, 259–63
Regularity, 18, 266–67, 273, 274
Religion, 142–43, 151, 153, 266; Catholic church, 18, 19; Christianity, 14, 17, 20, 22, 102; Judaism, 145–46, 149–50
Remarks on the Philosophy of Psychology (Wittgenstein), 139
Remembrance of Things Past (Proust), 234–35, 253
Renaissance, 62–63
Rhetoric, 270

Rousseau, Jean-Jacques, 38–39, 43, 45, 47
Russell, Bertrand, 13, 204–5, 210–11, 213–14

Sacred Fount, The (James), 147
Schema-rule, 285–86
Science: conception of philosophy, 288; Husserl on, 58–63, 65–66; as Kantian, 285; mathematical model, 61; modern, 285; Montesquieu on, 43; neuroscience, 228; and religion, 266; scientific and poetic speech, 228–29
Science of Logic (Hegel), 73, 91, 180, 268
Scientific model, 16
Scientific response, 2
Sein and Zeit (Heidegger), 118–34
Sense and foolishness, 169
Sense and Sensibilia (Austin), 1
Senses, delight in, 262
Shaped matter, 281–84
Siècle des lumières, 47
Smith, Adam, 47, 48
Social Contract (Rousseau), 43
Sociology, 15, 44, 45, 53
Socrates: Eros, 249–50; erotic revelation, 4; explanation of emergence of philosophy, 3; good, 236; knowledge of ignorance, 144–45, 152–53, 155; maxim, 246; nature of the good life, 3; *Phaedrus*, 72; piety, 153; such-and-such a kind, 246–47, 257–58; theory and practice, 3–4; wonder, 3
Software, mind as, 281
Soul, 51, 142
Speech, 250
Spinoza, Baruch, 146; antibiblical views, 23; censorship, 23; foundation for analysis of behavior, 51; interpretation of treatment of Judaism, 145–46; and Montesquieu, 22, 23, 27, 49; politics as mechanics, 27; revolutionary shift, 23; *Tractatus Theologico-Politicus*, 23
Spirit of the Laws (Montesquieu), 15–19, 22, 28, 45, 48, 51, 53, 250

Standard English, 170
Standard idiom, 163
Stimmung, 272
Stories, 241, 242–45, 253–56, 258, 289
Strauss, Leo, 135–58; and Al Farabi, 146; Al Farabi distinguished from, 145; analysis of Aristotle's *Politics,* 153; ancient Greeks, 160; Aristophanes, 138; Aristotle's influence on, 135; Athens versus Jerusalem, 136, 139, 143, 149, 151, 153, 158; on Austen, 145–47; charm of competence, 156; *The City and Man,* 153; deconstruction of philosophical tradition, 136; depths in surface, 147, 157–58; Descartes versus Moses, 151; desire, 142; differences with Wittgenstein, 143; disciples, 136; esotericism, 146–48; frankness and concealment, 147; on God, 151; Greek pretheoretical experience, 135–58; and Heidegger, 117–18, 135, 138–39, 147–49; historical perspective, 55; on Hobbes, 146; Judaism, 145–46, 149–50; and Kant, 139; knowledge of ignorance, 144–45, 152–53, 155, 157; on Kojève, 152, 156; on Locke, 44; on Maimonides, 146, 150, 152; on modern science, 153–54; *Natural Right and History,* 44, 148–49, 150, 153; on *Nicomachean Ethics,* 153; and Nietzsche, 135–36, 137, 146–47; noetic heterogeneity, 154–56; overview, 11–12; Paris and Jerusalem, 151; personality of, 136; as philosopher, 147; *Philosophy and Law,* 151; and Plato, 135, 148, 154–55; Platonic Ideas, 154–55; political views, 137, 145; pretheoretical political discourse of ancient Greeks, 135–36, 160, 302; reason and revelation, 137, 150–54, 157; religion, 151, 153; and Socrates, 135–58; on Spinoza, 145–46; surface and depths, 147, 157–58; *Thoughts on Machiavelli,* 139–40; Thucydides, 138; "What Is Political Philosophy?" 151–52; Xenophon distinguished from, 145–47

Substances, 209–10, 219, 280–81
Subtilitas legendi, 240–41
Such-and-such a kind, 164, 194, 246–47, 257–58, 277
Suicide, 84

Taminiaux, Jacques, 117
Tarski, Alfred, 237
Techne, 2, 220–21, 224
Technical discourse, 224–27, 230–32
Technical language, 6, 162–64
Technology, 220
Terminus, 245–49, 253–54
Text, 242–45, 252–53, 256. *See also* Stories
Third-man paradox, 284
Thoughts on Machiavelli (Strauss), 139–40
Thucydides, 138
Tocqueville, Alexis de, 44
Tractatus Logico-Philosophicus (Spinoza), 55
Transcendence, mystical experience of, 291
Truth, 172, 221, 224, 235–40, 245
Truth-predicate, 236–37
Twentieth-century philosophy, 4–5

Ulysses (Joyce), 234
Unity, 266–68, 273–74
Unity of experience, 207–9, 271
Universal homogeneous state, 39

Virgil's *Aeneid,* 28
Volpi, Franco, 117

War, 28–29, 39–40, 42–43
Washington, George, 254–55, 256
Well-ordered soul, 24
"What Is Political Philosophy?" (Strauss), 151–52
Wholeness, 244, 254
Wholes, 156–57, 210–12
Whole story, 242–44, 253–54, 258
Will to power, 295–96

Wittgenstein, Ludwig, 135–44; Athens versus Jerusalem, 143; and Austin, 6, 184, 190, 200; correcting errors of philosophical discourse, 233; desire, 142; destruction of philosophical conditions, 139; difference with Strauss, 143; disciples, 136; established discursive orthodoxy, 6; and Heidegger, 139; historical perspective, 55; intuition, 214; and Kant, 75, 137, 139; life-form, 75; linguistic therapy, 5; natural history, 140–41; nature, 140–41; and Nietzsche, 143; ordinary language, 6, 70, 137–44, 171, 233; overview, 11–12; personality of, 136; *Philosophical Investigations,* 140, 143; and Platonic dialogues, 141–42; pretheoretical discourse, 135–36, 139; *Remarks on the Philosophy of Psychology,* 139; on Spinoza, 55; surface, 140–41, 143, 149; technical devices, 137; world, 55–56

Wonder, 3

World, 55–57, 85

Xenophon, 145–47, 146, 147

Yeats, William Butler, 208